Beautiful Suffering

Beautiful Suffering

PHOTOGRAPHY
AND THE

This book is issued in conjunction with the exhibition *Beautiful Suffering: Photography and the Traffic in Pain*, held at the Williams College Museum of Art, January 28–April 30, 2006.

The University of Chicago Press
Chicago, IL 60637
Williams College Museum of Art
Williamstown, MA 01267

15 14 13 12 11 10 09 08 07 1 2 3 4 5 6

ISBN-13: 978-0-226-70950-5 (paper)
ISBN-10: 0-226-70950-7 (paper)

Library of Congress
Cataloging-in-Publication Data

Reinhardt, Mark.
Beautiful suffering / Mark Reinhardt, Holly Edwards, Erina Duganne.
p. cm.
ISBN-13: 978-0-226-70950-5 (pbk. : alk. paper)
ISBN-10: 0-226-70950-7 (pbk. : alk. paper)
1. Documentary photography—Exhibitions.
2. Suffering in art—Exhibitions.
3. Photographic criticism—Exhibitions.
I. Edwards, Holly. II. Duganne, Erina. III. Title.
TR820.5.R47 2007
779.092—dc22
2006035000

♾ The paper used in this publication meets the minimum requirements of the American National Standard for Information Sciences—Permanence of Paper for Printed Library Materials, ANSI Z39.48–1992.

MARK REINHARDT AND HOLLY EDWARDS

TRAFFIC IN PAIN

Photography's traffic in pain is heavy—a grave matter, a big business, a common form of social exchange.[1] This traffic is a crucial element of news reporting, obviously, but it also courses through the art market, tourism, even fashion and advertising. Without injured bodies and devastated landscapes, without scenes of death, destruction, misery, and trauma, the contemporary image environment would be nearly unrecognizable. These scenes of affliction are often formally striking or beautifully rendered: every day, without much effort, one may come across exquisite images of other people's suffering.

Perhaps this should not be surprising. In the contemporary United States, at least, stories and claims about suffering are as potent as they are pervasive. Ours is a moment of "wounded attachments" to affliction as a source of moral and political

1. The subtitle of this volume pays homage to Allan Sekula's influential essay "The Traffic in Photographs," and behind it, Gayle Rubin's foundational "The Traffic in Women: Notes on the Political Economy of Sex." Sekula's arguments have helped to shape both a generation of debates on photographic representation and the pursuit of alternatives to mainstream photo-journalistic ways of representing suffering. Although parts of this book will take issue with some of his assumptions, this project bears the stamp of his work. See Sekula, *Photography Against the Grain: Essays and Photo Works*, 1973–1983 (Halifax, N.S.: Press of the Nova Scotia College of Art and Design, 1984), pp. 77–101. For Rubin, see Rayna Reiter, ed., *Toward an Anthropology of Women* (New York: Monthly Review, 1975), pp. 157–210.

legitimacy.[2] Sentimentalism, a cultural form that has always been a major presence in American life, has metastasized in recent years, especially since September 11, 2001; accounts of trauma have become still more crucial to the formation of the social bond and the shaping of national identity. The images we see in the mass media are but one expression of those changes. But photographs engaging suffering people are also part of a much older and broader story. After all, much of what is called "culture" (in the West) has *always* involved elaborating the complex conventions and expressive forms that make suffering comprehensible and give it meaning. Ancient Greek tragedy and nearly two millennia of Christian painting and sculpture—to choose but two obvious examples—address the seemingly endless suffering at the core of human experience, making it somehow bearable and sometimes even grand. Given suffering's centrality in history, it is hard to imagine how its prominence in the sphere of representation could have been otherwise. What varies widely and significantly across time, space, and media are the forms those representations take and the uses to which they are put.

Photography is a complex case in point, presenting distinctive ethical, political, and aesthetic problems and possibilities. Susan Sontag, whose work is a critical touchstone for this book and the exhibit from which it arose, went so far as to call the mass-mediated witnessing of distant calamities "a quintessential modern experience," remarking that "ever since the invention of the camera in the 1839, photography has kept company with death."[3] The traffic in pain is not unique to contemporary photography; it is as old as the medium itself.

So, too, is anxiety about this traffic: worries about sensationalism and exploitation have always attended the taking, distributing, and viewing of certain kinds of photographs. Just decades after the birth of the medium, contemporaries of Matthew Brady expressed concerns about photographs of the dead that he exhibited during the Civil War.[4] Such concerns have hardly abated since then. As John Stomberg demonstrates in this volume, these quandaries animate formative controversies in the history of photography. The campaign launched by Walker Evans, James Agee, and their champions against Margaret Bourke-White's photographs of Southern sharecroppers was framed as a critique of her way of responding to suffering and deprivation. The debate concerned both divergent aesthetic approaches and the social effects that ostensibly followed from different visual forms. As Stomberg indicates, contemporary controversies echo—often unwittingly—these formative struggles.

If retrospect reveals a pattern of angst about witnessing and picturing suffering, it also documents the innocent and durable trust that photographs enjoy. That trust can harbor diverse illusions and excuses—for example, that the viewer need look no further to understand distant events; that structural violence requires only a personal emotional response; that the represented pain or calamity has already been resolved and can therefore be dismissed; or that addressing the problem is the privilege or the perquisite of the viewer. For the trusting, then, pictures of suffering may seem to convey the whole truth and also to confirm the viewer's power to rectify the wrong, to alleviate the pain, or simply to turn the other way.

2. The term "wounded attachments" is Wendy Brown's, from her influential account of the moral and political uses of suffering in contemporary identity politics. See Brown, *States of Injury: Power and Freedom in Late Modernity* (Princeton: Princeton University Press, 1995), pp. 52–76 and passim. We are also indebted in this discussion to Lauren Berlant's analyses of sentimentality and national membership and to Marc Seltzer's discussion of injury and the social bond in "wound culture." See Berlant, "Poor Eliza," *American Literature* 70:3 (1998): 635–63 and *The Queen of America Goes to Washington City: Essays on Sex and Citizenship* (Durham: Duke University Press, 1997), and Seltzer, *Serial Killers: Death and Life in America's Wound Culture* (New York: Routledge, 1998).

3. Sontag, *Regarding the Pain of Others* (New York: Farrar, Straus and Giroux, 2003) pp. 18 and 24. Sontag's precise dating to 1839, the year in which Daguerre's process was announced to the world at a conference in Paris, is familiar, but historians of photography offer a murkier and more complex story of multiple, contested—and earlier—origins. For an extensive and nuanced discussion, see Geoffrey Batchen, *Burning with Desire: The Conception of Photography* (Cambridge, MA: MIT Press, 1997).

4. For a discussion, see Sontag, *Regarding the Pain of Others*, pp. 62–3.

Contemporary visual culture, however, undermines that trust and complicates those choices. The authority of photographic witnessing has been corroded by competition from television, video, and other media. These corrosive effects have been intensified by the ease with which anyone with access to a computer and a cheap, digital camera can produce startling alterations in a photograph, mixing and matching bits and pieces from a potentially infinite image archive, presenting as "real" a scene that never actually existed. As this mass-mediated, digitally and synthetically contrived image world grows denser, its pace ever faster, and its networks ever more global, consumers face relentless, sometimes manipulated but always manipulative images of people in pain.

This confounding visual barrage is augmented and further complicated by testimony from previously silent or silenced individuals and interest groups. But if sites of pain seem to proliferate before the eye, they are also difficult to differentiate and categorize. Readily publicized and visually homogenized in the digital age, specific sufferings are seemingly diminished, deprived of nuance and urgency. The very process of picturing may even control or subdue that which it depicts. Alternatively, such acts of representation may serve to mobilize political action from interested or implicated parties, at times even helping to reshape identities and generate new constituencies.

These conflicting tendencies and controversies raise numerous questions about the very act of photographing and about the work that photographs can do. What forms of picturing, for example, respect the dignity and agency of those shown? What forms assault the integrity of the spectator? What will mobilize useful action and what will, instead, exacerbate the injury? How much do the answers depend on the site of the encounter between image and viewer—for example, newspaper, magazine, monitor, book, or museum?

The apparent symbiosis of suffering and spectacle has inspired some to claim that we are no longer capable of seeing the evidence of other's pain; benumbed or satiated, we watch it pass by in a blur. Nonetheless, photographers deny or defy the futility of picturing—dutifully, doggedly, or perhaps quixotically—even as they feed our visual appetites. Some photographers choose to augment the image itself with ancillary documentation, including, for example, the verbal testimony of the subject; others claim to empower the pictured individuals by paying them for posing. Some call themselves photojournalists, accommodating the exigencies and timetables of mass media; others call themselves artists, retaining control of their work and the format of its publication. As Erina Duganne notes in her essay, some photographers have sought to move from one camp into the other by forsaking the immediacy of 35mm cameras for slower, larger images.

Many practitioners and commentators freight such distinctions with enormous moral, epistemological, or even ontological significance, attributing to photojournalism a privileged access to the real or granting art, through its greater distance and reflexivity, a superior ability to bear witness to the complexities of social experience. As Duganne argues, however, such approaches typically obscure the ways in which photography's multiple modes of authority are entangled in diverse social practices and audience responses. By seeking to analyze some of these nuances, Duganne questions the adequacy of the metaphor of "witnessing."

By enumerating the diverse incarnations of a single image, as Holly Edwards does in regard to Steve McCurry's **Afghan Girl** (**PLATE 5**), it is possible to articulate still other dynamics—parsing image, context, caption, and social function as variables in the production of visual culture. Unpacked in this manner, the life cycle of a formally generic, though aesthetically pleasing, portrait can reveal numerous agents and multiple beneficiaries of the traffic in pain, be they journalistic, entrepreneurial, or philanthropic. But if the subjects, makers, and purveyors of photographs are all instrumental, the images themselves exercise the real power to configure and contain emotional response. Those of Sebastiao Salgado (**PLATE 49**) and of James Nachtwey (**PLATE 21**)—important points of reference for this project—have elicited critical comment for their troubling "beauty" and formal refinement. The installation of Alfredo Jaar (**PLATE 51**), by contrast, is often read as a retreat from the fraught seductions of the image to near total aniconism in the face of genocide.

It is just such readings that Mark Reinhardt seeks to complicate in his essay. In the critical discourses of aestheticization, he argues, legitimate insights into the ways in which particular images may pacify viewers or exploit the suffering of others are often distorted by more dubious anxieties about the aesthetic work inherent in photography, as in all forms of visual representation. What appears at first to be a concern about a particular kind of picture, then, often turns out, on closer scrutiny, to be a fear of picturing. Tracking those anxieties may make it possible both to identify more precisely the ways in which the traffic in pain is problematical and to understand more clearly the complex and, at times, politically productive work that photographs can do.

Mieke Bal's essay in this book further articulates that possibility, using extended readings of the images in the exhibition to elaborate a theory of political art. Bal's argument revisits—but also reinterprets and substantially reworks—Theodor Adorno's warnings about the barbarism of art "after Auschwitz." In exploring both the potential and the dangers of contemporary photographic responses to suffering, Bal also takes up the fraught act of exhibiting. If an image compounds or creates the suffering pictured, must not its display, even for critical purposes, repeat the very gestures and effects the critic would denounce? Bal acknowledges that "Beautiful Suffering" risked precisely this; however, she also reads the exhibition as a self-conscious response that, through its juxtapositions of specific images and contending visual strategies, summoned viewers instead into an uncomfortably open-ended and philosophical analysis of visual culture.

This book's consideration of photography's traffic in pain thus tries to account for many and diverse participants in transactions that transpire in myriad ways and moments. The book is not just about photographs, or even about photographers. It also involves those who suffer and those who look on, those who publish and those who purchase, and of course, those who talk about what it all means. We, the authors and curators, have sought to reflect these complexities with two discrete but yoked forms of address—book and exhibition. At the outset, then, it seems appropriate to articulate the different sectors of our project and to describe some of our intentions and choices.

The book grew out of an exhibition at the Williams College Museum of Art (January 28–April 30, 2006), and it reproduces the exhibition's images and wall texts as a discrete chapter. It is therefore not an exhibition catalogue in the traditional sense. This documentary approach is a pointed acknowledgment of the fact that museums are potent sites of tutelage in looking, their lessons surpassing the simple transmission of fact or the display of art. The refuge in the surface beauties or formal qualities of treasured artifacts—which often attend ritual viewing in the quiet, communal spaces of museums—can readily become effete apathy; this is one of the troubling patterns of contemporary viewing that we seek to address.

But if museums can foster and condone such aesthetic detachment, they can also direct the visitor toward other modes of engagement. More specifically, we wished not only to avoid the dangers of anesthetized viewing and exploitative voyeurism but also to thematize them; to this end, we crafted our rhetorical stance carefully for "Beautiful Suffering," admitting from the outset our curatorial culpabilities in the traffic in pain. By addressing explicitly in the exhibition texts "beauty" and the act of looking and by reiterating those issues and questions here, we hope to provide a foil for further consideration of the role of museums within larger social networks and pedagogies.

The book also ranges more widely in other ways, tracing some of the historical antecedents of today's debates and modes of representation. Focusing primarily on photographs produced since the mid-1980s, we explore the dilemmas of picturing suffering under contemporary conditions, examining some of the most prominent and revealing photographic and critical responses to those dilemmas. We felt it important to bring together the kinds of images from "photojournalism" and "art" that are often considered—or exhibited—separately. In that sense, this is not a typical selection. Nor is it statistically representative of what the average media consumer would be likely to encounter. In choosing works for the exhibition, we emphasized photographs that attempt, in one way or another, to depart from the most common forms of photojournalistic or mass-mediated imagery. The wager of both the show and the book is that we need to place exemplars of the most familiar forms of representation in dialogue with trenchant alternatives. In this way, we want to ask what the differences among them are and what difference, if any, these differences might make.

Because book space affords greater discursive latitude than wall space, we have dilated more generously between these covers on non-visual and contextual issues, including the making, circulation, and reception of photographs. Both our curatorial and authorial processes, however, have involved asking endless and varied questions of ourselves, questions intended to pinpoint the sites of power, pain, agency, and complicity. The reader will encounter many of those queries toward the end of the book as they appeared in the exhibition texts—unanswered. We settled on that open-ended strategy for the museum venue to reflect the images' obdurate resistance to curatorial omniscience and to invite active engagement with the issues on the part of each and every museum visitor.

Like the exhibition, this book offers neither sustained polemics nor even a single, tidy answer to its major questions. It does aim, however, to pose those questions with care and to offer up more forceful, sustained, and analytical replies—albeit, from diverse vantage points. Taken as a whole, our text delves into the historical antecedents of contemporary photographic genres and critical discussions; elaborates sustained readings of specific pictures; traces image life cycles as they move across contexts and serve different functions; reflects on the ethics and politics of different visual choices and approaches; and argues for particular ways of understanding the aesthetic domain. The reader, in turn, is invited to contemplate how images of suffering are made, how they should be made, how they circulate, the effects they have, and the dilemmas they pose for thoughtful producers and spectators. In the end, we hope that the exhibition and the book serve to foster a more reflective awareness of how we represent and address the rampant suffering and the corollary spectatorships that characterize our time.

MARK REINHARDT

PICTURING VIOLENCE: AESTHETICS AND THE ANXIETY OF CRITIQUE

> The critical image...must not only
> fail to capture its referent but show its failure.
>
> —JUDITH BUTLER

> The second commandment is all
> the more terrifying since there is no way to obey it.
>
> —BRUNO LATOUR

Photographers who take pictures of people in pain or in situations of danger or degradation sometimes aim to arouse concern, to provoke indignation, perhaps even to move viewers to action. In such cases, the image is an indictment; the outrage is directed at the scene depicted. The photograph's solicitations may fail, of course. Viewers may remain unmoved, unpersuaded, or simply uninterested. Doubtless, this is the likely outcome: it happens every day. But the aim is reasonable enough, for it is grounded in long experience. Repeatedly, pictures that expose the sources and conditions of injury have, in inciting horror at affliction or anger at injustice, helped to change what Elizabeth Spelman called "the economy of attention to suffering."[1] Photographs of this kind burn into memory: it is hard to forget them, even when we want to do so. Nor are these indelible images easy to avoid. They often come to us unbidden and unanticipated, with the turn of a page, a glance at a screen—a brief look, and the contours of consciousness are changed. Receptivity to such photographs is partly a matter of individual temperament and conviction but also a matter of social location, collective identification, and political affiliation. The meaning and effects of the images are at once singular and shared, intimate and public. As you read these words, you can, I'd wager, call to mind photographs that have worked in just this way. I suspect that, especially if you are an American of a certain age, the memory pictures include dogs and fire hoses turned on peaceful protestors; screaming children shedding napalmed clothes; a single, defiant demonstrator dancing before an advancing tank; clouds of black smoke billowing from two towers; and citizens stranded on rooftops awaiting rescue as floodwaters flow beneath them. Interpreting such icons can play an important role in the articulation of moral concerns and the making of political claims.[2]

1. Elizabeth V. Spelman, *Fruits of Sorrow: Framing Our Attention to Suffering* (Boston: Beacon Press, 1997), p. 7.

2. On this point see, among other sources, Mieke Bal's rich discussion of Vik Muniz's *Memory Rendering of Tram Bang Child* in the final essay of this book, and Susan Sontag, *Regarding the Pain of Others* (New York: Farrar, Straus and Giroux, 2003), pp. 84–6.

When the subject of a photograph is suffering, however, viewers also may respond with dismay or indignation to the manner of depiction. Something about the picture may strike some viewers as obscuring or falsifying the nature of the situation. Or the picture may seem to diminish the suffering in question. Conversely, it may be that, when suffering is conveyed most vividly, the photograph itself arouses the greatest ire: an image may even be a kind of violation of privacy, say, or of dignity, adding insult—another kind of injury—to the injury that is pictured. The depth of concern—even anger—aroused in these circumstances suggests that the stakes in the photographic representation of suffering are high. And surely they are, not only because the issues in the world beyond the image are as large as life and death but also because of the dilemmas involved in the framing of pictures themselves. The very qualities through which photographs may draw and hold our attention, and their power to enter and alter individual and collective memory, provide good reason for worrying when the representation of something as serious as suffering is somehow off.

Off in what way? The very imprecision of my language begins to suggest a theme that will concern me throughout this essay: for all of the unease that is rightly generated by photography's traffic in pain, providing a satisfactory account of where the troubles lie and how they are best addressed proves to be a vexing undertaking. One common, even dominant, term for expressing concern about ways in which photographs can fail in response to human suffering is "aestheticization." The challenge to the aestheticization of suffering in photographic representation runs through much twentieth-century criticism, from the recent work of, for instance, Abigail Solomon-Godeau, Martha Rosler, Allan Sekula, and Susan Sontag back through some of the formative early writings of the Frankfurt School. The ways in which this critique is framed vary from critic to critic and era to era, but all share a sense that, to put the matter in the starkest terms, aestheticizing suffering is inherently both artistically and politically reactionary, a way of mistreating the subject and inviting passive consumption, narcissistic appropriation, condescension, or even sadism on the part of viewers.

It is hard not to feel the force of such worries. The exhibition at the center of this book was organized, in no small part, in order to explore them. Yet, I have come to doubt that "aestheticization" is an entirely satisfactory—or even altogether coherent—concept for addressing what might be problematical in photographs of suffering. There are certainly times or ways in which turning the suffering of another human being into a beautiful or formally elegant image seems somehow indecent. Insofar as it is the aesthetic character of the picture that leads to denigration of the subject or spectatorial passivity, the vocabulary of aestheticization may, to a certain extent, help us to understand how these effects are produced. But more often, the term undercuts or dilutes the critic's best insights, and critique risks oversimplification even when the target is narrowed to the more specific problem of beauty in the representation of suffering. In this essay, I try to show how and why this is the case. By revisiting the work of some familiar critics in the company of many of the photographs gathered in this book, I explore both the conceptual limits of the idea of aestheticization and the anxieties that underwrite it—anxieties that, I contend, ultimately prove to be about the very nature of photographic representation itself. My hope is that clarifying a few issues will help to put critical worries on a sounder footing and will also help foster recognition, even affirmation, of the fruitful ways in which certain aesthetic strategies can help to deepen engagement with and understanding of suffering's meaning, sources, effects, and implications for the spectator.

My initial approach to this problem will be oblique. I turn first to the grisly archives of Abu Ghraib, a case in which the problem of the aesthetic is of peripheral importance but which reveals, in extremis and hence with unusual clarity, the capacity of photographs both to mobilize political sentiment over the suffering represented and also to produce suffering through the very act of representing it. Thinking through this example thus helps us begin to frame the issues that the subsequent inquiry must address more directly.

FIGURE 1
IRAQI CHILDREN KILLED BY AMERICAN BOMBS

ABSENCE, PRESENCE, AND THE FACES OF SUFFERING

Extending the indirection one step further, let us begin with some photographs that one *cannot* see—for, as a response to suffering, the refusal to picture may pose the most basic problems of all. Consider one conspicuous absence from the early days of the Iraq war (**FIG. 1**). This "image" stands in for the reluctance of the news of the United States' media—widely noted by critics of the American occupation of Iraq—to present photographs that would reveal the death and violence that the invasion of 2003 visited upon ordinary Iraqis. It is not that such photographs were never taken, but that American media outlets typically declined to show them, even when they were available. Images of destruction were instead presented, as Judith Butler has pointed out, through the distancing—even imperial—framing offered by the aerial view.[3] Such a criticism, of course, suggests that this was a politically costly evasion: the perspective and imagery adopted in most reporting made the consequences of American policy and the humanity of those afflicted less evident and, thus, the administration's claims about the nature of the conflict harder to contest. On this account, pictures showing the intensity and individual-

3. Judith Butler, *Precarious Life: The Powers of Mourning and Violence* (New York: Verso, 2004), p. 149.

ity of suffering had at least the potential to alter popular perceptions and understanding, opening more space for critical analyses of and opposition to the war.

In the widely circulated photographs from the Abu Ghraib prison—which are all too full of examples of intense suffering, showed close up—those hopeful assumptions about the consequences of picturing are both confirmed and complicated. Take the case of this familiar image: a hooded man, wearing what appears to be blanket as some kind of makeshift poncho, stands on an upended cardboard box, arms outstretched, electrical wires attached to each hand (**PLATE 57**). It scarcely needs repeating that this photograph has become iconic, appearing not only in the mass media but plastered on walls and placards from Los Angeles to New York to London to Tehran to Baghdad (**PLATE 56**). Clearly, it has joined the memory pictures catalogued above.[4] Responses to the image were, of course, hardly uniform (like so many global icons, it is a site of politically charged interpretive contestations that have taken different forms in different settings). In the United States, the most pugnacious conservative commentators went so far as to direct *their* indignation not at the horrifying scene itself but at those who suggested it revealed something important about the conduct and character of the war. Still, it is easy enough to sketch, in crude outlines, the dominant American response: the publication of the Abu Ghraib pictures in this country in late April and early May of 2004 prompted outrage and political challenges even from many who had supported the war and its conduct. Although certain political actors and interests tried to redirect the anger, the extent to which the pictures threatened the war's popularity can be seen in the efforts to keep the images out of circulation altogether. We might note, first, that the news organs most partisan in advocating for the Bush administration and its policies were reluctant to reproduce the pictures or give much space to their discussion, and, second, that the Defense Department not only continues to refuse journalists access to much of its archive of photographs documenting American abuse of Iraqi prisoners but vigorously contested the ACLU's Freedom of Information Act (FOIA) lawsuit requesting the material's release.[5] In these respects, the political effects of the pictures are clear enough.

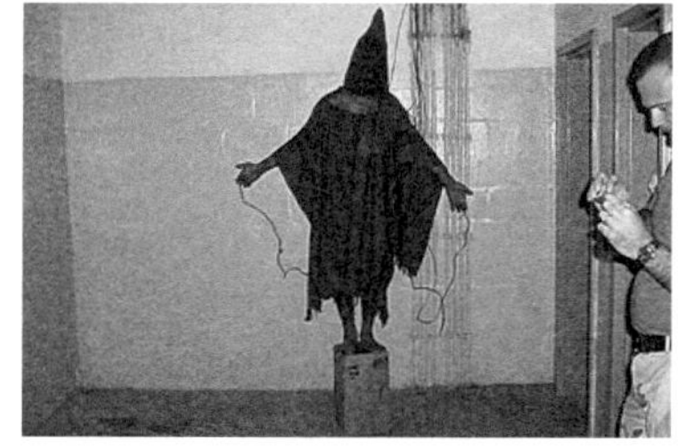

FIGURE 2
DETAINEE, WITH STAFF SERGEANT IVAN FREDERICK II IN FOREGROUND

Yet, it is just as obvious that the taking of pictures was not incidental but *integral* to the notorious events at Abu Ghraib. Torture in the prison could, of course, have been carried out without the aid of photography, as it has been on countless other occasions throughout history, but the cameras that were, in this instance, ubiquitous did not merely record what happened: they were instruments used to abuse and humiliate prisoners. Nor was that use exhausted in the initial encounter. In many pictures, the faces of the tortured stare out at us in a moment not only of fear and pain but also of shame, as we, by looking, prolong the shaming. Viewing and disseminating these pictures thus complete the rituals of degradation first enacted in the prison. The guards who showed pictures to prisoners in their cells or threatened to send copies to the victims' families understood this well enough, even if those guards who took, posed in, and circulated the pictures among friends evidently had no idea how shameful *they* would appear in the eyes of most viewers

4. That it has done so may seem to speak against my suggestion that questions of aesthetics are unimportant in the case of Abu Ghraib, for surely the emergence of *this* particular picture as the icon of Abu Ghraib is largely due to its striking simplicity at the level of form, along with its absence of nudity and obvious echoes of the Crucifixion. For my purposes, though, what matters is that the aesthetics of the image are not in any important respect constitutive of the violations involved; given when, how, and why the prison pictures were taken, there is no conceivable aesthetic quality that could alter what is objectionable about them.

5. *New York Post*, *The Weekly Standard*, and Fox News all gave considerably less attention to the photographs than did most major news outlets. See Timothy Noah, "The Right's Abu Ghraib Denial. Is the Liberal Outrage Really Worse than the Torture?" *Slate*, May 11, 2004. In February 2006, and then more completely the next month, *Salon* magazine published an archive of leaked material from the United State's Army's Criminal Investigation Command (CID). Mark Benjamin, "The Abu Ghraib Files," *Salon*, February 16, 2006. http://www.salon.com/news/feature/2006/02/16/abu_ghraib/ and Joan Walsh, "The Abu Ghraib Files," http://www.salon.com/news/abu_ghraib/2006/03/14/introduction/index.html

when the pictures became public (**FIG. 2**).[6] Insofar as photographs of this kind are performative artifacts that help to create or prolong the very suffering they document, we have good reasons—rather different from those, say, of Fox News or the *New York Post*—for hesitating over their re-presentation now.

None of this entails that either the interests of the individual victims or the imperatives of justice would have been met if the American media in April 2004 had simply refused to reproduce the images from the prison, as it did those of bombing casualties in 2003. After all, the pictures were crucial for turning reports of prisoner abuse into a major international scandal. In the three months between January 2004, when the events in Abu Ghraib were reported by American newspapers for the first time, and the publication of the photographs, the story had basically vanished from the press and failed to generate significant public discussion; in the two years since the first release of the pictures, revelations of still worse atrocities, unaccompanied by further visual evidence, have not created comparable levels of concern, or even awareness, in the United States. As Anthony Lewis has noted, "it was *seeing* the mistreatment that produced the outrage."[7] Still, while the dissemination of the photographs as news and their reframing as signs of protest have clearly been important, the way in which this traffic may also extend the pictures' capacity to humiliate suggests that when and how to present them requires careful consideration.

This problem loomed large during the organization of "Beautiful Suffering." Our ultimate willingness to exhibit the **Abu Ghraib image** reproduced here (**PLATE 57**) was partly due to our sense that anyone who came across it in this context was likely to be familiar with it and, furthermore, to have easy access to it in many other places. But such is the case with all of the most familiar of the prison pictures (for instance, the widely circulated photograph in which Lynndie England holds a leash tied around the neck of a prone and naked prisoner). More important to our decision was a feature distinguishing this particular photograph from many others that were published: one form of abuse inflicted upon the man pictured—his forcible hooding with a black sandbag—now preserves his anonymity. Press coverage of the prison scandal did not protect all prisoners in this way. True, American newspapers and magazines did conclude that decency required the suppression of many photographs and the alteration of others, but these editorial decisions appeared to be focused more on the readership's sense of propriety than on the dignity of the tortured. One can hear that emphasis, for instance, in *The Washington Post* executive editor Leonard Downie Jr.'s comment that many pictures were "in such bad taste," particularly because of "the extensive nudity," that they were unfit for publication. This concern about nudity was pervasive; routinely, papers and magazines reproducing the pictures deliberately blurred genitalia to the point of illegibility. Faces, however, apparently required no such digital drapery: in the *Post*, as in most other publications, they were not altered. And so the victims were identifiable and—since many of these photographs remain in circulation—anyone may still look at them, endlessly extending the moment of violation.[8]

When it comes to the faces of *American* sufferers, in contrast, the idea that photographs may compound affliction or injure dignity has been pervasive from the war's beginning, in 2003. In order to be embedded with the American forces, photographers

6. Helpful reports on, analyses of, and speculations about the strategic role played by photographs in the humiliation of prisoners at Abu Ghraib can be found in the following sources: Susan Sontag, "Regarding the Torture of Others," *The New York Times Magazine*, May 23, 2004; Dora Apel, "Torture Culture: Lynching Photographs and the Images of Abu Ghraib," *Art Journal* 64.2 (Summer 2005): 88(13); Ian Fisher, "The Struggle for Iraq," *The New York Times*, May 5, 2004, p. A1; Hassan M. Fattah, "Symbol of Abu Ghraib Seeks to Spare Others His Nightmare," *The New York Times*, Saturday, March 11, 2006, p. A1; Seymour Hersh "Photographs from a Prison," *Inconvenient Evidence: Iraqi Prison Photographs from Abu Ghraib* (New York: International Center of Photography).

7. Anthony Lewis, "The Torture Administration," *The Nation*, December 26, 2005, p. 13. Connie Coyne documented the scant newspaper coverage given to the story between the first, brief reports and the release of the photographs. See Coyne, "Photos Aren't the Most Shocking Part of the Abuse Story," *The Salt Lake Tribune*, May 8, 2004, p. B2. Since Coyne and Lewis wrote, there has been further confirmation of their views. For instance, *Salon*'s vast archive of images has, in the absence of replication in major publications, had little visible effect on public discourse or opinion.

8. The remarks from Leonard Downie Jr. are cited in Apel, "Torture Culture," p. 98. Downie's comments were made in an online forum. See: http://www.washingtonpost.com/wp-dyn/articles/A44952-2004May21.html. Pressed by readers, Downie insisted that editorial choices *were* driven by a concern with prisoners' "dignity" (and surely the nakedness of the prisoners was one aspect of their humiliation). I believe, however, that the entirety of his remarks and the broader context of the *Post*'s coverage at the time make it clear that the paper was more sensitive to the problem of offending viewers than to the ethical question of how to protect those visible in the pictures. As Sontag remarked about such editorial decisions more generally, "good taste" is "always a repressive standard when invoked by institutions." Sontag, *Regarding*, p. 69.

must agree not to take pictures showing the faces of dead or wounded servicemen. Nor, more generally, are dead American soldiers easy to find in the photographic record of the war as produced by the American media. Indeed, figure one above could just as accurately have been titled *American Military Casualties*—for while reportage in this country offered virtually no visual record of the suffering of Iraqi civilians during the invasion (when public support for the war was high, and the Bush administration promised a speedy victory followed by a heroes' welcome), in more recent journalistic coverage of the continuing violence there have been more pictures of Iraqi than of American casualties. According to a comprehensive *Los Angeles Times* study of the contents of major news sources from September 11, 2004, through February 28, 2005, neither that paper nor *The New York Times* and *The Washington Post*, nor *Time* and *Newsweek* magazines published a single picture of a dead American soldier.[9] When running stories on soldiers killed in combat, most papers and magazines illustrated them with pictures of grieving families or memorial services back home. The rare instances in which a photographer sought to take or a (minor, regional) newspaper printed pictures in which the American dead are visible provoked, respectively, fierce resistance from soldiers or outrage from readers.[10] As Susan Sontag remarked, "The more remote or exotic the place, the more likely we are to have full frontal views of the dead and dying."[11] (This attitude about the "exotic" dead is one of the conditions that facilitated the making and, certainly, the circulation of Luc Delahaye's stunning **Taliban** (**PLATE 4**), a work that, unlike some images gathered in this book has, to the best of my knowledge, generated no public controversy.)

Obviously, then, my initial contrast between the political costs of the dearth of images of Iraqi suffering and the potentially transformative effects when such pictures are widely circulated grossly simplified the problem. Is there a fundamental tension here, in the politics of exposure? Is the problem that the dissemination of images that are broadly useful as a means of informing and mobilizing relevant publics nonetheless does some kind of injury to the specific individuals pictured (and perhaps, by extension, to the group or culture or cause for which such individuals are taken to stand)? Although it would appear to be supported by much of the foregoing, that suggestion, too, understates the ethical and political complexity that marks this case of abusive representation and fraught circulation. We can see this by noting, however briefly, two additional episodes in the strangely twisting-and-turning story of who can and cannot be seen in the photographs from Iraq. The first involves the professed (and, to say the least, belated) recognition by the masters of the prison that torture by camera raises issues about the politics of representation and circulation. Despite the obvious ironies of the gesture, it is still revealing that government lawyers fought the FOIA lawsuit filed by the ACLU by arguing that releasing photographs from Abu Ghraib would be a form of public humiliation and would thus constitute a violation of the Geneva Conventions.[12] The argument marks the ways in which the recognition that photographic representation can radically undermine the dignity of those pictured has been codified in the discourse of international law, even as this particular iteration shows how that recognition can also be deployed opportunistically against those whose interests are ostensibly being protected.

9. James Rainey, "Portraits of War, Unseen Pictures, Untold Stories," *Los Angeles Times*, May 21, 2005, p. A1. Rainey reported that, in the period covered, the *Los Angeles Times* alone printed forty-one pictures of dead Iraqis.

10. Rainey, "Portraits of War."

11. Sontag, *Regarding*, p. 70.

12. In ruling against the government, Federal District Court judge Alvin Hellerstein noted that this problem could be avoided if the faces of the prisoners were obscured, thus protecting their identities. The government appealed his ruling. On March 29, 2006, after I had drafted this essay, the government dropped its appeal, agreeing to turn over 77 items requested by the ACLU, but also said it reserved the right to fight requests for any other images from the prison. Meanwhile, some news agencies have followed Hellerstein's recommended practice in recent coverage. See, for instance, BBC news and CNN coverage of February 15, 2006: http://news.bbc.co.uk/2/hi/middle_east/4715540.stm, http://www.cnn.com/2006/WORLD/meast/02/15/abughraib.photos/

The other development, worth a slightly longer recounting, concerns the appropriation and redeployment by former prisoners of the photographs. On March 11, 2006, *The New York Times* ran a picture on page one, identifying Ali Shalal Qaissi as the hooded man "who became the indelible symbol of the torture at Abu Ghraib." The exposure of his identity was not initiated by the *Times*: Qaissi had already publicly identified himself as the man in the photograph and had begun granting interviews to Western publications and television stations. Qaissi had founded the Association of Victims of American Occupation Prisons with other former prisoners who figured in published photographs. He then had traveled through the Middle East presenting slideshows of images from Abu Ghraib and talking about the severity and extent of prisoner abuse. The *Times* account quoted him as saying, "I never wanted to become famous, especially not in this way," but it also characterized Qaissi as someone who "clearly understands the power of the image," observing that he had reproduced it on his business card (**FIG. 3**).[13] It would appear, then, that any moral or political scruples about revealing the identity of those pictured must be complicated by a recognition of both the right of victims to identify themselves at a time of their choosing and also their capacity to re-frame the images for their own purposes, so that an image originally constructed for its power to humiliate may take on a very different meaning.

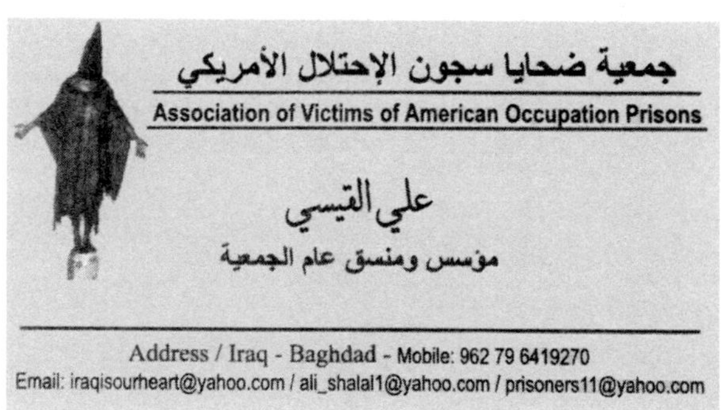

FIGURE 3
ALI SHALAL QAISSI AND BUSINESS CARD, *THE NEW YORK TIMES*, MARCH 11, 2006, P. A1.
COURTESY *NEW YORK TIMES*.

Yet, the story did not end there. One week later the *Times* ran a second article retracting the first, explaining that American military evidence indicated that another man was the figure in the notorious photograph that Qaissi had held in his hands for the *Times* photographer, and that Qaissi himself now conceded that it was a different man in this particular picture.[14] There was still no doubt that Qaissi had been a prisoner at Abu Ghraib. There was good reason to believe that he, too, had been hooded and then photographed—without electrical wires or being forced to stand on a box—on the same day and with the same cameras. But there was no publicly available evidence to support his claim that he was the subject of photographs virtually identical to the now-famous one, and there was considerable evidence that, over time, he had substantially changed his account of his experiences at Abu Ghraib. Qaissi had begun claiming to be the man in the famous picture more than a year after he first began talking about his imprisonment, and he had evidently risen to prominence as a political spokesman for victims largely on the basis of that claim. He had not only resignified the photograph but had used his acts of resignification to build something of a career.[15] Meanwhile, the *Times* reported that the whereabouts of the prisoner now believed to be "the man on the box" were unknown, and he had not at any moment after his release come forward to identify himself publicly as the subject of the photograph.[16] Based on the preceding incidents and reflections, we may say about photographic absences what Michel Foucault had to say about silences in general: "There is not one but many...and they are an integral part of the strategies that

13. Fattah, "Symbol of Abu Ghraib."

14. Kate Zernike, "Cited as Symbol of Abu Ghraib, Man Admits He Is Not in Photo," *The New York Times*, Saturday, March 18, 2006, p. A1. I had intended to use the photograph as a figure illustration, but the photographer, Shawn Baldwin, refused to grant permission. His communications indicated that, because the story was retracted, he does not want the image to be reproduced anywhere. (Meanwhile, the picture continues to have vigorous afterlife on the internet.) The attitude that a picture based on false or dubious claims should be withdrawn from circulation reflects, I think, the long tradition of seeing photojournalism as having privileged access to truth and the real. For a discussion of that tradition, see Erina Duganne's essay in this volume.

15. For a retroactive account, on which I draw in my discussion here, see Michael Scherer, "The Wrong Man," *Salon*, March 18, 2006 (http://www.salon.com/news/feature/2006/03/18/torture_photo_update/)

16. Zernike, "Cited as Symbol." In this second story, the *Times* maintained that much of Qaissi's testimony on many other details of his imprisonment were credible, but the coverage in *Salon* suggested that there are more pervasive problems with Qaissi's reports on his imprisonment. Scherer, "The Wrong Man."

underlie and permeate discourses."[17]

These cases from Iraq drive home some of the most important effects that photographs of suffering can have and vividly reveal how photography's traffic in pain can compound the injuries pictured. They further intimate the elasticity of photographic meaning, the importance of the context of circulation or display, and the related opportunities for reframing. The total absence of imagery with which I began and the violent picturing at Abu Ghraib mark the outer limits of the arena I will explore for the remainder of this essay. The questions of photographic representation on which most critics rightly seek to concentrate tend to concern neither the use of the camera as one more tool in the torturer's kit nor the refusal to picture. Rather, these questions concentrate on those murkier issues that arise in assorted, more common forms of journalistic and artistic picturing—in which even photographs that might come to seem highly problematical present themselves to us with, as it were, some kind of moral or political alibi. Yet the examples I have just considered are not so easy to set aside, even when we turn to photographs taken with the purpose of informing, or deepening understanding, or provoking uncomfortable reflection, or aiding in the struggle to identify and undo injustice. Such pictures often confront us in more subtle and complex ways with either the move of withholding—of turning from or refusing to display certain painful circumstances of the human body—or that of displaying in a manner that preserves or compounds injuries and oppressions. And it is this problematic of withholding and display that stands at the center of both the critique of aestheticization and the anxieties that, I will argue, shape that critique in ways that can obscure the ethical and political problems of and possibilities in the representation of human suffering.

17. Michel Foucault, *The History of Sexuality, Volume One: An Introduction*, trans. Robert Hurley, (New York: Vintage, 1980), p. 27.

THE WORK OF AESTHETICIZATION IN THE AGE OF MECHANICAL REPRODUCTION

In 1934, in his brilliant and influential essay "The Author as Producer," Walter Benjamin bemoaned the inability of photography "to convey anything about a power station or a factory other than, 'What a beautiful world!'" Benjamin's lament was at once highly specific and sweeping. He was reflecting in particular on the then-current movement known as New Objectivity, but his analyses identified dangers that seemed both broad and fundamental. Photography in his time, he thought, had "succeeded in transforming even abject poverty—by apprehending it in a fashionably perfected manner—into an object of enjoyment." What this revealed, he continued, was that it was "one of [photography's] political functions to renew from within—that is, fashionably—the world as it is."[18] Here, Benjamin linked political quiescence to a particular kind of pleasurable consumption. Obscenely, the extremities of human suffering or injustice ("*even*" abject poverty) are the raw materials of this form of spectatorial gratification. And it is the nature of the picture that plays a key role.

18. Benjamin, "The Author as Producer," *Walter Benjamin: Selected Writing, Volume 2, 1927–1934*, Michael W. Jennings et al., eds. (Cambridge, MA: Harvard University Press, 1999), p. 775.

Which picture? Does the problem reside in photographs of a certain kind or in photography itself? What precisely, for that matter, *is* the problem? As a point of entry, we might consider a line from Sontag's *On Photography*, a work in which worries about the moral and political failings of photographic images run especially deep. "Photographs can and do distress," she writes, "but the aestheticizing tendency of photography is such that the medium which conveys distress ends by neutralizing it."[19] Here, we encounter a criticism of photography *tout court* in which the limitations of the form are explicitly grounded in the problem of aestheticization. Photography tends to aestheticize, and aestheticization prompts passivity or contentment in the face of trauma and injustice. This is no small claim. To my mind, it is neither obviously true nor even obviously clear. To begin with, then, we might ask what aestheticization entails.

19. Sontag, *On Photography* (New York: Delta, 1978), p. 108.

Some clarification can be found in the work of those Anglo-American analytical philosophers who, at least since the mid-twentieth century, have sought to characterize "the aesthetic attitude." This kind of philosophical work is preoccupied with neither photography nor suffering, and it differs fundamentally in both vocabulary and sensibility from the critical approaches that most interest me here. Despite this, accounts of "the aesthetic attitude" can help us to see why it is that "aestheticizing suffering" can be a term of opprobrium, and how it is that aestheticization might be thought to produce the moral and political ills attributed to it. Extending a tradition rooted in Kant's *Critique of Judgment*, such thinkers make disinterested pleasure the defining characteristic of the aesthetic. Jerome Stolnitz, for instance, characterized the "aesthetic attitude" as one in play when "we pay attention to a thing simply for the way it looks or sounds or feels," when we are engaged in "disinterested and sympathetic contemplation" of an "object of awareness...for its own sake alone." More recently, Marcia Muelder Eaton wrote that the point of such acts of attention is "delight," for "delight in what resides intrinsically in something is a mark of the aesthetic generally."[20] Such a response is one, plausible way to respond to, say, a painter's beautiful still life (the kind of example these thinkers tend to have in mind). When photographers approach real human beings in their moment of affliction, however, things may get trickier. If such a circumstance becomes the occasion to produce an image offering pleasure, and only pleasure, through an exclusive focus on the work's formal or internal properties—so that not only the causes of and responsibility for suffering but also its meaning and implications are wholly obscured while being used as resources for gratification—then the aestheticizing work of photography would obviously be an especially unproductive, indeed pernicious, response to the world's calamities and injustices. If this kind of response is *all* that the critics of the aestheticization of suffering aim to capture, then their reasons for taking on that target seem sound enough. Better no photographs at all than photographs like that.

20. Jerome Stolnitz, "The Aesthetic Attitude," p. 79, and Marcia Muldar Eaton, "Locating the Aesthetic," p. 87, both in Carolyn Korsemeyer, *Aesthetics: The Big Questions* (Oxford: Blackwell Publishing, 1998). For all the narrowness of his understanding of what art can be and despite his disputable account of the disinterested character of judgments of taste, Kant's own position was considerably more complex and ambitious than the arguments I am engaging here. If that difference makes his work ultimately more fruitful and enduring, it makes these recent variations more helpful for identifying some of the confusions that mark contemporary critical discourse.

Again, however, it seems important to ask, "What photographs are like that?" All photographs of human sufferers? *Must* a photographic representation of a person in pain draw us away from a consideration of how to understand or address the problem and toward taking unadulterated pleasure in the way that the circumstances of the person's misery are given visual form? Or, to put the point more modestly, must the formal features of a photographic image in some way blunt critical engagement with the social dynamics of the scene depicted?

I suspect few viewers really believe this, at least not consistently. And yet, when struggling to articulate what disturbs them about particular pictures or photographic tendencies, some critics (Sontag among them) are sometimes tempted by this position and, more often, are drawn to language that, against their own best insights, logically entails such a view. It is this tendency, above all, that makes "aestheticization" an overly blunt tool for getting at what is most troubling about certain photographs of suffering people. Establishing how and why this is so will take some work, as we move back and forth between specific images and moments of critical reflection. It may help to begin with what appears, at least at first glance, to be the narrowest version of the aestheticization critique.

The terms suggested by the philosophers of the aesthetic attitude are more or less those in which the most hostile critics have often judged the work of photographers such as **James Nachtwey** (PLATE 21) and **Sebastião Salgado** (PLATE 49). Repeatedly, viewers have found something inherently objectionable in these extraordinarily vivid and exquisitely composed images that document the plight of human beings in assorted situations of extremity.[21] The consistent charge is that the aesthetic satisfaction of the images is a source of the pictures' failures to provide genuine understanding of the situations and suffering of those pictured: the aesthetic qualities are often cited as causes of the pictures' tendency to misdirect the viewer's attention, to place the emphasis of the glance on the quality of the image or, at least, to leave us with not much more than a sense of how striking the sufferers look in their moments of affliction. "What a beautiful world" indeed.

It is worth asking how well, in practice, this line of analysis captures what might be objectionable in the photographic representation of suffering. Let us look more closely—although this may not be easy to bear—at Nachtwey's **Sudan** (PLATE 21). It is one of the pictures in this volume that I find most troubling, and my conversations with viewers of the "Beautiful Suffering" exhibition have made it clear to me that this is by no means an atypical response. Is the trouble a matter of aestheticization? One thing militating against the charge is that it is hard to imagine a viewer who does not recoil in dismay at the scene depicted—does not, for a moment at least, look past the manner of depiction and simply find something unacceptable, even criminal, in the mere existence of circumstances such as these. It would be hard—and unfair—to read this photograph as inviting indifference or purely formal analysis. Still, part of what disturbs me is the character of the representation itself. Certainly, the composition draws our notice. The formal satisfactions—if one may speak that way of a picture that is so difficult, indeed excruciating, to look at—are directly reliant on the bodily ravages and contortions that signal the man's affliction. The photograph seems framed to take maximum advantage of the crossing diagonals, the contrast of light and dark, the interplay between the texture of the skin and that of the coarse cloth wrapped (so ineffectually, one imagines) around it. Is there something indecent about that? While we cannot justly say that such strategies seek to provide only disinterested formal pleasure, does the manner of composition subtly suggest that one redemptive reason for the existence of suffering of this kind is its presentation in just such a photograph? Are we supposed to be cheered by the triumph of artistry?

Nachtwey obviously would contest such a reading. He is widely quoted for his understanding of himself as not a "war photographer" but an "anti-war photographer" whose acts of witnessing contest the oppressions and atrocities he so consistently documents. He clearly intends **Sudan** and similar images to bring aid to the afflicted by challenging

21. See, for examples representing a wide range of opinion, Michael Kimmelman, "Can Suffering Be Too Beautiful?" *The New York Times*, July 13, 2001; David Levi-Strauss, *Between the Eyes: Essays on Photography and Politics* (New York: Aperture, 2003), pp. 4–7 and 42–50; Peder Jansson, "Photography's Dissidents: Documentarism vs. Visual Art? The Aesthetic Transformation of the Documentary Photograph," *Katalog*, Vol 13, no. 1, p. 42–6; Ingrid Sischy, "Good Intentions" *The New Yorker* Sept. 9, 1991, pp. 89–95; Sontag, *Regarding*, pp. 78–9.

the complacency of those who have the luxury of only encountering such extremity second hand.[22] I find it revealing, though, that even some of Nachtwey's greatest admirers seem anxious about the formal means through which he seeks to bear witness. In his introduction to *Inferno*, Luc Sante protested that the consistent formal virtuosity of the compositions "should not be mistaken for anything like aestheticization." In elaborating that claim, he argued that Nachtwey does not freight his images with heavy symbolic burdens and that his photographs merely reveal "what he sees, apparently in the order in which he sees it."[23]

22. See, for example, James Nachtwey, "Afterword," *Inferno* (London: Phaidon, 1999), pp. 468–71, and Steve Appleford, "The Eyes of Perpetual War," *LA Weekly*, November 20, 2002.

23. Luc Sante, "Introduction," Nachtwey, *Inferno*, p. 10.

In order to show that Nachtwey does not somehow justify or exploit or blunt awareness of the suffering he pictures, Sante not only denied the allusion and symbolic associations that so often mark Nachtwey's pictures (such as the resonances of the Crucifixion and the Pietà in **Sudan**), but he wrote as if the compositions are somehow natural or without artifice, even while he also acknowledged, as anyone must, how consistently striking and distinctive they are. What interests me about this is why Sante would be driven to make such claims, why—at least for a rhetorical move or two—he felt pressure to disavow the elements of mediation. The answer seems to be that an acknowledgment of the works' willed formal complexity and allusive range are what would validate the seemingly trivializing charge of aestheticization. But if this is the case, then there seems to be a slippage between, on the one hand, aestheticization in the sense of "inviting only pure formal pleasure" and, on the other, aestheticization in the sense of having any kind of formal properties whatsoever. A suspicion of a kind of morally obtuse obscuring or exploitation of pain slides into an anxiety—inchoate or unstated, but perhaps more powerful for that—of the formal choices and rhetorical conventions, and the resulting transformative work, of representation itself.

This slippage is not an isolated instance. The potential for it inheres in the very terms of critique. Consider the way "aestheticization" is defined in the *Oxford English Dictionary*: "To render æsthetic, or agreeable to a refined taste, to refine." Are the latter senses additional meanings or clarifications of the first? Does rendering a scene "aesthetic" necessarily make it agreeable, and agreeable specifically to the refined? One might, of course, turn to the meaning of the adjective "aesthetic," but here, too, we find a wobble: aesthetic means both "pertaining to sensuous perception received by the senses" and "pertaining to the appreciation or criticism of the beautiful."[24] The range of possible meanings is as narrow, then, as beautification-in-the-service-of-pleasure and as broad as sensory perception and all of the diverse ways in which images and the work of representation engage it. How much does that range affect or inflect critical discourse? Do indictments of aestheticization in the narrowest sense shade into a challenge to photographs' sensory engagement itself? Is it the work of giving photographs aesthetic form, as such—is it the very nature of the photographic image—that provokes anxiety? I suggest that something like this is often the case.

24. In fairness, I should note that the first definition of "aesthetic" is listed as obsolete, but my contention is that this sense lingers as an important presence or entailment in discussions of photography and broader questions of visual representation.

We can track the slippage, for instance, in the important and influential work of Allan Sekula. This work is often unusually acute, and nowhere more so than in his landmark essay "Dismantling Modernism, Reinventing Documentary (Notes on the Politics of

Representation)." Here, Sekula developed a devastating critique of the forms of quiescence and mystification invited by the dominant traditions in socially concerned documentary photography. He critically dissected the rhetoric of "objective" reportage that tends to reify and simplify the social dimensions of the scenes depicted and to "naturalize the eye of the observer." He was equally sharp in analyzing the particular subjectivist turn taken by many who accept that kind of critique: he illustrated how, when "documentary is officially recognized as art," all questions of reference are displaced by pure expressivism, and the attention of the viewer "is directed toward mannerism, toward sensibility."[25] Sekula, then, would have us accept neither images whose promise of access to the real involves problematical forms of reification and disavowal nor pictures that frankly give themselves over to aestheticization (in the narrow sense). Instead, he called for a more epistemologically complex, politically subversive approach to both the making and the exhibiting of photographs. A pivotal moment in this argument came when he issued the following complaint: "Documentary photography has amassed mountains of evidence. And yet...the genre has simultaneously contributed much to spectacle, to retinal excitation, to voyeurism, to terror, envy and nostalgia, and only a little to the critical understanding of the social world."[26]

25. Sekula, *Photography against the Grain: Essays and Photo Works, 1973–1983* (Halifax, NS: Press of the Nova Scotia College of Art and Design, 1984), pp. 56, 58.

26. Sekula, *Photography against the Grain*, p. 57.

In assessing photography's traffic in pain, Sekula's emphasis on critical understanding of the social world is indeed appropriate.[27] Many of his terms might be employed fruitfully in explaining where the representation of suffering falls short. I want to linger, however, on his stress on the "retinal" (with its echoes of Marcel Duchamp's "retinal flutter"), for it names, I think, a recurrent anxiety in those who write about photography and suffering, an anxiety about the relationship among vision, aesthetics, and understanding. Much of Sekula's argument appears to rest on a distinction between the purely visual or aesthetic and the critical or metacritical, and to worry about the capacity of the former to produce the latter. Even when explaining how an image *can* do the work of critique, challenging both prevailing social relations and the perceptual codes that sustain them, Sekula turned to text. He praised the way in which some artists "openly bracket their photographs with language" in order to "go beyond the meaning offered by the images themselves" and—in the case of his primary example, the work of Martha Rosler—to resist "the pornography of the 'direct' representation of misery" by placing language between the viewer and "'visual experience.'"[28]

27. This is only fitting since, as noted in our introduction to this volume, the title is in part an acknowledgment of Sekula's contributions to the topic and to his landmark essay, "The Traffic in Photographs." in *Photography against the Grain*.

28. Sekula, *Photography against the Grain*, p. 62.

This fear of the visual and privileging of the linguistic enter into even the work of Benjamin. Now, fundamental suspicion of images is surely neither the most important nor the most prevalent tendency in his work. Benjamin, after all, is a critic who lodged extraordinary hope and wrote with exceptional intensity about the potential radicalism and subversive power of a visual culture shaped by what he famously called "mechanical reproduction."[29] But that provides all the more reason to find it telling that when such a critic worries about aetheticization, he turns, for redress, to the word. In "The Author as Producer," Benjamin remarked: "What we require of the photographer is the ability to give his picture a caption that wrenches it from modish commerce and gives it a revolutionary use value. But we will make this demand most emphatically when we—the writers—take up photography."[30] In context (to be fair to Benjamin), this declaration was both an indictment

29. Walter Benjamin, "The Work of Art in the Age of Mechanical Reproduction," in Hannah Arendt, ed., *Illuminations* (New York: Shocken, 1969), pp. 217–52.

30. Benjamin, "Author as Producer," p. 775.

of the interrelationship between the formal and political conservatism of *writers* and a call for casting off intellectual restraints and radically transforming the apparatus of cultural production. Still, Benjamin's reliance not merely on the caption as the source of radical meaning but on writers as the ideal photographers betrays an anxiety about the shortcomings of both images and those for whom they are the preferred medium. Though Sontag was no stranger to this anxiety—to which, indeed, she succumbed more thoroughly than he—her observation on Benjamin rings true: "Moralists who love photographs always hope that words will save the picture."[31]

Of course, photographic meaning is hardly produced in isolation. All photographs, including solitary images displayed without caption or title, take their meaning only from the broader economy of statements and discourses (which, surely, include other images as well as written texts), as critics such as Sekula, John Tagg, and Michael Shapiro have shown so well.[32] Benjamin understood this, and shared with—helped engender in—those writers a sense that the critical value of a photograph lies in its ability to disrupt prevailing discursive economies and denaturalize or contest dominant codes. But how are these disruptions effected? Can it really be the case that images unsupervised by words are ill suited to the task? Is there not something in images that resists or eludes every effort to fix meaning through language? Might *that* be the underlying source of anxiety?[33] We can begin to explore these questions by comparing the very different ways in which Joel Meyerowitz and Thomas Ruff responded to the destruction of the World Trade Center.

A TALE OF TWO TOWERS

Perhaps because the events of September 11, 2001, were among the most photographed in world history, they stand out for the extent to which their portrayal in the mass media brought questions about the ethics of representing suffering into broad popular circulation: after this event unfolded, live, on television, it was broadly agreed that there were limits to what ought to be shown. Rudy Guiliani was responding to popular anxiety about the invasiveness and indecency of the camera when, on September 25, he banned photographic and video equipment from Ground Zero; signs posted on the perimeter of the site warned passersby that the taking of photographs was cause for prosecution.[34] Despite this ban, Joel Meyerowitz persuaded the city to grant him sole, unimpeded access to the site to photograph the clean-up operation. Over eight months, he took more than eight thousand photographs.[35] A model of careful composition, **North Tower and Woolworth Building** (**PLATE 16**) is among the most striking that Meyerowitz produced. The sharpness of the pipe at the lower left, the remnant of the wall above it, and the excavator on the right stand in dramatic contrast to the clouds and smoke that blur much of the image. The spray of water draws our eyes toward the center of the picture, and although no person is visible, it suggests the work of reconstruction. The resulting photograph conveys a sense not only of destruction and loss but also of active, even heroic, recovery. This rendering owes much to the conventions of history painting. But while these conventions underwrite the moral legibility of the image, shaping its field of connotations, they do so unselfconsciously, behind the scenes, as it were: the way in which they frame our reception is not thematized,

31. Sontag, *On Photography*, p. 108.

32. John Tagg "The Currency of the Photograph," in Victor Burgin, ed., *Thinking Photography* (London: Macmillan, 1982), pp. 110–41; Michael Shapiro, *The Politics of Representation: Writing Practices in Biography, Photography and Policy Analysis* (Madison: The University of Wisconsin Press, 1988), pp. 124–78.

33. I thank Susan Buck-Morss for pressing me to see this point (personal conversation, March 10, 2006). I also thank my colleague Christian Thorne for calling to my attention Buck-Morss' related writing on the ways in which the "meaning" of "photography's material trace" inevitably "surpasses the predetermination of the word." Buck-Morss, *Thinking Past Terror: Islamism and Critical Theory On the Left* (New York: Norton, 2003), p. 25.

34. Elisabetta Coletti, "City: No More Photographs of World Trade Center Site," AP, 9/26/01 *Boston Globe*

35. A selection of these images was subsequently sent to more than sixty countries, many of them in the Middle East and North Africa, as part of an exhibition initiated by the United States Department of State.

not part of what the picture invites us to think about.

In this regard, Thomas Ruff's **jpeg ny01** (**PLATE 17**) could not be more different. While Meyerowitz gained exclusive access to the World Trade Center site, Ruff required only access to the Internet, where he found Patrick Sison's Associated Press photograph of the Empire State Building and the burning towers (**FIG. 4**). By massively enlarging a JPEG of Sison's picture, Ruff altered the pixel structure and distorted the coloration. Seen in a large room at the photograph's full size (101 x 74 inches), these distortions are striking; the image changes, moreover, with proximity, looking almost entirely conventional when seen from a great distance and becoming more wildly pixelated as one gets closer. While Meyerowitz's picture effaces its governing conventions, Ruff's image calls attention to the digital processing that made it possible, thereby marking its distance from the event it putatively records and inviting reflection on the layers of mediation structuring perceptions of such events as 9/11. Thus, while it is a work of great visual power, Ruff's photograph also invites doubt or anxiety about its own labor. (The work is part of a recent series of similarly enlarged and pixelated JPEGs. Ruff first thought of the larger project as a "visual encyclopedia" of contemporary history, but as the work developed, he renounced as unachievable the aspiration "to explain the whole world in images.")[36]

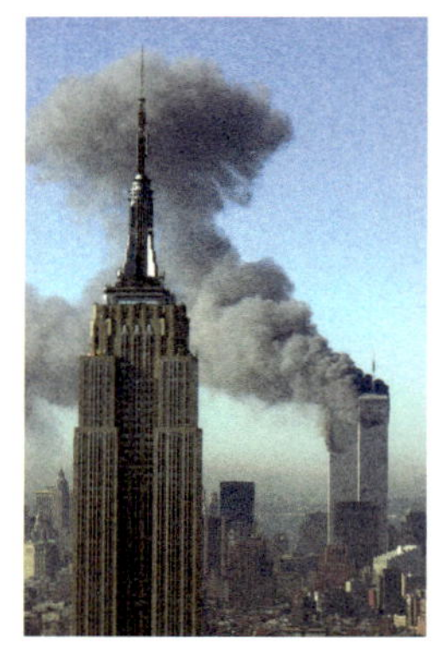

FIGURE 4
PATRICK SISON, "WORLD TRADE CENTER CRASH," 2001. COURTESY ASSOCIATED PRESS.

This pairing should trouble Sekula's framework for criticizing the limits of documentary photography and his rejection of the "pornography" of suffering. The ways in which **North Tower and Woolworth Building** confirms that framework are of course obvious and important. The picture naturalizes the code or visual rhetoric it employs. Although one might use that observation as part of a critical examination of problems in visual representation more generally or the representation of suffering in particular, to do this is to resist the solicitations of the image, to read it "against the grain." Photographing "after the fact," as Erina Duganne puts it in her exploration of other photographers elsewhere in this book, Meyerowitz is by no means fixated on the moment of injury or death; again, no bodies are visible in this picture. And such social information as the photograph conveys is produced in part through the dramatic framing—one agent of this work's "retinal excitation." What the aesthetics of this image do not do, however, is to promote critical vision or deepen understanding. Yet, Ruff's work should make it hard to treat that failure as an indictment of the aestheticizing tendency of the photograph. We could say that Ruff "aestheticizes" the suffering of others in that an occasion of extreme violence became the subject of a photograph that insists one pay sustained attention to its formal features. Although they are in no way visible in his photograph, great numbers of dying people were inside the buildings at the moment Ruff's source image was produced. One might experience moral unease in response. (In some moods, I do.) It is precisely *through* its aesthetic strategies, however, that this remarkable photograph invites both critical engagement and a kind of metacritical reflection on the mass-mediated character of disaster, the fascination such spectacles tend

36. "Thomas Ruff in conversation with Vicki Goldberg," *The Brooklyn Rail*, June, 2005.

to inspire, and the confidence they tend to invite in their reality—a confidence undermined by the image's flagrant distortions. Certainly the title of the work and the background information to which it points (for example, that Ruff began with an appropriation of someone else's photograph) accentuate these features, but this is a picture that would solicit critique even without the aid of the word.

Perhaps this reading is obvious. Yet, by highlighting the complex responses invited by Ruff's photographic approach, this account pushes against all those moments in which the critics of aestheticization slide from their narrowest charges to their broadest anxieties about photographs and aesthetics as such. Consider, one last time, the case of Benjamin. In the same passages from "The Author as Producer" that I have cited above, he complained about photography's inability to "record a tenement block or a refuse heap without transfiguring it."[37] Here, we seem to have reached the heart of the matter, for what, after all, is the alternative to transfiguration? Could it be avoided? As David Levi-Strauss noted in a cogent reflection on these issues, "to represent is to aestheticize; that is, to transform."[38] It is not as if a photograph of human suffering could simply be without aesthetic properties, thus *avoiding* the employment of a visual rhetoric or the generation of thought and feeling through the interaction between—for want of better terms—form and content. Although these points may seem self evident, we have seen how they are belied by assumptions or entailments integral to the discourse of aestheticization. In the grip of anxiety about aesthetics and the photographic image, critique ends up in some peculiar positions. This is what gives Bruno Latour's epigram about the terrors of the Second Commandment—with which I began this essay—its pertinence and its force.[39]

In *Regarding the Pain of Others*, Sontag seemed at times to recognize something like this, reacting against the critical discourse to which she had so formatively contributed. She wrote with some skepticism about the moral disapproval of spectacle. Noting the inevitability of aesthetic transformation, she complained about critiques (she could have included any number of passages in *On Photography*) that offer "remarkable exaggerations about what photographers ought or ought not to do." Yet, the pages that immediately follow this remark repeatedly shift back and forth between analysis founded on the irreducibility of the aesthetic and further claims about the ways in which aesthetics displace political and moral commitment.[40] Even when critical anxiety is explicitly recognized and renounced, it may be hard to shake. If moralists who love photographs hope the word will save the image, what is it about the image that is in need of saving? Perhaps, in the end, the relevant anxiety is rooted in one the oldest sources (along with the Second Commandment) of iconoclasm—a fear that the image is an extra step removed from truth and is likely to corrupt those ill suited to truth's rigors. In her own critique of Salgado's "aestheticised photographic imagery" of human catastrophes, Abigail Solomon-Godeau remarked on the dangers such aestheticism poses, adding that "as Plato insisted two thousand years ago, it is not by means of the image that moral, ethical, or political knowledge is produced." The sweep and bald simplicity of this iconophobic assertion are unusual—as is the unembarrassed evocation of a philosopher so intent on controlling art, and undercutting the authority of artists and images, but sentiment and source may,

37. Benjamin, "Author as Producer," p. 775.

38. Levi-Strauss, *Between the Eyes*, p. 7. Levi-Strauss is as acute on this point as any commentator I have read and has, for that reason, been a significant resource for my own thinking throughout this essay. I think, however, that he proceeds too swiftly once he has established the futility of seeking to avoid the aesthetic work of transformation: he does not pay much critical attention to the persistence or sources of the temptation to denounce aestheticization in the broad sense. And, because he has concluded that photographers such as Salgado and Nachtwey must of course produce images that are "aesthetic," he is too quick to gloss over the ways in which their framing of their subjects and solicitation of their viewers can be problematical.

39. Latour, "What Is Iconoclash? Or Is There a World beyond the Image and the Image Wars?" in Bruno Latour and Peter Weibel, eds. *Iconoclash: Beyond the Image Wars in Science, Religion, and Art* (Karlsruhe: ZKM; Cambridge, MA: MIT Press, 2002), p. 23. Using the notion of "iconoclash," Latour's essay offers a brilliant taxonomy of the repeated struggles between iconoclasm and iconophilia. A fuller, better version of my own essay would link the discussion of "aestheticization" to Latour's larger analytic framework and arguments.

40. Sontag, *Regarding*, pp. 74–81.

in less obviously recognizable ways, shape the whole discourse about the "aestheticizing tendency of photography": long after Platonic metaphysics has lost plausibility, some of its worries seem to linger.[41]

41. Solomon-Godeau, "Lament of the Images: Alfredo Jaar and the Ethics of Representation," *Aperture* no. 181 (Winter 2005): 42. While expressing bemusement at such an unembarrassed invocation of Platonism, I want to add that Plato's texts are far more complex than such references allow. Hostility to art is one powerful voice, but not the only one, in the elaborate ensemble that is the *Republic*; if that work clearly denigrated painters as far from truth, it also modeled the philosopher's apprehension of truth through a series of visual metaphors and distinguished truth in part by the magnificence of its aesthetic appeal. Similarly, the *Symposium* made the visual perception of beauty a key, if preliminary, step on the road to loving moral goodness. That strand in his texts has helped to inspire such recent critical works as Elaine Scarry, *On Beauty and Being Just* (Princeton, NJ: Princeton University Press, 1999), a work that in its reductive links between aesthetic beauty and the commitment to justice is something of a mirror image to the anxiety I have been analyzing. Two opposing critical tendencies thus share the same source: Plato is vast, containing multitudes.

BEAUTIFUL WORLD?

Despite the title of this volume, I have so far given beauty only passing mention in these reflections. Placing the emphasis elsewhere is justified, I think, in that to focus solely or primarily on the question of beauty and suffering would be to miss both the scope of the problem that has concerned me and the range of issues raised by the images gathered in this book. The critical anxiety I have sought to trace and resist seems to be aroused, as we have seen, by the photographic image and the aesthetic in the broadest sense. Yet simply to subsume beauty in the aesthetic would distort the analysis, too. While the idea of a representational photograph without any aesthetic properties is incoherent, a picture involving suffering obviously need not be beautiful—and many of the images exhibited in "Beautiful Suffering" are *not*, rigorously speaking, beautiful, though almost all of them are in some way formally striking, and many engage the spectator through aesthetically complex modes of address. It is important to ask, then, whether there are special difficulties that arise when loss or pain or affliction become the occasion for a beautiful image. If there are such difficulties, furthermore, then given the way in which the beautiful—one aesthetic modality among many—has so often monopolized discussions of the aesthetic as such (leading at times to a conflation of the one with the other), it is worth wondering whether concerns more appropriately aroused by beauty in particular have seeped into the broader discourse about aestheticization.

Consider, for example, the following observation by Arthur Danto: "'How beautiful those mourning women are beside the shattered pots of their burned and bombed houses, standing against the pale morning sky' is not a morally permissible vision. If, that is, one were to see a sight like this in reality and find it beautiful one would wonder what kind of moral monster one had turned into, and quickly think instead what could be done to help."[42] Danto here presented an ideal-typical case of taking "the aesthetic attitude" in an appallingly inappropriate situation, and the question he invited is whether something about beauty in particular inherently solicits such a misplaced response to moments—and representations—of extremity. One of the most nuanced and philosophically probing commentators on the place of beauty in art, Danto is by no means ideologically hostile to beautiful representation as such. He wrote skeptically of "the widespread sense that in some way beauty trivializes what possesses it" and the related modernist tendency "to make the simple grainy snapshot the paradigm of photographic purity."[43] But his analysis nonetheless gives us cause for moral and political concern about the conjunction of suffering and beauty.

42. Arthur C. Danto, *The Abuse of Beauty* (Chicago: Open Court, 2003), p. 110. Danto is writing about Motherwell's *Elegy for the Spanish Republic 172 (With Blood)*, a work in which one might see mourning women but which does not, he argued, solicit a morally monstrous response.

43. Danto, *The Abuse of Beauty*, p. 27.

Danto suggested that, as a general matter, it "may be the pragmatic function of beauty to inspire love toward what an artwork shows."[44] Even if beauty's tendency is to produce precisely this effect, there are, of course, many circumstances in which prompting that response is unproblematical. There are even cases in which beauty's solicitations are precisely those appropriate to a situation of suffering: obviously, from some Christian points

44. Danto, *The Abuse of Beauty*, p. xv.

of view, a painting's beautification of the suffering of Jesus may appropriately inspire love of God and recognition of the love prompting divine sacrifice. Yet, Danto's account of the pragmatics of beauty suggests that the ethical and political risks of making beautiful images from human suffering are significant. Might beauty, in particular, breed passivity? Perhaps by beautifying suffering, photographs cannot help but urge us to want the scene before our eyes always to remain just as it is. Sontag seemed to have something like this in mind when she claimed that "beautifying" in photography "tends to bleach out a moral response to what is shown."[45] Even if the photographer's express intent is to arouse indignation at injustice, will the beauty of a picture instead transmute the sorrow of the subject into the pleasure and satisfaction of others? Danto went so far as to worry that beauty might become "a relish, a device for enhancing the appetite, for taking pleasure in the spectacle of suffering."[46] Must something like this be the case? Does the distinction between "aestheticization" and "beautification" finally locate the proper target, narrowing the field of dubious images while more precisely identifying what makes them problematical? Should beauty simply be shunned in the photographic representation of suffering? Let us bear these questions in mind while looking at Shimon Attie's **Steinstrasse 22 (Berlin)** (PLATE 37), one small instance of his multi-media project *The Writing on the Wall.*

45. Sontag, *Regarding*, p. 81.

46. Danto, *The Abuse of Beauty*, p. 114.

In 1991 Attie, newly arrived in Berlin, began collecting photographs of life in Scheunenviertel, Berlin's prewar Jewish quarter. He then projected slides of these photographs at the addresses where they originally had been taken in the 1920s and 1930s. For about a year, in 1992 and 1993, Attie pursued this project, displaying an image for a night or two and then moving on to the next site. The work was, among other things, an act of haunting: block by block, the specters of a vanished population reappeared—uninvited and unexpected—confronting the city's contemporary residents as if the stone, wood, cement, and glass of the built environment harbored memories of their own. The language of confrontation seems appropriate in that the "memories" were highly disruptive, potentially uncomfortable. Marking as they did the shameful and irreversible destruction of a population, the specters were not always welcome. On multiple occasions they provoked denial, anger, or outright denunciation from current residents.[47] Yet, the projections that provoked these (and of course diverse other) responses created scenes of great beauty.

47. For accounts of the circumstances in which Attie produced the work and the responses of those who encountered it, see Shimon Attie, "The Writing on the Wall, Berlin, 1992–93: Projections in Berlin's Jewish Quarter," *Art Journal* (Fall 2003); Shimon Attie, *The Writing on the Wall: Projections in Berlin's Jewish Quarter* (Heidelberg: Edition Braus, 1994). I am especiallyindebted to James Young's introduction to Shimon Attie, *Sites Unseen: Shimon Attie European Projects: Installations and Photographs* (Burlington, VT: Verve Editions, 1998), pp. 10–17.

We know this because Attie photographed each projection and then exhibited the photographs in galleries and museums and had them reproduced in books. These photographs are not just artless records of a primary work—the moment of performance—but rather exist as a separate form or level of the work itself. The pictures are less disruptive, less potentially confrontational, than the street installations they capture (primarily because they do not haunt residents where they live), but their visual rhetoric is anything but self-effacing. Typically, as in **Steinstrasse 22 (Berlin)**, the lighting is stagy and the color saturation is intense beyond what could be perceived by any spectator on the scene. The photographs are breathtakingly beautiful. Responding to this exceptional beauty is intrinsic to recognizing the photographs' power; a version of **Steinstrasse 22** that austerely abjured beauty would be a very different work, with very different affect and meaning. Even as it invites visual pleasure, the image also expresses and arouses sorrow. Attie's reclamation of the Scheunenviertel is *only* spectral, and we are meant to recognize that; in bringing the past briefly back into the present, the photograph does more to mark history's fissures and disjunctures than to fill them in. The picture invites reflection on place and displacement, loss and erasure, and photography's role in the making of collective memory, in sustaining the presence of the past. The beauty of the work shapes and intensifies the invitation.

Even mentioning beauty—let alone pleasure—in conjunction with the topic of genocide is, of course, enough to raise suspicions of exploitation or moral obtuseness. But a critique of **Steinstrasse 22** along these lines would miss the mark. Surely this is not an instance in which beauty trivializes the suffering that is engaged. Nor can we conclude that beauty must rob suffering of its dignity, for dignity is a signal quality of these photographs. **Steinstrasse 22** invites nothing like Danto's hypothetical response to the mourning women. Attie's work does not displace our attention from the moral gravity of the historical episodes with which it is engaged; still less is the pleasure of the picture in the suffering of the victims of the Shoah. It is not the Shoah that is made beautiful in this photograph.

This last point cuts two ways. Though the picture responds to suffering that took place on an unimaginable scale, we do not know that the individuals pictured in this series were in any kind of pain. The images that Attie projected in the streets of Berlin were taken well before the deportations and the death camps, in some instances before the Nazi rise to power. Those later events are part of the meaning Attie makes from his found material; his projections and subsequent photos cannot but conjure the policy of systematic murder responsible for the destruction of the Scheunenviertel as a Jewish quarter and the death or displacement of so many who lived there. But if Attie had brought beauty of this kind to the death throes of those slaughtered, we would have considerably more reason to question his aesthetic choices and the ethical and political force they give to the work.

The beauty in Attie's photograph brings it into the general neighborhood of elegy, a form in which, Danto noted, beauty gives sorrow public form and enables it to become shared, thereby helping to constitute a community of mourners; elegy is "a way of responding artistically to what cannot be endured or what can only be endured."[48] This response can elevate death's importance and lend it meaning. It can prompt deep reflection. But elegy is not generally a provocation to either action or outrage, and Danto asked whether beauty is the right aesthetic quality to bring to representations that seek—or that ought to seek—to mobilize indignation.[49] When violence is ongoing, when the situation represented calls not for mourning or enduring what has passed and cannot be changed but instead for intervening, or holding the relevant parties accountable, or at least passing judgment, must beauty be an impediment to the generation of those responses?

48. Danto, *The Abuse of Beauty*, pp. 110–11.

49. Danto, *The Abuse of Beauty*, pp. 113–16.

Perhaps. We should be wary, though, of making too quick or sweeping a claim. Attie's projections, too, were beautiful, and we have seen that they prompted anger and judgment of a certain kind (though not necessarily *because* of their beauty, and perhaps not the kind of anger at injustice for which one might hope). Nor is it obvious that beautiful renditions of suffering must take the form of acquiescence-inducing elegy or that such renditions are acceptable only when they look at suffering with a kind of retrospective glance. Ruff's beautiful, pixelated JPEG of the burning towers is neither elegiac nor retrospective—again, there are burning bodies in that building, though they are not visible to us—and though the image may rightly induce moral anxiety or squeamishness, it also invites complex and pointed critical reflection on the ways we spectators tend to witness the kind of event it records. That is, I think, *politically* useful work. But it is hardly in any straightforward or instrumental sense a call to action. And so we are back to Danto's thought that such calls are not part of the pragmatics of beauty: it seems likely that beautiful images of suffering are suited to the generation of only certain kinds of effects. At issue, then, is the relationship between what the image asks of the responsive viewer and the kind of response the situation of the sufferer demands. What kind of solicitations ought we to expect from a photograph?

THE AESTHETICS OF ACKNOWLEDGMENT

In some moods, at least, the Sontag of *On Photography* wanted far more from photographs than she thought they could give. Repeatedly, she underscored just how much the photographic image cannot account for or convey. This line of complaint culminated in her remark that "photographs do not explain; they acknowledge."[50] And it *was* a complaint: in context we may fairly read it as saying, "*unfortunately* photographs do not explain; they *merely* acknowledge." Sontag's resistance to beauty in particular, or aesthetic qualities more broadly, flows from that sense that photographs do not or cannot tell us what we need to know.

Perhaps she was looking for the wrong thing. Her resistance to what she took to be the effects of the image appears misguided if we view it through the lens provided by Stanley Cavell, a philosopher who has, for half a century, returned again and again to reflecting upon what is entailed in the act of acknowledging. For Cavell, acknowledgment is precisely what it is that we must offer when confronted with human suffering. It is the difficult, often painful, and thus often avoided act of responding appropriately to the pain of others.[51] "The acknowledgment of another," he wrote, "calls for recognition of the other's specific relation to oneself," a recognition that "entails the revelation of oneself as having denied or distorted that relation." To avoid acknowledgment is, fundamentally, to refuse to grapple with one's relation to another. In terms that are more or less the inverse of Sontag's, Cavell suggested that recognition of such relations can come *only* through acknowledgment; the work can never be undertaken by knowledge alone.[52] In response to problems of suffering, photographs fail when they solicit responses that fall short of acknowledgment in this sense of the word. Dickens, Cavell noted, worried that the images conjured by his fiction might fall short in just this way, for he realized that "he could get the Pecksniffs and Murdles of the world to cry over the pictures he presented of poverty and the death of children, but this did not get them to see their connection with these pictures."[53] The solicitations of an image may, of course, be ignored. (It is not clear what *could* lead a Pecksniff or Murdle to a morally or politically satisfying acknowledgment.) But photographs fail morally and politically when what they invite from a responsive viewer is something less than acknowledgment; this ethical and political failure is tied to the pictures' aesthetic strategies and effects.

We might, with this in mind, return to Nachtwey's **Sudan** (**PLATE 21**). I would like

50. Sontag, *On Photography*, p. 111.

51. Stanley Cavell, *Must We Mean What We Say? A Book of Essays*, updated edition (New York: Cambridge University Press, 2002), p. 263.

52. Cavell, *The Claim of Reason: Wittgenstein, Skepticism, Morality, and Tragedy* (New York: Oxford University Press, 1979), p. 428 and 338.

53. Cavell, *The Claim of Reason*, p. 354.

to read its problems as failures of acknowledgment, failures to which the visual strategies and aesthetic choices of the image contribute but which are not precisely instances of "aestheticization" in either the broad or the narrow sense of the term. Earlier I noted that Nachtwey seeks to give us something more than just a spectacular image (though this picture, like so many of his photographs, is specacular). He wishes to aid those afflicted by famine in Somalia by making of such afflictions a scandal and thus shocking the conscience of his (presumptively) privileged spectators. This image is not an elegy; it invites not just mourning but outrage. One question to ask, then, is what it means to scandalize privilege in this particular way.

What do we learn, for instance, about the man in this photograph? We are not told his name; he apparently *is* his condition of suffering, a victim pure and simple.[54] Even though, without caption or sufficient enlargement, the precise nature of what is being passed from hand to hand (hydration salts) remains obscure, the image alone makes it hard to doubt this man's status as recipient, even supplicant. For all of the picture's specificity—it is a picture containing only one man in full, a man into whose eyes we can gaze even if he does not glance directly at us—this man is portrayed as an incarnation (one among so many photographic incarnations) of Africa as site of misery and helplessness. That the helping hand comes from above, while leaving the helper largely outside the frame, invites the viewer to equate the act of viewing with the offering of assistance and to shirk the more difficult questions of the relationship between the world of this man and the world of the most likely viewers. The truncated body, indeed, helps make this photograph a kind of allegory of its own mode of address. The encounter between donor and recipient inside this image is an enactment of the relationship that the photograph proposes between the condition it pictures and the external audience it is likely to reach: absolute, anonymous benevolence encounters pure, individual-and-yet-anonymous (hence generic) powerlessness.[55]

Sudan thus exemplifies what Cavell wrote of as a "too thin" and confused humanitarianism, in which the "intention is to acknowledge the outcast as a human being," while the "effect is to treat the human being as an outcast."[56] This is a picture in which nothing, it seems, is held back. The photographer shows no inclination to avert his eyes. We are asked to join him: the imperative proposed seems to be, "You must look at this, you must not turn away." For all that, it is hard to fathom what the looking achieves or effects. We, the spectators, may (most likely, will) cringe before it; we may even weep. Our feeling of disturbance will in all likelihood confirm, in a gratifying way, our sensitivity and our compassion. But it is it not at all clear how the photograph asks us to assess our relationship to—our complicity in—the situation. The image issues no proposal or invitation on this matter. It is a failure of acknowledgment.

Alfredo Jaar's **The Eyes of Gutete Emerita** (PLATE 51) responds, too, to crisis in Eastern Africa. Jaar visited Rwanda in the immediate aftermath of the 1994 genocide, interviewing and photographing many people he encountered. He then drew upon those images and experiences to produce *The Rwanda Project*, a series of works presented over a seven-year period (1994–2000). Like Nachtwey's work, Jaar's offers a kind of indictment. But the nature of his response to what he saw and his way of working on viewers are radically different.

54. Sontag pointed out Salgado's tendency to present his subjects in this way, an insight that has helped me think about Nachtwey's work. Sontag, *Regarding*, pp. 78–9.

55. One might instead argue, as Diane Rubenstein has to me, that this comfortable reading will, for many white Western viewers, be undermined or destabilized by the fact that the helping hand is black, not white (personal communication, March 10, 2006).

56. Cavell, *The Claim of Reason*, p. 437. As he put it elsewhere in the same passage, "The hand handing out its alms can look like a fist."

Jaar confronts genocide in a manner at once pointed and elliptical; his work is about seeing and the failure to see and about how *both* implicate his audience in the situations to which the work responds.

The Eyes of Gutete Emerita is an installation; of all the works reproduced here, it loses the most by being presented in book form, for it has a temporal structure and achieves somatic effects that cannot be experienced apart from its installation setting (**FIG. 5**). That setting is a room with bare black walls illuminated only by the glow of twin light boxes placed side by side. For most of the duration of the piece, the boxes contain text. The text offers brief accounts of the Rwandan genocide, of the experience of Gutete Emerita—a woman who watched as her husband and sons were murdered before her eyes—and of Jaar's encounter with her as she told her story to him and he took her picture on more or less the spot at which she had witnessed the killings. This text comes in three installments, each one shorter than its predecessor—ten lines per box, then five, then one (**PLATE 51**). The transitions between texts are virtually instantaneous, but the words themselves linger with a deliberate and painful slowness: Jaar keeps each passage on screen for far more time than is needed to read it (forty-five seconds, then thirty, then fifteen). After the final lines, "I remember her eyes. The eyes of Gutete Emerita," the text gives way: Emerita's eyes flash on screen for the briefest of instances... then they're gone, and immediately, the piece begins again.

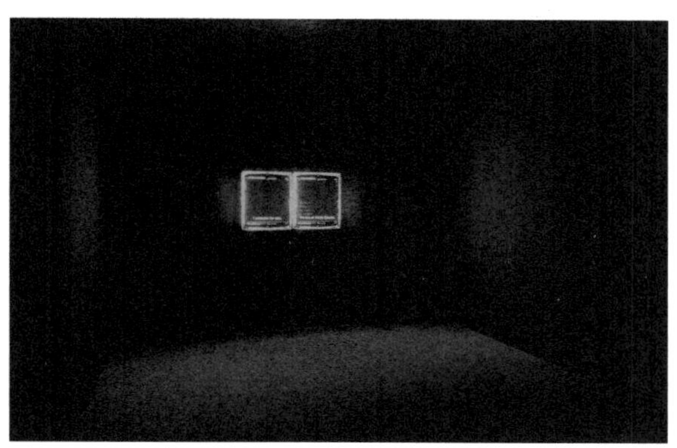

FIGURE 5
ALFREDO JAAR, *THE EYES OF GUTETE EMERITA*, FROM "*THE RWANDA PROJECT*," 1996. COURTESY OF THE ARTIST AND GALERIE LELONG, NEW YORK.

Jaar explained the pace of the work as an attempt to resist the habits of museum-and-gallery goers who tend to move every few seconds from work to work, image to image.[57] The slowness with which the text moves courts frustration, impatience. This makes all the more startling the swiftness with which the eyes come and go. After the relentless text, the image is a kind of payoff, or reward, but it is over practically before it begins. The immediate disappearance of the eyes may prompt a desire to view the cycle again and again just so the image can sink in. But the surprise is not just a matter of sequence and timing; it also concerns what we see. Understandably, the words conjure up scenes of the most extreme violence (for example, "corpses on the ground, rotting in the African sun"). Viewed, as it must be, in the context provided by the long tradition of photographing African misery, the piece invites the expectation—or at least the speculation—that the images will show something of the terrible incidents the text describes. By refusing to meet these expectations, by showing not the acts of violence but eyes that witnessed so much of it, **The Eyes of Gutete Emerita** engages the limits of representation in situations of extremity—and not as an abstract philosophical question but as one in which viewers of the work are implicated. Viewers are prompted to place their imagined or wished for or feared images against those we are typically shown and against the simple, haunting, image Jaar provides. This image underscores the importance of Emerita's own witnessing, even while it underscores all that "the West" refused to see while the slaughter was underway. The work, furthermore,

57. Alfredo Jaar, lecture at Williams College, April 19, 2006. Many commentators have discussed the way that the work seeks to slow perception. See, for example, Mieke Bal's essay in this volume.

models or performs that acknowledgment of implication. The labor involved in seeing the pictures—waiting through the long textual prelude, the burst of concentration required to extract something from Emerita's (quite beautiful) eyes—offers instruction in the difficulties of responsible viewing. It is also crucial to the meaning and effects of the piece that the eyes we see are what *Jaar* is able to "remember," as the text puts it. The photographer thematizes his own relationship to the subject, but the power of the image and the focus of the piece on the scope and character of the genocide ensure that this implication does not thereby devolve into narcissism or solipsism on his part, just as the piece offers viewers little opportunity for self-congratulation or for equating the act of watching with the delivering of aid.

The Eyes of Gutete Emerita is both hugely ambitious and self-undercutting. It is, to borrow from Judith Butler's epigraph to this essay, a work that shows its own inability to capture its referent.[58] In this, it is of a piece with the larger *Rwanda Project*, a series animated by a fundamental paradox or tension. The project was born of Jaar's anger that much of the world turned away from adequate intervention in the few short months in 1994 during which a million people were slaughtered. He attributes that failure, in part, to insufficient pressure from the mass media: in this sense, he suggests that we needed more pictures. Yet Jaar also sees the graphic pictures of suffering people in the mass media—pictures such as **Sudan**, for instance—as contributing to our failures of perception.[59] In response to what was in some senses a dearth of images, he makes work to get us to see what we missed as the events unfolded, yet he does so without picturing those events directly. Although he took many photographs that would reveal the carnage, nowhere does *Rwanda Project* present them: much of the work depends upon, even stages, Jaar's withholding of the images he took. *Rwanda, Rwanda* (1994), one of his first responses, consisted of forty light boxes distributed in public spaces across Malmö, Sweden, containing simply the name "Rwanda", repeated multiple times in large, black type on a white background. *Real Pictures* (1995) was the first to employ the photographs he had taken in Rwanda, but it did so in such a way as to make viewing them impossible: Jaar placed a color photograph of a scene of destruction inside each of 550 black boxes, allowing the images to be "read" only in the form of written descriptions silk screened on the boxes' exteriors.[60] Over time, Jaar made the images more available. Indeed, another version of **The Eyes of Gutete Emerita** presents one million images in the form of 35mm slides—each an identical picture Emerita's two eyes—piled on a white light table, accessible for viewing by loupe.

This movement over time from an absence toward a surfeit of images recapitulates my argument and also raises a question: Is Jaar, in the end, Benjamin's writer-turned-image-maker? After all, like some other complex and provocative works in this book—such as Michael Nye's **Doris** (PLATE 33) and Faisal Sheikh's **Bashia Gababo Sharamu** (PLATE 24)—it draws much of its power from the way in which the story or voice of the subject of a portrait is paired with an image. Does this mean that the ability of Jaar's project to engage us with the ethics and politics of seeing could not succeed without the agency of the letter? And do such examples validate Sekula's broader privileging of the bracketing of image with text (an emphasis that, among other things, reflects his sense that purely visual portraiture tends to sacrifice the subject's "self-authorship")?[61] Of course, even in works such as the

58. Butler, *Precarious Life*, p. 146.

59. Alfredo Jaar, lecture at Williams College, April 19, 2006.

60. For a fuller description and astute commentary on the previous two works, see David Levi-Strauss, *Between the Eyes: Essays on Photography and Politics* (New York: Aperture, 2003), pp. 92–3. I am indebted to his account.

61. Sekula, *Photography against the Grain*, p. 73. I hope it is obvious that I am nowhere arguing that the incorporation of text is not a meaningful or potentially productive approach. One reason why "Beautiful Suffering" included pieces by Jaar, Sheikh, and Nye was precisely to explore what effects the use of sound and words enable photographers to produce. Mine is not a case, then, for the necessary purity of the image. My claim is simply that, when yielding to the—strangely persistent—critical anxieties about the aesthetic and the visual, commentators often impute power to the word in a way that denies the complex effects that can be produced through photographic images themselves.

version of **The Eyes of Gutete Emerita** included in "Beautiful Suffering," the text functions as something other—something more—than a caption or a context. The image is not simply an illustration of the words; nor is its meaning containable by them. Jaar seeks to provoke complex political reflections, but the conceptual work of the piece depends on its aesthetic strategies and the visceral experience provided to viewers inside the installation space. Still, the undeniable importance of text to **The Eyes of Gutete Emerita** suggests that it might be helpful to conclude these reflections on anxiety about images and aesthetics by examining one final photograph, one that invites from viewers comparably complex critical engagement through more purely visual means.

Alan Schechner's **It's the Real Thing—Self Portrait at Buchenwald** (PLATE 41) is a fruitful example.[62] It is one of the images in the exhibition that has drawn the most objections for its approach to the representation of suffering. Best known for its inclusion in "Mirroring Evil" at the New York's Jewish Museum, in 2002, it was among those works most often singled out in protests and hostile reviews of that much-criticized exhibit.[63] A work of web-based art, **It's the Real Thing**—far more than Jaar's project—directly presents suffering people in a situation of extremity, and it is the manner in which it does so that has drawn so much criticism. Schechner digitally inserted himself into one of Margaret Bourke-White's famous photographs of the liberation of Buchenwald. He stands in the foreground, surrounded by emaciated prisoners, most of them lying in rows of bunks. Though he has donned a prisoner's striped uniform, Schechner looks well fed and is holding a gleaming can of Diet Coke; unlike the rest of the photograph, the can is in color. What fueled the hostile responses? Surely the ironies of the image were partly responsible. In all likelihood, too, the mere fact of altering a documentary photograph from the death camps violated many understandings of how such materials should be used, and the reframing of such an image as a work of art does so all the more. What purposes might be served by that alteration, and what should we make of them?

Like Attie's photograph, Schechner's engages with historical memory, but this is an engagement of a very different mood, pursued by very different means. As a self-portrait, the work functions as an act of both identification and dis-identification. As a Jew, Schechner projects himself into the kind of scene in which some of his relatives perished, thereby forging an imaginative connection between his circumstances and theirs as he ponders being in a situation of such desperation. It is a way of making the burden of that history his own, the better to take on its lessons. At the same time, the photograph would lapse into obscene and imperial sentimentality if it were simply to appropriate the survivor experience in a way that collapsed the radical disparity between historical moments and social locations. Yet, this is no simple appropriation: Schechner highlights those disparities, pressing the viewer to acknowledge the absurdity of his effort and of any facile identification. The Diet Coke can that Schechner holds aloft for our inspection is the most obvious marker of how far he is from the situation into which he has placed himself: though surrounded by people who have known extreme hunger and privation, *he* comes from a world in which millions of people pay to drink a beverage precisely because it provides no nourishment. Radiant and in color, the can is more "alive" than anything else in the picture.

62. I have, of course, just reproduced Schechner's *title*, one that reinforces the way in which the work signifies. And the image also contains the words "Diet Coke" on the can that Schechner holds. My wager, however, is that were the words on the can unreadable (but the brand still identifiable) and were the piece untitled, it would still invite, by and large, the same responses and function as a comparably complex intervention.

63. See for instance, George Will (who saw the work and show as "evil"), "Genocide as Art," *The Washington Post*, June 20, 2002, and Michael Kimmelman, "Evil, the Nazis and Shock Value," *The New York Times*, March 15, 2002. The controversy was not limited to the Jewish Museum showing. A few years earlier, when Schechner sought to have a slightly different version of the work printed as a photograph in England, the lab he hired ultimately refused to produce a print. See Francis Frascina and Jonathan Harris, "Social Control and Permissibility: A Case History," *Art Monthly* #194 (March 1996): 40–41. Not all responses have been hostile, however. Art historian Linda Nochlin, for instance, gave the piece an appreciative and thoughtful reading in her review of the Jewish Museum's show. Nochlin, "Mirroring Evil: Nazi Imagery/ Recent Art," *Artforum* (Summer 2002): 168, 207.

The Diet Coke can functions as sign of consumerism and the attendant forms of fetishism. The raising of this theme through the vehicle of genocide may appear to be a crude trivialization, a failure to recognize the relative weight of two problems of radically different magnitudes. Insofar as the piece uses the Shoah to talk about consumption *tout court*, such a critical response might be justified. But Schechner's gesture of bringing that theme to this context offers something more specific. It renders him a consumer of the very scene into which he has thrust himself, raising questions about what such consumption might be about. It thus engages the viewer with questions about the circulation and ideological function of Holocaust imagery. What does it mean—for Jewish culture and politics—to consume images of the Shoah as a way of forming or shoring up one's identity or moral claims? What uses, and what users, of such pictures are authorized?

These questions about the traffic in pain are sharpened by the kind of photographic appropriation that enabled **Self-Portrait at Buchenwald**. Although many commentators recognize the source image, there is a tendency to look right through it, as if the artist has placed himself in the barracks of a notorious death camp. And on one level, of course, he has: his effort both to imagine inhabiting the prisoner's position and to show the radical limits of his access to that position requires this reading of him as being, or projecting himself, physically on site. On the other hand, it is also internal to the meaning of the work that Schechner has not literally placed himself there; he has put his digitized image not in Buchenwald but in a *photograph* of the camp. It matters, too, that it is a *famous* photograph. Through this means, Schechner engages questions of how the Holocaust has been represented in visual culture and what moral and political effects those representations have. Furthermore, Bourke-White, the photographer, was fiercely attacked over the appropriate photographic response to suffering. As John Stomberg shows in his essay in this book, the disputes were one key source of the critique of aestheticization that resonates to this day. Yet Schechner's revision of the image makes clear what was often obscured in that earlier debate, namely the power of certain visual strategies and forms of aesthetic address to lead thought and affect to a deeper response to problems of suffering. Edgy in its provocations, it is not—does not aim to be—a soothing picture. For many viewers, it will arouse disturbing, uncomfortable, even angry reflections. In its capacity to do so, however, this image provides reasons for relaxing the aesthetic anxiety of critique.

JOHN STOMBERG

A GENEALOGY OF ORTHODOX DOCUMENTARY

Transforming is what art does, but photography that bears witness
to the calamitous and the reprehensible is much criticized if it seems 'aesthetic;'
that is, too much like art. —SUSAN SONTAG

In 1938 a small group of men determined to change the course of contemporary photography and succeeded. That group included Walker Evans, Lincoln Kirstein, James Agee, and Thomas Mabry. Together, they began a sustained campaign to redefine the dominant mode of late-1930s photographic practice so that it more clearly supported the idiosyncrasies of Evans' particular style. Though this was at heart an aesthetic dispute, Evans and his friends often presented their aesthetic preferences as ethical principles, arguing that some formal approaches to photography were inherently morally superior. Since then, the contentious evolution of the multiple aesthetics of suffering has continued to demark the critical arena in which most contemporary documentary projects operate.

The campaign started in defense of Evans' 1938 exhibition at the Museum of Modern Art, in New York. Though modestly effective at the time, the efforts of the group gained widespread acceptance after the 1960 edition of *Let Us Now Praise Famous Men,* the book on which Evans had worked with Agee in the 1930s. The group's establishment of an orthodox definition for documentary practice has diminished the contribution of Erskine Caldwell and Margaret Bourke-White, whose 1937 book *You Have Seen Their Faces*, dominated the narrow field of photo-textual books during the late 1930s. It is the goal of this essay to trace the reception of these two key books as a reflection of how 1930s documentary-style photography was understood during the decade, what factors shaped these understandings, and how these factors have since influenced the literature on the subject.

Indeed, much of the ethical weight that critics today attach to the different aesthetic programs in documentary photography evolved through Evans' early battles to position the Bourke-White approach in opposition to a code of conduct more to his own taste. Writing in 2003, Susan Sontag referred to this very issue in a key passage of *Regarding the Pain of Others*: "The dual powers of photography—to generate documents and to create works of visual art—have produced some remarkable exaggerations about what photographers ought or ought not to do. Lately, the most common exaggeration is one that regards these powers as opposites."[1] Sontag, here, contextualized an important underlying assumption at work in much of the current criticism on documentary photography—one that strongly supports the Evans code. For decades, the polarization she described has informed discussions regarding images of the "calamitous" and the "reprehensible"—documentary photography, in short, without benefit of careful analysis.

1. Susan Sontag, *Regarding the Pain of Others*, (New York: Picador, 2003), p. 76. * Note: This is also the citation for the Sontag quote that begins this essay.

Criticism on the subject today often works to reinforce the largely unwritten stipulations of the Evans code and to denounce its transgressors without consideration for the derivation of its value system. Writing for *The New Yorker* in 1991, for example, critic Ingrid Sischy derided the work of contemporary Brazilian photographer Sebestião Salgado as "emotional blackmail fueled by a dramatics of art direction" and asserted that Salgado was the "polar opposite" of Evans.[2] Sischy's position regarding these two photographers made it clear that she operated from within this system of imperatives, but her essay did not reveal an awareness of its historical origins or evolution.

2. Ingrid Sischy, "Photography: Good Intentions," *The New Yorker* (September 9, 1991): pp. 95, 93.

Sontag herself wrote both about and from within this system of values. She identified Salgado as "the principal target of the new campaign against the inauthenticity of the beautiful" and noted that he also stood accused of profiting from his work and using "sanctimonious" visual rhetoric.[3] In conclusion, she noted that "morally alert photographers and ideologues of photography have become increasingly concerned with the issues of exploitation of sentiment (pity, compassion, indignation) in war photography and of rote ways of provoking feeling."[4] Her brief essay—clear and well considered as it was—left unanswered several of the central questions in the dilemma of documentary ethics. Which photographers have earned the right to be called "morally alert," and who decided? What were the criteria by which they were judged? When were the visual characteristics of exploitative sentiment separated from acceptable uses of pity, compassion, and indignation? Was Sontag's problem with the fact that some "ways of provoking feeling" in photography were "rote" or was the very act of "provoking feeling" the issue?

3. Sontag, *Regarding the Pain of Others*, p. 78.

4. Sontag, *Regarding the Pain of Others*, p. 80.

Sontag's brilliantly articulated argument offers a portal into the belief system at work in much of today's writing on documentary practice. With characteristic prescience—or perhaps just uncanny coincidence—Sontag included a footnote at the end of the paragraph cited above that referenced both the individuals and the projects that originally launched the ethical debates on which her book focused. In the note, Sontag discussed the role of "spectacle" in relation to the picture's degree of effectiveness. She proposed that anonymous images of concentration camps might "seem more valid" than those produced by professional photographers by virtue of the very lack of professionalism displayed in the anonymous works. Significantly for our purposes, she briefly mentioned that this criticism was not a "recent view," citing that Walker Evans "detested the work of [Margaret] Bourke-White," whose photographs of concentration camps exemplified the professional approach.[5] Sontag left the subject there, despite the fact that the two photographers she mentioned had played crucial roles in the establishment of criteria for the documentary practice of photography and had done so more than sixty years earlier.

5. Sontag, *Regarding the Pain of Others*, p. 77.

FORTUNE AND THE BACK STORY

By the early 1930s, three important developments fostered a marked expansion in the documentary mode of photographic practice: the social uses of photography, camera technology, and the mass media used to disseminate images. Writing in 1938, Beaumont Newhall was one of the earliest critics to cite social uses as the most important aspect of this expanding practice. Newhall described the relatively new mode in photography as the "documentary approach," borrowing the term from the literature on film.[6] He also carefully differentiated this approach in film from most "newsreels and travelogues" in two critical areas: intended use and form. He described the first of these, the "social significance," as the key trait and stressed that the documentary films on which he based his definition of photography were "produced for definite sociological purposes."[7] Although these works were not unified by any one style, Newhall defined the aesthetic of this form with a comparison to Emile Zola's "document-novels" and emphasized the "dramatic presentation of fact" as their salient formal quality.[8] Documentary photography—as defined by Newhall at the time—combined dramatic image making with defined social goals.

6. Newhall noted that the term "documentary" did have precedents dating to 1906. Beaumont Newhall, "Documentary Approach to Photography," *Parnassus* 10 (March 1938): 4, 5.

7. Newhall, "Documentary Approach to Photography," p. 3.

8. Newhall, "Documentary Approach to Photography," p. 3.

The technological developments of the era also made the medium an increasingly practical rhetorical tool. Candid photography grew out of opportunities first made available in the 1920s. Though there were others, the Leica camera—which featured roll film and a small body—was crucial in making it possible to document people and places quickly, sometimes unobtrusively; the camera's success also fed the growing appetite for candid photography. Whereas older formats typically required collaboration between the subject and the photographer, the Leica allowed for a stealthier approach. Further, the style of candid photography expanded into some of the larger formats—that is, it developed as the Leica approach but soon became an aesthetic goal that informed photographic work in a variety of formats.

Finally, in the early 1930s, documentary photography attained a greatly increased level of participation due to its unprecedented access to vehicles of dissemination—particularly magazines and newspapers. Newhall cautioned that this access could be a mixed blessing: while filmmakers could control their presentations (with the possible exception of editing on moral grounds by some theater owners), photographers faced the problem that their work could be "produced together with any other photograph, and with any caption."[9] Newhall astutely highlighted the importance of both the presentation and the presenting agency in the shaping of meaning with the documentary approach.[10] He also cited the importance of the German illustrated press, *Vu* in Paris, and *Life* in the United States as important vehicles for photographic documentary projects in the late 1930s. Earlier in the decade, the singular and premier outlet for documentary photography in the United States—based on the quality of its reproductions; its pioneering role in the use of the photo-essay; its dedication to photography; and perhaps most surprisingly, its attention to liberal social causes—was *Fortune* magazine. Both Bourke-White and Agee worked there.

Though conceived in the late 1920s as a paean to business, the magazine had been subtly transformed in its first year (the first issue was February 1930) in response to the crises of the Depression. Archibald MacLeish, a staff writer at the time, recalled that "*Fortune* [by 1931] became a more accurate and reliable historian of the period than any other publication in the country."[11] He continued:

> Where the old *Fortune*, in other words, was to have concerned itself with business for business' sake, the new *Fortune* would report the world of business as an expression—a peculiarly enlightening expression—of the Republic, of the changing world.[12]

The magazine was not transformed dramatically, or even officially, but during the early years of the Depression, *Fortune* ran frequent stories in support of President Roosevelt's New Deal programs. In 1934 the magazine's founder and publisher, Henry Luce, decided to show the devastation caused by the drought that year, and he specifically asked his editor, Ralph Ingersoll, to put Bourke-White on the assignment.[13] Ingersoll did so and assigned the writing to Agee.[14]

For Bourke-White, the drought assignment marked the beginning of her difficult path to a documentary style of photography (**FIG. 1**).[15] She often commented that the industrial photography of the early 1930s had come naturally to her, as though she were predisposed to create imagery of factories. Her industrial photography involved light, forms, angles, and sometimes movement, but not the emotional response that she experienced on the drought assignment. Bourke-White later wrote: "I had never seen people caught helpless like this in total tragedy. They had no defense. They had no plan... I was deeply moved by the suffering I saw."[16] This assignment led her to largely abandon her growing advertising career to allow more time for meaningful assignments—in fact, it feuled to her desire to work with Caldwell on the project that became *You Have Seen Their Faces*.[17]

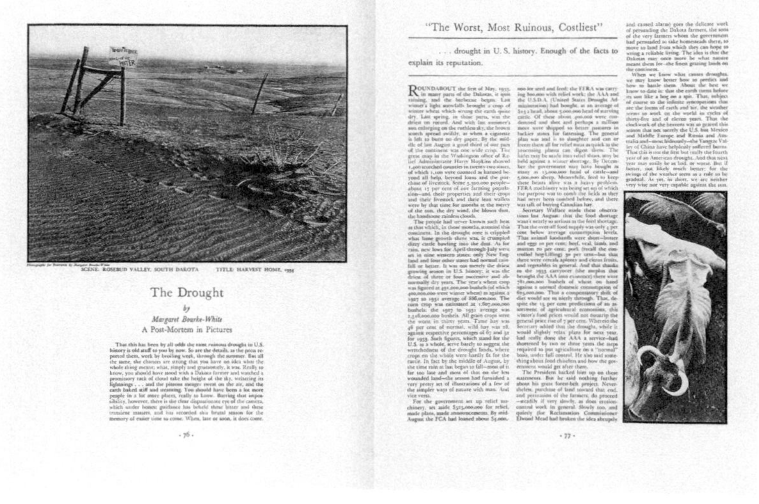

SCENE: ROSEBUD VALLEY, SOUTH DAKOTA   TITLE: HARVEST HOME, 1934

The Drought

by

Margaret Bourke-White

A Post-Mortem in Pictures

That this has been by all odds the most ruinous drought in U.S. history is old stuff to you by now. So are the details, as the press reported them, week by broiling week, through the summer. But all the same, the chances are strong that you have no idea what the whole thing meant; what, simply and gruesomely, it was. Really to know, you should have stood with a Dakota farmer and watched a promissory rack of cloud take the height of the sky, weltering its lightnings . . . and the piteous meager sweat on the air, and the earth baked stiff and steaming. You should have been a lot more people in a lot more places, really to know. Barring that impossibility, however, there is the clear dispassionate eye of the camera, which under honest guidance has beheld these bitter and these transient matters, and has recorded this brutal season for the memory of easier time to come. When, late or soon, it does come.

· 76 ·

"The Worst, Most Ruinous, Costliest"

. . . drought in U. S. history. Enough of the facts to explain its reputation.

· 77 ·

FIGURES 1 AND 2
MARGARET BOURKE-WHITE, "THE DROUGHT," *FORTUNE* 10 (OCTOBER 1934), PP. 76–79. COURTESY THE ESTATE OF MARGARET BOURKE-WHITE AND *FORTUNE*.

9. Newhall, "Documentary Approach to Photography," p. 4.

10. This observation continues to inform the literature on the subject. Maren Stange, for example, succinctly described that it was "not the photograph alone . . . but the image set in relation to a written caption, an associated text, and a presenting agency...[that] constituted the documentary mode." Maren Stange, *Symbols of Ideal Life: Social Documentary Photography in America, 1890–1950*, (New York: Cambridge University Press, 1989), p. xiv.

11. Archibald MacLeish, "The First Nine Years," In *Writing for Fortune* (New York: Time, Inc., 1980), p. 7.

12. MacLeish, "The First Nine Years," pp. 7–8.

13. Luce wrote to Bourke-White soon after her assignment was completed in August 1934 and said, "To tell the truth I, too, was quite pleased with myself for having the idea of asking you to record the most famous drought for all time." Henry Luce, Letter to Margaret Bourke-White, August 31, 1934, Margaret Bourke-White Papers, George Arents Research Library, Syracuse University. And Ingersoll wrote to her that "the idea was Harry's and had my enthusiastic support as soon as I heard of it." Ralph Ingersoll, Letter to Margaret Bourke-White, September 4, 1934, Margaret Bourke-White Papers.

14. Bourke-White had been hired by Luce to work at *Fortune* in 1929, before the magazine even began publication; Agee had started in 1932 as a writer fresh out of Harvard University. See Vicki Goldberg, *Margaret Bourke-White: A Biography* (New York: Harper & Row, 1986), pp. 101–03; Laurence Bergreen, *James Agee: A Life* (New York: E.P. Dutton, Inc., 1984), pp. 106–09.

In keeping with the published story's obvious emphasis on images, Agee's text—primarily extended captions—betrayed his strong emotional response to the photographs.[18] In Agee's opening caption, he chastised the reader with the admonition that, despite their reading, they still could not "know" about the suffering. "Really to know," Agee wrote, "you should have stood with a Dakota farmer and watched a promissory rack of cloud take the height of sky, weltering its lightning...and the piteous meager sweat on the air, and the earth baked stiff and steaming. You should have been a lot more people in a lot more places, really to know."[19] Agee then dwelled on photography's power to capture the scene, complimenting Bourke-White's integrity in her use of the medium: "Barring that impossibility [of standing with the Dakota farmer], however, there is the clear dispassionate eye of the camera, which under honest guidance has beheld these bitter and these transient matters, and has recorded this brutal season for the memory of easier time to come."[20] This essay revealed Agee's belief that photography's "dispassionate eye" was the essence of successful documentary and did so in a discussion of signature Bourke-White photographs.

At *Fortune*, in 1934, the predilection continued for photographs of factories, machines, buildings, land, animals, and equipment—all part of the magazine's corporation stories. The brief editorial shift toward subjects more directly involved with people's lives developed abreast of an evolving interest in candid photography and accelerated at the time Agee and Bourke-White worked on the drought story.[21] The most visible result of this shift was the introduction of a new story format at the magazine called "The Life and Circumstances," which focused on individual working families. Bourke-White received the first assignment for this series, and approximately one year later, Agee and Evans received the last. This series led directly to the two key projects under consideration: Bourke-White created her photographs for *You Have Seen Their Faces* on the rebound from the stinging criticism she received for her submission from her editors at *Fortune*, and Agee and Evans turned their assignment (repeatedly rejected by the magazine) into *Let Us Now Praise Famous Men*.

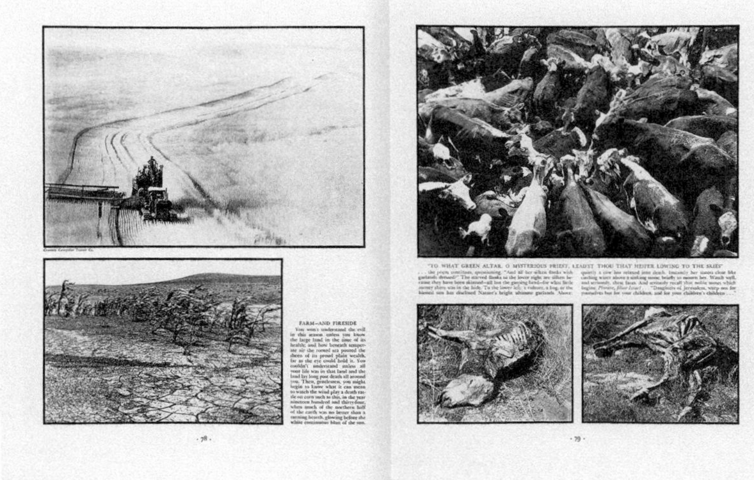

Bourke-White began work on *You Have Seen Their Faces* partly to follow through on the personal epiphany she had had after working on the drought assignment. In 1935 she submitted an article to *The Nation* that testified to her growing sympathy for people struggling to subsist in conditions that made doing so practically impossible. The essay, "Dust Changes America," recounted her return a year later to the drought-stricken regions of the central United States. She wrote, "By coincidence I was in the same parts of the country where last year I photographed the drought. As short a time as eight months ago there was an attitude of false optimism. 'Things will get better,' the farmers would say...But this year there

15. "The Drought," *Fortune* 10 (October 1934): pp. 76–83.

16. Margaret Bourke-White, *Portrait of Myself* (New York: Simon and Schuster, 1963), p. 110.

17. Goldberg, *Margaret Bourke-White: A Biography*, p. 155.

18. According to his biographer, though, Agee expressed worries about Bourke-White's objectivity: "The resulting article, published in *October*, featured, to his [Agee's] dismay, photographs by Margaret Bourke-White, a rapidly rising young photojournalist whom Luce had recently discovered." Lawrence Bergreen, *James Agee: A Life* (New York: E. P. Dutton, 1984), p. 145.

19. "The Drought," p. 76.

20. "The Drought," p. 76.

21. Largely due to their enthusiasm for the photographs of the German photographer Dr. Erich Salomon, whose candid approach received special notice and ample fanfare in the magazine, the editors encouraged their own photographers to try out smaller format cameras, noting the gain in credibility through the perceived candor of the photographic style. The magazine extolled Salomon's candids as "historic documents." "Statesmen of Europe," *Fortune* 4, (November 1931): pp. 143–46.

is an atmosphere of utter hopelessness."[22] Bourke-White's own trademark optimism, based on her faith in industry's ability to provide an abundant future for all, had been severely altered by her experiences of 1934 and 1935. These experiences left her—like the magazine that had employed her since before the beginning of the Great Depression—searching for ways to make a difference. She wanted her photographs to be catalysts for change and not "dispassionate" records.

22. Margaret Bourke-White, "Dust Changes America," *The Nation* 140 (May 22, 1935): 597.

At the same time, in 1935, Bourke-White began to speak of her interest in candid photography—a marked departure from her previous large-format work. She wrote to *Fortune*'s art editor, Eleanor Treacy, "I had never thought to mention to him [editor Ralph Ingersoll] before my growing interest in the lives of workmen," continuing:

> It seems to me that while it is very important to get a striking picture of a line of smoke stacks or a row of dynamos, it is becoming more and more important to reflect the life that goes on behind these photographs. This fringes on the candid camera type of photography, and also represents a point of view which I think is becoming increasingly important in regard to photography, and is something I have given much thought to lately.[23]

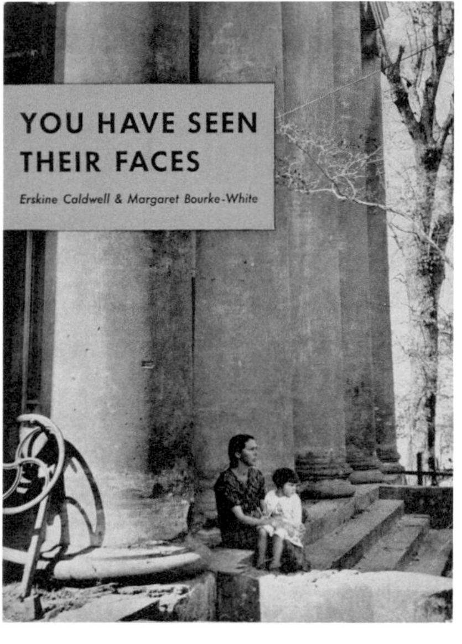

FIGURE 2
ERSKINE CALDWELL AND MARGARET BOURKE-WHITE, *YOU HAVE SEEN THEIR FACES*, (COVER), 1937. COURTESY SIMON & SCHUSTER, INC.

Bourke-White's expressed interest in developing candid photography, paired with the social awareness that began the previous summer when she met with organized farm workers, led her to consciously change both the approach and subject of her work.

The pictures she produced for the magazine's first "Life and Circumstance" story were utter failures at keeping the controlling hand of the photographer invisible. The magazine's harsh response to the work had far reaching implications for her. In a letter to Bourke-White, Treacy detailed the problems:

23. Bourke-White to Eleanor Treacy, July 9, 1935, New York, and Eleanor Treacy to Bourke-White, July 2, 1935, New York, Margaret Bourke-White Papers.

> I think I should pass on to you some criticisms that have been made here of your automotive family set. There was a general feeling that the pictures were too stiff and posed-looking, and I certainly think that you didn't get the spontaneity in your candid shots that there might have been. After all, the only reason for candid photography is the ability to catch people unawares and to get natural expressions and actions which cannot be caught in any other way. I do think if you are interested in going on with candid camera work you ought to concentrate on taking lots of pictures without the subjects' knowledge if possible. Never mind if the technical quality of the prints is not as high as you would like to have it for a while. I think it is better to sacrifice that a little in order to get life and action into your pictures.[24]

24. Treacy to Bourke-White, October 21, 1935, New York, Margaret Bourke-White Papers.

This criticism appears to have become the guiding principle for Bourke-White's work on *You Have Seen Their Faces*, especially the implication that only through catching her subjects "unawares" could she achieve a greater, more candid form of truth.

As her editor at *Fortune*, Ralph Ingersoll had known Bourke-White for years. He was, in fact, working with her during the spring of 1936, using her photographs in mock-ups for the new magazine that would become *Life*. She confided to him her interest in turning to photographic projects that focused on working people and the tenor of their lives. She described her plans to travel with Caldwell to work freelance on a book specifically about sharecroppers, and they even discussed the possibility of using her work from this trip in the new magazine.[25] That very month, Ingersoll gave Agee and Evans an assignment for *Fortune* to travel south and work on sharecroppers, knowingly setting up a second team competing to cover the same story. He also initiated a rivalry, the extent and longevity of which he could not have foreseen at the time.

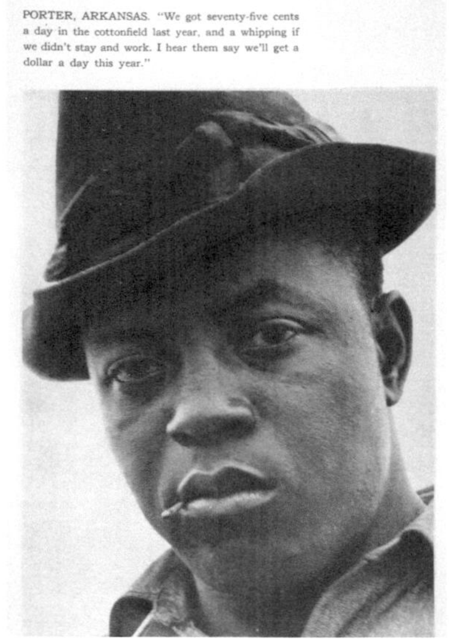

FIGURE 3
MARGARET BOURKE-WHITE, *PORTER, ARKANSAS*, FROM *YOU HAVE SEEN THEIR FACES*, 1937. COURTESY THE ESTATE OF MARGARET BOURKE-WHITE AND SIMON & SCHUSTER, INC.

YOU HAVE SEEN THEIR FACES

Caldwell and Bourke-White's book came out first and was such a commercial success that the publisher printed multiple editions during its first year (**FIG. 2**). The book included seventy-five of her photographs and his fifty-four-page essay. Each image was accompanied by a "legend" penned collaboratively by Bourke-White and Caldwell. Despite being largely overlooked at the time, this last invention has come to be the focus of heated debate on the book. The authors included a note at the beginning, stating:

> No person, place, or episode in this book is fictitious, but names and places have been changed to avoid unnecessary individualization; for it is not the authors' intention to criticize any individuals who are part of the system depicted. The legends under the pictures are intended to express the authors' own conceptions of the sentiments of the individuals portrayed; they do not pretend to reproduce the actual sentiments of these persons.[26]

Despite this disclaimer, and judging by the published reviews, many readers understood the "legends" as quoting the individuals pictured. The captions gave the images a textual framework that directed interpretation in stark contrast to the manner in which Evans' photographs, appearing in *Let Us Now Praise Famous Men* without captions, left meaning more open-ended (**FIGS. 3** and **4**). This heavy-handed editorializing would eventually earn *You Have Seen Their Faces* strong rebukes, but at the time it was first published, the concern was seldom raised.

The book was widely reviewed across the country, first in newspapers, soon followed by magazines, and within its first year, by academic presses. The critical responses were strongly favorable, with the complaints coming mostly from Southern press outlets exasperated by the biased, Northern viewpoint of

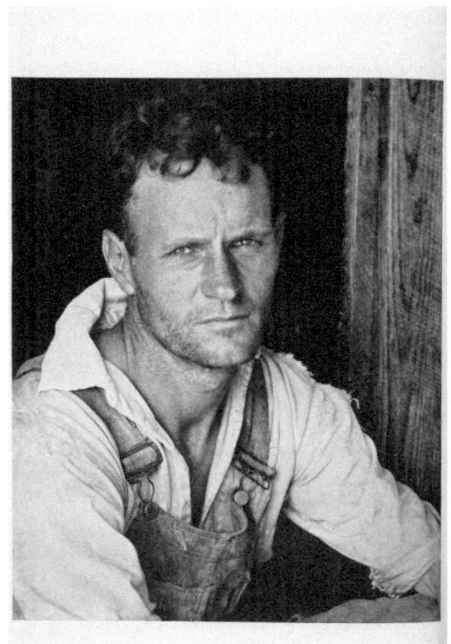

FIGURE 4
WALKER EVANS, UNTITLED, FROM *LET US NOW PRAISE FAMOUS MEN*, 1941 COURTESY HOUGHTON MIFFLIN COPMANY.

25. Bourke-White, *Portrait of Myself*, p. 119.

26. Erskine Caldwell and Margaret Bourke-White, *You Have Seen Their Faces* (New York: Viking Press, 1937), un-paginated front matter.

the book. Of particular note, none of the reviewers used the term "documentary," though some referred to the photographs as "documents" and several used the term "candid photography." The majority singled out the photographs for *You Have Seen Their Faces* exactly for their drama and passion. Also, the ability of the photographs to carry the narrative more profoundly than the text received frequent comment, with some critics even arguing that the images proved more literary than the literature. The word "simplicity" was used by critics who found that the straightforward nature of the poses lent added gravitas and poignancy to the images. And almost all the critics acknowledged that a strong point of view was expressed and contended that persuasion was a key part of this new form of communication (text and images working together).

In the "Books of the Times" section of the *The New York Times*—one of the first newspapers to publish a review—Ralph Thompson placed *You Have Seen Their Faces* in the context of the growing trend to use "the camera to mold public opinion" and noted that the authors "were not after fair impartiality."[27] In remarking that "the pictures produce such an effect, indeed, that it is no exaggeration to say that the text serves principally to illustrate them," Thompson shared with many other critics the notion that the images could, maybe should, carry the weight of the argument—they were the foremost bearers of information; this was the essence of their art. Arthur Ellis' review of the book a few days later in the *The Washington Post* started off with the declarative sentence: "Photography today stands firmly entrenched in its position of importance on the American scene."[28] Ellis introduced what would become an oft-repeated notion, that the images are "proof," working to verify the claims made by the text.

27. Ralph Thompson, "Books of the Times," *The New York Times*, November 10, 1937, p. 29.

28. Arthur Ellis, "Photographer Shares Honors With Writer in New Book," *The Washington Post*, November 14, 1937, p. T9.

Both *The Nation* and *The New Republic* covered the publication enthusiastically. Writing for the former, Margaret Marshall focused primarily on Caldwell's text, which she found a bit timid, though correct in its essentials. Toward the end of her discussion, she asserted: "Many will see these faces; and the beautiful photographs by Miss Bourke-White are not so beautiful that the reader will miss the tragedy of worn-out faces and depleted soil—their texture, under the lens, is amazingly similar—or find more pleasure than pain in the lines and surfaces that make a woman share-cropper's face a triumph of photographic art."[29] For Marshall, the text did not push hard enough for concrete changes, but the photographs struck a healthy balance between art and rhetoric.

29. Margaret Marshall, "You Have Seen Their Faces," *The Nation* 145 (December 4, 1937): 622.

Malcolm Cowley raved about the book in *The New Republic*; for him, the "quotations printed beneath the photographs are exactly right; the photographs themselves are almost beyond praise."[30] Importantly, he continued by calling for new "standards" by which to judge the images, as they amounted to nothing less than a "new art." He argued that "the important qualities are those which used to be conveyed in words rather than pictures—drama, for example, and class conflicts, and stories to the extent that they are written in the gullied soil, the sagging rooftree of a house or the wrinkles of a tired face." It is essential to note that Cowley cited drama as an exemplary attribute of this new art, as it would become one of the very characteristics for which Bourke-White would be criticized in the decades that followed.

30. Malcomb Cowley, "Books in Review: Fall Catalogue," *The New Republic* 93 (November 24, 1937): p. 78.

Not surprisingly, given Bourke-White's longtime association with Luce's publishing empire, *Time* ran a relatively long review and included a reproduction of the female portrait identified in the book as "Locket, Georgia."[31] The essence of the review was: "After a year and a half of investigation they returned with a skeletonized [sic], unemotional array of case histories, native opinion, commentary and camera evidence on the dreariness and degradation of plantation workers' lives."[32] The case histories and commentary referred to Caldwell's text, but the "native opinions" were the legends, clearly mistaken here—as they had been by Thompson and Cowley—as the words of the people in the photographs. The magazine printed several quoted captions as though they were indeed the words of the people in the photographs, transcribed verbatim in the book. In the context of this review, these quotes held the same evidentiary weight as the photographs.

In the *Time* essay, the author mentioned the likelihood that the book would "chill the stomachs of Northern readers," acknowledging the unwritten assumption of a predominantly Northern audience. The book certainly met with a different reception in some of the Southern press, perhaps best exemplified by a long essay written by poet Donald Davidson, which appeared the following year in *The Southern Review*.[33] After a passage on Caldwell's past transgressions—most notably, *Tobacco Road* and *God's Little Acre*—the author offered moderate admiration for the photographs and their legends. Though he lamented the probable confusion over their authorship, he conceded that "here [in the legends], as in the pictures, the average Southern reader, if not the Northern one, is compelled to admit that Mr. Caldwell has behaved a little more handsomely than might have been expected... they are quite near to the genuine country idiom, and are surprisingly nonrebellious and uncomplaining."[34]

Davidson then divided Bourke-White's photographs into three groups, with "realistic" forming one end of a binary opposition framed at the other end by "romantic." The former he defined as "those pictures that show some notable excess of rags, dirt, disease, bad housing, or depressing environment; or that are meant, possibly, to suggest some brutality."[35] The latter included "pictures that give us faces smiling, happy, cheerful, vigorous, that tell or imply a sentimental or humorous story, or that suggest the fallen grandeurs and lush natural abundance traditionally associated with the 'Deep South' and the 'Cotton Kingdom.'"[36] The "neutral" images, those that occupied a middle zone between the two poles, were defined simply as not presenting bold, obvious meanings. Davidson tallied the images to show that they were fairly equally clustered at either end, with a smaller portion forming the "neutral" group. He wrote that he had seen some tenant farmers living in true comfort and others whose homes resembled animal dens, but Bourke-White's "photographs hit between these two extremes."[37] Davidson summarized his thoughts on the photographs by claiming that Bourke-White's images were "camera studies done with a fine eye for composition" and "not candid camera shots."[38]

In a review in *The Journal of Negro Education*, W. P. Robinson, a political science professor at Howard University, focused on Caldwell's essay, stating, for example, that he was in "complete" agreement with Caldwell's bleak assessment of the emotional reasons for lynching.[39] For Robinson, Caldwell and Bourke-White had avoided sentimentalizing the facts; the book was a cry to action. For him, *You Have Seen Their Faces* derived its power precisely from its strong rhetorical style and its authors' willingness to apply their style to a

31. "Speaking Likenesses," *Time* 30, November 15, 1937, p. 94–6.

32. "Speaking Likenesses," p. 95.

33. Donald Davidson, "Erskine Caldwell's Picture Book," *The Southern Review* 4 (1938–39): 15–25.

34. Davidson, "Erskine Caldwell's Picture Book," p. 16.

35. Davidson, "Erskine Caldwell's Picture Book," p. 17.

36. Davidson, "Erskine Caldwell's Picture Book," p. 17.

37. Davidson, "Erskine Caldwell's Picture Book," p. 18.

38. Davidson, "Erskine Caldwell's Picture Book," p. 18.

39. W. P. Robinson, "You Have Seen Their Faces," *The Journal of Negro Education* 7 (October 1938): 562. Caldwell's assessment, to which Robinson referred, was: "In a land that has long gloried in the supremacy of the white race, he [the white tenant farmer] directed his resentment against the black man.... When his own suffering was more than he could stand, he could live only by witnessing the suffering of others." Caldwell and Bourke-White, *You Have Seen Their Faces*, pp. 19–20.

clearly stated purpose (in lockstep with Newhall's assessment of documentary in general). Robinson echoed the book's inherent confrontation with its readers at the end of his own essay: "The book suggests the challenge. What are we going to do about it now?"[40]

40. Robinson, "You Have Seen Their Faces," p. 563

You Have Seen Their Faces had a very public life in the first years after its publication—the waning years of the 1930s.[41] Its images became the best-known exemplars of the new mode of photography described in Newhall's 1938 essay, which he published just months after the book's release.[42] In that article, Newhall cited Bourke-White's work as an exemplary instance of the new approach. He referred to the book as among "the most penetrating photo-documents" and quoted at length from the notes Bourke-White published in the back of her book. Newhall also mentioned the work of the government agency by then called the Farm Security Administration (FSA, formally the RA, the Resettlement Administration) and acknowledged that Evans, along with a list of other FSA staff photographers, also practiced the documentary approach.

41. For a further account of the responses to the book, see Robert E. Snyder, "Erskine Caldwell and Margaret Bourke-White: You Have Seen Their Faces," *Prospects* II, (1987): 397–406.

42. Newhall, "Documentary Approach to Photography," pp. 2–6.

Bourke-White never worked for the FSA, but she had become one of the original four photographers for *Life* while she was still working on her book. The combination of her magazine work and the book's extravagant success made her famous. When, for example, *Life* published a group of images from *You Have Seen Their Faces,* it emphasized that she was part of the story by titling the article: "The South of Erskine Caldwell is Photographed by Margaret Bourke-White."[43] This sort of fame, achieving celebrity status for a book aimed at social justice, provoked Agee and Evans to work toward superseding her accomplishments with a book of their own.

43. *Life*, November 12, 1937, p. 51.

LET US NOW PRAISE FAMOUS MEN AND *AMERICAN PHOTOGRAPHS*

The events leading up to the publication of *Let Us Now Praise Famous Men* also started at *Fortune* (**FIG. 5**). Agee was just returning to the magazine after a leave—designed to ease his deep dissatisfaction with his work—when Ingersoll offered him a "Life and Circumstances" story.[44] This assignment was not considered a plum, as it involved extensive travel in the rural South during the hottest months of the year, but it attracted Agee: he was from the South and the subject seemed to have more literary potential than most of his *Fortune* assignments. He was to find a farmer's family whose story would personalize the larger issue of sharecropping and tenant farming. For this assignment, the magazine hired Evans, then still working for the Resettlement Administration, under Roy Stryker. Evans' work had appeared sporadically in the magazine in the previous few years, and Agee seems to have been happy about the pairing.[45] In order to secure the arrangement, the RA would get to keep for their files all the photographs that Evans made, but only after *Fortune* had run the article.

44. Bergreen, *James Agee: A Life*, pp. 156–7.

45. Bergreen, *James Agee: A Life*, p. 159.

Agee and Evans returned from their trip to the South to discover that Luce had decided to impose a new order at *Fortune* and that there had been an editorial shift at the magazine. The editors who had overseen the original assignment were no longer responsible for the magazine—in fact, the new management team had already cut the "Life and Circumstances" series by the time Agee delivered his first draft. Evans, in the meantime, had lost his position at the FSA due to cutbacks in the program. Taking advantage of this unexpected time off, he organized his negatives and made prints from his trip. Over the next several months, Agee submitted further versions of the essay, but his editors rejected each one.[46] Finally, at his request, *Fortune* relinquished its claim to the project, allowing Agee to pursue a book deal instead. Stryker, who also supported the book format for the project, was willing to wait a while longer for the debut of Evans' photographs.

46. Jeff L. Rosenheim, "'The Cruel Radiance of What Is:' Walker Evans and the South," in Maria Morris Hambourg, et al., *Walker Evans* (New York: Metropolitan Museum of Art, 2000), pp. 95–6.

The book that became *Let Us Now Praise Famous Men* was mostly completed by 1937, but complications in his personal life continued to keep Agee from committing to a finished text.[47] By the end of that year, he had an agreement with Harper & Brothers to publish the work under the title *Three Tenant Families*, but following considerable wrangling over changes that Agee found unacceptable, the publisher rejected the work outright.[48]

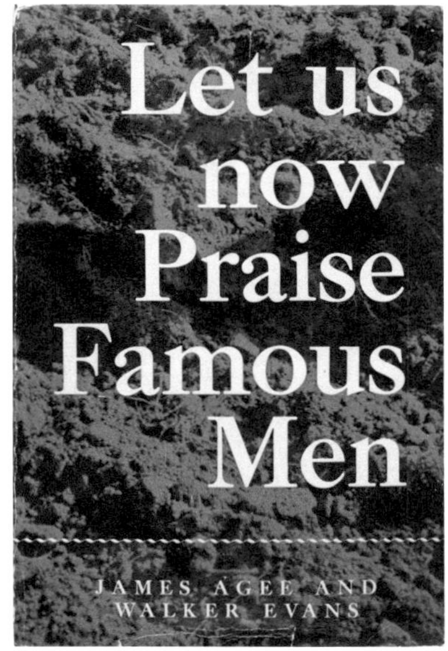

FIGURE 5
JAMES AGEE AND WALKER EVANS, *LET US NOW PRAISE FAMOUS MEN*, (COVER), 1941. COURTESY HOUGHTON MIFFLIN COMPANY.

47. Bergreen, *James Agee: A Life*, pp. 182–3.

48. Bergreen, *James Agee: A Life*, pp. 233–35

While Evans waited for his partner to complete the text, he produced the book that would establish his reputation as the master of modern documentary photography in the United States. It started when his longtime friend Lincoln Kirstein helped him get an exhibition at the Museum of Modern Art (MoMA), in New York. Evans worried that his show would fail critically. Since his first exhibiting experience in New York, he had been compared to Bourke-White and not to his benefit—the success of *You Have Seen Their Faces* only promised to exacerbate the situation.[49] As well, Newhall's essay on the subject had just been released, and it made Bourke-White more central than Evans to the very practice he sought to dominate. Lincoln Kirstein recalled that Evans' obsession with Bourke-White's success reached the level of paranoia and that he complained that she might try to steal his ideas and leave him in obscurity.[50] Evans took no chances with his MoMA show. His father was in the advertising business, and one lesson the young photographer understood was the power of marketing to shape public perception.

49. In 1933, for example, Kirstein had helped get him a show in a commercial gallery with Bourke-White and Ralph Steiner. The gallerists, John Becker and Thomas Mabry, commissioned a short essay by Condé Nast editor Dr. Mehemed Agha, who singled out Evans for faint praise while heartily endorsing the work of Bourke-White and Steiner. Belinda Rathbone, *Walker Evans: A Biography* (New York: Houghton Mifflin Company, 1995), p. 67. Later that year, when being considered for a job photographing Cuba for a book by Carleton Beals, the art director at Lippincott (slated to publish the book) wrote encouragingly: "I feel perfectly sure that Evans has the possibilities for [being] another Margaret Bourke-White," as long as "he did as good a job on Cuba as [she] did on Russia." Quoted in Rathbone, *Walker Evans: A Biography*, p. 79.

50. Rathbone, *Walker Evans: A Biography*, p. 84.

The MoMA show was arranged through Kirstein's friend Thomas Mabry, now working at the museum. Probably worried about attendance at the museum's temporary quarters at Rockefeller Plaza (the Fifty-third Street building was undergoing renovations), Mabry organized a brilliant publicity campaign for Evans. He began with a "whispering campaign" and followed up with overtures to periodicals, offering them exclusives on certain images in exchange for coverage.[51] He not only told people about the show but also explained how they should understand the photographs.

51. Rathbone, *Walker Evans: A Biography*, p. 157.

As Mabry planned for the exhibition catalogue, he held Kirstein to an earlier promise to write for it. In a letter to Kirstein containing a reminder of this commitment, Mabry outlined the particular slant he expected for the essay, including how clearly Evans was to be differentiated from Bourke-White, in particular. He wrote:

> I should think that you might want to define as simply and clearly as possible the difference between Walker's work and the majority of photographers both 'documentary' and 'lyric'....The canonization of the commonplace that documentary photography has turned

into (Margaret Bourke-White, "Life" photographers, and much of the Federal Art Project photography) is just as bad to me as any kind of Herald Tribune beautiful baby contest photography.[52]

As well, Mabry wrote several reporters directly to garner attention for the project and often colored his pitch in moral terms. For example, in his letter to Belle Rosenbaum at the *Herald Tribune*, he wrote, "Photographs are so often corrupt and fake that I think of these particular photographs as being the real thing."[53] This was the essence of his campaign: Evans as pure and real, others as corrupt and fake. Despite the simplistic terms of his argument, it proved effective and lasting. Indeed, the notion of the "modern" in the context of photography clearly owes much to this differentiation, and the debates surrounding contemporary photographic representations of human suffering derive, almost unaltered, from these polarities invented in 1938.

Mabry also wrote his press release—a four-page, single-spaced opus—in the same tone but with much greater clarity. Without mentioning Bourke-White by name this time, Mabry described many of the more obvious characteristics of her style and cited them as the antithesis of Evans, who had "the 'purest' eye of any photographer of our generation."[54] He introduced this discussion on the first page, writing:

> It is the power to create an austere drama from America *as it is* that gives to Evans' work its unique character. There is no trick about his photographs. He never exaggerates by angle shot or unusual perspective. He never sentimentalizes the 'beauty' of the industrial machine, and he respects the industrial worker too much to exploit his pathos. He abhors such easy camera melodrama.[55]

Bourke-White, of course, was famous for her angled shots, unusual perspectives, beautiful images of industry, and most recently, for her photographs of workers. Mabry continued that Evans was "the antithesis of the candid-camera man, that anomalous being of modern times who, with his pretensions to truth, succeeds most often in merely distorting it."[56] Much of the press release was consumed with adumbrating all the things Evans was not; among these was the note that his work was "meaningful because of its order, its morality."[57] Here, he had introduced a theme, not too subtly neoclassical in its argument, which would accompany Evans' work for decades—order implied morality, austerity denoted truth, and the combination represented virtue.

Mabry circulated his press release with the traveling version of the exhibition. Each venue could receive fresh copies with blank areas at the top to insert the name of their institution and the duration of their exhibition—after MoMA, there were ten venues around the country. Mabry's opinions became the framework for reviews from New York to San Francisco. He succeeded in selling Evans' approach as pure and uncontrived. Gilbert Seldes' report for *Esquire* was pretty typical of how thoroughly most writers bought the press release; his headline read: "No Soul in the Photograph: Walker Evans' pictures are not posed, nor bitterly candid, they simply show American people and places as they are."[58] Mabry could hardly have hoped for a better representation of his ideas; his campaign on behalf of Evans was already beginning to shape a much broader critical orthodoxy for documentary aesthetics and ethics.

52. Thomas Mabry to Lincoln Kirstein, April 29, 1938. Registrar Exhibition Files, Exh. #78, The Museum of Modern Art Archives, New York.

53. Thomas Mabry to Belle Rosenbaum, August 26, 1938. Registrar Exhibition Files, Exh. #78, MoMA Archives, NY. Mabry also offered several of the papers the names of possible reviewers and included Agee.

54. Thomas Mabry, "Walker Evans' Photographs of America," typescript, unpaginated and undated, Registrar Exhibition Files, Exh. #78, MoMA Archives, NY.

55. Mabry, "Walker Evans' Photographs of America."

56. Mabry, "Walker Evans' Photographs of America."

57. Mabry, "Walker Evans' Photographs of America."

58. Gilbert Seldes, "No Soul in the Photograph," *Esquire* (December 1938). Clipping at Department of Public Information Records, [MF43; Frame 276]. The Museum of Modern Art Archives, New York.

These ideas were further consolidated in the exhibition catalogue on which Evans and Kirstein collaborated. They worked together on the design, and Kirstein provided an essay that pointedly separated Evans' work from the rest of contemporary photography—he carried further Mabry's idea of defining a set of criteria for the use of his readers which, when applied to Evans' photography, confirmed the singular greatness of the work. Kirstein's text provided Evans with much-needed ammunition in his fledgling battle to supercede Bourke-White's position of dominance in American photography. The essay for *American Photographs* covered not only what Evans' photographs were, but even more importantly, what they were not—again, essentially, Bourke-White photographs. Throughout the essay, Kirstein defined new criteria for photography and decried a list of attributes that, under the new regime, were inexcusable. These newly defined transgressions included many attributes for which Bourke-White was famous, from angled shots and monumentalizing images of machinery to her latest trials with candid-camera work.[59]

59. In a sub-section on candid photography, he wrote: "The candid camera is the greatest liar in the photographic family.... It is anarchic, naïve and superficial" (p. 189), but Evans creates work of order, simplicity and permanence. He also pointed out that "Evans is less concerned with the majesty of machinery than with the psychology, manners and looks of the men who make it work." (p. 193) Lincoln Kirstein, "Photographs of America: Walker Evans," in *Walker Evans: American Photographs* (New York: Museum of Modern Art, 1938), pp. 187–195.

The combination of Mabry's well-articulated marketing campaign and Kirstein's work on both the image selection and the interpretation of their significance aided greatly in introducing the idea that Evans' dispassionate approach was a truer expression of his subjects' suffering than the passion evidenced in Bourke-White's photographs. It was in this context that some of Evans' photographs for *Let Us Now Praise Famous Men* made their public debut—exhibited in a museum of art, accompanied by a museum catalogue, and supported by a publicity campaign that defined their particular aesthetics in terms of "truth" and the "real."

Perhaps Evans' growing reputation contributed to Agee's finally being able to interest a young editor at Houghton Mifflin in their book, now complete and with a new title. With little further editing, *Let Us Now Praise Famous Men* was published in 1941. Recurrent in Agee's writing was the idea that words would never be able to fully transport his readers to the scene as well as photography could. At the beginning of the book, Agee considered at length the appropriateness of writing about his subjects. He repeatedly described the vast gulf that lay between the subjects and his readers, explaining that his subjects were human beings, "investigated, spied on, revered, and loved, by other quite monstrously alien human beings, in the employment of still others still more alien."[60] He continued, in what has become a paradigm for documentary self-awareness: "If I could do it, I'd do no writing at all here. It would be photographs; the rest would be fragments of cloth, bits of cotton, lumps of earth, records of speech, pieces of wood and iron, phials [sic] of odors, plates of food and of excrement."[61] Agee, here, demonstrated his desire both to remove his own presence from the work and to forgo the problematical process of representation. Naively, he wished for his readers an experience unmediated by an author. Agee's text followed, including notes, asides, and appendices—his protests about the shortcomings of writing notwithstanding, his text ran to well over four hundred pages.

60. James Agee and Walker Evans, *Let Us Now Praise Famous Men*, originally published 1941(Boston: Houghton Mifflin, 1960), p .13.

61. Agee and Evans, *Let Us Now Praise Famous Men*, p. 13.

With their book, Agee and Evans established a new ethic of disengagement and an aesthetic of artlessness. In one oft-quoted passage, Agee wrote that his book was "written for all those who have a soft place in their hearts for the laughter and tears inherent in poverty viewed at a distance, and especially for those who can afford the retail price; in the hope that the reader will be edified, and may feel kindly disposed toward any well-thought-out liberal efforts to rectify the unpleasant situation down South."[62] This passage, like several others in which he expressed his disdain for using his art to bring about social change, was likely aimed directly at Bourke-White and Caldwell and their well-publicized good intentions. It was also a swipe at the general understanding of documentary practice as then reflected in Newhall's essay and one that today continues to drive the ethical debates surrounding documentary practice. Note, for example, the vehemence with which Martha Rosler recently countered what she described as "artists' pantomimes of social disengagement" with the rejoinder: "I stress that the community of artists has a responsibility to involve itself actively in social matters with some dedication to the ideal of positive social transformation."[63] According to their published statements, Agee and Evans had no intention of working toward "transformation" through their work. Neither did they intend to make art. Agee insisted that they had worked to distance their efforts (both the writing and the photography) from ideas of art and requested of his readers: "Above all else: in God's name don't think of it as Art." Evans' photographs nevertheless established an aesthetic that has dominated certain types of photographic practices ever since, one brilliant in its ability to simultaneously maintain a virtual hegemony on documentary photography while essentially denying its own existence.

62. Agee and Evans, *Let Us Now Praise Famous Men*, p. 14.

63. Martha Rosler, "Ethics and Aesthetics in Documentary Photography" in Ine Gevers, *Voorbij Ethiek en Esthetiek (Beyond Ethics and Aesthetics)* (Nijmegen: Sun, 1997), p. 390.

Agee's text posited a high level of believability in the objectivity of Evans' photography—the images have the same relative weight as facts as did the variety of field specimens he discussed. The 1941 edition contained a suite of thirty-two images notable for the relative paucity of human representations and the abundance of architectural views, interiors and exteriors. Most were Evans' signature, large-format work, though some bore the characteristics of 35mm exposures (many of which were cut from the second edition). Unlike the photographs in *You Have Seen Their Faces*, Evans' photographs were grouped without captions at the beginning of the book. This bold departure from the norm has become one of the creative hallmarks of their book, as it encouraged a more-or-less unmitigated visual experience for the reader prior to the text.

The first review appeared that August in *The New York Times*. Written by Ralph Thompson, the reviewer who had previously written about *You Have Seen Their Faces*, the piece was far from favorable. Though Thompson singled out the photographs for acclaim, he did so at the expense of the text: "There never was a better argument for photography. Mr. Evans says as much about tenant-farmers in the Cotton South in his several dozen pictures as Mr. Agee says in his entire 150,000 word text."[64] According to the criteria by which Thompson evaluated the text, it was a failure. The singular accomplishments of Agee's style—the self-obsessiveness, the lack of narrative structure, even the run-on sentences—all came in for harsh critique. Essentially, the book was dismissed as being simply "the choicest recent example of how to write self-inspired, self-conscious, and self-indulgent prose."[65]

64. Ralph Thompson, "Books of the Times," *The New York Times*, August 19, 1941, p. 19.

65. Thompson, "Books of the Times," p. 19.

Most major-market newspapers continued to ignore the book, probably for a variety of reasons, not least of which were the accelerating war in Europe and the fact that farm tenancy and sharecropping were no longer the burning issues they had been in 1936. As a countermeasure, Agee's friends cobbled together a public relations campaign, submitting reviews to journals on speculation and encouraging their editor friends to pay attention to the book.[66] This worked. Though many of the reviews were still mixed, the campaign gained the book some much-needed critical attention. Agee biographer Laurence Bergreen identified Selden Rodman's piece in the *Saturday Review of Literature* and Harvey Breit's in *The New Republic* as results of this effort. In one telling passage, Rodman wrote that the book "will be spat upon—and years hence (unless the country is given over to the fascists or the faith-healers or 'far away' democracy) read."[67] And in a similar tone Breit wrote, "Whatever the case, whether attracted or repelled, whether for or against, it is a rich, many-eyed book and ought to be looked into."[68] At *Time*, editor T. S. Mathews published his own review after rejecting one written by a friend of Agee's on the staff. Mathews declared *Let Us Now Praise Famous Men* "the most distinguished failure of the season."[69] He also took Agee to task for "bad manners, exhibitionism, and verbosity," before complimenting the "delicacy and power" of his prose.[70]

66. Bergreen, *James Agee: A Life*, p. 258.

67. Selden Rodman, "Let Us Now Praise Famous Men," *Saturday Review of Literature* 24 (August 23, 1941): 6.

68. Harvey Breit, "Cotton Tenantry," *The New Republic* 105 (September 15, 1941): 349.

69. T. S. Mathews, "Let Us Now Praise Famous Men," *Time* 38 (October 13, 1941): p. 104.

70. T. S. Mathews, "Let Us Now Praise Famous Men," p. 104.

Not until Lionel Trilling's passionate response to the book was published in the winter of 1942 did Agee and Evans get a hint of what would become—in the decades to follow—the more standard, if conflicted, take on their work.[71] It was Trilling who publicly introduced the moral dimension to discussions of their documentary project. He wrote: "What always immediately strikes me about [Evans'] work is its perfect *taste*, taking that word in its largest possible sense to mean tact, delicacy, justness of feeling, complete awareness and perfect respect. It is a tremendously impressive moral quality."[72] For Trilling, ironically, this form of morality included passion. He speculated that *Fortune* rejected their work because an "attitude of clear, cool investigation had been manifestly impossible. You cannot be cool about misery so intense, nor clear about people with whom you have lived."[73] Trilling raved about Evans' photographs—which he called "wholly successful"—but critiqued Agee's text as marred by "a failure of moral realism." Trilling argued that Agee wrote "of his people as if there were no human unregenerateness in them, no flicker of malice or meanness, only a sure and simple virtue, the growth, we must suppose, of their hard, unlovely poverty."[74] Despite its shortcomings, he concluded that the book was "the most important moral effort of our American generation."[75] Neither Trilling's review, nor any of the others, did much at the time to help the book commercially, and it was remaindered after selling fewer than a thousand copies.

71. From a commercial standpoint, Trilling's piece was ill timed: It appeared in the winter of 1942, the very moment that the United States struggled to respond to the twin instigations of its participation in World War Two: the attack on Pearl Harbor and Hitler's declaration of war—both occurred in December 1941.

72. Lionel Trilling, "Greatness with One Fault In It," *Kenyon Review* 4, (Winter 1942): 100.

73. Trilling, "Greatness with One Fault In It," p. 99.

74. Trilling, "Greatness with One Fault In It," p. 102.

75. Trilling, "Greatness with One Fault In It," p. 102.

THE LEGACY

The reputation of *Let Us Now Praise Famous Men* rose again, phoenix-like, in the years following the 1960 edition. By then, their cool approach could find a warm reception in an art world weaned on Evans' brand of photographic modernism and a literary community now accustomed to Agee's confessional mode of exposition. The reissue was precipitated by the growing interest in Agee—who had died in 1955 and won a Pulitzer Prize posthumously in 1958—and by Evans' own continuing ascendance in the world of photography. Starting with Granville Hicks' 1960 proclamation that *Let Us Now Praise Famous Men* was "one of the great books of our time," interest had grown.[76] T. S. Mathews returned to the subject in a 1966 review in which he called the work "an accurate, profound, and vivid report on

76. Granville Hicks, "Suffering Face of the Rural South," *Saturday Review of Literature* 43 (September 10, 1960): 18.

the life of sharecroppers (besides being a most disturbing reflection on the whole human condition)."[77]

77. T. S. Mathews, "James Agee—Strange and Wonderful," *Saturday Review of Literature* 49 (April 16, 1966): 22. Quoted in Leonidas Betts, "The 'Unfathomably Mysterious' *Let Us Now Praise Famous Men*," *The English Journal* 59 (January 1970): 44.

By 1973, when William Stott brought out *Documentary Expression and Thirties America*, his trailblazing book, *Let Us Now Praise Famous Men* was already enjoying cult status. Stott's book overtly shut out any further competition between *You Have Seen Their Faces* and *Let Us Now Praise Famous Men*; he dedicated a sizable portion of his study to the latter. Following the critical arguments established by Mabry and Kirstein in their 1938 campaign for the MoMA exhibition, Stott demonstrated how Bourke-White's photographs for *You Have Seen Their Faces* were not only inferior to Evans' work but also inherently flawed. Stott's analysis influenced a generation of readers—his book's position as the first comprehensive text on the subject, and the timing of its publication at the beginning of the expansion in photography studies, established it for decades as the authority on documentary.

Stott's essay included extended quotations from an interview with Evans in which the photographer's old obsession with Bourke-White's success came to the fore. Stott embraced Evans' assessment of *You Have Seen Their Faces* and his explanation of why the book had so outraged him and Agee—namely, that they felt Caldwell and Bourke-White had exploited their subjects and profited from their book. Writing about the short article on Bourke-White that Agee and Evans had decided to reprint in *Let Us Now Praise Famous Men*, Stott noted:

> Mean it was—'vicious,' Walker Evans says—but it was not gratuitous. One must remember the huge critical acclaim that greeted *You Have Seen Their Faces*...The book sold excellently...Evans' work in contrast was generally thought idiosyncratic, old-fashioned, cold, insufficiently reformist. While Bourke-White went from triumph to triumph, Evans was fired from the FSA Photography Unit (March 1937) and for years thereafter did not have a steady job.[78]

78. William Stott, *Documentary Expression and Thirties America*, originally published 1973 (Chicago: University of Chicago Press, 1986), p. 222.

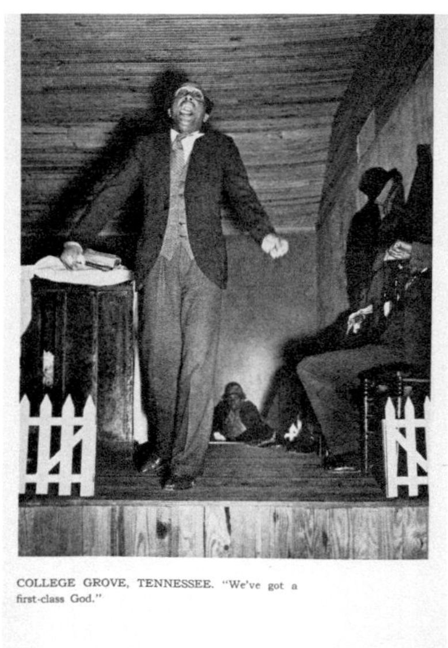

FIGURE 6
MARGARET BOURKE-WHITE, *COLLEGE GROVE, TENNESSEE*, FROM *YOU HAVE SEEN THEIR FACES*, 1937. COURTESY THE ESTATE OF MARGARET BOURKE-WHITE AND SIMON & SCHUSTER, INC.

The fact that the Bourke-White/Caldwell book sold well made it a less valid (truthful) document for Stott and opened it to criticism based on the motivation of the creators.[79] Stott's argument that vicious attacks on successful works were justified by virtue of their success has—like the attacks themselves—carried into the debates surrounding current photographic practices.

Stott avoided careful comparison of the formal attributes of the photographs in the books, but he did generalize enough to perpetuate the version of difference established by Mabry and Kirstein. He listed again the visual touchstones of dishonest photographs (angled vantage points, flash lighting, candid work, even industrial scenes) but went the step further of doing so directly in a discussion of Bourke-White's work.[80] He argued that beauty existed in the scene before the photographer recognized it and that the photographer should do nothing more than passively record what lay in front of the camera—as Evans did. Bourke-White—whose work Stott used throughout

79. Yet, to the extent that motive can be established, Bourke-White did not make her book—as noted above—with a profit motive in mind. See Goldberg, *Margaret Bourke-White: A Biography*, pp. 190–94.

80. This differentiation becomes recurrent in the literature on Agee and Evans; in his 1984 biography of Agee, Bergreen went so far as to describe as "Margaret Bourke-Whiteism" those attributes deemed unacceptable in documentary work as defined by Agee and Evans. Bergreen, *James Agee: A Life*, p. 164.

his discussion as the antithesis of Evans'—"over dramatizes virtually everything she treats. She shoots from bizarre angles and in operatic lights."[81] Unlike Davidson, Stott discerned no range in the selection of images in *You Have Seen Their Faces*; he saw only unrelenting defeat: "These people are bare, defenseless before the camera and its stunning flash...we see them spotlit in raptures of a revival meeting...we see a preacher taken in peroration, his mouth and nostrils open like a hyena's." (**FIG. 6**)[82] Following his extended list of her specific photographic transgressions, he concluded that Bourke-White's work was "a sentimental cliché," and he added that, "Bourke-White wanted—too obviously—to move her audience; Evans characteristically seemed not to care."[83] Caring, as revealed photographically by the use of flash and dramatic angles, had become an indicator of disingenuousness. Not caring, evidenced by camera angles close to level with the sitter's eyes and the use of available light, had become honesty's hallmark. Though simplistic, this dichotomy continues to drive critical interpretation of documentary photography.

81. Stott, *Documentary Expression and Thirties America*, p. 220.

82. Stott, *Documentary Expression and Thirties America*, p. 220. This passage was not atypical in its use of strident language to color the reader's understanding of the image.

83. Stott, *Documentary Expression and Thirties America*, pp. 270–71.

In the first three sections of his book, Stott redefined the criteria by which the images should be judged, and he dedicated the last section to an extended justification of Evans' solitary position in the world of documentary projects, as Evans himself would have it defined. He concluded his chapter on Agee's text for *Let Us Now Praise Famous Men* with the following assessment: "There can be no doubt that *Let Us Now Praise Famous Men* is a classic of the thirties' documentary genre."[84] The notion of the term "classic" deserves attention in this context. If Stott's point was that the book was an example of late-1930s documentary art as defined after the fact, then his assertion holds. But if by "classic" he meant that moment in the flow of a civilization's cultural output when the product of a creative act stands as a crystalline example of that civilization's aspirations at the time, then his case seems hard to defend. *Let Us Now Praise Famous Men* was not a key documentary project as it was defined in the mid-to-late 1930s; only after the terms of success had changed did it receive recognition. At a basic level, the essence of the documentary format also must be communication, a two-part process of transmission and reception. Though the photographs were taken in 1936, and a few were seen in the years that followed, the book had very little public life—that is, its pages were not the subject of any widespread or shared cultural experience—until 1941 (and even then its circulation was extraordinarily limited). More realistically, the *Let Us Now Praise Famous Men* of 1960, with its new preface by Evans and the expanded and re-edited photography section, was a "classic," but of a later era.[85]

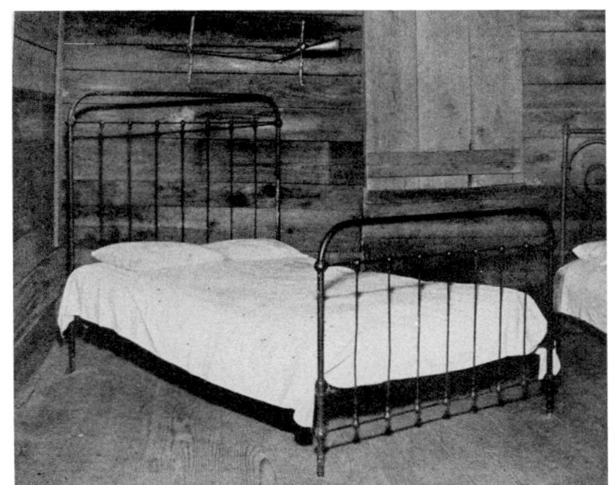

FIGURE 7
WALKER EVANS, UNTITLED, FROM *LET US NOW PRAISE FAMOUS MEN*, 1941. COURTESY HOUGHTON MIFFLIN COMPANY.

84. Stott, *Documentary Expression and Thirties America*, p. 266.

85. By then, too, it was celebrated by so-called New Journalists who saw in Agee's prose a justifying heritage of their own approach to journalism

Among the revisionist texts that began to emerge in the 1980s were some that appeared to present counterarguments to the hegemony of the Agee/Evans definition of a moral documentary. In a prime example, James Curtis and Sheila Grannen demonstrated that "Evans often arranged subject matter in ways that directly contradicted his self-proclaimed documentary creed." (**FIG. 7**)[86] He moved furniture and objects within his compositions to

86. James C. Curtis and Sheila Grannen, "Let Us Now Appraise Famous Photographs: Walker Evans and Documentary Photography," *Winterthur Portfolio* 15 (Spring, 1980): 2. In the interior view reproduced in my figure 7, for example, Evans had moved the bed away from the wall to make the flies gathered on the bedspread more apparent.

make them more compelling, to more effectively reveal the beauty he found in poverty. Curtis and Grannen, though, argued that this took nothing away from Evans' photographs, despite refuting one of the major claims—the purity of process—that both he and his supporters had maintained for decades. Evans, they pointed out, had to "become the creative artist who saw a larger significance in the particular details of poverty. He had to discover the universal symbols beneath the welter of their everyday existence...he made life into art."[87] Indeed, but this leaves unanswered the question of why rearranging the furniture in a house about to be "documented" did not represent a moral lapse—did not alter the truthfulness of the depiction—but using an angled point of view or a flash did.

87. Curtis and Grannen, "Let Us Now Appraise Famous Photographs: Walker Evans and Documentary Photography," p. 3.

88. Bourke-White, *Portrait of Myself*, pp. 126–7.

Ironically, and significantly for our discussion, in 1963 Bourke-White had already weighed in on this issue. She reported that she and Caldwell had discussed the appropriateness of rearranging objects early during their first visit to the South after she had composed the articles on a woman's dresser for a picture; her reminiscence makes it clear that they considered this behavior "violence" to both the scene and the subjects.[88] Both photographers, then, moved objects within their view (either physically or through vantage point and framing) to better tell the truth of the scene as they saw it—rendering problematic ethical distinctions based on this criterion alone.

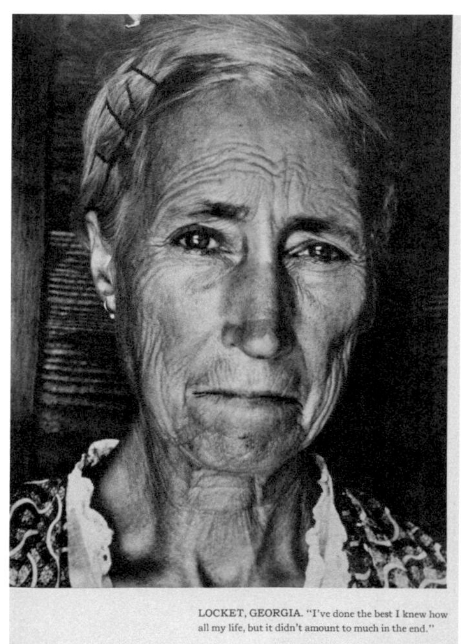
LOCKET, GEORGIA. "I've done the best I knew how all my life, but it didn't amount to much in the end."

FIGURE 8
MARGARET BOURKE-WHITE, *LOCKET, GEORGIA*, FROM *YOU HAVE SEEN THEIR FACES*, 1937. COURTESY THE ESTATE OF MARGARET BOURKE-WHITE AND SIMON & SCHUSTER, INC.

Some critics have claimed, though, that the major ethical line crossed by Bourke-White, but maintained by Evans, had to do with the relationship between the photographers and their subjects. Carol Schloss, for example, stated that "Agee's point [about Bourke-White] was that these photographic subjects were being used and that they were exploited in the very act that purported to help them."[89] She returned to one of the central ethical tropes perpetuated against Bourke-White, arguing that photographers had to get to know their subjects before photographing them. But how this process of familiarization would guarantee the subjects' protection from exploitation was not made clear. At what point did picture taking not connote exploitation? Did the fact of familiarization alter the fact of the picture? Clearly, every photograph of a person involved some level of exploitation—a taking—whether the image depicted a long-loved family member or a total stranger.

89. Carol Schloss, *In Visible Light: Photography and the American Writer: 1840–1940* (New York: Oxford University Press, 1987), p. 184.

The essence of the argument was that not spending time getting to know your subjects was necessarily exploitative and led to images that were less truthful. Rosler also addressed this dilemma, noting that "photographers often think that either they must become 'participant observers'...or they must have otherwise intense visiting relationships with their subjects."[90] She went on to identify the perceived ethical difference between this practice and "'parachuting photo-journalists,' the stereotypical figure of irresponsibility to the subjects."[91] Agee and Evans typified the former; they lived with their subjects for days or weeks. This,

90. Rosler, "Ethics and Aesthetics in Documentary Photography," p. 384.

91. Rosler, "Ethics and Aesthetics in Documentary Photography," p. 384.

they felt, brought them closer to the truth of the lives they depicted. Caldwell and Bourke-White, though cordial, were, at best, barely acquainted with their subjects; for them, getting too close interfered with the objectivity (truthfulness) of their observations—a value more consistent, according to Rosler, with photojournalism.[92] Both systems had advantages and disadvantages—but these were, again, relative and not polar extremes (**FIGS. 8** and **9**). In both cases photographs were taken and images were made, and the nature of the relationship between photographer and subject at the moment of the shutter release could not change that fact. The exploitation occurred at the moment the shutter was released.

92. Rosler, "Ethics and Aesthetics in Documentary Photography," p. 382.

If the argument was that the exploitation came after the fact—in other words, if it was not the taking of the picture but its use that denoted the immoral act—then, again, the differences between the Agee/Evans project and that of Caldwell/Bourke-White can hardly have evidenced the ethical differences that Stott and others purported. The books were different, but not in an ethical sense. Jefferson Hunter has argued that the idea of ethical ramifications in photography was undeveloped, at best, in the 1930s.[93] That is, *You Have Seen Their Faces* could not be unorthodox in advance of the establishment of documentary photography's orthodoxy. If the exploitation came from profiting—a result of better sales—would this not equal a higher ethical good due to wider distribution of the message? And, if this were true, the moral scoreboard might appear as follows: *You Have Seen Their Faces* would register as both self-serving and helpful—the authors made money and achieved fame due to their book's success, but the book brought widespread awareness of a major social problem affecting the country; *Let Us Now Praise Famous Men* would only have been self-serving.

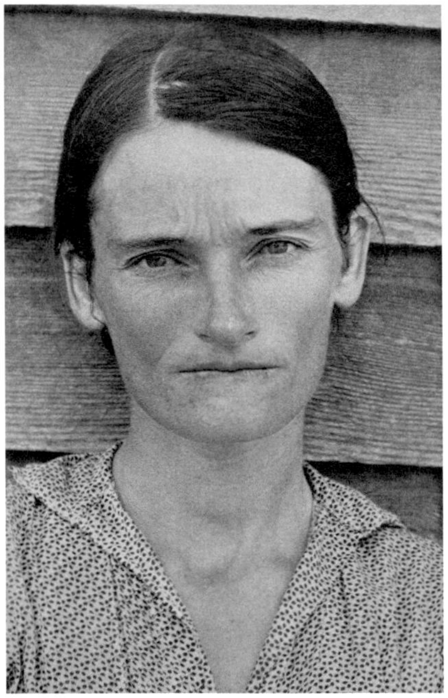

FIGURE 9
WALKER EVANS, UNTITLED, FROM *LET US NOW PRAISE FAMOUS MEN*, 1941. COURTESY HOUGHTON MIFFLIN COMPANY.

Hunter's was among the first balanced responses to the books published since the second edition of *Let Us Now Praise Famous Men*. He conceded readily to Bourke-White's use of visual rhetoric, noting that *You Have Seen Their Faces* "arranges facts, verbal and photographic, in a way calculated to impress. It manipulated its human subjects. But it does not transform them into 'entirely piteous' creatures, as William Stott claims. They are not brutalized in the text, [nor] rendered abject in the photographs."[94] In fact, Hunter—like Donald Davidson, writing in 1938—saw as fairly even the distribution of despair and hope in the photographs. *Let Us Now Praise Famous Men*, he suggested, was atypical—largely a reason for its elevation among modernists to its status as art. It was clearly innovative, even in its failings as either collaboration or journalism. Hunter concluded: "*Let Us Now Praise Famous Men* stands by itself, admirable and infuriating, un-influential now, unsuccessful in 1941, 'experimenting' with the idea of collaboration by spurning it."[95] In other words, it was an atypical, creative, and idiosyncratic work of art.

93. Hunter wrote: "Social investigation now seems more methodologically and ethically complicated than it did, say, to Erskine Caldwell and Margaret Bourke-White." Jefferson Hunter, *Image and Word: The Interaction of Twentieth-Century Photographs and Texts* (Cambridge, MA: Harvard University Press, 1987), p. 198.

94. Hunter, *Image and Word: The Interaction of Twentieth-Century Photographs and Texts*, p. 70.

95. Hunter, *Image and Word: The Interaction of Twentieth-Century Photographs and Texts*, p. 79.

In John Tagg's recent analysis of Evans' photographs, he concluded that the most salient difference between Evans' work and that of Bourke-White was the level of interest each photographer displayed in fixing meaning within their images.[96] Evans worked in a manner that did not offer obvious meanings—that leaned heavily toward the austerity of modern art. Bourke-White's assignation of clear significance to her subjects derived from her personal aesthetics and her political goals. Tagg, though, disparaged the ethical freight that has so often accompanied discussions of their work. He argued: "The production of a difference was what Evans' supporters worked for, as part of a discursive strategy to institute a particular status for his work. Within that context, the ethical terms of the contrast have a function. Outside it, they are not only questionable, but also essentially beside the point."[97] Tagg, here, offered a fresh assessment of both projects, focusing on interpretation without the moralizing that Mabry, Agee, and Kirstein had managed to attach to the subject.

Let Us Now Praise Famous Men, then, is best understood as a comment on, and not an active participant in, the American tradition of documentary photography in the 1930s. Its rise to the status of exemplar of the very mode it critiques represents a sustained campaign that took a generation of partisan reinterpretation to achieve. *You Have Seen Their Faces* deserves reexamination in the context of its role as the key photo-textual document of the 1930s. The obfuscation of its meanings, methodology, and cultural significance has contributed to the many unreflective assumptions that continue to inform contemporary debates about the ethics of documentary aesthetics. Partisan criticism of this sort reinforces the very hegemony Agee and Evans sought for their brand of "documentary style" and reduces the arguments involved from a complex matrix of contending visual strategies and social agendas to a simplistic, falsely ethical opposition of good and bad. To understand documentary practice today, it is critical to recognize the degree to which artists and photographers who deal with the subject of suffering in their work continue to embrace, critique, or transform visual codes established by *You Have Seen Their Faces* and *Let Us Now Praise Famous Men*, just as the critics who consider these contemporary works continue to engage in debates that emerged in the context of the efficacy and ethics of Bourke-White's and Evans' images and image-making practices.

96. John Tagg, "Melancholy Realism: Walker Evans' Resistance to Meaning," *Narrative* 11 (January 2003): 3–77.

97. Tagg, "Melancholy Realism: Walker Evans' Resistance to Meaning," p. 58.

ERINA DUGANNE

PHOTOGRAPHY AFTER THE FACT

Photojournalism is often thought to have a special relationship to the real. It records the important political and social issues that affect our world, and because of its assumed immediacy to the palpable "facts," we tend to believe that it is reliable and, hence, authentic. The legendary advice of photojournalist Robert Capa substantiates this assumption: "If your pictures aren't good enough, you're not close enough." In this statement, Capa implied that photojournalism's reportorial powers derive largely from the physical and emotional proximity of the photographers to their subjects and their ability, thereby, to witness events firsthand.

Due, however, to the recent influx of such technologies as television, video, and digital media, contemporary photojournalism seems to have lost much of its witnessing authority. A number of scholars have attributed this shift in photojournalism's identity to the Gulf War of 1991. Because most of the images from this war were taken by digital imaging systems and then dispersed through military spokespeople, often via television, many argue that photojournalism relinquished the traditional position of witness that it had previously served, especially during Vietnam.[1] Photography historian David Campany explained: "Today it is very rare that photographs actually break the news. The newspaper constitutes only a second wave of interpreted information or commentary."[2]

1. The bibliography about the highly orchestrated nature of the Gulf War as spectacle is extensive; on its implications for photography, see David Campany, "Safety in Numbness: Some Remarks on the Problem of 'Late Photography,'" *Where is the Photograph?*, ed. David Green (Manchester: Photoworks / PhotoForum, 2003), pp. 123–32; Ian Walker, "Desert Stories or Faith in Facts?" *The Photographic Image in Digital Culture*, ed. Martin Lister (London and New York: Routledge, 1995), pp. 236–52; John Taylor, *Body Horror* (New York: New York University Press, 1998); William J. Mitchell, *The Reconfigured Eye: Visual Truth in the Post-Photographic Era* (Cambridge: MIT Press, 1992); and Fred Ritchin, "The End of Photography as We Have Known It," *PhotoVideo: Photography in the Age of the Computer*, ed. Paul Wombell (London: Rivers Oram Press, 1991), pp. 8–15.

2. Campany, "Safety in Numbness," p. 127.

A number of contemporary photographers have responded to this situation by forgoing traditional photojournalism's reliance on the lightweight, 35mm or digital handheld camera with its ostensible ability to freeze events quickly. Instead, they have turned to medium- or large-format cameras, the larger frames and cumbersome sizes of which require a slower process and produce more detailed images of what comes "after."[3] The large-scale, panoramic photographs entitled *History* that former Magnum and *Newsweek* photographer Luc Delahaye began in 2001 seem consistent with this tendency (**PLATE 4**). This series depicts such newsworthy subject matter as the war zones in Afghanistan and Iraq, the G8 summit in Genoa, and a memorial service at Ground Zero, to name just a few. Yet, rather than photograph these subjects spontaneously, as he had done in numerous images taken while on assignment for *Newsweek* (**PLATE 3**), Delahaye instead depicted them from the distant and oblique perspective assumed as intrinsic to his medium-format Linhof Technorama 612 panoramic camera.

A number of critics have read this shift in Delahaye's production as a direct confrontation of traditional photojournalism and, more particularly, its voyeuristic tendencies. Photography curator Carol Squiers, for instance, argued that the "slowness" and "detachment" of the Linhof panoramic camera enable Delahaye to focus on peripheral information frequently "excised or ignored by the media's focus on sensational incident." In so doing, Squiers claimed that Delahaye overturns Capa's insistence on the "immediacy" and "instantaneity" of photojournalism and the sensationalism that she believes is implicit to this approach: "By implementing this reversal, Delahaye alters his relationship to the human subjects caught in newsworthy events, often refusing to spectacularize the pain written on the faces and bodies of the strangers he photographs."[4] Likewise, art historian Michael Fried maintained that the "distance" and "withdrawal" that Delahaye adopted in relation to his series *History* cause viewers to become "aware that a basic protocol of these images rules out precisely the sort of feats of *capture*—of fast-moving events, extreme gestures and emotions, vivid momentary juxtapositions of persons and things, etc.—that one associates with photojournalism at its bravura best."[5]

Delahaye has also contributed to this reading of *History* as an implicit challenge to photojournalism. According to Delahaye, he prefers the Linhof panoramic camera because of the explicit distinction that it makes between art and photojournalism and the responses required of them. In particular, Delahaye believes that the monumental and highly detailed images produced by the Linhof panoramic camera counter the diminution of meaning that occurs in photojournalism, especially when its images are reproduced in the print media. Because of the smaller frame of photojournalism's 35mm or digital handheld cameras, which have a 3:2 aspect ratio, Delahaye maintains that these prints promote rapid scanning when reproduced in the chaotic context of newspaper or magazine pages. The generous proportions and 1:2 aspect ratio of the Linhof frame, on the other hand, encourage a more detached relationship to the subject matter—one that is necessarily, as Delahaye explained, "incompatible with the economy of the press"—especially when, as in *History*, they are enlarged into eight-by-four foot prints and placed within the context of an art museum or gallery.[6]

In making these distinctions about *History* and its relationship to photojournal-

3. In "Desert Stories or Faith in Facts?" (p. 240), Ian Walker used the term "post-reportage" to define this shift in photography: "I use that term 'post-reportage' to suggest not what photography cannot do, but what it can: document what comes after, what has been left when the war is over." David Campany, "Survey," *Art and Photography* (London and New York: Phaidon, 2003), p. 27, reiterated this observation: "Whatever its indexical primary, photography is now a secondary medium of evidence.... This is the source of the eclipse of the realist reportage of 'events' and the emergence of a photography of the trace or 'aftermath.'"

4. Carol Squiers, "The Stranger," *Strangers: The First ICP Triennial of Photography and Video* (New York: International Center of Photography and Göttingen: Steidl, 2003), p. 17.

5. Michael Fried, "World Mergers," *Artforum* 44, no. 7 (March 2006): 64.

6. Luc Delahaye, quoted in Bill Sullivan, "The Real Thing: Photographer Luc Delahaye," *Artnet Magazine* (April 10, 2003) www.artnet.com/magazine/features/sullivan/

ism, these critics—as well as Delahaye—assume that photojournalism and art involve, as Squiers elucidated, "Different preoccupations and different freedoms."[7] Since photojournalism remains bound to newspaper or magazine pages, its photographers necessarily and automatically "capture" the real without any self-reflexivity or critical detachment. Artists, on the other hand, due to the self-sufficiency and distance of their images from the real, can think about the nature of representation and its depiction of reality in a more oblique and, hence, contemplative manner. Delahaye explained this in relation to *History*: "To voice the real and at the same time to create an image that is a world in itself, with its own coherence, its autonomy and sovereignty; an image that thinks."[8] In other words, whereas photojournalism must adhere to the "immediacy" and "instantaneity" of the "facts," the "slowness" and "detachment" of art allow it to function, as David Campany further explained, "Both as and of a trace."[9] Such distinctions, however, imply that these systems of image making and the types of responses that they elicit are both steadfast and resolute. Photography's ability to bear witness cannot be reduced to either a "trace" of the real or even a "trace of a trace" of the real. Instead, the evidentiary and testimonial authority of the medium depends on complex habits of observation and a set of assumptions and beliefs that continually shift according to the culture and interests of those who use and read them, as well as those who make them.

7. Carol Squiers, quoted in Nancy Princenthal, "Forty Ways of Looking at a Stranger," *Art in America* 91 (December 2003): 42.

8. Luc Delahaye, quoted in Susan Bright, *Art Photography Now* (New York: Aperture, 2005), p. 181.

9. Campany, "Survey," p. 27.

EVIDENCE

Having worked extensively as a Magnum and *Newsweek* photographer, Luc Delahaye has had firsthand experience with the loss of meaning that occurs when photographs are reproduced in the print media. For a project on post-Communist Russia, for instance, he spent four months during the winter of 1998–99 riding with a translator on the Trans-Siberian railroad from Moscow to Vladivostok. Along the way he stopped to photograph the daily hardships of the Russian people whom he encountered and the equally stark and dreary landscapes of a nation struggling to survive economic crisis. In 1999, four photographs from this trip were published in *Newsweek* with the headline "The Faces of Russia's Agony" and a text describing the "grit and grim fatalism" with which Russians "scrape by."[10] Through this format, *Newsweek* editors used Delahaye's pictures to illustrate Russia's bleak and damaged existence, as the letter of one reader attested: "Your dark and moving photographs convey far more despair than words ever could."[11]

Not all *Newsweek* readers, however, appreciated the anguish depicted in Delahaye's photographs. The letter of another reader, for instance, criticized the images for focusing exclusively on the squalor and suffering of Russia and its people: "Yes, there are many harsh realities, but there is also a beauty about Siberia, Novosibirsk, and the Russian people that was not fairly credited. I urge you to take a deeper look."[12] What this reader did not realize (since *Newsweek* editors neglected to disclose it) was that Delahaye's four photographs actually represented only a small portion of a larger, more extensive project on Russian life. Like many of his predecessors and contemporaries—including Mary Ellen Mark, James Nachtwey, and Sebastião Salgado—Delahaye frequently used his photojournalistic assignments as the basis of larger, more personal projects.[13] Thus, the same photographs

10. "The Faces of Russia's Agony," *Newsweek*, December 20, 1999, pp. 24–6.

11. Timothy Shenk, "Letters," *Newsweek*, January 31, 2000, Atlantic Edition, Lexis-Nexis http:web.lexisnexis.com/universe/form/academic/s_guidednews.html

12. Grigory Ioffe, "Letters," *Newsweek*, January 31, 2000, Atlantic Edition, Lexis-Nexis http:web.lexisnexis.com/universe/ form/academic/s_guidednews.

13. Mary Ellen Mark addressed the relationship between her personal and commercial work: "I am always thinking of the different ways that I can finance my own work. Because without personal projects, what's the point? The self-assigned project is your heart and soul.... The ideal situation is when a magazine assignment overlaps with your body of personal work." "Mary Ellen Mark: Streetwise Photographer," *Witness in our Time: Working Lives of Documentary Photographers*, ed. Ken Light (Washington, D.C: Smithsonian Institution Press, 2000), p. 82.

by Delahaye that appeared on the pages of *Newsweek* also circulated as part of a larger project, in a traveling exhibition as well as in the more intimate format of the art book *Winterreise*, which he designed.[14] Within these frameworks, the images were not appended with descriptive captions fixing their meaning; instead, they were placed within a larger sequence of photographs that led viewers along a more visually complex journey through Russia than allowed by the photo-essay in *Newsweek*.

Realizing that merely re-situating his photographs from a photojournalistic to an artistic context was not enough to offset the supplementary and frequently compromising purposes of the print media, Delahaye took a different approach for *History*. During his tenure in Afghanistan in 2001, for instance, Delahaye decided to produce two different sets of images. He made one set as a photojournalist; this set was subsequently circulated, among other frameworks, in *Newsweek* and on its web site as well as in such publications as Magnum Photo, Inc.'s *Arms against Fury: Magnum Photographers in Afghanistan*.[15] Delahaye concurrently took another set of images as an artist, using his Linhof panoramic camera; these photographs have been exhibited in art museums and galleries as well as reproduced in art books.[16] These distinctions—as well as the announcement in the January 31, 2004, issue of the British newspaper *Guardian* that, as of three years before, he had "officially" become an artist—reflect Delahaye's ongoing effort to extricate himself and his pictures from photojournalism and the "distracting" context of the print media to which this field is inexorably tied.[17] In short, Delahaye believes that this shift in his identity will ensure that his photographs "have [their] own coherence, are a world in themselves."[18]

In spite of Delahaye's effort to position his series *History* as art, many precepts considered fundamental to photojournalism continue to inform his work. For instance, even though Delahaye has rejected the "immediacy" and "instantaneity" of photojournalism and its use of the quicker and more immediate 35mm or digital cameras, he still remains influenced by its ostensible commitment to "bear witness." For Delahaye, though, "bearing witness" does not include a moral obligation. Unlike many photojournalists, he claims not to be driven by a desire to communicate social ills or to use his images to produce social change: "The majority of photojournalists tell themselves they do this work because it is important, that if people can just see these problems in these parts of the world they will do something about them. I have never believed this. I even think that that is a con."[19] What has instead attracted Delahaye to photojournalism's "bearing witness" is the privileged relationship to the real that he assumes is implicit in this approach. In other words, Delahaye wants to separate the evidentiary function of "bearing witness" from the "sentimentality" and "vulgarity" that he believes arises when it is used as a form of testimony. To do this, Delahaye has chosen to align himself as an artist with the "reticent, understated, and impersonal" documentary practice of Walker Evans.[20] In so doing, Delahaye believes that, like Evans, he can remove himself from his picture-making process and thus allow his camera to create detached and impartial representations: "I am not making commentaries on the battlefield. My approach is direct, like a simple recorder."[21]

What Delahaye fails to realize is that this self-effacement, along with the panoramic format and monumentally sized prints of *History*, which he likens to "tableaux," are not the

14. Luc Delahaye, *Winterreise* (London: Phaidon, 2000).

15. "The Fall of the Taliban," *Newsweek*, November 26, 2001, pp. 22–9; and Robert Dannin, ed., *Arms against Fury: Magnum Photographers in Afghanistan* (New York: PowerHouse Books, 2002), pp. 166–185.

16. Images from Delahaye's *History* series have been circulated in exhibitions at the Ricco/Maresca Gallery, New York City; The Cleveland Museum of Art; National Museum of Photography, Film & Television; International Center of Photography, and the Huis Marseille, among other places. They have also been reproduced in the limited edition *History* (London: Chris Boot, 2003) as well as in Brooks Johnson, ed., *Photography Speaks: 150 Photographers on Their Art* (New York: Aperture; Chrysler Museum of Art, 2004); and Bright, *Art Photography Now*.

17. Peter Lennon, "The Big Picture," *Guardian*, January 31, 2004, p. 24.

18. Luc Delahaye, quoted in Patrick Henry, "Luc Delahaye: Photographs," *RPS Journal* 144, no. 3 (April 2004): 122.

19. Delahaye, quoted in Sullivan, "The Real Thing."

20. Luc Delahaye cited the importance of Evans to his work: "Walker Evans was important to me, as his work showed me that there were possibilities other than those with which I had grown up: the vulgarity of sentimentalism, the dumbness of trying to have a 'style.'" Chris Booth, ed., *Magnum Stories* (London and New York: Phaidon, 2004), p. 106.

21. Delahaye, quoted in Henry, "Luc Delahaye: Photographs," p. 122.

22. Delahaye described the making of "Taliban" in Delahaye, "Luc Delahaye: Snap Decision," *Art Press* 306 (November 2004): 29.

23. See note 15 above.

product of his camera's unique vision or photography's supposed intrinsic documentary capacity; instead, they are formal conventions whose meanings cannot be separated from the circumstances in which they were made or circulated. For instance, Delahaye took **Taliban** (**PLATE 4**) in November 2001, while traveling on foot with Northern Alliance soldiers as they forged their way into Kabul, Afghanistan. Before taking the picture, he spent two weeks living with these soldiers on a farm not far from the Taliban front line. When the Taliban began to yield their positions and the Northern Alliance initiated their final assault on Kabul, Delahaye accompanied the soldiers and took pictures of the fighting, surrender, and death—including the recently killed Taliban soldier depicted in the image.[22]

FIGURE 1
LUC DELAHAYE, TALIBAN FROM *NEWSWEEK*, 26 NOVEMBER 2001

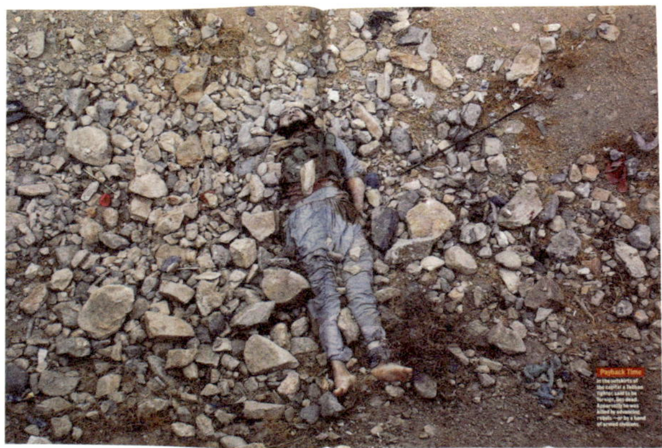

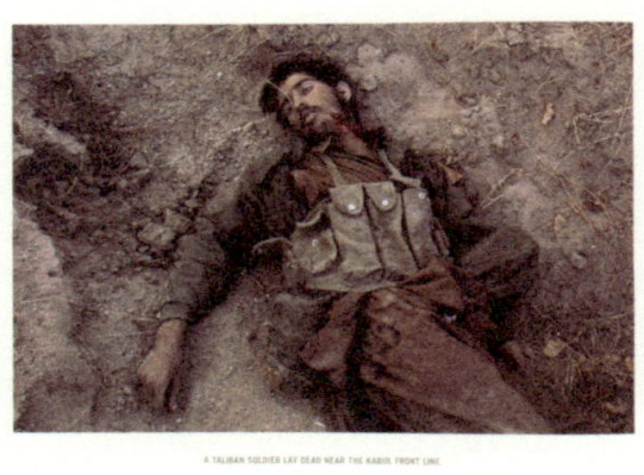

FIGURE 2
LUC DELAHAYE, *A TALIBAN SOLDIER LAY DEAD NEAR THE KABUL FRONT LINE*, 2001 FROM *ARMS AGAINST FURY: MAGNUM PHOTOGRAPHERS IN AFGHANISTAN*. EDITED BY ROBERT DANNIN.

Yet, as I mentioned previously, **Taliban** was not the only photograph that Delahaye made while traveling with the Northern Alliance in Afghanistan. Since he was still functioning at this point as a *Newsweek* and Magnum photographer, Delahaye also took a series of pictures that were subsequently published in an article in *Newsweek* entitled "The Fall of the Taliban" and in the book *Arms against Fury*.[23] Included in these publications are images by Delahaye whose straightforward point of view and blurring of subject matter suggest the "immediacy" and "instantaneity" of traditional photojournalism and its use of the smaller and quicker handheld 35mm or digital cameras (see **PLATE 3**).[24] At the same time, the publications also included images by Delahaye that are remarkably similar in form and content to his artistically conceived **Taliban**, which he took with his Linhof panoramic camera. Specifically, the *Newsweek* article included a photograph of another dead Taliban soldier reproduced as a double-page spread (**FIG. 1**), which Delahaye took from the same oblique and detached point of view as **Taliban**. Likewise, *Arms against Fury* includes a different version of the dead solider depicted in **Taliban** but nonetheless still photographed from a comparable perspective (**FIG. 2**). The visual affinities suggest that Delahaye made both of these images with his Linhof as opposed to a handheld camera. Why, then, were these images not included in Delahaye's series *History*?

24. Delahaye's *Newsweek* photograph of the Northern Alliance troops ambushed by retreating Taliban won first place in Spot News Singles in the 2001 World Press Photo Contest. This further attests to the extent to which the convention of spontaneity is privileged within the field of photojournalism. Delahaye's *Newsweek* photographs from Afghanistan also won the Robert Capa Gold Medal, in 2001.

25. Luc Delahaye, quoted in David Schonauer, "Fallen Enemy," *American Photo* 13, no. 5 (September 2002): 23.

According to Delahaye, the images in *History* "needed to be seen in a different way. The format of the image decided how it should be used."[25] Delahaye implied here that these photographs were the product of the clear-eyed, dispassionate view imparted by his camera's panoramic format. Therefore, it was the Linhof camera, as opposed to human agency, that dictated the photographs' use in Delahaye's lavish, limited-edition, and oversized book *History* as well as in the various museum and gallery exhibitions where they appeared as eight-by-four-foot, "tableau" color prints. Still, even if the panoramic format mandated these decisions, the question of why Delahaye elected to only reproduce as art certain photographs taken with the Linhof camera while relegating the rest to photojournalism remains unanswered.

Delahaye wants to define his photographic practice as "reticent, understated, and impersonal" to perpetuate the idea that his images transparently reflect the real: "I restore [the suffering] more effectively if I am able to adopt a certain detachment."[26] Here, Delahaye assumed that the oblique and distanced perspective provided by his Linhof camera allowed "the suffering" in his images to "speak for itself." Yet, how Delahaye actually encodes "the suffering" in his pictures, and the manner in which it is subsequently decoded, are not intrinsic to the photographs that he takes, to the camera that he uses, or even to the subjects that he photographs.[27] Delahaye may attempt to establish the objectivity and impartiality of his *History* series in terms of the "slowness" and "detachment" of his Linhof camera and its generously sized prints. However, like the "immediacy" and "instantaneity" of traditional photojournalism, these are visual tropes whose meanings are shaped as much by the culture and interests of those who read them as by the intent of those who make and use them. As Victor Burgin explained: "Regardless of how much we may strain to maintain a 'disinterested' aesthetic mode of apprehension, an appreciation of the 'purely visual', when we look at an image it is instantly and irreversibly integrated and collated with the intricate psychic network of our knowledge."[28]

Many critics, nonetheless, continue to read the clarity, precision, and detachment of images such as **Taliban** as unmediated and the product of a "neutral" vision. As one critic noted: "This mode of absence is what allows Delahaye to act 'without presumption' and 'without regard for outcome'; to become in-phase with the situation and open to its possibilities; in short, to become as present as possible to the reality before him."[29] In arguing that Delahaye's detachment facilitates more "realistic" depictions, this critic assumed that the "slowness" and "detachment" of the Linhof necessarily enabled him to objectively and impartially record his subject matter. In actuality, this "slowness" and "detachment" are visual conventions that offer little insight into the intricacies of how the subject, in fact, appeared in front of the camera or what a viewer would have seen had she or he "been there." This is in part because, as photography historian Joel Snyder remarked in reference to the tendency to interpret the sharply focused compositions of Walker Evans as "real," "We do not—because we cannot—see things in this way."[30] Human vision is immensely more complex than what the camera records; yet, because Delahaye has chosen pictorial strategies—"slowness" and "detachment"—that, due largely to our habits of looking at pictures, seem transparent to the subject of a dead Taliban soldier, the photograph appears unmediated and hence "real."

If Delahaye had depicted the Taliban soldier in a blurred or distorted manner or photographed an American soldier, the picture would have likely engendered a different response. The reaction to the photographs of bloated and decaying bodies that Sally Mann took in 2000 for her series **What Remains** (**PLATE 19**) speaks in part to this bias. According to *The New York Times* critic Sarah Boxer, Mann's photographs of decomposing corpses "have something of the grave robber in them."[31] Boxer attributed this irreverence to two causes. First, she argued that Mann, like all who photograph the dead, violated "the privacy of the decency of the dead." Here, Boxer couched her critique in terms of the ethics of representing

26. Delahaye, quoted in Sullivan, "The Real Thing."

27. I use the terms "encode" and "decode" to refer to the dual process through which meaning is produced and received. See Stuart Hall, "Encoding/decoding," *Culture, Media, Language: Working Papers in Cultural Studies*, 1972–79 (London: Hutchinson in association with the Centre for Contemporary Cultural Studies, University of Birmingham, 1980), pp. 128–38.

28. Victor Burgin, "Photography, Fantasy, Fiction," *Screen* 21, no. 1, (Spring 1980): 70.

29. Paul Tebbs, "Conflict Zone," *Art Review* 1, no. 11 (2003): 62.

30. Joel Snyder, "Picturing Vision," *Critical Inquiry* 6, no. 3 (Spring 1980): 505.

31. Sarah Boxer, "Slogging Through the Valley of the Shutter of Death," *The New York Times*, July 23, 2004, p. E30. For a counterpoint to this article, see Eleanor Heartney, "The Forensic Eye," *Art in America* 93 (January 2005): 50–55.

the dead. This criticism is frequently evoked when photographers depict the dead without showing them proper respect. The conviction and imprisonment of Cincinnati photographer Thomas Condon, in 2001, is a case in point. When Condon, without obtaining the proper formal permission, took photographs at the Hamilton County morgue for an art project on the cycle of life and death, he was arrested and tried for "corpse abuse."[32] Since, as Boxer knew, Mann had permission to photograph the dead in her pictures, and since, unlike the photographs by Condon confiscated by the police, none of their identities are discernible, it would seem that morals were not really what were at stake for Boxer.

32. For information on Thomas Condon, see Stephen Kinzer, "In Cincinnati, Art Bows to the Privacy of Death," *The New York Times*, August 3, 2002, p. 7; and Eleanor Heartney, "Is the Body More Beautiful When It's Dead?" *The New York Times*, June 1, 2003, p. 37.

According to Boxer, the second irreverence of Mann's images stemmed from "the dreadful things that Mann has done to surfaces of her photographs." Here, Boxer criticized Mann's photographs in terms of aesthetics. But what began as a critique of representational choices quickly turned back to the morals of representing the dead. This was largely because, for Boxer, Mann's prints distort instead of clarify her subject matter and thus create ambiguity rather than certainty: "You have to stare at some of them for quite a while to make out what exactly is in the picture." Implicit in Boxer's argument is the idea that, since photography is a mechanical medium that shares a unique relationship to the real, it should provide an accurate or "factual" record of the dead that, as the image is enlarged, should only get more exact. Accordingly, the dead bodies in Mann's photographs, even if in a state of decomposition, should be clearly defined. This of course is the opposite of what happens in Mann's photographs, since, as Boxer further complained, "The larger the photograph, the coarser and harder it is to read, as if the eyes, opened wide in horror, can't see at all."[33] This criticism then led Boxer, in a manner similar to the charges of "corpse abuse" levied against Condon, to accuse Mann of literally committing violence to the bodies she represents: "In many ways it's hard to see where the violence of death itself ends and where the violence in the picture making begins. Ms. Mann seems to be assisting in the decomposition."[34]

33. Boxer, "Slogging Through the Valley," p. E30.

34. Boxer, "Slogging Through the Valley," p. E30.

To some, the circumstances under which Mann initially took her photographs of the decomposing corpses may justify Boxer's complaints. Even though these images have been exhibited and published as part of her series **What Remains**, Mann first took them while on assignment for *The New York Times Magazine*.[35] Mann generally does not accept editorial work, but she made an exception in this case because the subject matter—decomposing bodies at the University of Tennessee Forensic Anthropology Facility, or Body Farm—aligned closely with work on death and decay that she had begun a year earlier when her beloved greyhound Eva died.[36] As part of this project, Mann had wanted to photograph corpses at the Body Farm, but as an artist, she had been denied permission. With the access provided by the *Times Magazine*, Mann was able to enter the facility and photograph the decaying human corpses for a story about scientists who study these bodies so as to better learn how to assess, from decomposition, times of death.[37]

35. A selection of Mann's photographs of decomposing corpses is reproduced in Lawrence Osborne, "Dead Men Talking," *The New York Times Magazine*, December 3, 2000, pp. 105–108. Even though Mann initially took these photographs under the aegis of *The New York Times Magazine*, the director of the Body Farm allowed her to return several times to photograph for her personal project *What Remains*.

36. Sally Mann, *What Remains* (Boston: Bulfinch Press, 2003).

37. For more information on this assignment, see Heartney, "The Forensic Eye," p. 53.

In taking her photographs, however, Mann did not act like a traditional photojournalist. She neither depicted the bodies instantaneously nor did she use a 35mm or digital camera. Instead, she photographed them with an eight-by-ten-inch view camera and then developed the negatives using the time-consuming, nineteenth-century process known wet-collodion printing. In using this large-format camera and the antiquarian process as well as focusing on the remains of the dead, Mann seems to share commonalities with Delahaye's "slow" and "detached" approach to photography. What distinguishes her is an interest in photography's memorial capacities. For Mann, photography is not determined by its relationship to the real. Instead, it is a form of representation that allows her to "fashion an object" from the real.[38] Accordingly, her use of the "bearing witness" of photojournalism offers not a way of "being there"—she is, after all, not a forensic scientist who photographs the bodies every three hours to record how the body rots—but as a means to memorialize and remember the dead.

38. Sally Mann, "The Angel of Uncertainty: An Interview with Sally Mann on the Lure of the Poured Image," in Lyle Rexer, *Photography's Antiquarian Avant-Garde: The New Wave in Old Processes* (New York: Harry Abrams, Inc., 2002), p. 81.

Mann's use of a large-format camera and the wet-collodion process visually enhances this quality in her prints. Mann does not try to create clear and concise prints. Refusing to be a slave to technique, she instead embraces the inconsistencies and accidents that occur in the printing process. For Mann, these irregularities and ambiguities in the surfaces of her prints are formal devices that allow her to heighten the physicality of her photographs and, in so doing, to explore the process through which one remembers the dead. The problem for Boxer was that Mann's interest in these memorial capacities of the medium compromises the assumed indexical nature of photography. Yet, what Boxer failed to realize is that photography's evidentiary authority cannot be reduced to its relationship to the real. Instead, as Eleanor Heartney elucidated in relation to Mann's photographs, it is determined "as much in memory and imagination as in fact."[39]

39. Heartney, "The Forensic Eye," p. 55.

Due to the high level of clarity in Delahaye's **Taliban** (**PLATE 4**), this image seems to more closely meet Boxer's expectations for representing the dead in photography. At the same time, since every detail of the dead corpse, including his face, is rendered with absolute precision, and since it is doubtful that Delahaye acquired "formal" permission to photograph him, one could argue that Delahaye should have also been condemned as a "grave robber." Interestingly, this ethical complaint is distinctly absent from the critical responses to Delahaye's photograph. Instead, as I have already mentioned, critics maintained that the "slowness" and "detachment" provided by his Linhof panoramic camera enabled Delahaye to impartially record "the reality before him." But is the objectivity of his Linhof camera in fact what has absolved Delahaye from discussions about the ethical quandaries of representing the dead?

In *Regarding the Pain of Others*, Susan Sontag argued that "the more remote or exotic the place, the more likely we are to have full frontal views of the dead and dying."[40] Sontag alluded here to a contradiction in recent photographic representations of the dead and dying. The print media will, largely out of moral decency and respect for families, obscure the faces of American and European dead. But, as Sontag further explained, "This is a dignity not thought necessary to accord to others."[41] Delahaye's "full-frontal" photographs of dead Taliban soldiers, published in November 2001 as part of the *Newsweek* article, "The Fall of the Taliban," substantiate Sontag's claim (see **FIG. 1**). No one has questioned the ethics behind the widespread circulation of these images. Instead, along with other images of dead Taliban soldiers distributed concurrently in the print media, they have provided one of the most popular means through which the American public has learned about the

40. Susan Sontag, *Regarding the Pain of Others* (New York: Farrar, Straus and Giroux, 2003), p. 70. The representation of foreign, dead and dying bodies by the Western press is also discussed in John Taylor, "Foreign Bodies," *Body Horror*, pp. 129–56.

41. Sontag, *Regarding the Pain of Others*, p. 70.

war in Afghanistan and, more particularly about the defeat of Islamic fundamentalism by the Northern Alliance.[42]

Delahaye believes that, once in front of *History*, the audience will suspend all of these prior habits and expectations of looking just as he does when taking pictures. "Witnessing wars and mayhem," Delahaye explained, encourages "a sort of cool indifference to myself, which lets me have a cool sensibility to the world."[43] Yet, just as the "slowness" and "detachment" are visual tropes used by Delahaye to signify the real, so too is the ostensible "realism" of **Taliban** dependent upon larger interests and assumptions about the representation of the dead, and more particularly Afghan dead, in photography.

TESTIMONY

Like Delahaye, Alfredo Jaar also has expressed dissatisfaction with the circulation of photography in the print media. Yet, whereas Delahaye dislikes photojournalism because it compromises photography's assumed evidentiary authority, Jaar objects to the manner in which its distribution promotes passive and disinterested viewers: "I have always felt that we suffer from a bombardment of images through the media, a bombardment that has completely anesthetized us."[44] Because of this aversion, a number of critics have interpreted Jaar's work (**PLATES 50** and **51**) as a direct confrontation with photojournalism. "Implicit in his approach," argued H. Ashley Kistler, "is a critique of 'concerned' photography and the patented responses to social tragedy that its distancing, voyeuristic stance too frequently provokes."[45] Kistler implied here that Jaar intends his work to render explicit the moral inadequacies of photojournalism and more particularly the ethically suspect form of photojournalism known as "concerned photography." Madeleine Grynsztejn extended this argument when she claimed that "Jaar's works are driven by the desire to expose 'the misrepresentation' that 'lies' beneath the surface of photographic representations...the most insidious ways in which our dominant western culture has misrepresented the Other is through 'concerned photography'."[46]

In making this argument about Jaar's practice, both Kistler and Grynsztejn rely on the definition of "concerned photography" posited by Martha Rosler, which identified this practice as "the weakest possible idea of [substitute for] social engagement, namely *compassion*."[47] Whereas documentary photography had once functioned as a form of social and political critique as well as an oppositional practice, Rosler—along with critics such as Allan Sekula and Abigail Solomon-Godeau—argued that "concerned photography" has brought attention to the sensibility (compassion) of the photographer at the expense of the subjects depicted. Such photography, Rosler further argued, "Leans toward the self-congratulatory and the cathartic and invites projection and puts the viewer into a voyeuristic position to the depicted."[48] Rosler ignored here the specific set of historical conditions under which the practice of "concerned photography" was actually developed and instead uses the term to substantiate the moral corruption of documentary photography through its appropriation into the tradition of "fine art" photography.

When Cornell Capa coined the term "concerned photography," he intended it as a way to memorialize his brother Robert Capa and Cornell's friends and colleagues, David

42. For more information on journalism's photographic coverage of the killing of the Taliban by the Northern Alliance during the war in Afghanistan, see Barbie Zelizer, "Death in Wartime: Photographs and the 'Other War' in Afghanistan," *The Harvard International Journal of Press/Politics* 10, no. 3 (2005): 26–55.

43. Luc Delahaye, quoted in Vince Aletti, "Making History," *Village Voice*, March 11, 2003, p. 46.

44. Alfredo Jaar, "Violence: The Limits of Representation," an interview in Rubén Gallo, *Trans Arts, Cultures, Media* ¾, 1997), p. 59.

45. H. Ashley Kistler, "Re-Visions: An Introduction to Geography=War," *Alfredo Jaar: Geography=War* (Richmond, VA: Virginia Museum of Fine Arts, 1991), p. 4.

46. Madeleine Grynsztejn, "Illuminating Exposures: The Art of Alfredo Jaar," *Alfredo Jaar* (La Jolla, CA: La Jolla Museum of Contemporary Art, 1990), p. 21.

47. Martha Rosler, "in, around, and afterthoughts (on documentary photography)," in *3 Works* (Nova Scotia: The Press of the Nova Scotia College of Art and Design, 1981), p. 83, n1.

48. Martha Rosler's remarks made during a lecture, "The Look of War Photography," at Walker Art Center, November 16, 1981. Quoted in Adam D. Weinberg, *On the Line: The New Color Photojournalism* (Minneapolis: Walker Art Center and the University of Pennsylvania Press, 1986), p. 31. See also Allan Sekula, "On the Invention of Photographic Meaning," *Artforum* 13, no. 5 (January 1975): 45; and Abigail Solomon-Godeau, "Who is Speaking Thus? Some Questions about Documentary Photography," *Photography at the Dock: Essays on Photographic History, Institutions, and Practices* (Minneapolis: University of Minnesota Press, 1991), p. 301, n11.

(Chim) Seymour and Werner Bischof, who had all been killed while on assignment in the 1950s. Due to the diminishing interest in their work after their deaths, Cornell Capa wanted to preserve their archives and to cultivate public awareness in the production of these and other recently deceased photojournalists. Yet, the function of this term quickly exceeded this purpose. With television increasingly placing restraints on—and even replacing—picture magazines, Capa realized that photography, as a form of witnessing, was dying. In 1967, to offset this situation, Capa founded The Fund for Concerned Photography so that photojournalists could "bear witness" without having to worry about the constraints imposed on them by the print media.[49] "It is my personal conviction," Capa explained, "that the production demands and controls exercised by the mass communications media on the photographer today are endangering our artistic, ethical, and professional standards and tend to obliterate the individuality of the witness-artist."[50]

Like Capa, Jaar also has objected to the restrictions that the print media impose on photojournalists and to the manner in which these limitations tend to prohibit them from "bearing witness" to their subjects. "Photojournalists," Jaar noted, "always maintain a certain distance because they work in a hurry."[51] Wanting to get as physically and emotionally close to his subjects as possible, Jaar instead adopted an approach much like a "concerned photographer," whose role—as Capa declared in the introduction to the catalogue of his 1967 exhibition *The Concerned Photographer*—"is to witness and to be involved with his subject."[52] This commonality is evident in the amount of time and emotional energy that Jaar spends getting to know his subjects and the circumstances in which they live. To prepare himself for this involvement, Jaar conducts research, often in several languages, about a place or situation. After reading extensively about the subject, he then travels to that location to develop direct contact with the people and the particularities of their situation before he begins to photograph them.[53] Jaar adopted such an approach for his 1986 installation *Gold in the Morning*. Before traveling in 1985 to Serra Pelada to photograph there the workers who were mining for gold, Jaar read at length about the discovery of gold in what was then Brazil's largest, open-pit mine. He then traveled to Brazil, and after getting to know the miners, he took more than one thousand images of them and their surroundings.[54]

Bearing witness, however, is not the only function of "concerned photography." Lewis Hine's quotation in Capa's definition of "concerned photography" clarifies this distinction: "There were two things that I wanted to do. I wanted to show the things to be corrected. I wanted to show the things that had to be appreciated."[55] This dual concern of social reform and aesthetics is also evident in photographs that Jaar took of the Serra Pelada miners. In many of these pictures, Jaar used such formal devices as cropping, the close-up, and lighting to construct highly composed images that simultaneously attest to his intimate knowledge of the plight of his subjects and to his admiration of the formal properties of their mud-covered bodies (**PLATE 50**). Thus, despite Kistler's and Grynsztejn's claims, Jaar's work appears to share numerous parallels with "concerned photography." The formal similarities between Jaar's Serra Pelada images and those taken of the same miners by "concerned photographer" Sebastião Salgado further support this reading (**FIG. 3**). In fact, the commonalities between their photographs are so extensive that, despite the fact that Jaar took his pictures a year

49. It is generally assumed that Capa coined the term "concerned photography" in 1966. However, he did not actually use this term until 1967, when he changed the name of the Fund from "Werner Bischof—Robert Capa—David Seymour Photographic Memorial Fund" to "The Fund for Concerned Photography, Inc." to signal the broadening of the Fund's goals. In 1970 Capa changed the title again to "The International Fund for Concerned Photography, Inc." See Cornell Capa, "The Concerned Photographer," *Infinity* 16, no. 10 (October 1967): 5–6; and Harvey V. Fondiller, "ICP: Photography's Fabulous New Center," *Popular Photography* 76 (April 1975): 49–53, 110–11, and 114–15.

50. Cornell Capa, "To the Concerned Photographer," *Camera* 48 (May 1969): 9.

51. Jaar, "Violence: The Limits of Representation," p. 59.

52. Cornell Capa, introduction to *The Concerned Photographer* (New York: Grossman Publishers, 1968), not paginated.

53. For more information on Jaar's picture-making process, see Alfredo Jaar, "Acts of Responsibility: An Interview with Alfredo Jaar," interview by Stephen Horne, *Parachute* 69 (January/March 1993): 28; Jaar, "Violence: The Limits of Representation," pp. 55–7; Alfredo Jaar, "The Art of Inclusion: Alfredo Jaar—an Interview," interview by Kate Davidson, *Photofile* 46 (Novemer 1995): 15–16; and Alfredo Jaar, "The Aesthetics of Witnessing: A Conversation with Alfredo Jaar," interview by Patricia C. Phillips, *Art Journal* 64, no. 3 (Fall 2005): 12–14.

54. For more information on Jaar's *Gold in the Morning*, see Grynsztejn, "Illuminating Exposures," pp. 12–17.

55. See Capa, introduction to *The Concerned Photographer*, not paginated. David Vestal elucidated this dual concern: "These photographers have more in common than their involvement with the people and places in their pictures. Each brings an intimately personal vision to his work: the concern is photographic as well as human." "Concerned Photographer," *Popular Photography* 61 (October 1967): 106.

prior to those by Salgado and used a different type of film, a number of Jaar's photographs of the Serra Pelada miners have been mistakenly attributed to Salgado.[56]

The confusion between the Serra Pelada photographs taken by Jaar and by Salgado is largely a product of their distribution. Even though Salgado also dislikes the limitations and, more particularly, the rapid working conditions required by most picture magazines, he—unlike Jaar—actively distributes his work in the print media. Issues of funding have partially driven this decision. For instance, to finance the photographs that he took of the Serra Pelada miners, Salgado used money that he received working concurrently on assignments in South America for two German magazines.[57] Salgado has also used the circulation of his images in the print media to secure funding for future projects. This was the case for his Serra Pelada images that, because of their distribution in London's *The Sunday Times*, led twenty-five other picture magazines, including *The New York Times Magazine*, to buy and circulate these photographs. As a result, as British photography editor Colin Jacobson explained: "[Salgado] made his name on that story."[58] This recognition allowed Salgado to secure financial backing for his personal project *Workers: An Archeology of the Industrial Age*, for which he spent six years photographing manual laborers in twenty-six countries.[59]

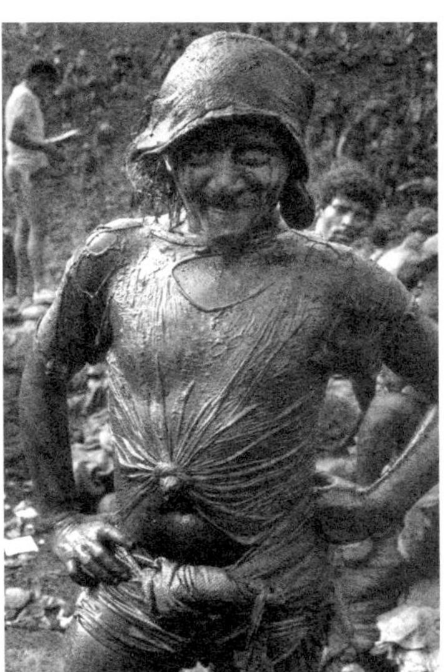

FIGURE 3
SEBASTIAO SELGADO, *SERRA PELADA MINE, BRAZIL*, 1986. COURTESY THE YANCEY RICHARDSON GALLERY.

Finances are not the only reason that Salgado distributes his work in the print media. For him, photography's greatest potential lies in its ability to depict the human dimension of a situation in a natural and uncomplicated way: "Everything that happens in the world must be shown and people around the world must have an idea of what's happening to the other people around the world. I believe this is the function of the vector that the documentary photographer must have, to show one person's existence to another."[60] Newspapers and magazines, despite their limitations, remain fundamental to this communication process, since they ensure the most extensive circulation of photography. Here, Salgado assumed that viewers would instinctively identify with the humanistic content of his images, provided that the images were distributed to as wide an audience as possible. This belief in the intrinsic communicative potential of photography parallels that of Capa, who, in spite of his reservations about the print media, also believed in the transparency and universality of the medium. Capa elaborated: "[Photography] provide[s] an undistorted mirror of man's actions, thereby sharpening human awareness and awakening conscience."[61] For Jaar, on the other hand, the act of "bearing witness" cannot be separated from issues of distribution, consumption, or the marketplace. And so, while he may initially approach his subjects like a "concerned photographer," he differs in terms of the control he exerts over how his images are seen and experienced.

In preparing his *Gold in the Morning* installation for the 1986 Venice Biennale, Jaar spent close to a year perusing more than one thousand photographs that he took in Serra

56. Jaar, "The Art of Inclusion," p. 16.

57. To finance his Serra Pelada photographs, on the other hand, Jaar used funding that he received in 1985 from the John Simon Guggenheim Memorial Foundation.

58. Collin Jacobson, quoted in Ian Parker, "A Cold Light: How Sebastião Salgado Captures the World," *The New Yorker*, April 18, 2005, p. 154.

59. For his *Workers* project, to ensure that he could work without the constraints imposed by the print media, Salgado secured annual guarantees from magazines and newspapers against the photographs he was taking. He also secured a generous grant from Kodak. See Liz Jobey, "Elevating the Common Man," *Independent*, November 28, 1993, p. 12; and Parker, "A Cold Light," pp. 15456. In 1993 Salgado's *Workers* project, which included the images he initially took at Serra Pelada, was published as a 400-page book and was circulated internationally as an exhibition of the same name. See Sebastião Salgado, *Workers: An Archeology of the Industrial Age* (New York: Aperture, 1993).

60. Sebastião Salgado, "Sebastião Salgado: Workers," in *Witness in our Time: Working Lives of Documentary Photographers*, ed. Ken Light (Washington and London: Smithsonian Institution Press, 2000), p. 111.

61. Cornell Capa, introduction to *The Concerned Photographer 2* (New York: Grossman Publishers, 1972), not paginated.

Pelada. From them, Jaar selected five images that he then displayed as color transparencies in thirty-by-forty-six-inch light boxes, four of which he appended with like-sized, gilded-metal boxes (**FIG. 4**). By placing his images within these light boxes and in a darkened room, Jaar heightened the aesthetic appeal of the miners by using the light that emanates and reflects against the boxes to emphasize the sculptural qualities of the workers' bodies. At the same time, Jaar disrupted the visual pleasure of looking at the miners by installing the sets of boxes above or below eye level. In relegating the miners to the peripheral spaces of the room, Jaar physically obstructed their passive consumption as art and forced viewers to interact with the representations in ways that were difficult and unfamiliar. Jaar's placement of an ornate, gold-leaf picture frame filled with gold nails on the floor directly in front of one of his light boxes facilitated this active involvement as well (**FIG. 5**). Like the formally composed yet marginally positioned miners, the lavishly carved, golden frame—enclosed by a wide band of abrasive, black nails—simultaneously seduced and frustrated viewers, encouraging them to become more self-aware of the process and conventions through which people and objects are transformed into and read as art.[62]

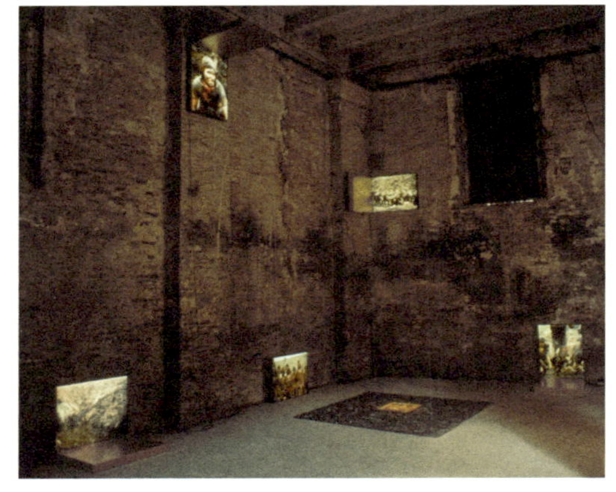

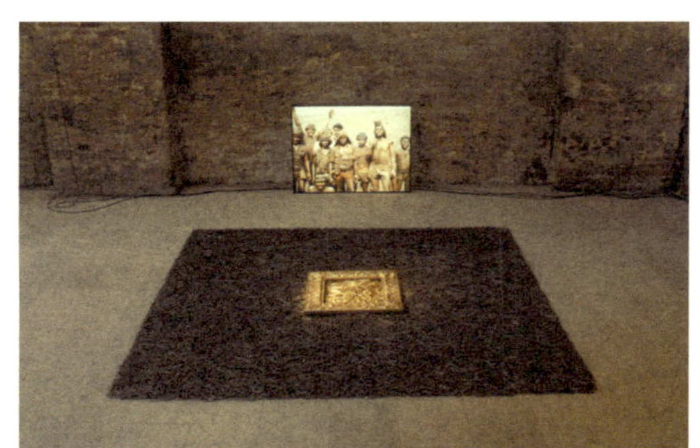

FIGURES 4 AND 5
ALFREDO JAAR, INSTALLATION VIEWS OF *GOLD IN THE MORNING*, VENICE BIENNALE, 1986. COURTESY OF THE ARTIST AND GALERIE LELONG, NEW YORK

In placing his Serra Pelada photographs within the space of this intricately conceived installation, Jaar created a physical and conceptual framework—or mise-en-scène—to engage viewers and to provide a context for them to begin to think about some of the political and aesthetic ramifications of representing the "other."[63] Yet, not everyone has interpreted Jaar's works in this manner. For instance, in response to the inclusion of one of Jaar's Serra Pelada photographs entitled *Unframed* in the exhibition *1 Plus 1 Plus 1: Works by Alfredo Jaar* (**FIG. 6**), Roberta Smith, *The New York Times* critic, argued that the plight of the miners "would be better elucidated by an exhibition of many normal-size photographs or of a newspaper article." Smith contended here that the installation strategies that Jaar used—pinning the life-sized image to the wall unframed and then placing a black frame (half mirror and half glass) over each of the miners—detracted from the image's ability to effectively communicate information about the social circumstances of the miners: "*Unframed* is impressive without being either completely convincing or, in the end, very visually satisfying." In other words, Smith was troubled because the representational strategies that Jaar chose for his photographs of the miners did not seem to match the plight of their social circumstances. As Smith further explained: "The miners themselves end up seeming glamorous, like exotically costumed and made-up *Vogue* models."[64]

To ensure that the social circumstances of the miners were made explicit, Smith believed that their photographs should be circulated in a straightforward and transparent manner. The images that Salgado took in Serra Pelada—and which circulated in such contexts

62. For more information on this installation, see note 54 above and Jaar, "Acts of Responsibility," p. 30.

63. Jaar frequently cites the following quotation by Jean-Luc Godard: "It may be true that one has to choose between ethics or aesthetics, but it is no less true that, whichever one chooses, one will always find the other one at the end of the road. For the very definition of the human condition should be in the mise-en-scene itself." See Jaar, "The Aesthetics of Witnessing," p. 15; and Jaar, "Alfredo Jaar: A Conversation," pp. 41 and 46–47.

64. Roberta Smith, "Alfredo Jaar's Work: 'Us' and 'Them'," *The New York Times*, January 17, 1992, p. C29.

65. See "In the Hellhole," *The Sunday Times*, May 24, 1987, pp. 26–31; "An Epic Struggle for Gold," *The New York Times Magazine*, June 7, 1987, pp. 34–41; and Salgado, *Workers: An Archeology of the Industrial Age*.

66. It is interesting to note that while Jaar incorporated commercial strategies from advertising into installations such as *Rushes*—in which he temporarily displayed computer prints of his Serra Pelada photographs in an advertising space in the Spring Street station of the New York City subway—Salgado approached the advertising photographs that he took for Silk Cut cigarettes and Le Creuset as a "concerned photographer." For more information on *Rushes*, see Grynsztejn, "Illuminating Exposures," pp. 17–18. For more information on Salgado's advertising work, see Matthew Soar, "The Advertising Photography of Richard Avedon and Sebastião Salgado," *Images Ethics in the Digital Age*, ed. Larry Gross, John Stuart Katz, and Jay Ruby (Minneapolis: University of Minnesota Press, 2003), pp. 269–93.

67. Alfredo Jaar, quoted in David Levi-Strauss, "A Sea of Griefs Is Not a Proscenium: On the Rwanda Projects of Alfredo Jarr," in Alfredo Jaar, *Let There Be Light: The Rwanda Project 1994–1998* (Barcelona, Spain: ACTAR, 1998), not paginated.

68. For more information on "Real Images," see Levi-Strauss, "A Sea of Griefs;" Debra Bricker Balken, *Alfredo Jaar: Lament of the Images* (Cambridge: List Visual Arts Center, Massachusetts Institute of Technology, 1999), pp. 24–6; and Jaar, "Violence: The Limits of Representation," p. 61. For a critique of this work in terms of its use of Western-based art strategies to represent subaltern culture, see Nicholas Mirzoeff, "Invisible Again: Rwanda and Representation After Genocide," *African Arts* 38, no. 3 (Autumn 2005): 87–8.

as *The New York Times Magazine* and *The Sunday Times* of London as well as in the exhibition and catalogue *Workers*—seem to meet such expectations (**PLATE 49**).[65] Even though one could argue that the miners in Salgado's photographs are depicted in an equally "glamorous" and "exotic" manner, their circulation as like-sized images in the pages of news magazines and on museum walls—with accompanying texts that elucidate the particularities of their social circumstances—is more in keeping with the passive consumption that Smith expects when she encounters depictions of the "other." For Smith, Jaar's *Unframed* was "visually" dissatisfying precisely because it forced her to acknowledge such conventions and standards as "glamour" and "exoticism," which would otherwise go unnoticed in the picture-reading process.[66]

Jaar believes that controlling the environments in which his photographs are exhibited and experienced will lead to more attentive and more critical viewers. In so doing, Jaar does not try to prescribe what viewers see; instead, he attempts to slow down their habits of consumption and make them more aware of how they see and, by extension, of what they cannot see. This sensitivity to the nature and complexity of the representational process is most apparent in the series of works that Jaar made in response to the Rwandan genocide. As with his Serra Pelada photographs, Jaar initially approached this project like a "concerned photographer": he informed himself about the situation; traveled to Kigali, Rwanda, in August 1994; and spent time getting as "close" as possible to his subjects before he photographed them. As part of this process, Jaar spent two or three hours speaking at length with his subjects about the tragedies that they had experienced. For Jaar, these interviews—"the feelings, words, and ideas" that the people he met used to describe their horrific experiences—rendered explicit the sheer impossibility of representing this tragedy.[67] To begin to address this inadequacy among what his subjects had experienced, the personal impact on him of these stories and what he saw, and the photographs that he took in Rwanda, Jaar initially decided not to show any of the images. Instead, in 1995 he created his first "Real Images" installation at Chicago's Museum of Contemporary Photography, carefully selecting his "best" Rwanda photographs and then "burying" them in one hundred, black, linen archival photo-storage boxes with a description of the picture silk screened on the top of the box. The boxes were then arranged within the darkened space of the gallery so as to create a "cemetery of images" (**FIG. 7**).[68]

FIGURE 6
ALFREDO JAAR, UNFRAMED, 1985. COURTESY OF THE ARTIST AND GALERIE LELONG, NEW YORK.

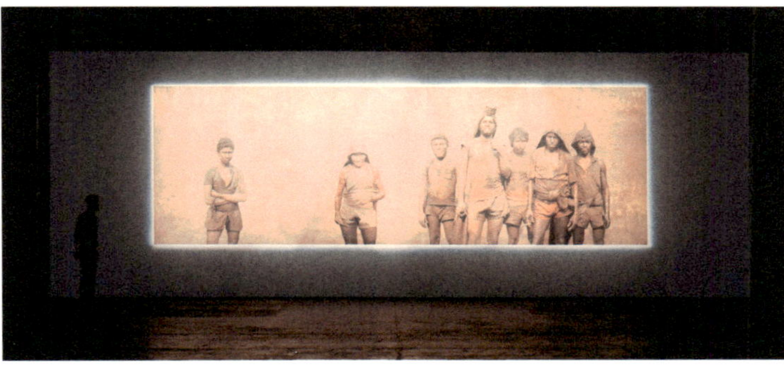

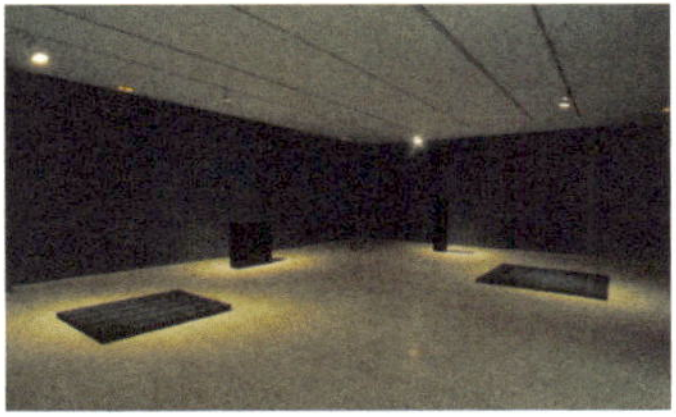

FIGURE 7
INSTALLATION VIEW OF *REAL IMAGES*, MUSEUM OF CONTEMPORARY PHOTOGRAPHY, CHICAGO, 1995. COURTESY OF THE ARTIST AND GALERIE LELONG, NEW YORK.

In 1996 Jaar decided to try a different representational strategy for circulating his Rwandan photographs. Rather than exhibit the devastation and suffering that he had witnessed there, Jaar selected two photographs for his installation **The Eyes of Gutete Emerita**, each depicting the eyes of a woman he had met in

Rwanda (**PLATE 51**).[69] In a manner similar to that used for his Serra Pelada photographs, Jaar displayed these two photographs as color transparencies in quadvision light boxes mounted next to each other on the wall. At the same time, Jaar did not limit the light boxes only to photographs. Prior to the images of Emerita's eyes, three sets of text transparencies appear in the light boxes for forty-five seconds, thirty seconds, and fifteen seconds, respectively. These texts describe, from the point of view of Emerita, the brutal killing of her husband and children. After the texts, the photographs of Emerita's eyes flash in the light boxes for a fraction of a second, after which the sequence of texts begins again.

Several critics have interpreted Jaar's use of texts and images in **The Eyes of Gutete Emerita** as an explicit critique of photojournalism. Photography critic Mark Durden, for instance, argued: "The eyes of Gutete provide a subjectivized counterpart to the objectivity and distance of media coverage."[70] Durden implied here that looking into the eyes of Emerita necessarily allows viewers to bear witness to the pain and horror of the Rwandan genocide in ways that the "distanced" and "dehumanizing" images of the print media have prohibited. Though Jaar is also concerned about the print media's lack of coverage of the genocide in Rwanda, in this installation he was less interested in having viewers "see" or even "feel" Emerita's pain than in making them aware of their inadequacies as witnesses. The placement of the two light boxes within an enclosed and darkened twenty-by-sixteen foot space reinforces this distinction. In order to access the light boxes, viewers must first enter a narrow, dark corridor. After they walk through this passageway and turn the corner, their sight is momentarily impaired by the light emanating from the boxes. In placing his images from Rwanda within this space, Jaar physically disrupts their easy or immediate consumption. He heightens this effect by giving viewers sufficient time to read about Emerita's painful experiences but then allowing them to see only for a fraction of a second the eyes that witnessed this tragedy. This disruption again frustrates viewers and forces them to consider that which they cannot see and by implication that which remains impossible to represent.

By using his installation to call attention to the limitations of representation—or its "failure," as Jaar claims—he is not suggesting that images have completely lost their power or function in today's society. In fact, Jaar recently said that he "believe[s] images are more necessary than ever."[71] For Jaar, then, the problem lies not with photojournalism or "concerned photography" per se but with the contexts in which these images are disseminated and consumed. This is because, according to Jaar: "Journalistic information and presentation actually discourage action. Much of the media overwhelms us with a sense of being present; we feel we know, and because we think we know, we think we care. But it stops there."[72] Jaar implied here that, since we are continually confronted with such a vast number of images in the print media, there is a tendency to pass over them quickly and without much critical awareness. To counter this situation, Jaar believes that it is the responsibility of artists who use "the real" in their works to create alternative frameworks for their images, ones that encourage viewers to become aware, in an active and inquiring manner, of the nature of representation. But the question remains: Can such an environment—one that implicates viewers as critically engaged participants—be produced within the context of the print media, the traditional vehicle for distributing and consuming photojournalism?[73]

69. For more information on *The Eyes of Gutete Emerita*, see Balken, *Alfredo Jaar*, pp. 28–39; and Strauss, "A Sea of Griefs."

70. Mark Durden, "Eye-to-Eye," *Art History* 23, no. 1 (March 2000): 128.

71. Jaar, "Alfredo Jaar: A Conversation," p. 47.

72. Alfredo Jaar, "The Peripatetic Artist: 14 Statements," *Art in America* 77 (July 1989): 131.

73. It is important to note that Jaar is not completely opposed to the distribution of his work in the print media. For instance, his public project "How can I make art out of information that most of you would rather ignore?" was reproduced in *Saturday Night* 106, no. 3734, (September 1991): 27–30; and "Rwanda, 5 years later" was published in *Wereldwijd* 293 (April 1999): 1–13. In allowing his work to be distributed in these contexts, however, Jaar assumed complete control over its layout and design. The extent to which more well-known newspapers and magazines would be willing to grant such authority remains in question.

FABRICATION

The June 12, 2005, cover of *The New York Times Magazine* featured an unidentified figure dressed in black (**PLATE 53**). Represented up from the shoulders and positioned in the center of the composition, the figure shared certain formal parallels with individuals depicted in mug shots. But a mug shot typically uses—to disclose an individual's unique and distinguishing features—even and consistent lighting, a neutral background, and a fixed distance between camera and sitter. In this photograph, however, an angular, green sandbag covering the figure's head and neck masks the subject's identity. Moreover, the dramatic lighting; the intense, red-painted background; and the shallow depth of field lend the figure an ominous and dominating presence. This association is reinforced by the four sets of questions, printed in small, white type, that flank the figure's head as well as by the headline: "What We *Don't* Talk About When We Talk About Torture," which runs along the bottom of the page. Containing such words as intimidation, interrogation, prison, and torture, the *Times Magazine* cover leaves unclear whether one should read the figure as the subject or the object of torture.

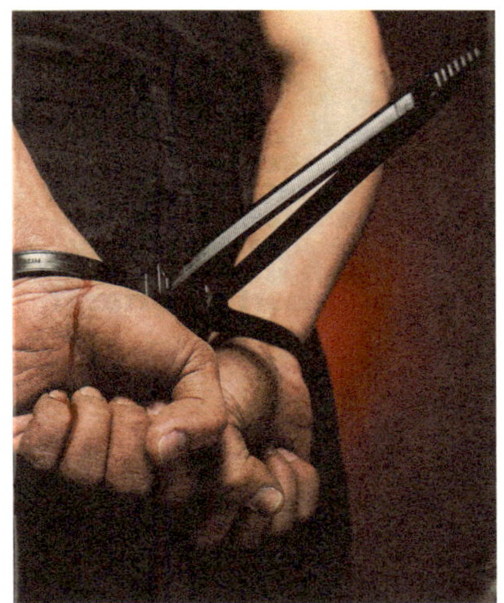

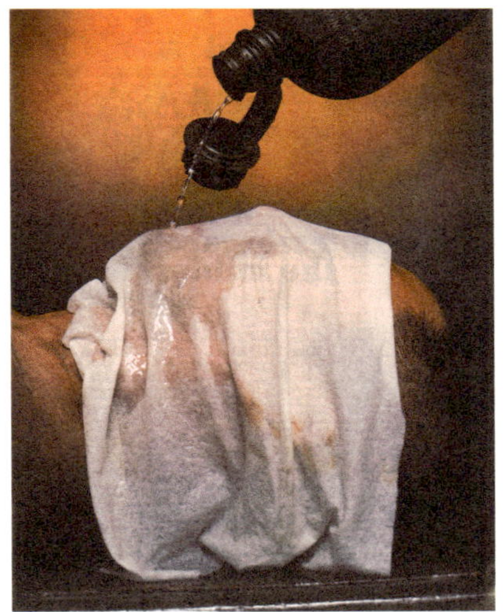

FIGURES 8 AND 9
ANDRES SERRANO,
NEW YORK TIMES MAGAZINE,
12 JUNE 2005. COURTESY
OF THE ARTIST AND *NEW YORK TIMES*.

The visual parallels between the angular, green sandbag and those depicted in the widely circulated photographs of tortured Iraqi prisoners at Abu Ghraib (**PLATE 57**) offset this ambiguity and encourage one to read the hooded figure as suffering and in pain.[74] The article, "Interrogating Ourselves," to which this *Times Magazine* cover photograph referred and the two additional, full-page color photographs that accompanied this essay corroborate this association.[75] Unlike the cover picture, both the article and the images explicitly referenced tortured subjects. In the essay, for instance, Joseph Lelyveld discussed the coercive techniques that Americans have used to interrogate detainees in the war on terror. The photographs seem to provide graphic visual support for this discussion: the first image depicts a close-up of a figure's arms, which have been forcefully handcuffed behind his back, while the second depicts the head of a reclined figure whose face is covered with a wet, white cloth over which water is being poured from a canteen (**FIGS. 8** and **9**).

At the same time, the article and its accompanying photographs also contained certain ambiguities. For instance, rather than offering a clear, moral position regarding the use of interrogation procedures, Lelyveld instead raised many perplexing and uncomfortable questions about our beliefs and assumptions regarding what constitutes torture when it is used in the war on terror. The stylistic conventions used to depict the figures in the photographs parallel these uncertainties. The sheer beauty and scrupulous details of the

74. The caption for the cover image in "Back Story," *The New York Times Magazine*, June 12, 2005, p. 6, further supports this reading: "The hooded figure has a long history as an icon of torture. But what once indicated the executioner has now come to symbolize the prisoner."

75. Joseph Lelyveld, "Interrogating Ourselves," *The New York Times Magazine*, June 12, 2005, pp. 36–43, 60, and 66–67.

photographs; the use of rich saturated colors and dramatic overhead lighting; and the manner in which the compositions are meticulously composed—right down to a trickle of blood running down one of the handcuffed hands—suggest that the suffering may, in fact, not be "real." That the photographs were taken by artist Andres Serrano—whose name appears in a caption on the table-of-contents page as well as on the first page of Lelyveld's article—heightens this association. Known for highly stylized and carefully staged images that often depict bizarre, morbid, and what some consider offensive subject matter (**PLATES 22** and **23**), Serrano's name—one that many *Times* readers would find familiar—also placed into question the "realism" of what is depicted.[76]

76. Besides the notoriety of *Piss Christ* (1987), Serrano is frequently commissioned to take portrait photographs for the *Times* and his name is often listed in its captions.

This ambiguity between the real and the fabricated in Serrano's torture photographs has troubled a number of individuals. For instance, *The New York Times* public editor, Byron Calame—whose job entails responding to complaints and comments from the public and monitoring the paper's journalistic practices—criticized the *Times Magazine* editors Kathleen Ryan and Gerald Marzorati for not appending more concise labels to Serrano's pictures. Finding the "realism" of the handcuffed arms especially perplexing, Calame argued that the inclusion of Serrano's name and "Backdrop painting by Irina Movmyga" in the caption on the table-of-contents page failed to clarify for readers what the images actually depicted. According to Calame, a more appropriate credit line would have read "Depiction by Andres Serrano," since this text would make clear that his photographs were fabrications. To support his argument, Calame cited *The New York Times* "Guidelines on Our Integrity," which states that "images in our pages that purport to depict reality must be genuine in every way," and those in which "the slightest doubt is possible" must offer an explanation.[77]

77. Bryon Calame, "Pictures, Labels, Perception and Reality," *The New York Times*, July 3, 2005, p. 10.

In response to Calame's critique, editors Ryan and Marzorati called attention to the "conceptual" nature of Serrano's images and to their "over-the-top" qualities, which they felt would ensure that no one would mistake them as "real."[78] Moreover, the *Times Magazine* editors argued that a vast majority of readers had interpreted them as such; as one of the published responses to Calame's column suggested, this was the case at least for some readers: "I am astonished by your suggestion that a typical *Times* reader could look at the Andres Serrano photographs and not realize that they were staged."[79] For Calame, however, the readers of *The New York Times* should never have to question the authenticity of images; instead, he believes that consistent labels should make readily apparent to readers "whether images are real or manipulated." Moreover, Calame maintains that the *Times* should establish a standardized system that can "be used across all parts of the paper and online to describe the various categories for images, depending on the way they have been created or manipulated."[80] This conviction mirrors the goals that Calame stated, when he took over as public editor in June, 2005, of making the journalistic process "more transparent to readers" and holding "the *Times*' news staff more accountable."[81]

78. Calame, "Pictures, Labels, Perception," p. 10.

79. John S. Hall, "Photographs and Labels," *The New York Times*, July 24, 2005, p. 12.

80. Calame, "Pictures, Labels, Perception," p. 10.

80. Calame, "Pictures, Labels, Perception," p. 10.

81. Bryon Calame, "The New Public Editor: Toward Greater Transparency," *The New York Times*, June 5, 2005, p. 14.

Calame's support of explanatory captions is largely a product of his belief in the fundamental truthfulness of the journalistic field—hence his citation of the *Times* "Guidelines on Our Integrity." Therefore, what ultimately rendered Serrano's photographs problematic for Calame was their relationship to the real, or more accurately, how they compromised the integrity of photography's assumed realism. After all, the *Times* Magazine editors went to great lengths—securing "authentic" sandbags and constructing, for instance, the water-torture composition in terms of "actual" photographs taken in Vietnam—to ensure that what Serrano depicted was accurate. What concerns Calame, then, is not what Serrano represents but how he depicts it, and more particularly, how these representational strategies weaken what former *Times Magazine* picture editor Fred Ritchin labeled "photography's putative capacity for reliable transcription" and—by extension—the overall journalistic integrity of the *Times*.[82] Calame believes that, like *The New York Times*, photography has a moral obligation to render reality transparent and understandable; he is troubled by Serrano's photographs because of the uncertainty that they raise in terms of photography's evidentiary and testimonial authority.

82. Fred Ritchin, "Photojournalism in the Age of Computers," *The Critical Image*, ed. Carol Squiers (Seattle: Bay Press, 1990), p. 28.

What Calame fails to realize is that it is not Serrano's photographs that have compromised photography's ability to bear witness; instead, it is the photographs from Abu Ghraib to which Serrano's photographs refer—and, more particularly, the circumstances under which these images of torture were taken and circulated by American soldiers—that have undermined longstanding beliefs in photography's position as witness. A number of critics—Susan Sontag, Brian Wallis, and more recently, Andy Grundberg—have addressed this aspect of the production and distribution of the snapshots from Abu Ghraib. "Where once photographing war was the province of photojournalists," Sontag argued, "now the soldiers themselves are all photographers—recording their war, their fun, their observations of what they find picturesque, their atrocities—and swapping images among themselves and emailing them around the globe."[83] As deliberate acts of maltreatment, humiliation, and domination that were not supposed to be seen (at least by the larger general public) the Abu Ghraib photographs, these critics maintain, represent a direct violation of the traditional function of photojournalism. Grundberg elucidated: "These photographs tell us that the codes of objectivity, professional ethics, and journalistic accountability we have all relied on to ensure the accuracy of the news—at least in rough draft form—are now relics. In their place is a swirling mass of information, written as well as visual, journalistic as well as vernacular, competing to be taken as fact."[84]

83. Susan Sontag, "Regarding the Torture of Others," *The New York Times Magazine*, May 23, 2004, p. 27.

84. Andy Grundberg, "Point and Shoot: How the Abu Ghraib Images Redefine Photography," *American Scholar* 74, no. 1 (Winter 2005): 108.

For Grundberg, the most disturbing aspect of this "uncontrollable flow of digital images" is the manner in which it compromises a crucial feature of how we make sense of the world—namely, "our ability to distinguish what is real from what is fabricated and what is important from what is irrelevant."[85] Calame's critique of Serrano's torture photographs seems to parallel this concern. At the same time, in making this association, Calame overlooked a crucial difference between the two sets of images. Whereas recognizing the ambiguity between the real and the fabricated is intrinsic to the meaning of Serrano's photographs, the uncertainty of the Abu Ghraib photographs is much more troubling, since, as Grundberg also pointed out: "No one (at least no one this side of paranoia) has questioned the veracity of what they depict...the pictures never ask to be read as anything but snapshots."[86] In today's free-floating and over-saturated media world, it is precisely this distinction that lends their import to Serrano's photographs of torture.

85. Grundberg, "Point and Shoot," p. 109.

86. Grundberg, "Point and Shoot," p. 108.

By staging images that reference the torture at Abu Ghraib and elsewhere but do not literally represent them, Serrano's photographs ask viewers to think more carefully about what the representation of torture means, and if it is even something that can be depicted. This is a different kind of work than that performed by the recent widespread and rapid appropriation into contemporary art and public displays of photographs from Abu Ghraib (**PLATES 55** and **56**).[87] Instead of offering a space in which to object and to resist the horrific actions that the snapshots from Abu Ghraib both depict and represent, the visual ambiguities in Serrano's photographs provide a framework in which viewers can think critically about their assumptions and expectations regarding the use of coercion tactics and the extent to which we believe that these techniques, like Serrano's photographs, "actually" constitute torture. The conflict between the real and the fabricated in Serrano's images—a tension heightened by their circulation in the ostensibly reliable journalistic context of the *Times Magazine*—forms an essential part of this representational strategy. Assigning Serrano's photographs a caption like "depiction," "illustration," or something similar limits this potential, since it necessarily defines them in relation to what they are not—the "facts." Rather than undermining photography's ability to bear witness, the circulation of Serrano's photographs in *The New York Times Magazine* poses a more challenging task: it encourages viewers to more closely examine the conventions and the set of beliefs upon which photography's evidentiary and testimonial authority ultimately depend.

87. For a discussion about how the Abu Ghraib photographs have been appropriated and transformed into protest images by such artists as Salaheddin Sallat, Forkscrew Graphics, and Richard Serra, and others, see Dora Apel, "Torture Culture: Lynching Photographs and the Images of Abu Ghraib," *Art Journal* 64, no. 2 (Summer 2005): 94–100.

HOLLY EDWARDS

COVER TO COVER: THE LIFE CYCLE OF AN IMAGE IN CONTEMPORARY VISUAL CULTURE

Afghan Girl by Steve McCurry (**PLATE 5**) first appeared on the cover of *National Geographic* in 1985 to epitomize the plight of refugees displaced by the Soviet invasion of Afghanistan. Since that time, the image has been republished frequently in diverse contexts, its meaning altered and augmented with each reincarnation. The photograph and the photographer gained fame, even as the girl (Sharbat Gula) survived seventeen years of flight and repatriation, unaware of the use of her image. During the Taliban era, **Afghan Girl** became the focus of renewed interest. *National Geographic*, seeking to recapitulate Afghanistan's suffering, launched a campaign to find the person behind the famous face and to tell her life story. The photograph was reprised and revised, serving as the visual lynchpin of philanthropic efforts to raise money for the education of Afghan girls after Taliban power collapsed.

The success of that humanitarian campaign, coupled with the protracted story of Sharbat Gula and her widely disseminated image, pose some important ethical issues: the abuse and suffering that Afghan women and children have undergone in recent decades are incontrovertible; the rhetoric and performance of the resulting charitable campaigns and the role of photography for documentary and philanthropic purposes, however, are more vexed and contestable. By tracing the story of **Afghan Girl** over time, I hope to call attention to a few of the moral complexities that reside in the overlap between visuality and human rights.[1]

Embedded within that story are myriad quandaries involved in the acts of photographing, exhibiting, and even viewing the suffering of others; standing without the story are other, equally complex issues relating to the more general production and elaboration of visual culture. Positioning **Afghan Girl** at the crux of these two domains underscores the intimacy between ethos and image over time, sustained and complicated by the ever more sophisticated technologies of image production.

My strategy will be to trace the meandering life cycle of a mechanically reproduced image episodically functioning as (but not limited to) document, "art," advertisement, and fundraiser, thereby articulating the traffic in pain that is endemic to contemporary visual culture. My starting point is nebulous and even banal: What is it about this photograph? Why has it enjoyed sustained currency in the public arena and served so many diverse functions? Why have so many people responded to the image in such extravagant, diverse, and personal ways? Men have written to McCurry seeking to marry the girl; couples have offered to adopt her. Most importantly, many people have contributed money to the Afghan cause in response to her image.

That numerous people *have* responded monetarily is striking; that **Afghan Girl** has become a virtual icon in a visually saturated society also demands comment. Countless images (some of them "beautiful," powerful, dangerous, or otherwise provocative) have simultaneously come and gone without a trace in the visual blur to which we are accustomed. Somehow, against the odds, this one has repeatedly reached benumbed and satiated audiences, eliciting fascination and even activism.[2] I would argue that diverse and multiple dynamics must have coincided to keep the image in the public eye over time; no single factor can explain its sustained power and currency.

In order to tease apart those forces, it is useful to consider the photograph not simply as a discrete visual document but rather in/as a relational matrix encompassing image, maker, audience, and era. This matrix is exponentially expanded by the reproducibility of the medium, the encounter between viewers and image endlessly reenacted and constantly recalibrated. Such an approach is doubly pertinent to the study of a portrait, a visual type that activates a peculiarly interactive force field among multiple agents—subject, maker, viewers.[3] Underlying this strategy is the conviction that the image is an agent as well as a manifestation of culture and the viewer is a vector of changing meaning.

This study is loosely diachronic. Such an approach reflects the constantly renewed and revealing topicality of the image, arising out of one of the most symbolically charged and politically complex encounters of the era. **Afghan Girl** gained currency in the context of Afghanistan's struggle against the Soviet Union, the corollary refugee crisis, and America's escalating involvement in Afghanistan; it enjoyed augmented relevance during the Taliban era. What this suggests is that the fame of **Afghan Girl** is part of a larger picture, in which Afghanistan served as a strategic proxy in the burdened contest between the Soviet Union and the United States and then as a charged focal point in the protracted encounter be-

1. Other images have enjoyed similarly protracted and revealing life cycles. See Liz Wells, "Image Analysis: The Example of Migrant Mother," *Photography: A Critical Introduction* (New York: Routledge, 1996), pp. 37–48; Stephen Biel, *American Gothic: A Life of America's Most Famous Painting* (New York: Norton, 2005); Donald Sassoon, *Becoming Mona Lisa* (New York: Harcourt, 2001).

2. Susan Sontag's trenchant engagement with the issues surrounding the image glut, as well as the pertinent theories of DeBord and Baudrillard resurface in Susan Sontag, *Regarding the Pain of Others* (New York: Farrar, Straus and Giroux, 2003), pp. 104–13.

3. Richard Brilliant, *Portraiture* (Cambridge, MA: Harvard University Press, 1991), pp. 7–21.

tween the Islamic world and the United States. Indeed, it seems likely that **Afghan Girl** has enjoyed prolonged currency in no small part because of its resonance with core narratives of American political dominance in the late twentieth century.

The observation that the fame of **Afghan Girl** is related in some way to the diverse entanglements between the United States and Afghanistan (and by extension, the Islamic world more generally) has certain implications. Most obviously, it points to the relevance of the voluminous discourse generated by Edward Said's *Orientalism*.[4] McCurry's photograph is, after all, about a very specific case of "beautiful suffering"—that of a Muslim, Afghan woman; the manner in which it extends a long tradition of representing the "Orient" or the "East" by means of an exoticized, eroticized female undergirds the following argument in diverse ways. Indeed, this is on some levels a case study of Orientalism in its narrowest sense of defining, documenting, and controlling the (albeit changing) "Orient" as that process has been enacted in the visually aggressive culture of the late twentieth century.

4. A recent and insightful overview of this protracted discourse appears in Zachery Lockman, *Contending Views of the Middle East* (Cambridge and New York: Cambridge University Press, 2004), pp. 182–215.

That the photograph depicts a girl widely deemed *beautiful* invokes another matrix of analysis. Following Danto,[5] we must consider the possibility that perverse pleasures factor in the sustained charisma of **Afghan Girl**. Are we relishing her suffering because of her appealing appearance? Are we consoled by seeing one so pretty survive? On the other hand, is she ennobled by this portrait or is she being victimized by our gaze? How do beauty and morality overlap in this viewing experience?

5. Arthur Danto, *The Abuse of Beauty* (Chicago: Open Court, 2003), pp. 108–15. There is a mushrooming consideration of the meanings and functions of beauty in contemporary visual culture that is beyond the scope of this essay. Danto's work is the most useful point of reference for the present purpose.

While it might be easy to contemplate her beauty and her predicament in a detached (or reverent) fashion, (there is certainly ample precedent in the history of Christian art for this[6]), the next step would be to consider the voracious consumption of beauty in the present tense. This is beauty in the vernacular sense of a pretty face in the here and now, the experience of physical attraction that is a matter of our tastes, social conventions, and somatic experiences. This kind of immediate arousal has underlain the impact of countless images in the past,[7] but the sustained power of **Afghan Girl** to elicit strong response is augmented by the medium in which she is rendered—photography. She is *"real"* to the average viewer in part because of the presumed veracity of photographs that is, in turn, corroborated by the shared viewing experience afforded by multiple iterations of the easily reproduced image.[8] When many people see the same image, a consolidated truth value for the image coalesces in the public arena. The image functions as an active agent—shaping and often homogenizing taste and public opinion.

6. Elaine Scarry, *The Body in Pain*, (New York: Oxford University Press, 1985).

7. Arousal by image is discussed in detail in David Freedburg, *The Power of Images* (Chicago: University of Chicago Press, 1989), pp. 317–45.

8. The implications of mechanically reproducing images were articulated by Walter Benjamin in the 1930s. For an array of related issues and commentaries, see Andrew Benjamin, ed., *Walter Benjamin and Art* (New York: Continuum, 2005).

This, then, suggests a final nest of significance—the marketplace. Beauty, in a vernacular rather than in a philosophical sense, is the lynchpin of a vast industry and the currency of consumer society. By embedding the life cycle of **Afghan Girl** in that socio-economic context, I seek to trace the syncopated processes by which the image became simultaneously icon and commodity and to tabulate the benefits that have accrued to those who are needy and those who are safe, thanks to this photograph. In the end, I think, we (the comfortable viewers) are ineluctably forced to confront a hard and basic question: how is our privilege related to her suffering?

When Steve McCurry took the photograph known as **Afghan Girl**, he was an unknown, young photographer with a college degree and some freelance experience.

His impressive career as a photojournalist affiliated with Magnum was launched when he covered the refugee situation on the border between Pakistan and Afghanistan. Now, one can peruse and purchase McCurry's work online and encounter it in magazines, galleries, and museum exhibitions; recently, a glossy monograph on his work was published.[9] Indeed, according to his early 2006 web site, McCurry is "universally recognized as one of today's finest image makers."[10] Clearly, over the years, he has refined his promotional strategies as well as his art.

9. Anthony Bannon, *Steve McCurry*, (New York: Phaidon, 2005).

10. http://www.stevemccurry.com

On the same web site, McCurry presented a selection of his photographs and singled out one for further comment. Approximately contemporaneous with **Afghan Girl**, this photograph shows a tailor in Porbandar, India, carrying a sewing machine on his shoulder down a flooded street (**FIG. 1**).[11] The neck-deep waters hide everything but the man's head and juxtaposed sewing machine, both of which appear to simply float on the surface of the water in a seemingly whimsical if slightly surreal decapitation. It is an audacious, compelling image and, like **Afghan Girl**, it appeared on the cover of *National Geographic*. That exposure in a high-profile magazine generated, in turn, a showy act of charity—the sewing-machine manufacturer magnanimously replaced the tailor's ruined equipment so that he could recoup his losses and carry on with his life.

11. This image appears with short commentary in Bannon, *Steve McCurry*, not paginated.

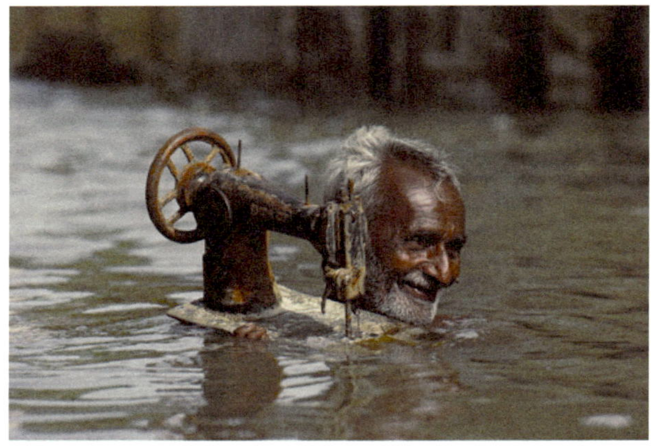

FIGURE 1
STEVE McCURRY, *PORBANDAR, GUJARAT, INDIA*, 1983. COURTESY STEVE McCURRY AND MAGNUM PHOTOS.

McCurry used this exemplary image to articulate his personal stance: "We photographers say that we "take" a picture, and in a certain sense, that is true. We take something from people's lives, but in doing so, we tell their story. In this case, I took his picture, others saw it, were moved, and reached out to help the man. That is the best possible result." Thus, for McCurry (and others), it is valid and even laudable to photograph the plight of someone else rather than to alleviate it, for by this means, others are inspired to altruism. It is, in effect, the rationale for a division of humanitarian labors: the moment must be captured visually so that the suffering can be remembered, rectified, and (hopefully) not repeated.[12]

12. This reasoning resonates with David Levi Strauss, *Between the Eyes* (New York: Aperture, 2003), pp. 42–9.

The story of **Afghan Girl** entails a more complex rendition of the same attitude. The life cycle of that image involves comparable (and also contradictory) dynamics of witnessing and charity, and it poses vexing questions about exploitation and voyeurism. But in the end, it is more revealing of the embedded ethical quandaries than is the case of the photograph of the stoic tailor. Its unique status and sustained currency are evident on the web site and corroborated in McCurry's other promotional materials, where the image is overtly and repeatedly showcased. It is mentioned specifically in the biography, where it is described as "the most recognizable photograph in the world today." It serves as the icon for the online gallery of McCurry's coverage of Afghanistan, and it reappears as the emblematic image for a link to a charitable foundation, ImagineAsia, set up by McCurry and others to support educational opportunities in rural Asia.[13] It was also the centerpiece for "Face of Asia," an exhibition of McCurry's photographs mounted and circulated by Eastman

13. http://www.imagine-asia.org

Kodak House; the accompanying brochure featured Kodak products in conjunction with a brief biography of the photojournalist and an elaborate time line of **Afghan Girl** entitled "Image to Icon."[14] By the year 2006, then—two decades after its initial appearance—**Afghan Girl** is still resonant and recognized; it has become advertisement, icon, and professional attribute, while McCurry enjoys accrued blessings—monetary and otherwise—as do various commercial and institutional concerns. What follows is, in part, an effort to trace the processes by which that happened.

14. Nathan Hogan "Face of Asia: Steve McCurry's Photographs," *Afterimage*, vol. 31 (July–August 2003). Exhibition at George Eastman House, April 19–August 31, 2003.

Afghan Girl is a riveting portrait of a female looking over her right shoulder; her eyes blaze. Apart from a few ragged holes in the shawl covering her hair, there are no indications of her status or identity. She is mute and even frozen, but the protective hunch of her shoulder and the slight obduracy of her mouth suggest resilience, or perhaps resistance. Ultimately, it is the eyes that confront and mesmerize. Their color is not inconsequential—they are neither commonplace brown nor crystalline blue, nor does one think to dismiss them as merely hazel. Serendipitously enhanced by the shawl's contrasting hue and the color of the garment underneath, they are a vivid, surprising green.[15]

15. The cymbal clash of red and green and the riveting eye color are so deterministic that McCurry's testimony about their authenticity is worth quoting: "Just by sheer luck, the background from the tent was a certain shade of green and her shirt was green as well; so there's a wonderful color thing happening." Simon James, "Steve McCurry: Humanity in Color," *RPS Journal*, vol. 142, no. 6, (July–August 2002): 48–51. The extent to which the palette was enhanced or manipulated in subsequent iterations is open to question: even cursory comparison of the many incarnations of the image reveals considerable variation.

If she seems bound, so are we—held captive by the girl's unflinching, verdant gaze. We do not look up to her or down to her but rather directly at her, and that face off is crucial to the impact of the image. Indeed, it is her piercing glare that dictates the terms of the encounter and forces a declaration of intent. Looking at her, we must admit ourselves.

Of course, it is more complicated than that. Her gaze is not really directed at us; it is an artifact of her encounter with Steve McCurry and his camera. That instant of eye contact is central to this story, for the terms of that confrontation affect every subsequent reading, whether replicatory, divergent, or contesting. What can be said about that critical encounter?

To answer that question in retrospect, we have recourse to the verbal testimonies of participants. McCurry's description, the publication of which will be addressed later, goes like this:

> I remember the noise and confusion in that refugee camp 17 years ago. I knew that Afghan girls, just a few years away from disappearing behind a traditional veil, might be reluctant to have their picture taken by a male Westerner. So I proceeded carefully. I asked the teacher for permission to enter the girls' school tent and photograph a few of the students. The shyest of them, Sharbat, said I could take her photograph and I shot a few frames.[16]

16. This story is recounted in various contexts; I quote it from Cathy Newman, "A Life Revealed," *National Geographic*, April 2002, where the story was published for the first time.

Sharbat Gula's version of the encounter is problematical. Indeed, it cannot legitimately be equated with McCurry's more discursive, personal testimony, as it has been summarized, directed, and stylized by interviewers, translators, and editors. Already the quandaries abound. Do I quote it and gloss over those interventions, or do I resist the reductionist voice-over and delete the report? Condone or erase? For the moment, I will recount it, noting in the process its compromised nature:

> She remembers the moment. The photographer took her picture. She remembers her anger. The man was a stranger. She had never been photographed before. Until they met again 17 years later, she had not been photographed since.[17]

Setting aside the contrived ventriloquism, it is clear that there are asymmetries (age,

17. See note 15.

gender, power) inherent in this meeting. The picture was taken in a setting in which gender segregation was normative and image making was fraught. She was angry and he was an outsider; he "took" her picture. Without presuming to pinpoint her emotional response to this or any other social complexities involved, it seems safe to state that McCurry's codes of propriety and visuality (not hers) dictated the terms of the encounter; that encounter, in turn, left traces on the resulting image.

I go back now to the image itself. Ironically and significantly, the famous photograph is of limited value as a piece of reportage, conveying little of the girl's situation. The image shows a female of indeterminate age against an undifferentiated backdrop; aside from a few ragged places in her shawl, there are no definitive sartorial clues as to her circumstances. Her expression telegraphs unspoken emotion, but it is (already) veiled and—without the accompanying narrative—somewhat enigmatic. In its generic and generalized quality, it is richly ambiguous.

By contrast, other images of the same person from McCurry's roll of film are considerably denser with circumstantial detail (**FIG. 2**).[18] The thick hands, grimy fingernails, and furtive gestures caught in other images betray the youth, the vulnerability, and the hard life of the girl in ways that preclude fantasy or even multiple readings. These (not surprisingly) less-well-known frames convey more information about the girl but sustain less projection from the viewer. They are not general but rather specific visual notes about a particular person. By contrast, the famous image invites diverse readings and sustains complex projections by virtue of its capacious, generalized character.[19]

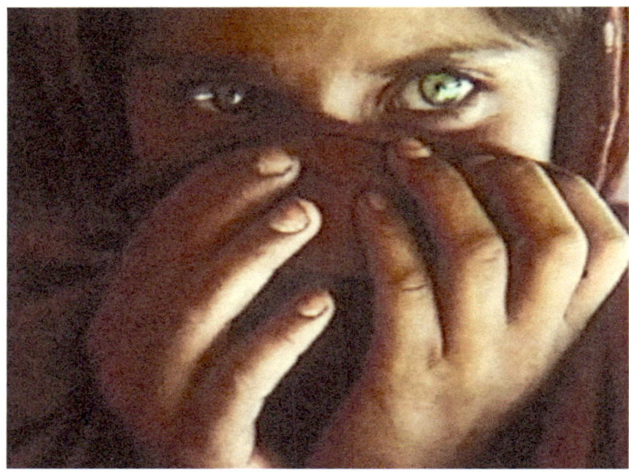

FIGURE 2
NATIONAL GEOGRAPHIC, APRIL 2002, N.P. COURTESY STEVE McCURRY AND MAGNUM PHOTOS

This receptivity, while critical to the longevity of this particular image, is not unusual; rather, it is commonplace in commodity culture, especially among stock images of the advertising industry that are archived and sold for diverse marketing purposes. Characterized by aesthetic/technical refinement, generalized content, and lack of explicit "meaning," such images are useful precisely because they can be "branded" or glossed to convey disparate messages in varied commercial contexts. From one iteration to the next, the stock image can change considerably in connotation, depending on the needs of the purveyor.[20]

In this milieu of generic image and protean meaning, the connotational valences of **Afghan Girl** have been specified and can, in turn, be gauged by the varied captions applied to the mechanically reproduced and widely disseminated image. Roland Barthes described this as the "anchorage" function of a caption, tying a picture to certain meanings and drawing it away from others.[21] As cues, captions serve to turn the enigmatic appeal of the portrait to varying ends; as clues, they reveal sponsors and beneficiaries. By considering different iterations of the portrait in conjunction with their appended captions, I will articulate changes in the image's meaning, tune in to its social resonances, and identify the ideological and commercial engines of its dissemination.

18. Fig. 2, for example, has been reproduced frequently without acquiring fame and fortune. It appears in *National Geographic*, April 2002, as well as on the back cover of *Steve McCurry, Portraits* (New York: Phaidon, 1999).

19. The connotative receptivity I refer to was also a formative factor in the life cycle of Dorothea Lange's *Migrant Mother* (see note 1).

20. Anandi Ramamurthy, "Commercial photography, image banks and corporate media" in Liz Wells, ed. *Photography: A Critical Introduction* (London: Routledge, 2004), pp. 201–04. See also Douglas Holt, *How Brands Become Icons: The Principles of Cultural Branding* (Boston: Harvard Business School Press, 2005). Following the latter, this brand of suffering has become an icon, a successful campaign of culturally resonant identity construction.

21. Roland Barthes, "Rhetoric of the Image," in Stephen Heath ed. *Image, Music, Text* (New York: Hill and Wang, 1977), pp. 39–40.

First, I want to consider the initial incarnation of **Afghan Girl** and the frame in which it appeared, in June 1985—the immediately recognizable yellow border of *National Geographic*'s cover (**PLATE 6**). As an artifact of the era, the conjunction of image and frame is complexly potent, merging the social charisma and rhetorical style of the magazine with the power of a new and arresting image to capture the attention of the viewing public, thereby projecting a particular worldview. While the growth and character of *National Geographic*'s representational traditions as well as its more general cultural clout have inspired considerable comment,[22] the magazine's rendition of Afghanistan has escaped detailed scrutiny. That project lies beyond the scope of the present essay; let it be said simply that a distinct representational template emerges, beginning in the 1920s, particularly with regard to Afghan women.

22. The most sustained analysis is in Catherine Lutz and Jane Collins, *Reading National Geographic* (Chicago: University of Chicago Press, 1993). See also Linda Steet, *Veils and Daggers, A Century of National Geographic's Representation of the Arab World* (Philadelphia: Temple University Press, 2000).

For example, photographs that accompany Thomas Abercrombie's lead story entitled "Crossroads of Conquerors," in the 1968 issue of *National Geographic*, can typify that rhetorical tradition for present purposes. The cover image is an earth-toned riff on the Madonna and Child (**FIG. 3**); the second (embedded within the article itself) reprises the common trope of veiled woman as caged bird (**FIG. 4**). The general prominence and aesthetic virtuosity of both images are dissonant with their minimal captions and narrative insignificance. Indeed, the reader never learns anything substantive about either of the women. They serve circumscribed visual roles indicative of culturally specific tastes—one is a cover girl, the other is a photogenic veil. **Afghan Girl**, appearing on the magazine cover on two separate occasions, conformed to and extended these tropes;[23] in so doing, the portrait fulfilled readers' expectations, even as McCurry's image won acclaim in the public arena.

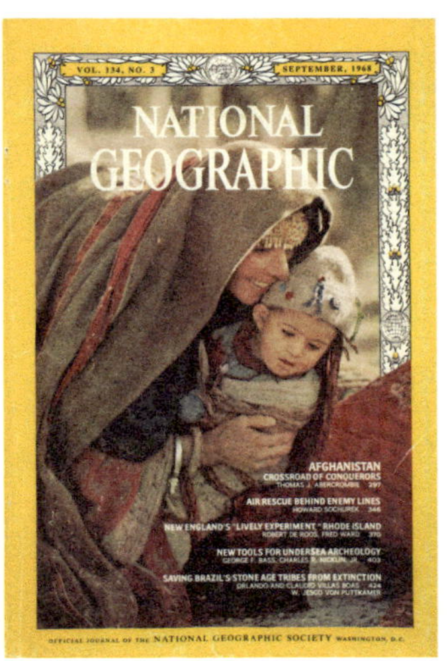

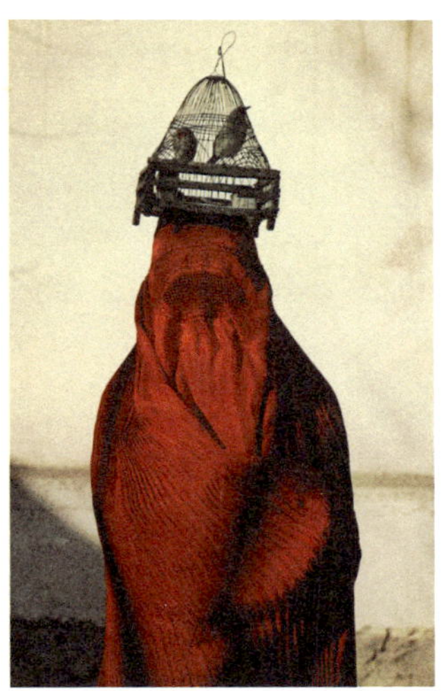

FIGURES 3 & 4
NATIONAL GEOGRAPHIC, SEPTEMBER 1968, COVER AND P. 303. COURTESY *NATIONAL GEOGRAPHIC* MAGAZINE

23. April 1985 and April 2002; Lutz and Collins, *Reading National Geographic*, addresses myriad issues relating to cover design at *National Geographic*. These provide useful analytical context.

But these are general observations. In its initial appearance on the cover of the June 1985 issue, **Afghan Girl** was cast in a more particular role, signaled by a few, carefully placed words at the lower-right corner of the image. Those words served to corral the viewer's imagination and focus attention on one particular set of associations: "Haunted eyes tell of an Afghan refugee's fears." With this directive act, *National Geographic* imposed a reading on McCurry's photograph, unilaterally labeling the girl's state of mind and effectively personifying Afghan refugees with a fearful, female victim. Her appearance is critical and critically limited as well. Most obvious is the fact that she posed beautifully on the cover and then played no further role in the magazine's description of the plight of Afghan refugees. Nowhere in the article is her name given, nor is her flight from the invading forces recounted. Visually enshrined but personally erased, she is no different from any other cover girl on any fashion magazine.

The resonance between **Afghan Girl** and the ethos of beauty and consumption that dominated America in the 1980s and 1990s was perhaps the critical factor in the photograph's subsequent rise to fame. It was a boom time. Americans were voracious consumers of new goods and new experiences, and affluent yuppies avidly welcomed the beautiful and the exotic as intriguing consumer experiences.[24] Controversy, however, was as endemic as consumption:[25] Robert Mapplethorpe's exquisitely scandalous photos and Andre Serrano's provocative images (**PLATE 22**) called into question the very codes of conduct that were operative in American visual culture—what was proper and what was off limits? Who had the right to determine (fund) what could be made visual/visible?

In actuality, these questions are central to the study of any visual culture,[26] and not coincidently, they were the same issues (albeit transposed into a trans-cultural key) that underlay the encounter between McCurry and the Afghan girl and would eventually resurface in the diverse iconoclasms of the Taliban and their impact on **Afghan Girl**. But that will be the climax of the story and we are only just beginning. For the moment, the issue is the beauty of the Afghan girl and how it played in consumer culture.

In the mid 1980s, the general receptivity to other cultures and new looks was manifest in myriad ways in the world of fashion. John Galliano, for example, launched a collection entitled "Visions of Afghanistan: Layers of Suiting, Shirting and Dried Blood Tones" just three months prior to the appearance of the Afghan girl on the cover of *National Geographic*.[27] With hints like this, one begins to suspect that the Afghan girl might have been perceived not simply as a frightened refugee but also as an exotic, intriguing beauty.

This is borne out by evidence of a larger shift in American tastes in the 1980s and 1990s, a move away from the blond-haired, blue-eyed stereotype toward a more inclusive notion of "beauty." A contemporaneous article in *Newsweek* documented this growing acceptance of "overtly ethnic girls," citing in particular Puerto Rican Talisa Soto, "the first to break into modeling's inner sanctum."[28] In heralding this relaxation of norms ("Paper dolls, indeed!"), the article went on to admit that cover-girl status remained a remote possibility for those who did not conform to old stereotypes: "Brunettes who get there tend to have blue eyes." Enter the Afghan girl, a green-eyed brunette—multi-cultural beauty personified. If she had aspired to be a fashion model, she could not have asked for a more auspicious moment to make an appearance.

If the Afghan girl were well cast to be a cutting-edge cover girl of the 1980s, she was well launched by *National Geographic* and Steve McCurry: a comparison of the magazine's cover with contemporaneous *Harper's Bazaar* or *Vogue* covers reveals a striking similarity (**FIGS. 5** and **6**).[29] Not only do these magazines share a similar page composition—closely cropped portrait surmounted by magazine name and bracketed along the sides by a list of headlines—but also a comparable approach to presenting a beautiful face. Large striking eyes, straight nose, and

FIGURES 5 & 6
NATIONAL GEOGRAPHIC, JUNE 1985, COVER. COURTESY *NATIONAL GEOGRAPHIC* MAGAZINE.
HARPER'S BAZAAR, MARCH/APRIL 1985, COVER. COURTESY HEARST COMMUNICATIONS, INC.

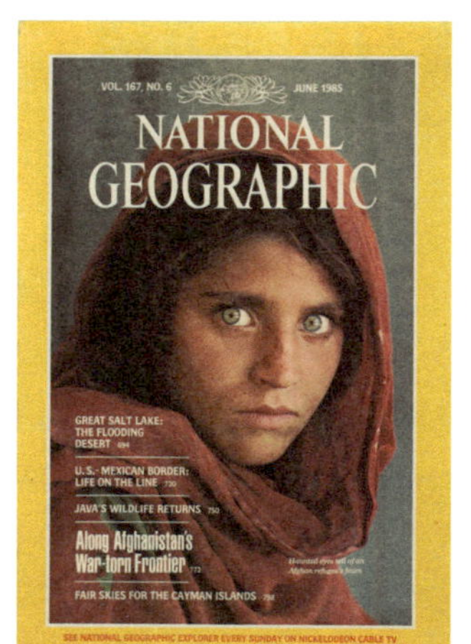

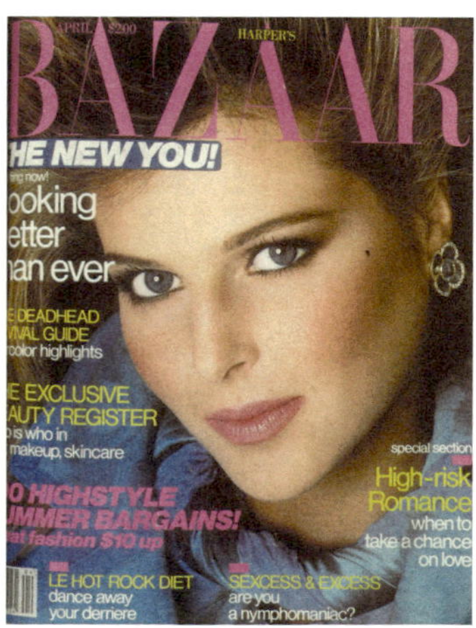

24. Kate Mulvey and Melissa Richards, *Decades of Beauty* (London: Hamlyn, 1998), pp. 172–205.

25. For an overview of some of these issues see Wendy Steiner, *The Scandal of Pleasure* (Chicago: University of Chicago Press, 1995).

26. W. T. J. Mitchell, "Showing Seeing: A Critique of Visual Culture" in Michael Ann Holly and Keith Moxey, *Art History, Aesthetics, Visual Studies* (Williamstown, MA: Sterling and Francine Clark Art Institute in collaboration with Yale University Press, 2002), pp. 231–50.

27. Colin McDowell, *Galliano* (New York: Rizzoli, 1997), pp. 79–81 and 91. Galliano's references to Afghanistan are complex—arising in part from history (King Amanullah's dress reforms in the 1920s) but also from a more general interest in what the designer called "wearing two different cultures."

28. Eloise Salholz, "More than a Pretty Face." *Newsweek*, January 14, 1985, p. 74. See also Jennet Conant, "Black Models Back to Stay," *Newsweek*, September 12, 1988, p. 78; Eva Pomice, "Putting Their Best Face Forward," *U. S. News and World Report*, vol. 106, no. 23, (June 12, 1989), p. 45.

29. For example, *Vogue*, January–February 1985; *Harper's Bazaar*, March and April 1985.

full mouth are shown to best advantage posed just so—the face turned slightly down and looking sideways over the shoulder, the body caught in a moment of arrested action directed elsewhere. Most striking is the emphasis on vivid eye color.

One might digress further on the conventions of fashion photography here or, alternatively, shift analytical gears and consider the image in the context of visual anthropology by correlating the portrait with Catherine Lutz and Jane Collins' typologies of gaze in *National Geographic* photography.[30] **Afghan Girl** may pose like a cover girl of the mid 1980s, but she also conforms to a particular type—the non-Western subject that confronts the photographer. The girl looks into and simultaneously twists away from the camera; deemed coy or seductive in a fashion shot, this torsion between pose and gaze also suggests qualified engagement and silent resistance in the realm of visual anthropology.

That **Afghan Girl** occupies an overlap between fashion photography and visual anthropology is not unusual in late-twentieth-century commodity culture. Anandi Ramamurthy articulated this phenomenon in reference to fashion magazines in the late 1980s and early 1990s (for example, *Marie Claire*, *Company*), citing jewelry and makeup evoking "Arabia behind the Veil" and harem themes as exoticizing fads and marketing strategies.[31] In that larger convergence between fashion and ethnography, **Afghan Girl** effectively reversed those advertising ploys, absorbing the Other into the fashionable familiar.

The implications of this transposition are important. For the purposes of a fashion magazine, a woman is chosen to personify and project the current canon of beauty for its own sake, whereas in this case, the girl epitomizes that canon and simultaneously represents something else—the Afghan refugee. That she might epitomize beauty and typify "Afghan refugee" at the same time suggest that some of the image's power is due to a successful conflation of likeness and alterity. Perhaps the most significant manifestation of this doubled resonance is that the Afghan girl became the *poster child* for the tragic and intractable conflict in Afghanistan.

In order to understand her peculiarly postmodern and remarkably sustained ability to mobilize sympathy, it is useful to look at the history of media-fueled philanthropy. Beginning with Franklin Delano Roosevelt's birthday balls to benefit research for polio (ultimately known as the March of Dimes),[32] many charities have mounted fundraising campaigns that rely on the universal solicitude for and identification with children. Historically, these efforts revolve around images of overt pain or severe physical disability. Thus a "poster child" is often depicted in grim straits, the victim of disease, war, drought, or famine.

In the case of the Afghan girl, however, the mechanism has been shifted. She is not obviously injured or malnourished, nor is she depicted in a ghastly setting. Her suffering has not been valorized or ennobled; instead, it has been aestheticized. Thus, she epitomizes the updated poster child—the beautiful female victim. In image-conscious, voyeuristic America, this is more compelling viewing than graphically explicit deprivation, disease, or injury. She seems exotic, perhaps, but also appealing. In effect, the viewer can envy, relate to or, perhaps most pertinently, desire one so pretty and simultaneously help that person from a position of comfort and privilege. In the words of one online viewer: "McCurry's photograph of the Afghan girl makes her seem real—not an abstract "Muslim" girl, but a girl we might

30. Catherine Lutz and Jane Collins, "The Photograph As an Intersection of Gazes," in Liz Wells, ed., *The Photography Reader* (London/New York: Routledge, 2003), pp. 358–62.

31. Anandi Ramamurthy, "Commercial photography, image banks and corporate media," in Liz Wells, ed., *Photography: A Critical Introduction*, third edition, (New York: Routledge), pp. 229–35. This article discusses a particular time period, but there are many chapters in fashion history that might be cited.

32. Scott Cutlip, *Fund Raising in the United States, Its Role in America's Philanthropy* (Rutgers, NJ: Rutgers University Press, 1965), pp. 351–93. Related but tangential is Jack A. Nelson, "The Invisible Cultural Group: Images of Disability," in Paul Martin Lester, ed., *Images That Injure* (Westport, CT: Praeger, 1996), pp. 119–27. The notion of the "poster child" deserves further scrutiny. "Beyond Affliction: The Disability History Project," a four-hour, National Public Radio documentary directed by Laurie Block, began with a segment entitled "Inventing the Poster Child."

know and care about and want to help."[33]

That the Afghan girl looks like a cover girl but acts like a poster child is consistent with a rhetorically ambiguous realm between fashion photography, advertising, photojournalism, and humanitarian campaign, in which consumerism and morality overlap in peculiar and problematic ways. Also symptomatic of this complex arena are the controversial advertising campaigns entitled "**Colors of Benetton**." In one of the advertisements undertaken in collaboration with the World Food Program (**PLATE 44**), an Afghan female is posed frontally for the camera, twice; in the left-hand image, she is completely enveloped in a blue, embroidered *chadri*,[34] whereas in the adjoining image she is shown with the chadri folded neatly back to expose her face and to display the elaborate needlework on the fabric now framing it. Thus, the needlework becomes an attribute of the woman and vice versa. This nexus of commodities is where the consumer's eye rests. Immediately juxtaposed with the embroidery/face, a caption provides the imagination with a few factoids:

> Food for work.
>
> Basima, 16, is supported with food aid in Afghanistan. She now hopes to find work as an embroiderer in Kabul.

Like **Afghan Girl**, the advertisement leaves much unspecified and capitalizes on the striking appearance of the girl. In this case, however, the open-endedness is vested in the very process of encountering the spread. Simply by reading the page from left to right, as a literate European/American would do, the viewer participates in the act of unveiling the woman; thereafter, the limited palette and the asymmetry of the layout accelerate attention toward the face, then the embroidery, and finally, the color contrasts of the right-hand margin. Veiled and unveiled, the woman is offered up frontally as an object for scrutiny and delectation. Only after that do we focus on the adjoining text (which itself deserves more comment than current space allows).

The aggressive frontality of the figure is critical.[35] Due to this bluntness, the image arguably falls somewhere between police lineup, identity card, and employment agency listing, and we are left wondering how to relate to her. As a veiled victim? Potential employee? Respectfully depicted producer of the embroidery that she wears? All of the above?

Like so many Benetton images, contradictory readings are purposely fostered, and the viewer is variously implicated. While there may be some viewers who linger simply over the aesthetic audacity of the advertisement and others who indulge in fantasy (the perennial "harem" scene with a new twist?) before moving on, all viewers will, I think, be obliged to grapple with the idea of veiling, since that is the action depicted in the photograph. The targeted viewer is expected (presumably) to look long enough to read the words and construct a narrative based on the assumption that the girl, Basima, is the victim of a cultural system that veils (sequesters/abuses) women, leaving them without adequate food or gainful employment.

Thus, the rationale might go, the viewer is seduced and then challenged, prodded to acknowledge if not to alleviate the woman's suffering by contributing to the World Food Program or by buying Benetton products or both.[36] The caption provides further direction, yoking humanitarian organization, commercial backer, and beautiful beneficiary (who, in-

33. Tina Manley, posting to Leica Users Group, March 13, 2002. Tina Manley<images@InfoAve.net

34. In mass media, this garment is often called a "burqa." That word is not generally used in Afghanistan; the garment is typically called a *chador* or *chadri*.

35. John Tagg comments on frontality as a signal of inferiority. John Tagg, *The Burden of Representation* (Amherst, MA: University of Massachusetts Press, 1988), pp. 36–7.

36. Benetton advertising strategies over the last twenty years have been controversial. See Henry A. Giroux, "Consuming Social Change: The 'United Colors of Benetton,'" *Cultural Critique*, no. 26 (Winter 1993): 5–32. Regarding Benetton's collaboration with the World Food Program, see "Benetton ads take a sober look at world hunger," *San Francisco Chronicle*, March 8, 2003.

cidentally, looks not unlike the more famous Afghan girl). Can one rationalize this image, then, as an ethical spectacle, letting us look but encouraging us to give? Or not?

Rather than offering answers to such troubling questions, I have tried simply to pose them, situating **Afghan Girl** in reference to a larger ethos of charity, commodification, and consumption (specifically of female beauty) and simultaneously pointing to some concepts and contexts that are pertinent. I turn now to a diachronic consideration of remakings of the image. This, I hope, will serve to articulate how many different ways **Afghan Girl** functioned, to provide a case study in the production of visual culture, and to trace a spiraling process of canonization and commercial gain. For each instance of remaking the image, the applied caption will serve as the key to the recalibrated meaning of the portrait and to the embedded agendas of image purveyors.

Steve McCurry himself capitalized on the power and appeal of his photograph, republishing it in a book entitled *Portraits*, a selection of images depicting people whom he had encountered traveling around the world.[37] First published in 1999, the book has been reprinted at least six times since then, a remarkable entrepreneurial success. It is an album of portrait photographs, laid out to simulate direct and intimate encounters between viewer and sitter. Few words intervene. At the beginning, there is a very short preface written by the author, and each portrait is given a brief caption providing only the place and year that the photograph was taken. The images are, like **Afghan Girl**, mostly bust-length, close-cropped portraits of single individuals looking directly at the viewer from sites ranging from Los Angeles to Hong Kong. Described in the preface as "chance connections in a world of resilience," the pictures are intended to record "the essential soul peeking out, experience etched on a person's face."

37. Steve McCurry, *Portraits* (New York: Phaidon, 1999). Reprinted 1999, 2000 (twice), 2001 (twice), 2002.

Although McCurry began his career as a photojournalist and these images derive from his travels as a reporter, the purpose of such an album was clearly not journalistic but rather, universalizing. As the introduction instructs us, the images were explicitly intended to transcend particular circumstances and to address something more general or fundamental about the human condition. Exhibiting deracinated beauty in this manner effectively presents the anonymous individuals as exquisite objects in a handheld gallery. In the process, the journalist positions himself as a fine-art photographer, and the viewer implicitly becomes the worldly connoisseur. Publishing and captioning his work in this manner was thus an act of contemporary Orientalism in which McCurry recreated himself even as he represented others in the guise and consumption of the photographic image.

Easily McCurry's most famous photograph, **Afghan Girl** serves as the cover image for *Portraits*. While *National Geographic* had specified its meaning as the archetypal Afghan refugee, here the viewer is directed toward the universal appeal of a beautiful face by a new caption, the appended title *Portraits*. The names of publisher and photographer serve as supplemental captions of a promotional nature. ("Phaidon" is the most prominent word on the cover, underscoring the identity of the editor/producer and linking the book with the publisher's other, similarly marketed products.) Thus, the now-autonomously powerful picture functions in a new constellation of meanings to bring luster to its sponsors and affiliates.

If *Portraits* recast the Afghan girl, increasingly disengaged from the specific tragedy of Afghanistan and more complexly entangled in American consumerism, the book provided inspiration for yet another iteration of the photograph, this time on the cover of a glossy calendar for the year 2002 (**PLATE 9**). In this rendition, the image was cropped almost oppressively close and overprinted in the upper-left corner with the name of the sponsoring institution, Amnesty International, along with the name of the photographer. This act of captioning positioned **Afghan Girl** in a different constellation of meanings, detailed by a text printed inside the front cover.

That text describes Steve McCurry as "photographer, groundbreaker, risk-taker" and also discusses another inspirational figure to whom the calendar is dedicated—Aung San Suu Kyi, leader of Burma's National League for Democracy. After fulsome praise for these two individuals, Amnesty's executive director explained the resonance between his institution's mission and McCurry's photography:

> In the introduction to his book, *Portraits*, McCurry writes, 'The portraits...speak a desire for human connection; a desire so strong that people...open themselves to the camera, all in the hope that at the other end someone else will be watching—someone who will laugh or suffer with them.' Amnesty International's message is similar. To the torturers and executioners: know that we are watching. And to the survivors: take heart; we suffer with you and will never give up the struggle.

Thus glossed, the image was deployed as part of a larger promotional package: Amnesty International was, in effect, crafting its own image campaign, affiliating itself with famous people (and photographs) and publicizing its record of "More than Forty Years of Defending Human Rights." This is a significant pivot in the life cycle of the image, for at this juncture the convergence between consumption and philanthropy is most proximate. Amnesty International used **Afghan Girl** for humanitarian as well as promotional ends by marketing a carefully calculated artifact: "This calendar with its vibrant and moving portraits is a must have for any lover of fine photography." Moreover, placing **Afghan Girl** on the cover suggested that this was the finest of the fine photographs. Thus, the calendar provided a site of potent and generative contiguity between discriminating spectatorship and humanitarian activism. Simultaneously, the picture that initially served to illustrate a magazine article was propelled into "collectible" status.

The calendar owner's political convictions and aesthetic standards (solidarity with Amnesty's cause and appreciation of McCurry's photographs) were demonstrated in the act of exhibition, but the calendar itself is an artifact of some ambiguity. Amnesty's text claims a stance of witnessing; McCurry's photographs offer an opportunity for spectatorship. In bringing these positions together, the calendar poses a quandary. Ownership and exhibition, after all, entail the exercise of power and the enjoyment of privilege. What does one do? Look or give?

Some viewers, not satisfied with a mass-produced and disposable calendar but fascinated nonetheless by **Afghan Girl**, might seek to acquire a signed print of McCurry's photograph. Available for purchase through Magnum, McCurry's agency, for a considerably larger sum, with or without a frame, such an artifact is more commonly called "art," a status reinforced by that peculiarly powerful caption, "the artist's signature." Unlike a calendar, which is overtly time-bound and lacks a grand frame, such a signed print is authentic, unique, costly, and timeless; owning it is the option of an elite clientele with concern for posterity and status.

This tangle of image-making and remaking, witnessing and voyeurism, activism and ownership is emblematic of varied behaviors often termed "Orientalism," in which the visual and material evidence of contact with other cultures becomes the trophy, the treasured possession, the evidence of (Christian) charity. Whether a relic from the Holy Land, a bronze ewer from an "oriental" bazaar, a mass-produced wall calendar, an oil painting over the fireplace, or a signed photograph in the hallway, the transposition of culture into artifact enables the privileged owner to feel worldly, enlightened, and proprietary while maintaining a discrete and safe distance from those who ostensibly need help.[38]

38. For a general discussion of this phenomenon see Holly Edwards, *Noble Dreams, Wicked Pleasures: Orientalism in America, 1870–1930* (Princeton, NJ: Princeton University Press in association with the Sterling and Francine Clark Art Institute, 2000), pp. 11–57.

But consider also those who actively seek to help the distant disadvantaged. A photograph taken by Ron Haviv in the Taliban Ministry for the Prevention of Vice and the Promotion of Virtue (**PLATE 11**) suggests some of the complexities of humanitarian activism. It shows materials confiscated from the offices of Shelter Now—an American aid group accused of proselytizing Christianity in Afghanistan—strewn haphazardly across the floor in a still life of evangelical altruism. Here, **Afghan Girl** appears in note-card form with yet another caption: "Greeting [sic] from Afghanistan" and in the lower left in smaller letters: "Eyes of an Afghan (words following are illegible) speak about war and fear." Such a note card might connect an activist in Afghanistan with those in America. Juxtaposed with a two-dollar manufacturer's coupon for a Ross breast pump and the covers of two Christian videos ("Jesus," lauded for its "meticulous attention to authenticity," and "The Bible" on video, specifically the Book of Genesis), the note card closes the circle from journalism to confessional jingoism, undergirding the conviction that the war and fear endemic in Afghanistan might be alleviated by believing in Jesus. And so, we must ask, is this "help" helpful?

But the story is not over. If the saga began with a cover for *National Geographic*, it continued with the magazine's subsequent willingness to capitalize on the fame of **Afghan Girl**. As the photograph captivated public attention, *National Geographic* extended the iconic quality of the image by publishing the photograph in another context, this time in a coffee-table book reproducing the magazine's "best" photographs (**PLATE X**). Again, **Afghan Girl** is on the cover—now a full-fledged icon, a postmodern and endlessly reproduced Mona Lisa.[39]

39. Donald Sassoon, *Becoming Mona Lisa, The Making of a Global Icon* (New York: Harcourt, 2001) pp. 239–75.

As such, the portrait had tremendous marketing potential. Editors were clearly convinced that putting that icon on the cover would help to *sell* a book of *National Geographic*'s trademark, exquisite photographs. This is the appropriation of a famous, beautiful face for the purposes of making money as well as the fraught slide between art and sales pitch. The image was further absorbed into the arsenal of *National Geographic*'s marketing campaigns prior to Christmas 2002 (**PLATE 12**): *The 100 Best Photographs* (with **Afghan Girl** on the cover) was produced in a "Special Member's Edition" to be sent FREE to anyone who ordered a year of *National Geographic* at a forty-three-percent discount. A magazine subscription was trumpeted as "the perfect last-minute gift" and "the easiest gift selection you'll make all year long. Just add your love—let us handle the rest!" The same ploy was simplified for the year-round campaign wherein the potential subscriber was encouraged to "Remember someone special with a gift membership!" Save forty-three percent off the newsstand price and "Get a Free Gift! 100 Best Pictures." With such rhetoric, **Afghan Girl** functioned as a well-oiled cog in the machinery of *National Geographic* marketing and American consumption, in the guise of an image/object worth owning, a gift worth giving, a prize worth winning.

Arguably, at the height of her face-fame in America, the Afghan girl was still, on some level, the Afghan poster child. But she was an anonymous type, linked almost vestigially with her homeland. At the same time, she had become another type as well, one of the countless cover girls of American materialism, delegated to sell diverse causes and varied products. And so, one must ask, which culture does this image document most profoundly, that which it purports to represent or that which it serves most loyally?

The next layer of the story details an imbricated Orientalism, folded seamlessly over on itself and disseminated widely; in it, the image comes to function both in the culture that it fascinates as well as in the culture that it ostensibly represents. This non-linear phenomenon occurred against the backdrop of political events of the late twentieth century. Afghanistan's refugee crisis had continued to unfold in the late 1980s and 1990s, entailing a major diaspora and brain drain to the West. The Soviets had left Afghanistan ignominiously, the mujahideen ran rampant with weapons supplied by the United States, and finally, the Taliban achieved power in 1996, wresting control out of chaos and rubble. With ghastly implacability, the Taliban moved from moral to pious to rigid. They enacted abusive laws curtailing the actions and the very visibility of women, they prohibited most forms of public entertainment, and they outlawed photography and cinema. In the United States, 9/11 happened, Osama bin Laden was implicated, and Afghanistan was, throughout the process, on the front page.

At the height of Taliban power, press coverage of Afghanistan was replete with familiar tropes—barbaric warlords, iconoclastic mullahs, and veiled women predominating. But even a cursory glance at the mass media of that time suggests that the veil itself seemed to stand between cultures, a symbol of divergent social norms. Lifting the veil became the standard Western metaphor for explaining the situation; shedding the veil was deemed necessary for rectifying the situation.[40]

It was at this juncture that *National Geographic* mounted a campaign to find the Afghan girl. Previously, her anonymity had occasioned little comment. At this point, however, public outrage at the Taliban oppression of women mushroomed, and *National Geographic* sought to address the situation within the pages of the magazine. The goal was to find the girl and document her life as it had unfolded first under the mujahideen and then under the Taliban.

The result was the reappearance of the now-famous image on the magazine's cover—an enigmatic, even surreal contrivance, a picture within a picture (**PLATE 10**).[41] In its basic features, the composite is no different than the pictures taken earlier in the century: an unknown woman stands totally veiled and minimally contextualized. In this image, however, the woman is clutching a photograph of her younger self—in effect, a matron exhibiting her lost virginity.

40. The sheer number of headlines, book titles, exhibitions, and editorials invoking the veil would overwhelm these notes, but one useful collection of perspectives is David A. Bailey and Gilane Tawadros, ed., *Veil: Veiling, Representation and Contemporary Art* (Cambridge, MA: Massachusetts Institute of Technology, 2003).

41. Pictures within pictures have a long history, but in cases where the images are photographs-within-portrait-photographs, there is a grammar of honor, commemoration, and exposure that deserves further study.

If there is a sexual valence to this photograph, there is also a flexing of image-making muscle. In veiling and unveiling his subject and recording the results, Steve McCurry (sponsored by *National Geographic*) intervened in this woman's world to determine the terms of her visibility. Had she been left alone, she would have lived her life veiled and segregated, in conformance with indigenous canons of propriety. In this sequence, however, the veil did not provide the protection, status, or respectability that it would ordinarily bring her; instead, the veil effectively became the photographer's trophy and also the symbol of her subjugation for Western audiences.

The woman still remained an anonymous cover girl, in a sense, but this time her image was captioned with a single descriptor, "Found," a word that resonates more with a misplaced mitten than with a person. The primary message of such a gloss is to celebrate the accomplishment of tracking down the girl everyone knows, a victory for the journalist and, by extension, for the American institutions that participated in the search, such as the FBI, capable of finding anyone, anywhere, anytime.

Contrary to expectation, the composite photograph did not signal a feature article about the woman behind the veil. Preceding even the table of contents, the brief text was akin to a news flash—provocative, titillating, and, above all, open ended. In it, we begin to learn something about Sharbat Gula and her harrowing refugee experience in photographs that unceremoniously lay bare her domestic circumstances in a few glossy pages. We also learn quite a bit more about Steve McCurry, his collaboration with *National Geographic*, and cutting-edge forensic technologies. Ultimately, however, the story is effectively the trailer for a movie: "The Search for the Afghan Girl," a video narrated by Sigourney Weaver and available for sale at *National Geographic* stores or online.

In order to appreciate the tone and character of the movie, one need look no further than the cover of the video box. There, the famous photograph, held in the hands of the purple *chadri*,[42] is reprised yet again, framed in *National Geographic*'s signature yellow border. The new caption takes yet another tack, identifying the star of the show by her American name, "Afghan Girl," while the third line named the video's narrator, Sigourney Weaver. While it is a testament to the fame of **Afghan Girl** that Ms. Weaver got second billing, the captioning betrays the extent to which the icon eclipsed the living, breathing person—Sharbat Gula.

42. The color of the *chadri* that Sharbat Gula wears is critical to the impact of the image. While the garment's design is typical of Afghan production, the color is anomalous. Intended to counter visibility, these veils are usually reticent in hue—gray-blue, light green, sober gold, or plain white. I cannot help but wonder whether the bold purple of this one is an aesthetically motivated contrivance.

If the front cover resembles a movie marquee, the text on the back cover reads like a sensationalistic press release, heralding a drama of high suspense in which the viewer is invited to participate: "The search is on to find the nameless woman whose youthful image became a global symbol of wartime dignity, resilience and survival.... Journey to the Afghan-Pakistan border.... Follow clues and rumors through the twisting byways of a teeming refugee camp...witness FBI investigators applying cutting-edge technology to crack the ultimate "missing person" case...."

This punchy language is *National Geographic*'s characteristic strategy for providing "unmediated" and exciting encounters with things outside the American mundane, albeit updated for a new medium. Couching the story in mystery and situating it in the "twisting byways of a teeming refugee camp" is not-so-updated Orientalism serving as marketing ploy. All too familiar also is the contrived storyline itself: in a race against time, the enterprising male journalist penetrates the exotic culture and ultimately gets the girl. Predictable as well is the minimal role allotted to Sharbat Gula. Breathlessly described during the search as the Holy Grail, she occupies only a very few minutes at the end of a video when she is "Found." Otherwise, the video is almost entirely devoted to the experiences and stamina of Steve McCurry and the sophistication of American forensic technology.

While an analysis of this movie is beyond the scope of this essay, one point deserves particular attention. Earlier, I pointed out that Sharbat Gula became the poster child for the Afghan cause. In the context of the video, her potential to generate funds for that cause was deployed in the form of a narrative denouement. This transpires at the end of the video, after Sharbat Gula has been tracked down and definitively identified by examination of her vivid, green irises. Finally, she is interviewed, or having been "found," now she is miked. As the narrator explains, "The face that inspired so many to give now has a voice."

The newly granted "voice" (actually a translator's voice-over) then expresses a desire for her children to attend school. That statement, in turn, provides the rhetorical springboard for a representative of *National Geographic* to come onscreen and invite viewers to contribute to *National Geographic*'s Afghan Girls Fund, "created to assist in the development and delivery of educational opportunities for young Afghan women and girls."

Sharbat Gula's participation in this promotional campaign, perhaps levied at the expense of her personal privacy and local dignity, has attracted considerable attention in philanthropic circles. In an article entitled "Face of Afghanistan Prompts Thousands to Give," Tom Watson described how the campaign to find the Afghan girl earned *National Geographic* kudos among charity pundits:[43] in 2003, for its innovative approach to online contributions and direct aid to Afghanistan, The National Geographic Society was a finalist for a Blackbaud Technovation award. With a revised web site, diverse public programs, and an online campaign, *National Geographic* had generated more than half a million dollars for the Afghan Girls Fund at the time of the awards.

43. Tom Watson, "Face of Afghanistan Prompts Thousands to Give." www.onphilanthropy.com October 5, 2003.

In the article, the "viral effect" of this campaign was applauded: the story of the Afghan girl spread quickly and generated large contributions. In explaining these accomplishments, Watson pointed to the photograph of the Afghan girl as "the center of a pioneering fundraising effort," thereby proving the old fundraising maxim that "people give to people": "Her face has become an icon for photographers around the world—the keen, brave and vulnerable face of an Afghan teenager in a Pakistan refugee camp, her sharp green eyes staring at the lens with a directness that was astonishing in a culture that keeps its women veiled from the world." This testimony effectively recapitulated the manner and extent to which the Afghan girl came to serve America and to personify Afghanistan—as cover girl and as photogenic veil.

On one level, the Afghan girl's success as fundraiser highlights the vexed proximity between political activism and transgressive intervention and the fraught overlap between humanitarian aid and condescension. Clearly, the desire to fund schools for Afghan girls is laudable, and clearly, too, the need is great. The challenge, however, rests in the performance of that seemingly altruistic aspiration, for beneath the good intentions, there may be problematical transactions between benefactor and beneficiary in which, for instance, the charitable patron knows best what veiled women need, or the patron unilaterally overrides indigenous cultural norms to provide for those needs in the name of a greater good. In this case, Sharbat Gula knew nothing of the use of her image until she was "found," and its prior dissemination generated no income for her, even as it ran counter to her society's code of propriety and gender segregation. Indeed, Sharbat Gula's recompense (at least, that which is public knowledge) has been mostly abstract condolence—that her "discovery" seems to have had a verifiable and beneficial impact on humanitarian aid.

Significantly, when a similar sequence of events transpired in New York, the story took a rather different turn.[44] Philip-Lorca diCorcia (see his work in **PLATE 29**) photographed random faces in urban crowds over a period of two years (1999–2001), assembled the images in an exhibition, and published them in a catalogue. (Up to this point, the narrative recalls the account of Steve McCurry and **Afghan Girl**; subsequently, however, it betrays a lurking double standard.) When Erno Nussenzweig, one of diCorcia's anonymous subjects from New York, encountered his picture unexpectedly, he sued on the grounds of invasion of privacy and the right to practice a religion that forbids graven imagery. He could do so legitimately because New York State right-to-privacy laws prohibit the use of a person's likeness for commercial gain, advertising, or trade. The suit demanded the halt of catalogue sales as well as more than a million dollars in assorted damages. While the case is still unresolved, it was initially dismissed on the grounds that diCorcia had a right to artistic expression; this stance was defended with reference to the long tradition of street photography epitomized by the work of Walker Evans and Alfred Eisenstaedt.

44. www.nycourts.gov/reporter/3dseries/2006/2006_50171.htm

The parallels between the New York case and the Afghan one are numerous and (mostly) self-evident; what is less clear are the disparities and their implications. If Nussenzweig has a lawyer demanding compensation for damages, why doesn't Sharbat Gula? How is a New Yorker's right to privacy different than an Afghan's practice of gender segregation? Does the practice of one's art trump the practice of another's religion? What rights do Americans enjoy at the expense of Others?

There are countless other iterations of **Afghan Girl**—some legal, some bootlegged—many of which would add nuance and complexity to this story. However, two instances are particularly noteworthy, for they demonstrate how the photograph of an Afghan refugee taken by an American photographer has been absorbed back into contemporary Afghan culture. B. C. C. Breshna Card Company of Kabul, for example, produced a poster version of the image with yet another caption (**PLATE 8**). This time, the portrait was simply entitled "Afghanistan" in large letters, obliging the familiar face to stand for the country as a whole. It is not apparent what market this poster targeted, but it is clear that Afghan entrepreneurs deployed a female face, and an American icon, to represent their own country. Again, one wonders whether Sharbat Gula was consulted.

The extent to which the photograph has been interpolated back with a consumerist twist is evidenced in another incarnation of **Afghan Girl**, this one documented midway through the *National Geographic* video: McCurry's hunt is temporarily stalled and he wanders distractedly in a bazaar in Peshawar, not far from the refugee camp where Sharbat

Gula once lived. There, he unexpectedly encounters his own photograph, illegally reproduced and offered for sale in various different sizes. Stripped of its original narrative, its fundraising connotation, and its iconic (American) significance, the portrait is exhibited for sale in a Pakistani storefront, along with images of Bollywood stars and other items of consumer culture.

Such a shop and such a display would not have been possible under Taliban rule; indeed, it was precisely the plethora and power of such images that the Taliban feared and proscribed. That Taliban iconoclasm and stringent codes of veiling in Afghanistan coincided with the stardom and American exposure of **Afghan Girl** is not without significance. From one perspective in this story, the ideal was a cover girl; from another, the ideal was a covered girl. From yet another vantage point, the visibility and the agency of women are culturally limited in both cases, for while Taliban atrocities were obviously a more egregious transgression of women's rights than the stifling values of fashion-conscious America, declaring that these attitudes are *categorically* different is specious. Such a claim rests on Orientalist convictions about a benighted other and an enlightened self. What the case of **Afghan Girl** additionally reveals, however, is how mechanically reproduced images have contributed to the institutionalization and preeminence of peculiarly American attitudes and practices in the global arena.

A CODA

In closing and in passing, I note that **Afghan Girl**, with its original yellow frame, was recently reproduced in *The Abrams Encyclopedia of Photography*. There, the *National Geographic* cover serves as the emblematic example of travel photography, and the photographer adventurer/photojournalist is identified as a key player in contemporary visual culture. Similar publications, often gracing coffee tables, are categorized as "spectacle books," and the armchair traveler is named their primary consumer.[45] In this incarnation out of so many, **Afghan Girl** has been awarded the ultimate academic accolade—taxonomic status. Thus enshrined (and reduced) for the next generation to encounter, the portrait also still graces the cover of a box of note cards for sale at the store down the street in my hometown. This story has no end in sight.

45. Brigitte Govignon, ed., *The Abrams Encyclopedia of Photography* (New York: Harry N. Abrams, 2004), p. 178.

MIEKE BAL

THE PAIN OF IMAGES

FIRST ENCOUNTERS, SECOND THOUGHTS

When looking at a man looking at his mirror image showing his body devastated by disease and with an undefined look—resignation, assessment, or shock?—I feel overwhelmed by a turbulence of contradictory emotions (**FIG. 1**). Given the date of the photograph (1987) and the man's young, beautiful, but skeletal face and emaciated chest, the association with AIDS is inevitable, and I feel grief, compassion, and anger. But those feelings have nowhere to go. This is "just" a photograph, both real and distant, both private and utterly public, a moment both unique and extended beyond the grave. Alone, I am not witnessing anyone's suffering. In all likelihood, the man is long dead, and he will never know that, in 2006, someone unknown to him felt an emotion for him that might approximate grief.

FIGURE 1
NICHOLAS NIXON, *TOM MORAN*, OCTOBER 1987.
COURTESY OF THE ARTIST.

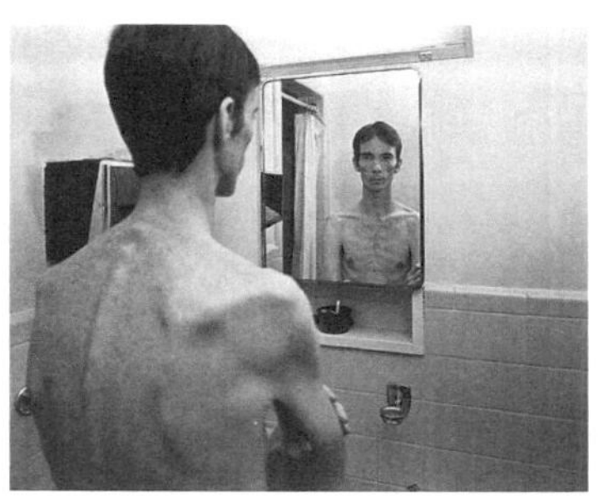

Even more than the obvious problem of the exploitation of suffering for pleasure or money, this diffuse quality of emotion is, for me, problem number one of the "traffic in pain" that the exhibition "Beautiful Suffering" analyzes and questions, and to an extent, inevitably and boldly performs. It is the problem of sentimentality, of an identification that either appropriates someone else's pain or exploits it to feel oneself feeling at a time when the overflow of visual representations of suffering tends to inure one to the confrontation—and thus to feel good about oneself. The resulting exchange is too unfair—twenty years ago this man was dying, and I am enjoying myself at a photography exhibition. And I am the one to benefit? Something is just not right.

Nicholas Nixon's photograph of Tom Moran also raises a second issue, evoked by the show's title: beauty, in its conjunction to suffering.[1] Both Moran and his mirror portrait are "beautiful." No doubt about it. His unreadable eyes and the perfectly arched brows draw attention to this quality. The iconography—man looking into mirror—invokes the endless numbers of beautiful women looking narcissistically into mirrors that punctuate the history of Western art. Venus is here, indeed; she is ironically invoked, then dismissed. Moran is standing, not lying on a lush bed. Most important, he is alone with his confrontational reflection. He is not looking at himself for narcissistic gratification. Nor is a chubby little putto enticing him into sexual traffic. But still, there is beauty in the photograph.

Once "beauty" is put on the table, the perfection of the black-and-white photograph adds its connotation of "art." The composition is quiet and perfectly balanced; the center of the image is divided between Moran's back (a bit to the left of it), and his face (a bit to the right). The shower curtain that is in the exact middle of the picture plane is decentered in depth but stubbornly imports the double notion of hygiene and hiding, subliminal elements in the ideological discourse of AIDS. The tones and lighting are also balanced to perfection, with an harmonious distribution of shining and muted (dull?) surfaces. And the coffee cup on the shelf—a prop in this theatrical setting—reminds us (we clearly need it) that Moran is real.

This is a work of art. Perhaps we can call it commemorative art, but given that it addresses an issue of public policy, it must be seen first and foremost as political art. It indicts the indifference to suffering that people dying of AIDS must encounter in a sex-phobic culture that is quick to blame such disasters on their personal Fall from Paradise. At least, I suppose the art work aims to perform such an indictment. In its function and status as political, committed, or concerned art, this photograph is fruitfully compared to the infamous Benetton poster of another AIDS victim, used by a multinational business to sell more clothes. That picture, too, was "beautiful." The question of art—including expertly made advertisements—in relation to pain is a question of aesthetics and its aloofness from, yet tenacious embeddedness in, the "real world." That question is particularly acute for the sub-genre that has that relationship in its very definition—political art.

Together, these two issues receive a specifically problematic nuance in the face of photography, the medium so troublesomely bound up with reality. With photographs of human subjects who suffer, it is not possible to be carried away in awe of artistic mastery. Tom Moran, at some point in history, "really" stood alone in his bathroom and faced himself, looking as sick as he does. He, as much as the artwork, questions the indifference of aesthetics and wonders about the politics that inform it, as well as the possibility of politically effective art.

Within walking distance, so to speak, is **Sudan**, James Nachtwey's indictment of another criminal indifference (**PLATE 21**). The photograph is less obviously "art," although also

1. Although the original checklist for "Beautiful Suffering" included *Tom Moran*, the picture was replaced late in the curatorial process by *Tony Mastrorilli* (Plate 25) another portrait from Nicholas Nixon's *People with AIDS* series. Nixon kindly granted permission to reproduce *Tom Moran* for this essay.

well made to an almost troubling degree. It clearly appeals to a scandalized awareness of the murderous nature of famine. The man in this 1993 photograph is not even able to see his own devastated body in the mirror. Even so, his pose is reminiscent of that of the traditional Venus. It reminds us, that is, of the impossibility of severing the ties between "art" and "life": a dying man in Sudan—a Venus in an art museum. But, living, if that's what it's called, in the street, he doesn't seem likely to own a mirror. Nor would he want to see himself, his skeleton more visible than anything he once embodied, one step before inevitable death. He can't stand up either. He is more dead than alive, and the hand that gives him something—money?—or to which he gives something—a plea for help?—seems to mock his incapacity to stand up and buy himself some food with any money that he might get. Is this political art, or is it voyeuristic journalism or journalism as political intervention? And what does it tell us that sometimes the difference is hard to tell?[2]

2. We know from textually supplemented information, not from the image itself, that famine victims received rehydration salts (and food) from volunteer aid workers, which makes this a likely act of handing out salts. But we cannot see this. See James Nachtwey, *Inferno* (London: Phaidon, 2000).

The questions of empathy, sympathy, or identification—of bottomless but directionless emotion as well as the seemingly opposite question of aesthetics and its required disinterestedness—are bound up with the most obvious problem of what the exhibition's subtitle pointedly calls "the traffic in pain." It concerns exploitation. When advertisements can change places with art, the one practice reflects on the other. The third problem this show raises, then, concerns the economic aspect of the noun "traffic." More than any other art form, photography of people confronts us with the economic unfairness of an exchange where the subject is exposed, even in the most painful and intimate moments, while the photographer cashes the earnings the viewer is willing to give.

Even if the man in Sudan got paid for Nachtwey's photograph—and I have no doubt that he did—the money, however much, didn't and couldn't save his life. The "subjects" in this exhibition may or may not have been paid—many of the photographs suggest nothing of the kind—but at any rate, they have disappeared. In some cases, a name belatedly remains, sometimes not even that. Yet, it is the *subjects'* imminent death—their pain, their poverty, disease, woundedness, or deprivation—that are exposed for the world to see but not to cure. Their exposure makes them vulnerable while the reason they are here on display is that they are already wounded. Their exposure, moreover, is someone else's merchandise.

In the face of the possibility that they do not get paid, or paid in proportion to their enduring exposure, or are given no chance to endorse the circulation of their image, this exposure can become a second suffering—a theft of their subjectivity, precisely, because they are is in pain. Looking at their pain is, in this sense, a secondary exploitation. In addition to emotional misdirection and the further abduction of subjectivity through the traffic in beauty, exploitation, then, is a third problem. All these and many more consequences of exhibiting images of pain move in the same direction: an art "of suffering" is a problem, not a given. This exhibition is an inquiry into that problem. In this essay, I will elaborate the notion that such art is only justifiable if it effectively qualifies as political art. To make that case, and to ponder what it may mean, I will expose some of the difficulties of the phrase "political art." By means of this exhibition, both its problems and its potential—though always partial and provisional—solutions, I hope to propose ways in which we can pursue thinking about political art in productive ways.

EXHIBITIONARY POLITICS

My first discussion concerns the exhibition—the theme, the title, the collected artifacts, and the mode of their display. Art exhibitions, routinely mounted to show a body of work—most frequently that of an artist, a movement, or a period but sometimes selected around a theme—are quite specific qua "visual events." As such, they both cater to a public and "dialogue" with that public; they are, potentially, forms of thought. It is worth considering the exhibition "Beautiful Suffering" as an episode within a recent tradition in the management of art's relationship to the public. It can be seen as continuing, modifying, and reconfirming the practice of self-conscious, creative curating.[3]

Personally, I know this tradition best from exhibitions in Europe, but it is much more widespread. Through exhibitions in the 1980s and 1990s of work by Rudi Fuchs, Harald Szeemann, Catherine David, and many others, the museum-going public was confronted with the retreat of the white cube and, instead, the creation of something like a *Gesammtkunstwerk* of a specifically designed combination of artistic objects. Examples are David's *Documenta X*, Szeemann's collective exhibition at the Venice Biennale, and—one of my favorites—"Parti pris," the series organized by Régis Michel in the 1980s and 1990s that made visitors rediscover the splendors of the graphic arts department at the Louvre. Another exemplary instance was the rare depth of a series of presentations, spanning almost two decades, curated in Toronto by collector Ydessa Hendeles from her own collection of photography and modern art. I consider "Beautiful Suffering" within this tradition.[4]

In connection to "Beautiful Suffering," Hendeles' practice is particularly relevant. An astounding connoisseur of modern art, particularly but not exclusively photography, she straddles the divide between "art" and "life" with unparalleled subtlety. For example, in her exhibition "Partners," held in the historically charged venue of the Haus der Kunst in Munich, she included icons of political photojournalism comparable to Nachtwey's, such as photojournalistic narratives of Malcolm Browne; *The Sacrificial Protest of Thich Quang Duc, June 11, 1963*; and Eddie Adams' *Murder of a Vietcong Suspect, February 1, 1968*, the last two twin emblems of that other war.

Because of its painful theme and its extension beyond art alone, the curatorial focus of "Beautiful Suffering" lies less on the works themselves and more on the issues they raise. In short, it focuses the difficulties of looking on looking at pain. For the visitors to this exhibition, these photographs are hard to look at. This difficulty is not, as is customary, naturalized. Here, the difficulty—undirected emotions, vicarious guilt, indifference as a shield to bear it, and secondary exploitation—is the principle but also the question underlying the show. Its proposed attitude or mode of looking, mobilized so that this mode of looking can be filled with—redirected toward—reflection and self-reflection. Don't misunderstand me; this exhibition is not didactic, because it doesn't have a single message to drive home. Instead, it is philosophical. In a visual discourse, it exposes thoughts without ending, problems without solutions, questions viscerally absorbed and not answered on the spot. True philosophy does not bear closing conclusions. As an exhibition—a public, visual discourse, concentrated in time and space—this show is conceived as an instance of critical visual

3. The term "visual event" is meant to draw attention to the specific situation in which a visual artifact appears, is looked at, absorbed, and further defined by its viewers. The term highlights a refusal to consider art works as autonomous objects that travel through time and space in self-same identity.

4. The exhibition by Hubert Damisch is worth considering as an intervention in this recent tradition. See Damisch, *Traité du trait* (Paris: Musée du Louvre, 1995). Damisch later curated a large exhibition at Museum Boijmans van Beuningen in Rotterdam. See Damisch, *Moves: Playing Chess and Cards with the Museum* (Rotterdam: Museum Boijmans Van Beuningen, 1997). After the projected five installments of the series at the Louvre were completed, Regis Michel continued with two exhibitions of his own design on gender's impact on art. See Michel, *Posseder et Detruire: Strategies Sexuelles dans l'Art d'Occident* (Paris: Musee du Louvre, 2000) and also Michel, *Painting as Crime: The Accursed Share of Modernity* (Paris: Musee du Louvre, 2002). In 2002–03, Hendeles curated *Partners*, her large-scale exhibition at the Haus der Kunst in Munich, with an important, comprehensive catalogue. Ydessa Hendeles, *Partners*, ed. Chris Dercon and Thomas Weski (Munich: Haus der Kunst, 2002). About Hendeles' exhibition, see Mieke Bal, "Exhibition as Film," forthcoming in *Exhibition Experiments*, ed. Paul Baru and Sharon MacDonald (Oxford: Blackwell Publishers, 2007). For more about this tradition, see Bal, "A l'Est d'Eden/East of Eden/Ten Oosten van Eden," *Marthe Wery: Les couleurs du monochrome*, ed. B. P. S. 2 Projects (Tournai: Musee des Beaux Arts, 2005) pp. 35–104 and 119–127.

reflection, an intervention in the field variously called "visual culture," "visual studies," or "visual analysis." Its concern is with the many meanings of "exhibitionism."

But this two-step process—where primary encounters and gut responses are redirected into cultural philosophy—may misfire. It may not work, at least not automatically, and what we would then be left with is precisely that dark complex of sentimentality, enjoyment, and superiority. In this section, I contend that the cultural genre of the exhibition itself cannot be simply refocused; it ushers in a heritage of precisely the problematic, culturally entrenched attitudes that I have indicated, even if the exhibition aims to undermine it. The inherent exhibitionism of exhibitions is one such element: the public flaunting of what is private, risking the destruction of the singularity of, in this case, suffering.

Moreover, an exhibition that is thematic rather than historical or monographic, requires, indeed imposes, a certain unification. Elements of framing provide this unity, without which the exhibition would make no sense at all. The title is not the only element that promotes, in the first instance, a troublesome mode of looking, although the fact that the title is what attracts visitors in the first place is food for thought. The combination, the collection as such, all but prescribes this highly problematic mode of looking as well. Let me phrase bluntly what the show is up against: put about one hundred such photographs together, and the hardship vanishes. One cannot sustain the difficulty through the confrontation with so many photographs, and hence, one must shed it and move on. Aesthetic appreciation, the standard mode of looking at exhibitions, is ready at hand to help out. This is a general issue that pertains to an exhibition itself as a cultural event. But the compilation of these images under this exhibition's concept poses an additional problem, namely, that of the (in?)visibility of suffering.

Some violence here, some famine there; a corpse lying about, a wounded figure and lots of blood (**PLATE 52**), a few veiled women, and a barely visible woman holding the photograph of—the title intimates—her dead son (**PLATE 43**). Or a bearded man with a turban (**PLATE 24**), some grenades lying about (**PLATE 18**), a soldier lying in a dune landscape (**PLATE 36**). Soon, the turbulent emotions vanish and either a customary ease or a profound unease sets in. Especially after the viewer is caught unaware pondering the beauty of certain images, the identificatory mode of looking may be replaced with even annoyance, a feeling of having been trapped. One element in my own unease is doubt, concerning the question of visibility. The images brought together under the banner of the show's title are "of suffering." We must trust the curators on faith. But can we?

After having confessed to sentimentalism, let me play my skeptical persona. How is the gorgeous woman in turquoise—so effectively promoting the beautiful colors of Benetton clothing—*suffering*? (**PLATE 44**). Because of the very tradition of clothing that the image exploits? Two female figures are dressed in the same color—one face invisible behind a veil, the other as beautiful as that of a movie star—in a color-coordinated image where the light-brown eyes enhance the nuanced coloring of a background changing from blue—enhancing the dress—to just a hint of brown, thus enhancing the eyes. I admire the artistry and the beauty of the face with its strong brows; perfectly shaped, large eyes; straight nose and full lips. Hear me assessing a woman's face like a casting agent for a modeling business! The woman we see could live a star's life and be an icon, like Marilyn Monroe. Not that that beauty didn't suffer. So the woman who keeps her face to herself might be better protected against the suffering that enforced unveiling might cause.[5]

I have responded as if there might be two different women in this image for, without the accompanying text, one could easily imagine that this is the case. The text, however, reveals that the two women are in fact one and the same: "Food for Work. Basima, 16, is supported with food aid in Afghanistan. She now hopes to find work as an embroiderer in Kabul." Through this supplement, we can know, or believe, that this is one woman, veiled and unveiled, who is currently out of work. Without the prosthetic writing—which tells of a form of suffering that the image does not show—the dilemma of either exposing or hiding beauty remains. It was this dilemma that the image conveyed when, lacking the biographical text, it was presented on huge European billboards and in the pages of Benetton's *Colors* magazine. For the viewer unwilling to pause over or take in the small, white, rather unobtrusive letters, it is what the exhibition image conveys, too.

More skepticism. Another image of the exoticizing school of confusing beauty and suffering shares many features with the Benetton advertisement. Made for a cover of *National Geographic*, the magazine that conquers the world by exotico-beautification, Steve McCurry's **Afghan Girl** from 1985 (**PLATE 5**), extensively analyzed in this volume by Holly Edwards, enhances the artsy principle of color coordination and composition that Benetton so cleverly deploys. Indeed, between *National Geographic* and its predecessors in the early twentieth century, on the one hand, and Benetton in our time, on the other, the affiliation is as blatant as that between art and journalism. As Edwards' analysis demonstrates, and as "Beautiful Suffering" highlights, this is a case of visual exploitation that goes beyond the commercial aspect of advertising. Of the many different ways this image has been exploited, some have been critically framed in this exhibition by showing the different uses and abuses of the photograph.

But, as the display of multiple images based on this generic one suggests, this exhibition is an attempt to question—not to reiterate—such exploitations. I therefore consider it an attempt to practice a critical visual analysis, or visual philosophy, not in the form of academic writing but in visual practice. One cannot avoid considering, however, adding to that list of exploitations the one in which, precisely, the framings are exposed. For, whatever the photograph says, taken out of context the image of the Afghan girl is infused, in many of its earlier uses *as well as* in this exhibition, with the idea of "suffering" that nothing in it specifically "expresses" or "represents." This is how the exhibition is inevitably exhibitionist, showing off a charitable sentimentality that nothing in the image promotes. Hence, the suffering can only come from the simple combination of the image's title with the exhibition's title. To make a shortcut to a primary message of this display: being Afghan, under Western eyes, equals suffering.

But with the tool of a critical visual analysis, this need not continue to be so. This exhibition, risking the pitfalls and the inevitability of visual ambiguity, is an attempt to perform such an analysis. The very uncertainty over whether it can escape those pitfalls makes it worthwhile pressing the issue of what collecting, exhibiting in juxtaposition, and

5. For a study of Monroe in the context of modernist art, see Griselda Pollock, "Killing Men and Dying Women: Gesture and Sexual Difference," *The Practice of Cultural Analysis: Exposing Interdisciplinary Interpretation*, ed. Mieke Bal (Stanford: Stanford University Press, 1999).

homogenizing images under the heading of suffering can and cannot achieve. This brings me back to the Afghan girl. Let's face it, or her: a saturated and tasty color scheme dominates the composition. First of all, there are the piercing, unsmiling, strikingly light-green eyes so harmonious with the color of the greenish-blue background. The eyes also harmonize with the small patch of the same color, from her dress, in the bottom-left corner of one version, where the color is repeated in a softer hue in the lettering of "A Life."[6]

The comparative perspective of the display of the multiple versions of this image allows us to realize how cropping alone is an aesthetic tool bound up with politics. In the 1985 version, less closely cropped, we can see that this artistic patch of dress actually shows through holes in the shawl, so that poverty and headscarf form as strong a pairing as earth- or blood-like red and Madonna-blue. Between 1985 and 2002, the girl received an individualizing name while losing the visibility of what Benetton-informed people would call poverty. What remained throughout that process of circulation, were the set mouth—colored to match the color of her scarf—and the shape of the headscarf, so elegantly leaving her hair visible.

For those who have been pre-programmed by Western traditions in visual culture, images of the Madonna—also a light-eyed sufferer wearing a headscarf—can start a dialogue about the culture of suffering in a Christianity-dominated Western world. Meanwhile, Manet's *Olympia* has something to add about the insolent look so contemptuous and dismissive of the viewer, his preconceptions, and his voyeurism. *Olympia*, in 2006, still goes around as the quintessential icon of a prostitute, while nothing in Manet's image strictly shows that she is. My guess is that this insistence must make the insolent look at the viewer more bearable. In this respect, the reflection of Olympia in the Afghan girl's eyes involves a measure of suffering on the part of the viewer, dismissed as indiscreet and intrusive. The mother of Jesus is venerated for her role, and her images are admired, not questioned as promoting suffering. But suddenly, that cult of pain is up for scrutiny. Like both these Western icons, Sharbat Gula will live her visual life as Afghan, "hence," suffering, if we fail to face up both to the contrived and prettified color scheme of the image and also to the resistance in her eyes against being stereotyped. This might make this photograph as good an emblem as any of the mission of visual analysis mission to critique. Visual analysis, I like to think, is about *facing*.[7]

Let's face, for example, the handsome man in Fazal Sheikh's 1992 photograph titled **Bashia Gababo Sharamu, Borana elder from Yabelo** (PLATE 24). He doesn't look happy, but whether, how, and why he is suffering are not *visible*. Only when we read the plea in the accompanying letter do we realize that he stands for an Ethiopian people threatened with violent destruction. The picture itself shows a different history. It is a typifying portrait, showing someone from the "family of man" who is different from "us" and, in that exotic otherness, precious. When read through the traditions of ethnographic photography, the image itself only says something like: look at how handsome these people are; no reason to get rid of them, but if we do, at least their image remains. Within this ethnographic tradition, the image is specified—by means of the turban, the sideways look escaping confrontation, and the beard—as Orientalist. In its visual aesthetic it is timeless, universal-

6. I will have to leave aside the question whether the fact that both this icon of Western charity and the woman in the Benetton ad have such strikingly light eyes might have anything to do with the images' success.

7. My view of visual analysis has been elaborated elsewhere. See Bal, "Visual Analysis," forthcoming in *Handbook of Cultural Analysis*, ed. Tony Bennett and John Frow (Thousand Oaks, CA: Sage Publications). I have elaborated the idea of facing as an important concept in visual analysis in a video installation, "Nothing is Missing." Stills of this video, and a related theoretical analsysis, will be published, under the title, "Facing Severance," in a forthcoming issue of *Intermédialités*. In the recent (2005) re-hanging of twentieth-century art in the Musée National d'Art Moderne (Centre Pompidou) in Paris, Olympia is at the center of a gallery entirely devoted to the theme of "the prostitute." The monumental piece, here, is Larry Rivers' 1963 sculpture *I Like Olympia in Black Face*. For a critique of the automatic interpretation of the figure as a prostitute, see Bal, *Double Exposures: The Subject of Cultural Analysis* (New York: Routledge, 1996), chapter 8.

izing its particularization of "others." This Orientalist tradition hence sets apart what only the Western world can unify as "the East."[8]

But this troublesome similarity to and embedding in an old and compromised visual tradition cannot be maintained in the face of the text that accompanies the photograph. This text is a letter, supposedly from someone of the same people. This letter insinuates both the present and the autobiographical into an image based on distancing in time and culture. That is, if the viewer bothers to read it. Again, the suffering is invisible, but it is readable. For the concept of the exhibition, the need to read—the insufficiency of the visuality of photographs—is one of many points of entry in a reflection on photography's claim to realism. The fact that nothing, in this image as in so many others, shows suffering, together with the addition of text, tells us how deceptive that mythical realism is.

Sheikh's photograph of **Qurban Gul** (**PLATE 43**) performs this visual insufficiency in a different way. The subject—the mother whose son has died—is blurred and dark, hardly visible. She looks like the dream image she describes in the accompanying text. Again, both the suffering and the subjectivity—here, in an autobiographical text of great restraint and intimacy—are introduced by the linguistic supplement. By contrast, the photograph of the son that the phantom mother holds is much clearer. This is an embedded photograph, a memento that the woman clings to and which is therefore utterly private. The suffering is visually muted, but the convention of the memento/photograph replaces it, telling us in a public language of convention what happened, and why the phantom woman suffers. Here, too, the autobiographical voice of the depicted woman disturbs the otherwise facile attraction of the image in its enigmatic aesthetic.[9]

Clearly, all these images raise an issue of the visibility of something so singular, individual, and private as suffering which, for that very reason, is too easy to deny or ignore. Thus, the theme visually addresses the rightly famous, profoundly moving analysis of pain developed by Elaine Scarry.[10] In addition to disease- and otherwise-induced pain, Scarry's analysis lucidly covered the political nature of such disturbing instances as torture and war. Tellingly the first subheading of her introduction is "The Inexpressibility of Physical Pain." In this regard, the question arises whether physical pain is easier to represent visually than to articulate verbally. "Beautiful Suffering," including the images I am questioning as expressive of pain, offers a reflection on this issue, while Scarry's study also suggested possible views.

On the basis of the exhibition, I submit that pain can be, but is not systematically, visible; it is differently but equally hard to represent visually as it is to express verbally. Reversing the perspective and siding with the sufferer is necessary ethically but also intellectually if we are to further our insight on this question. While relentless in her pursuit of an understanding of the real horror of her subjects, Scarry also attempted to offer insights that are potentially helpful for the sufferer. Her major tool is the *imagination*. In light of Scarry's study, I see works such as Sheikh's as struggling with the tension between the invisibility of pain and the need to "speak"—or what Scarry, in another of her eloquent subheadings called "the transformation of body into Voice." Voice, here, is one potential interface between the "radical subjectivity of pain," which comes with "the simple and

8. For a critique of *The Family of Man* (a 1955 exhibition at New York's Museum of Modern Art and a book), see Marianne Hirsch, *Family Frames: Photography, Narrative, and Postmemory* (Cambridge, MA: Harvard University Press, 1997), pp. 48–67. On the roots of Orientalism in Europe, see Edward W. Said's classical study *Orientalism* (New York: Pantheon Books, 1978), critically analyzed in *After Orientalism*, ed. Inge E. Boer (Amsterdam: Rodopi, 2004) and further in Boer, *Disorienting Vision: Rereading Stereotypes in French Orientalist Texts and Images* (Amsterdam: Rodopi, 2004). On the persistence of this discursive trend in art, see Holly Edwards, ed., *Noble Dreams, Wicked Pleasures: Orientalism in America*, 1870-1930 (Princeton, N.J.: Princeton University Press, 2000).

9. In a gallery show thematically close to the exhibition under discussion here, I came upon a similarly embedded memento. Martha Rosler's photo-collage *Wine (Muktada)*, from her 2004 series *Bringing the War Home*, shows a woman completely hidden by a burqa and holding a similar, framed photograph of, supposedly, her son. Also turbaned, the son could be a soldier, hence, a "terrorist." (Seen in Galerie Anne de Villepoix, Paris, September–October 2005).

10. Elaine Scarry, *The Body in Pain: The Making and Unmaking of the World* (Oxford: Oxford University Press, 1985). I cannot do justice to Scarry's extraordinary book, which underlies much of my take on the exhibition. For a short survey of the issues, "The Political Consequences of Pain's Inexpressibility," pp. 11–19 in the book's introduction is the best place to start.

absolute incompatibility of pain and the world" and the world of which, in our case, the museum-going public cannot help but be part. The metaphor of "voice" is interpreted, in Sheikh's works, as the play between the photograph of invisible pain and the text that gropes toward supplementation.

As a result of the visual "inexpressibility" of suffering, a doubt arises: where is the suffering here? This doubt might well be where the show is most keenly critical of its own status and theme. As a consequence of this doubt, many of the photographs in the exhibition confront the viewer with their own interpretation of the subject. Those images, for example, that suggest sexual suffering can do so only easily to those viewers who consider as a source of suffering any form of sexuality different from their own. Moreover, what is sexual about them is not clear. Philip-Lorca diCorcia's **Major Tom, Kansas City, $20** (**PLATE 29**), for example, opposes the figure lying on the street to the bus driving by and to the figure in the distance who walks on as if the foreground figure didn't concern him, or is even invisible. That leaves the viewer as the only one actually frontally exposed to the man. Mary Ellen Mark's **Edgardo Figueroa, Bronx, New York, USA** (**PLATE 31**) shows the beautiful face of a young man—that's all. Even the accompanying text, an autobiographical statement, doesn't tell us much, and suffering is really not an issue. Figueroa's denial of "going gay" may hint at the inhibiting social stigma, but then again, why would he have to open up to unknown readers? The confrontational look, here, seems to tell us to mind our own business.[11]

11. In relation to this doubt, Scarry, "Scenes of Wounding and the Problem of Doubt" in *The Body in Pain*, pp. 198–221, based on biblical discourse, is a useful reminder of the anchoring of the cult of suffering in this key Western heritage.

As an assemblage of images, then, the exhibition questions its subject in many ways, critically and self-reflectively. The critical edge in the title and subtitle indict the aesthetic and commercial exploitation of suffering. But, lest one tends to assume that the curators naively considered themselves able to step out of ideology (something only early Marxist thinkers might have thought), there is a display of the awareness that the exhibition itself is complicit in that exploitation. In this perspective, it is important that the selection of images even undermines the very "presence" or visibility of the theme—the possibility of display. As a result, viewer keep getting mirrored back to them the preconceptions that define not only "beauty" but also "suffering" itself.[12]

12. Although Louis Althusser is quite often read as a proponent of this naïve view of "science" standing outside of ideology, his discussion of the distinction between ideology and science is much more relativistic than that. He wrote explicitly that he warns the reader against such a misunderstanding. See Althusser "From Capital to Marx's Philosophy," *Reading Capital*, trans. Ben Brewster (London: Verso, 1979), pp. 11–69, especially pp. 56–69.

Scarry's primary thesis is the impossibility of expressing pain and the resulting absolute isolation of the suffering subject. This puts a public event such as an exhibition in an awkward position between collusion and the commitment to contribute to at least some measure of alleviation of that particular aspect of the suffering. The exhibition is a precarious but, it says, necessary balancing act between isolation and exploitation, denial and reveling. I see this commitment best expressed in an ongoing search for art—in the broader sense of the visual imagination—that is politically effective. This does not entail a naïve belief in the actual interventionist capacity of art but rather in its potential—precisely due to the role of intelligent imagination—to bring about shifts in public awareness and understanding, both intellectually and affectively, of political issues.

If this is true, then one of the primary tenets of this event is indeed its contemporary probing, through a visual "discussion" that interpellates its visitors as full participants in the concept of political art. I submit that—in its self-critical, analytical approach—the exhibition attempts to make a case for political art that is not defined in essence, but as a practice; not in what it is but in what it does. At the risk of stating the obvious, I would therefore like to revisit the different interpretations of this concept.[13]

POLITICAL ART?

The phrase "political art" traditionally possesses a number of meanings that I wish to discard or bracket. The first three are based on a distinction between politics and aesthetics. First, obviously, political art is not overtly and explicitly *about* politics. Such a thematic concentration would disempower art that may be more effective for not being explicit. Nor do I mean to endorse—and this is the second definition—state-sponsored and/or state-censored art. In fact, I tend to try to steer away from the sensitive issue of censorship that this conception entails. Both traditions limit the notion of political art as art that either resists or supports "official" politics.[14]

In an unfortunate misunderstanding of the phrase, the "conceptual overview" article in the *Encyclopedia of Aesthetics* based its conceptualization of the issues of political art on just such a simplistic relationship between art and politics.[15] In such cases, art and politics remain two separate domains that are more or less incidentally connected. The obsoleteness of those binaries—of support versus critique, and of public versus private—is one of the reasons why we need, I submit, to rethink political art. That this thinking is performed in an exhibition is itself an indication that the old binaries cannot be maintained. For, exhibitions are public events where each viewer brings along her own, private interests and obsessions. Especially when the exhibition confronts viewers in their deepest anxieties and sentiments, as is the case here.

Much of the art on display in "Beautiful Suffering" emphasizes how the very breakdown of the distinction between public and private is, in fact, an imposing feature of today's world and its ongoing state of war. This is one of many subliminal messages, for example, of Boris Michailov's work from **Case History** (**PLATE 30**), of Sheikh's **Qurban Gul** (**PLATE 43**), and in a different way, of Nan Goldin's disturbing photograph of herself, **Nan one month after being battered** (**PLATE 27**). Hence, rethinking reasons to protect these distinctions may well be the most poignant area for an inquiry into political art.[16]

A third sense of political art that I wish to disavow here is political art as *punctual protest*, as a singular, political statement presented within the framework of the art world. For such art is not political *qua* art; it just happens to have a political meaning. Its limited range may well hinder rather than enhance our understanding of how art can act politically. Such art may be effective—as effective as protest marches, lobbying, or actual warfare—but if so, it is not effective *qua* art. To anticipate what follows, the singularity of the suffering is primary and cannot be limited to the contingency of the protest against it. For such a punctual protest, in turn, is limited to partisan positions already taken before the confrontation with art; art, in such instances, has not much left to *do*.

These three senses in which the phrase "political art" functions also have a problematic feature in common. They all suggest, as their alternative, a universal and universally valuable kind of art that protects itself from political "contagion." This "non-political" art is pure, ethereal, and aesthetic only; perhaps appealing to Kant's "disinterested" contempla-

13. My use of the verb "to interpellate" resonates with Althusser's use of the term interpellation to explain ideology and its social effect. See, for a first use, Altusser, "Ideology and Ideological State Apparatuses," *Lenin and Philosophy and Other Essays*, trans. Ben Brewster (London: Monthly Review Press, 1971). Kaja Silverman took up this notion in her introduction to *Male Subjectivity at the Margins* (New York: Routledge, 1992). For an excellent discussion of political-art exhibitions in the context of the Israeli-Palestinian conflict, see Noa Roei, *Politics on Display: Three Contemporary Exhibitions in Israel* (Amsterdam: MA thesis in Cultural Analysis, University of Amsterdam, 2005).

14. For those who have forgotten, the inclusion in the exhibition of Serrano's *Piss Christ* (Plate 22) brings up the issue of censorship through reference to American restrictions of artistic freedom. On this piece, see Bal, *Quoting Caravaggio: Contemporary Art, Preposterous History* (Chicago: The University of Chicago Press, 1999), pp. 52–6 and references there.

15. John Stopford, "Culture and Political Theory," in *Encyclopedia of Aesthetics*, Michael Kelly, editor in chief (New York/Oxford: Oxford University Press, 1998), volume 4, pp. 16–19.

16. For a discussion of the breakdown of public and private in states of war, especially civil war, see Boer, *Uncertain Territories: Boundaries in Cultural Analysis* (Amsterdam: Rodopi, in press).

tion, or what Theodor Adorno disparagingly called "the work [of art] that wants nothing but to exist." It advocates forgetting that, as Adorno added, this fetishization of aesthetics is "an apolitical stance that is in fact highly political."[17]

There are three further meanings of political art, however, that are more difficult to discard, because they are not caught up in this false binary of the realm of the political versus that of aesthetics. These meanings emerge from another opposition, that between art and life. They emerged from post-Holocaust philosophy and have in common a delicacy, a modesty, a need to draw limits around the tragedy of "real life" so that victims are not re-victimized—a concern also central in "Beautiful Suffering." To bring this issue as close as possible to the relationship between art and what could be called "the cultural politics of suffering," I wish to situate the exhibition's critical as well as aesthetic thrust in relation to the concerns Adorno expressed on this matter so long ago.[18]

17. Theodor Adorno, *Can One Live After Auschwitz? A Philosophical Reader*, ed. Rolf Tiedemann, trans. Rodney Livingstone and others (Stanford: Stanford University Press, 2003), pp. 240–58. The publication of this collection of writings related to his initial indictment of "poetry after Auschwitz" (on which more below) will hopefully put an end to the indirect and decontextualized, often untraceable, citations of Adorno's position that have savaged critical theory for the last decade.

18. The ongoing relevance of Adorno's thoughts is manifest in the circuit of citations, especially in debates on Holocaust-related art and, in its wake, art of disaster, such as South-African, Palestinian, and other war-related art.

The first of these meanings is the kind of *aestheticizing* or, as Adorno would say, stylizing, of real-world politics such as violence, war, terror, domestic coercion, famine, and aesthetic and commercial exploitation—in short, of the topics highlighted in this exhibition. This stylizing is, in my view, the fourth meaning of political art that needs to be suspended in this little exercise in negativity: art that represents in beautiful form events or effects of violence. Beauty distracts, and worse, it gives pleasure—a pleasure that is parasitical on the pain of others. *Representation* is here perceived as turning violence—events, victims, consequences—into something that can be perceived as "art," which is different than documentation, journalism, or critical writing. "Beautifully" representing suffering is not in itself an act of political art, but on the contrary, it threatens to neutralize such acts of violence.

This fundamentally invokes the problem of representation that is at the heart of Mfon Essien's **The Amazon's New Clothes** (**PLATE 28**). The artificially glimmering skin of a figure of ambiguous femininity—nude drag, so to speak—is both exposed and withheld. The black-and-white aesthetic of part-objects simultaneously performs and addresses the anesthetization of racial stereotypes, along with that of femininity and fashion. Harking back to (self-?) stylized figures such as Josephine Baker and, later, Grace Jones, this figure capitalizes on the integrated stereotypes of blackness, gender ambiguity, and nudity. The title's reference to Hans Christian Anderson's tale suggests that the nudity is a form of ideological clothing. Like the mythical Amazon, the figure cannot be faced, literally, for his/her face is cropped. Like sculpture subjected to iconoclasm, her head is chopped off. These combined references—to the emperor, to the Amazon, and to classical art—empower the subject ambivalently: the emperor was stupid, the violence-thirsty Amazon didn't exist, and the art got iconoclastically damaged. Passive and encased in decorative contrast, representation is here indicted as the cultural strategy that makes suffering invisible.

Political art made under the banner of representation would either refuse art, limiting itself to the documentary, or refuse the representation (of suffering). This does not mean that representation in all its guises must be tabooed, as Adorno's initial statement has often been taken to mean. Thus, an exhibition that boldly highlights representation by selecting photography—and predominantly figurative photography—may be seen to take Adorno at his word instead of reiterating a flat interpretation of his statement. By definition, representation stylizes. In confrontation with this exhibition as a whole—in spite of some of its problematic examples of precisely what Adorno condemns—I submit that it does not, however, necessarily stylize violence *away*.[19]

One reason this Adornian problem is not inherent in representation is that stylizing can serve many different purposes, one of which is to question—not naturalize—itself. The mode of representation can be such that it works to "undercode" the violence it addresses. I contend that many of the artists represented in "Beautiful Suffering" have explored artistic languages that enable them to perform this double take on representation. For example, some of them undercode the violence so that its visibility in the resulting work, which is partly representational and partly anti-representational, is all the more tenacious and acute. Their tool is "metaphoring" between the particular and the general for the sake of promoting—sometimes even enshrining—the singular.[20]

19. Ernst van Alphen sums up and intervenes in the debate about representation of violence. See Van Alphen, *Caught by History: Holocaust Effects in Contemporary Art, Literature, and Theory* (Stanford: Stanford University Press, 1997). He argued strongly against a stark, flat acceptance of Adorno's warning and a subsequent taboo on imagination-based art.

20. For the notion of undercoding, see Umberto Eco, *A Theory of Semiotics* (Bloomington: Indiana University Press, 1976).

This seems a good frame for Nan Goldin's photograph, **Nan one month after being battered** (**PLATE 27**). This photo is overly quoted and its iconic status may have inured us to its singularity. The image, however, brings together the intertwining of three singularities. First, it is singular in content: the suffering it shows is singular, unique (not general), but not particular (we don't know the details of the life history; there is no anecdotal excess of information). In its frontal, close-up, and bare aesthetic and autobiographic framing, this image represents suffering without a shadow of a doubt. In this sense it is concrete and seems to be presented, not re-presented. Physical hurt still lingers in its visible traces, and we all know this is not all: a woman battered in domestic violence suffers more than physical pain. This possibility of translating from the unique woman to a condition of battered women, without losing sight of this woman's singularity, demonstrates how singularity differs from particularity, where the pain would be contingent upon the state of this particular woman. Her suffering, although endured by many, is singular in its loneliness.

The second singularity is aesthetic. This singularity answers Adorno's objection. The poignancy of the image is highlighted, not mitigated, by the form of "stylizing." Exceptionally bare in composition within Goldin's oeuvre, the image appears to be stylized, and as such, it draws attention to two aspects. On the one hand, we cannot fail to notice the damaged eye, doubly handicapping both the person looking at us and also the photographer, who needs her eyes more than most—even to make this very image. On the other hand, the beautifully shiny hair internally framing the face; the surrounding, light-green background; the well-tended brows repairing the symmetry damaged by the battering; the elegant, long earrings and the necklace show a woman more keen on her appearance than she is in many other self-portraits; and especially the bright-red lipstick all speak of a will to overcome the damage done to her face. The woman's attempt to reconquer beauty, here, is mobilized as a weapon *against* suffering. This stylizing against, not in favor of, a simplifying enjoyment of a neutralizing beauty gives the image its second singularity. This second singularity, proposing an aesthetic grounded in the entanglement of the woman's two states, imports a temporality, a duration of her pain, through the narrative of her efforts to overcome the devastation.

Thirdly, the image as such is singular. On all accounts, this photograph is emphatically made to be "beautiful," as an image as well as qua woman, in an oeuvre whose very different aesthetic it largely brackets. Goldin's anti-aesthetic affiliation with punk and other, related movements of the time is loudly discarded to make this image stand out, singularly, within her oeuvre. "Beauty," here, is not an incidental effect of artistic success but rather—in addition to that undeniable success—a message denoted by the traditional means of beautifying, used as signs. This phrasing is meant to make the shift from aesthetic to semiotic success. The meaning is the sign: /beautiful/ is, in turn, connected to its other meaning, /singular/. Standing out as, emphatically, *singular* in Goldin's oeuvre, this image does something by means of that exceptionality of the "beautiful suffering" it presents. I contend that its effect—its "doing"—is bound up with the exceptional double beauty of the image and of the woman's self-presentation.

What distinguishes singularity from particularity in this context is the possibility, indeed the almost irresistible compulsion, to translate. Translation opens up an experience to others without encouraging vicarious identification. For, translation maintains difference; it withstands assimilation. "Good" translation according to Walter Benjamin, safeguards the visibility of the remainder of the foreign. Here, that remainder is what makes one battered woman unique, since it is her subjectivity that has been hurt. It protects the unique subject from assimilationist appropriation. At the same time, the translation makes her experience accessible for others. It becomes understandable and, hence, open to comparison and to "conversation" with other experiences that share some of its features. Thus, through these three, insistent forms of singularity, the image "metaphors" the now-generalized notion of domestic violence into something uniquely singular. By means of this metaphoring, this singularity is accessible to others as in an attempt to remedy Scarry's diagnosis of pain as helplessly inexpressible.[21]

21. On the body of Goldin's work and its particular aesthetic within which this image was exhibited, see, for example, Nan Goldin, *I'll be your mirror*, catalogue of exhibition curated by Elisabeth Sussman and David Armstrong (New York: Whitney Museum of American Art, 1996). "Translation" is conceived here as a productive relationship with an "untranslatable" text or work that, nevertheless, requires mediation. See my analysis in *Traveling Concepts in the Humanities: A Rough Guide* (Toronto: University of Toronto Press, 2002). Walter Benjamin's essay, "The Task of the Translator" in *Illuminations*, ed. Hannah Arendt, trans. Harry Zohn (New York: Schocken, 1968) developed the normative concepts of "good" and "bad" translation. The latter is further developed in terms of the invisibility of the translator in Lawrence Venuti, *The Translator's Invisibility: A History of Translation* (London; Routledge, 1995). For the issue of cultural difference in relation to translation see Venuti, "Translation and the Formation of Cultural Identities" in *Current Issues in Language and Society* (1: 1994): 214–5. The concept of remainder, only implicitly present in Benjamin's essay, is developed in Venuti, "Translation, Philosophy, Materialism," in *Radical Philosophy* (79:1996): 24–34.

Hence, in its various formulations, Adorno's objection remains as paradoxical as it is valid. He argued that turning horror into beauty, far from being a civilized thing, is, indeed, barbaric. Allegedly, art would destroy the civilized world or at least be in collusion with that destruction, because it makes the violence palatable, even risks making it pleasurable. The effect is the total obliteration, even redemption, of the violence. For there is no more radical way of erasing violence than to make something appealing from it, thus mitigating it, giving it beauty, and unwittingly, redeeming it. The exhibition's theme is centrally derived from this contention and engages with Adorno's view.

POLITICAL ART AND MEMORY

Artists, the exhibition claims, do not wish to perform this erasure. On the contrary. And some of the most gripping images in "Beautiful Suffering" achieve their power, precisely, from the ingenious and thoughtful manners their makers devised to turn this threatening erasure upside down and to make the image a stark and performative memorial rather than a redemptively beautiful thing.

Here, I find Vik Muniz' work **Memory Rendering of Tram Bang** (**PLATE 39**) a compelling counter-example to Adorno's fear of erasure. The work is part of a series called *The Best of Life*, a title that strikes with bitter irony the image of a naked child running in horror while her skin is burning from napalm (**PLATE 38**). The burning girl is the poster child of the anti-war movement. In its time, it was one of those images that contributed to the increasing protests that ended the endless Vietnam War. The press photograph by Nick Ut, published many times in newspapers and magazines, is engraved on the visual memory of everyone who was old enough to read the papers. In his commitment to estrange the naturalized medium of photography as record, Muniz gleaned the image from visual cultural memory, a collective environment that the photograph never left, even long after the war—*that war*—had ended.

This image has been taken up by several artists working on visual memory. The latest I know of, besides that of Muniz, is by Polish artist Zbigniew Libera. This artist caused something of a scandal when, in 1996, he created *Lego Concentration Camp Set*. This became one of the scandals of a controversial but, to my mind, very important publication and subsequent exhibition at The Jewish Museum in New York: *Mirroring Evil: Nazi Imagery/Recent Art*.[22] Libera's strategy to counter Adornian erasure is to shift the mood, from appropriate—and thereby worn, ineffective—horror and mourning to inappropriate—and thereby shocking, effective—"toying." The resulting wavering of the previously fixed positions of perpetrator versus victim was what caused the scandal, but also what made the images effective tools in a fresh approach to cultural memory. Libera's 2004 photograph *Nepal*, from the *Positive Series*, includes the girl, now an adult, running naked with a cheerful group of people and laughing (**FIG. 2**). The identical body pose is all that recalls the napalm victim, but that is enough. Running, arms flapping, naked. The shock this image causes—its performativity—is the realization that even a healthy, adult, laughing player is capable of representing horror, unfixing it from the particularity and giving it a new singularity that connects to—but cannot substitute for—the burning child. Libera stages in order to deconstruct these icons of horror.[23]

22. Norman L. Kleeblatt, ed. *Mirroring Evil: Nazi Imagery/Recent Art* (New York: The Jewish Museum/New Brunswick: Rutgers University Press, 2001).

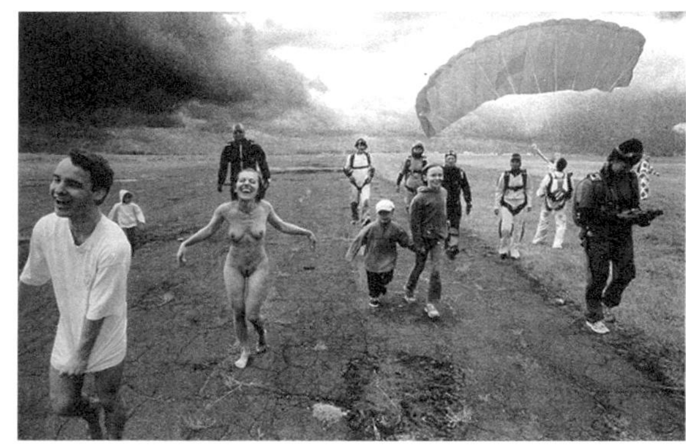

FIGURE 2
ZBIGNIEW LIBERA, *NEPAL*, 2003
FROM *POSITIVES* SERIES
COURTESY OF THE ARTIST,
AE FINE ART/PAULINA
KOLCZYNSKA, NEW YORK

Muniz also unfixes what seemed fixed, no longer effective. He does not, or not primarily, operate through shifting mood but by providing unnerving evidence of photography's capacity to indelibly insinuate images. Astoundingly, Muniz made a pencil drawing of the press photograph from memory, experimenting to "find out what a photograph looks like in your head when you are not looking at it."[24] The photograph in "Beautiful Suffering" was made after that drawing. The virtuoso achievement is incredible, but that is not the point. He seeks to address vision itself as colluding with the maintenance and *thereby* the erasure of horror from vision. This is what he had to say about his endeavor:

> ...to fuse two seemingly contentious media, photography and drawing, in a single image. When you blend these two kinds of representation, you create a perceptual rift—you are not just looking at something, you are actually *feeling vision* itself (emphasis added).[25]

Thus, like Libera, Muniz addresses the viewers affectively, but at the same time he compels the shift from a seemingly innocuous, perceptual appropriation of the suffering to an awareness of looking's active participation in what is seen. The visual grasp is turned from a transparent tool into a felt uncertainty. Both artists tamper with memory, but in different

23. As an attempt to meet the scandal head on and then diffuse it, the catalogue of *Mirroring Evil* was published one year before the exhibition opened. For an excellent explanation of the productive approach to memory through such mood shifts and other "toying approaches to the Holocaust," see Van Alphen's essay in the exhibition catalogue.

24. Vik Muniz, *Vik Muniz* (Paris: Centre National de la Photographie, 1999), p. 104.

25. Muniz, *Vik Muniz*, p. 104.

ways and with different results. Libera's picture makes us realize immediately how engraved such icons of suffering are, and how easily the mood attached to them can be put up for grabs. Muniz' approach uses his miraculously accurate memory to give us the contrary message. Instead of saying memory can be trusted, he shows how we are fooled.

Both Libera and Muniz can be considered as opposing the legacy of Adorno's indictment of art "after Auschwitz." That indictment has been extensively alleged in Holocaust studies, often to advocate documentation as the only "proper" way of representing the Holocaust.[26] Its influence has been such that it is worth revisiting as a frame for this exhibition. The primary reason is that there is a strong element of self-reflexivity at stake in the discussion, which has been under-illuminated in many references to Adorno's statements but is central in "Beautiful Suffering." Importantly in this respect, the original statement appears in the context of a rather savagely critical examination of what was to become cultural studies: the progressive, critical study of culture. One of the typical, enigmatic dialectical paradoxes Adorno refers to in this essay is something that cultural studies have taken to heart insufficiently: "Such [cultural] criticism is ideology as long as it remains mere criticism of ideology."[27]

26. Theodor Adorno, "After Auschwitz," *Negative Dialectics*, trans. E. B. Ashton (Frankfurt am Main: Suhrkamp, 1966]), pp. 361–65. Strangely, this essay is not included in *Can One Live After Auschwitz?*

27. Adorno, *Can One Live*, p. 153.

The reason for this severe judgment becomes clear in his later formulation, which states that the problem appears to lie with the definition of culture underlying this critique of ideology; "culture," in this context, is an entity rather than a process and can therefore be seen as outside or "other" than the violence it produces: "Such critical consciousness remains subservient to culture insofar as its concern with culture distracts from the true horrors."[28] Hence, Adorno prefigures Johannes Fabian's negative and dynamic concept of emerging culture as not an entity but a process of contestation within which violence must be positioned and understood.[29] This "distraction" is what some of the visual acts of metaphoring attempt to overcome. In that metaphoring, space is made available, a space for the confrontations which, for Fabian, constitute "culture." In line with these attempts, which I have characterized above as attempts at translation between the particular and the general, Adorno wrote that "the task of criticism must be not so much to search for the particular interest groups to which cultural phenomena are to be assigned, as to decipher the general social tendencies that are expressed in these phenomena and through which the most powerful interests realize themselves."[30]

28. Adorno, *Can One Live*, p. 155. The essay "Cultural Criticism and Society," from which this quote originally stems, was written in 1949 and first published in 1951.

29. Johannes Fabian, *Anthropology with an Attitude: Critical Essays* (Stanford: Stanford University Press, 2001).

30. Adorno, *Can One Live*, p. 158.

This is why I suspended above the punctual-protest approach to political art. And although some of Adorno's statements in this essay suggest that self-reflection is urgently necessary, he equally relentlessly pointed out the limitations of that activity: "Even the most radical reflection of the mind on its own failure is limited by the fact that it is only reflection, without altering the existence to which *its failure bears witness*" (emphasis added).[31] The continuing relevance of Adorno's thoughts on post-Holocaust art for cultural reflection resides within this last phrase. Is it possible, some of these photographs appear to ask, to deploy art not only as reflection but also as a form of witnessing that alters the existence of what it witnesses?

31. Adorno, *Can One Live*, p. 160.

But before witnessing can become a meaningful act, the principle of self-reflection that underlies this exhibition must be taken one step further, to confront Adorno's indictment and its exploitation in contemporary thought. For Adorno's famous indictment of poetry after Auschwitz first appears at the end of this in-depth and devastating commentary on radical cultural critique. In protest against the frequent isolation of this sentence, I quote the preceding and the following one as well, so as to highlight the fact that Adorno's addressee was the cultural critic, whether an academic or not: "Cultural criticism finds itself faced with the final stage of the dialectic of culture and barbarism. *To write poetry after Auschwitz is barbaric*. And this corrodes even the knowledge of why it has become impossible to write poetry today" (emphasis added).[32] Adorno wrote this in 1949. I don't think we are finished addressing this statement. Especially if we see it in the light of an even earlier, remarkable piece, pointedly and poignantly relevant for the state of the world today as "Beautiful Suffering" addresses it. It was published in *Minima Moralia* but written in the fall of 1944.[33]

In that short text, Adorno described, in one sweep, the world's permanent state of war, which we are only now beginning to notice; the role of the media in obliterating this state of war; and the financial interests of global proportions which sustain that war and even make it indispensable. In other words, Adorno addressed in 1944 the combined issues that, as I have outlined above, are inherent in the project of "Beautiful Suffering" and which the exhibition attempts to put on the table for today. It is no more able to come up with a non-contradictory answer than Adorno. But at the very least, it does attempt to address the situation on its own, real terms by deploying the fact that photography, too, is a medium. A medium that, embedded in traditions of (especially Western) art and—in spite of efforts to achieve the contrary—is still fiercely realistic in rhetoric, necessitates and sustains a further probing of the possibility of political art, including representation-based art. In the face of the realistic rhetoric and the predominantly figurative quality of photography—its commercial side as well as its facile appeal to the emotions—the question that needs to be asked yet again is: what can political art be and do, not outside of but in spite of the sentimentality so easily aroused by the images brought together in this exhibition?

POLITICAL ART AS SENTIMENTAL EDUCATION

In later writings, Adorno alleges three, slightly different reasons for his aversion, each entailing an alternative. In one of his most famous formulations, from *Negative Dialectics*, his negative judgment concerns his fear that art may suggest some sense where the horror did not and cannot make sense: "After Auschwitz, our feelings resist any claim of the positivity of existence as sanctimonious, as wronging the victims; they balk at squeezing any kind of sense, however bleached, out of the victims' fate." [34]

It is worth noting that, in terms of Adorno's conception of negative dialectics, the word "positivity" already points to a near-total ban on representation, at least representation with a claim to "matching" its object. Stylized representation makes matters worse, because it diminishes the suffering while rendering its representation enjoyable. "Sense," as Adorno used the word here, would emerge from stylizing representation. Stylizing, according to Adorno's reasoning, entails cutting off affect from meaning. This issue comes up again in contemporary theorizations of political art.[35]

32. Adorno, *Can One Live*, p. 162.

33. Adorno, *Can One Live*, pp. 145–7.

34. Adorno, "After Auschwitz," p. 361.

35. The logic seems highly dubious to me. Aesthetization or stylization can prettify away the horror, but it can also place it in the foreground in novel ways that do justice to the political content.

In a later, 1962 essay devoted to what Adorno calls "committed art"—and in which he again primarily discussed literature—the issue is not *sense*, as in entry into acceptance or even redemption but, plainly and disturbingly, *pleasure*: "The so-called artistic rendering of the naked physical pain of those who were beaten down with rifle butts contains, however distantly, the possibility that pleasure can be squeezed out from it."[36] That same verb, "squeezed," betokens the violent relationship between aesthetics and pain, whether sense or beauty is the blood squeezed out of the victims. The danger here, to put it bluntly, is akin to the effect of pornography. Due to the "double exposure" inherent in exhibitionary practice, this is part of the major challenge that "Beautiful Suffering" faces. But by means of a variety of strategies, it returns this risk to viewers made responsible for their own ways of seeing. I find this a hard, risky strategy, but perhaps it is the only one liable to work at all.

36. Adorno, "After Auschwitz," p. 252.

On the other hand, though, in both "After Auschwitz" and "Commitment," Adorno qualified his indictment almost immediately. The result is the fifth meaning of political art that I wish to bracket. This meaning is related to expressionism, to making the voices of the victims audible so that they can speak out and be heard. This possibility made Adorno nuance his original, forbidding formulation, albeit only to displace the burden from the poet to the survivor and from the ethical to the psychological domain. This shift not only gave his essay the status of a politico-aesthetic guideline but also showed his deep understanding of trauma.[37]

37. Adorno, "After Auschwitz," p. 362–3. The relation of this form of political art to expressionism anticipates my remarks in the concluding section regarding the "abstraction" within representational photography. For a critical overview of the literature on trauma, see Ruth Leys, *Trauma: A Genealogy* (Chicago: The University of Chicago Press, 2000). The best discussions of the difficult relationship between trauma and memory, and between trauma and art are Van Alphen, *Caught by History* and Jill Bennett, *Empathic Vision: Art, Politics, Trauma* (Stanford; Stanford University Press, 2005.

To summarize the issue tersely and in terms resonant with Scarry's analysis of pain, art as "scream," as expression, is both legitimate and, Adorno said, necessary. For, this expressionist view leaves open what art can *do*, which is something documentation, journalism, and critical writing cannot. More important, due to its focus on the artist-survivor, this view also remains caught up in a primary particularity that is confining and in tension with the need for art to mobilize "translation." As long as the photographic "expression"—which does not equal representation—remains caught up with the maker, the scream cannot really be heard. Nor can it be translated into a concern that can yield to action, where the viewer's body is directly addressed and mobilized—not into action but into an affective response that can compel the viewer to action. I see in this tension a good reason for the inclusion of advertising photographs and activist journalism—their affiliated "other"—in the exhibition.

Finally, the kind of art I am most at pains to distinguish from political art is the utterly particularizing, "sympathizing," sentimentalizing art that induces commiseration. As I have suggested above, compassion without a "feeling for" that is both specific *and* "heteropathic" leads us to an emotional realm where the fear of violence can be made objectless. Returning us to ourselves, this can compel us to endorse authoritarian governments, and it can be turned into a vague thrill of feel-good sentimentality about violence. Hence, between our gaze and the trace of life wrenched out of the victims yet visible in the traces that remain, a layer of glossy paper distorts and discolors the hyper-visible particularity. It is that layer that embodies the severance as well as the connection between the particular and the general, "translated" into our own particular experience of violence witnessed or undergone. Different, but able to be mobilized without facile sentiment. Roland Barthes called photographs "a skin I share." That sheet of skin allows the connection, up to a point.

Visitors to the exhibition are not in the place of the represented figures who, perhaps, suffer. But they do have skins that hurt, and eyes that see.[38]

Seeing is not an automatic ticket to identification, but it lends itself to it. But then, what is wrong with identification? Why is it not at all political but, instead, politically counter-productive, and what alternatives can be mobilized to shape an art that is truly political? In a recent book on the subject of political art, Jill Bennett brilliantly explained the traps of sentimentality that seem inherent in identification when suffering is at stake.[39] Bennett's account is clear and convincing and leads her to a position on political art to which I will affiliate myself in this essay. She followed the trail of a long discussion that started with feminist and postcolonial protests against the "double exposure" of objectionable images. The argument, hinted at above, was that showing, unlike rendering in language, cannot avoid repeating that which the author wishes to critique and dismiss. The discussion was further pursued in the 1990s, in the wake of studies of cultural memory, Holocaust studies, and trauma studies and is addressed once more in "Beautiful Suffering." This time, the attempt to critically engage this problem is performed visually on the basis of photography, the most visually "direct" of the still media.[40]

Identification is a mostly unreflective process, a response to seeing something emotionally charged. The term points to the act of putting oneself emotionally in the place of another. The process is well known and has been experienced by many. Just think of feeling that odd lump in the throat when watching a movie of great sentimental appeal. It is not something one does but rather something that happens to one on the basis of earlier psychic formations and tendencies or by socializing training under the pressure of ideological formations. And while such occurrences are a useful reminder of the untenability of the mind-body split and the culture-nature divide, three ethical traps threaten. First, identification can occur either on the terms of the self, who absorbs or "cannibalizes" the other, subsuming the self and thus neutralizing its difference or, on the terms of the other, so that the self risks alienation in "becoming" the other. The former is appropriative; the latter is potentially generous.[41] This leaves the question of identification still open.

POLITICAL ART, EMPATHIC UNSETTLEMENT, AND WITNESSING

In "Beautiful Suffering," the emotional realm in which identification may occur is that of suffering. This entails the second trap, frequently discussed within trauma studies. Mostly on the model of the cannibalizing form of identification, the viewer identifying with other people's (represented) suffering appropriates the suffering, cancels out the difference between self and other, and in the process, cheapens the suffering. Vicarious suffering, obviously, is an extremely lightened form, and if this lightening comes with the annulling of difference, in the end the suffering all but disappears from sight, eaten up by the commiserating viewer. To remedy this danger, Dominick LaCapra proposed a response he called "empathic unsettlement." Through this concept, he attempted to articulate an aesthetic based on both *feeling for* another and, as Bennett phrased LaCapra's view, "Becoming aware of a distinction between one's own perceptions and the experience of the other."[42]

The third, related trap concerns a predicament that lies at the heart of this exhi-

38. Roland Barthes, *Camera Lucida: Reflections on Photography*, trans. Richard Howard (New York: Flamingo, 1984), pp. 80–81. Here, Barthes speaks of photography in three metaphors, beautifully commented on by Janneke Lam in *Whose Pain: Childhood, Trauma, Imagination* (Amsterdam: ASCA Press, 2002), p. 252. For my argument here, the key phrase in the passage is "a skin I share."

39. Bennett, *Empathic Vision*.

40. Identification has a long history of theorizing within the framework of psychoanalysis. Lest I vulgarize this highly complex body of thought, I refrain from integrating it here, but refer, for an in-depth discussion indispensable for anyone interested in that field, to Kaja Silverman, *The Threshold of the Visible World* (New York: Routledge, 1996). A succinct, useful overview of forms of identification is offered in Laplanche, *Life and Death in Psychoanalysis*. Trans. Jeffrey Mehlman (Baltimore: Johns Hopkins University Press, 1976), pp. 79-81. In *Empathic Vision*, Bennett (partly critically) leans on Dominick LaCapra, especially *Writing History, Writing Trauma* (Baltimore: The Johns Hopkins University Press, 2001). I have written about this problematic myself in the context of postcolonial critiques of colonialist imagery. See Bal, *Double Exposures*, chapter 6. The literature in the three fields mentioned is immense. See Bennett for further references. Ulrich Baer, *Spectral Evidence: The Photography of Trauma* (Cambridge, MA: The MIT Press, 2002), is a useful study specifically on photography and trauma, but due to the kind of photography he examines and the questions raised, this book does not inform my position in the context of the exhibition in Williamstown.

41. This distinction is a summary rendering of Kaja Silverman's brilliant psychoanalytic theorizing of identification. See Silverman, *The Threshold of the Visible World*. Silverman called the former form idiopathic, the latter heteropathic identification, a term I have used above

42. LaCapra, *Writing History*, p. 41, discussed in Bennett, *Empathic Vision*, p. 8.

bition. On the one hand, suffering requires witnessing. This need made Adorno partly recant his indictment of art after Auschwitz. Without witness, the sufferer is irremediably alone, deprived of a social environment and all but dehumanized. This point joins Scarry's primary thesis. What suffering requires, then, is what Ernst van Alphen, in a study of art that mobilizes the experiences of the Holocaust, called "testimony's performative quality as a humanizing transactive process."[43] On the other hand, the production of what Geoffrey Hartman and others have denigrated as "secondary traumatization" poses the double danger of vicariousness and, conversely, of renewed hurt, of "trauma envy," and of art-induced suffering. Graphic imagery of suffering is especially liable to produce such an effect. The belated witness can experience a smaller dose of trauma. This can even be dangerous to the well being of the viewer.[44]

On the basis of these three problems pertaining to identification as a non-reflective process to which the art of suffering exposes the viewer, Bennett attempted to articulate what she calls an *aesthetic of relation*. Her framework is Deleuzian, mostly derived from *Cinema II* and *Francis Bacon* but also from Deleuze's early *Proust and Signs*. From the first, she derived the importance of *thought* in art as a weapon against unproductive sentiment. This is the subject of a recent book by Van Alphen that is closely relevant for my arguments as well as those of Bennett.[45] In this book, Van Alphen developed the notion that art actively "thinks" or shapes thought, a useful antidote against the unreflective quality of identification. For one can be held responsible for thought but not quite so easily for near-automated responses.[46] From Bennett's second Deleuzian source comes the importance of sense perception and sensation in our interaction with art. This idea helps us understand the visceral nature of response and the resulting difficulty in neutralizing damaging responses but, also, the possibility of diverting these and transform them into socially more responsible ones. This idea is also important to bridge the gap between highly figurative art—such as most, but not all, of the works in this exhibition—and other kinds of art, including abstraction. The concept of "encountered sign" completes Bennett's picture, which she summed up as "feeling is a catalyst for critical inquiry or deep thought."[47]

For Bennett, there is an additional difficulty with identification, and this brings me closer to the problematic of "Beautiful Suffering." The art that Bennett discusses, when not abstract, at least avoids realism. One of her key cases, for example, is the art of Doris Salcedo, a Colombian sculptor who uses altered household furniture to relationally address the violence of civil war in her country. The furniture is "real," but the violence is nowhere in (realistic) sight. Of course, photography can no longer be held to the naïve rhetoric of realism that characterized its beginnings. But given the works in this exhibition, I find myself compelled to remain attentive to that rhetoric, whose power still holds sway over the everyday discourse of photography and is inevitably entangled with the theme of this exhibition.

In this respect I will note just one element of her discussion. Bennett made a distinction between characters—which she understands as fully formed, pre-programmed roles—and the interaction or relation that she values in the encounter with art.[48] Characters, she argued, promote a naturalized and naturalizing effect. This objection is understandable. Characters are anthropomorphic and individualized. Relations, by contrast, do not need

43. Van Alphen, *Caught by History*, p. 153.

44. On secondary traumatization, see Geoffrey H. Hartman, "Tele-Suffering and Testimony in the Dot Com Era," *Visual Culture and the Holocaust*, ed. Barbie Zeliger (New Brunswick, NJ: Rutgers University Press, 2000), p. 119 and LaCapra, *Writing History*, pp. 135–6. The concept and its discontents are most profoundly discussed in Van Alphen, *Caught by History*, chapter 6, especially page 160.

45. Ernst Van Alphen, *Art in Mind: How Contemporary Images Shape Thought* (Chicago: The University of Chicago Press, 2005).

46. Bennett, *Empathic Vision*, p. 7. The term "relational aesthetics" is currently going around in a somewhat allusive version. See Nicolas Bourriaud, *Postproduction. Culture as Screenplay How Art Programs the World* (New York: Lucas & Sternberg, 2005). While Bourriaud, a curator, usefully indicated issues of art traffic, Bennett's approach is much more analytical and profound. My phrasing, in this paragraph, again skirts the entanglement with psychoanalysis. I avoid the term "unconscious" which, in the eyes of many, would suspend the ethical question and the viewer's responsibility more radically than I find acceptable. Note, though, that Silverman manages to articulate a psychoanalytical "ethics of vision" that goes pretty far in imputing ethical potential to the unconscious, while avoiding moralism See Silverman, *The Threshold of the Visible World*.

47. Bennett, *Empathic Vision*, p. 7. In addition to Bennett's book, these all-too-brief references are best expanded Van Alphen, *Art in Mind*.

48. Bennett, *Empathic Vision*, p. 17.

anthropomorphic figures. Characters are one of two elements in art that hamper rather than help an affective response capable of avoiding the traps of identification. The other element is the autobiographical posture, where the artist claims, or the viewer assumes, that the artwork transcribes personal experience. This aspect is helpfully undermined in Sheikh's two works (see **PLATES 24** and **43**), where the artist does not hold the voice that speaks in the texts, although he is the one who facilitated the supplementary relationship between image and text. Instead of these two modes of soliciting identification, politically effective art triggers a "direct engagement with sensation as it is registered in the work.[49]

49. Bennett, *Empathic Vision*, p. 7.

The argument against identification and vicarious suffering and in favor of a sense-based, close encounter leads to a conception of affect-based art as *political*. Only when we remain on the other side of the individual, the private, and the particular does it become possible to engage with the suffering of others in all its singularity, without trumpeting the moral line of indignation and without falling back into the simplistic, binary opposition between victim and perpetrator and avoiding the appropriative and diffuse gestures of sentimentality.

"Character," however, need not be considered the naturalization of moral roles that Bennett, in the wake of Nietzsche, maintained.[50] As literary theory has been arguing practically from its inception, characters can be evolving, complex, representational tools; figurations and "discussions" of ideas; and resting points on which the reader can hang a host of emotional and intellectual responses. The problem is not in character but in the forceful domination of the realistic tradition within which it—as much as photography—is caught up. Instead, for my purposes, I consider character a concept that facilitates the transition from the Deleuzian sensate, relational aesthetic that does not need figuration to photography, the art form most powerfully caught in realistic rhetoric.

50. Friedrich Nietzsche, *The Gay Science*, trans. Walter Kaufmann (New York, Random House, 1974 and 1982).

To make this point, I turn to those photographs in "Beautiful Suffering" that appear to heed Bennett's caution against character. Clearly, not all works in the exhibition deploy "characters." Some of the images do not show human figures at all. Shimon Attie's work (**PLATE 37**) only projects the place of suffering over the place of forgetting. Paul Seawright "translates" violence in the trace that projects forward, in an image of munitions casually scattered on an upward path between two hills only vaguely associative of a huge and sexualized human body (**PLATE 18**). Some images make the human figure faceless, addressing an old connection between portraiture and beheading that scrutinizes the humanistic "face value." Mfon Essien's **Amazon** is one example (see **PLATE 28**); Ashley Gilbertson's journalistic photo **One of Four Iraqis** is another (**PLATE 1**). Andres Serrano's **The Morgue (Gun Murder)** further reduces the figure to an extremely foreshortened body (**PLATE 23**). Yet most of the photos—even those that willfully make the figure hard to see—do represent human figures who, caught up as they are in a history leading to pain, are characters in the strict sense.

The figures we see on these walls are not individuals we can ever know, nor do they easily translate into universal icons of the human condition—even if some, such as the Afghan girl, have been pressed to do exactly that. Instead, they call for a political, affect-based response that—precisely by their anthropomorphism but combined with their unknowability—turns them into figurations of sensation-based thought. Their anthropomorphism and its highlighted limit can serve a political function. They are fleetingly anthropomorphic, but just as much, they are fanciful screens that enable viewers to project and share "seeing feeling" or "feeling into" the suffering we see. If that is, we see it.

SLOW LOOKING

But do we? As I have suggested, the visibility of suffering is an issue of figuration in its ongoing tension with abstraction. Many photographs in "Beautiful Suffering" emulate movements in modern painting in their attempt to mitigate a visibility that would be too stark—according to Adorno's warnings—by implementing tools of abstraction. And while I have argued that this exhibition lends itself to a revised notion of "character"—to a relational aesthetic of figuration—the insistence in many works on problems of visibility, of suffering, also invokes that tension in ways that can further illuminate the show's philosophy of photography. This philosophy finds its most open-ended expression in the careful balance of shocking, graphical representations of suffering; the invisibility of it in figures that ask viewers to reflect on why they would suffer; and images that withhold the human figure. I will conclude my interpretation of the exhibition through this perhaps controversial idea and deploy the concept of "abstraction" as a conceptual metaphor.

Ernst van Alphen recently summed up a number of conceptions of that tension, and of abstraction, in a useful train of thought that also leads us back to Deleuze. To summarize, the first, avant-gardist conception of abstraction in the early twentieth century was a metaphysical purification of form (Malevich, Mondrian). In "Beautiful Suffering," some images seem to present an updated and photographic version of this purification. This second, American wave of abstraction proposed the exploration of the flat surface as the essence of the medium (Jackson Pollock, Barnett Newman). This can be related to the images that "scream." The third way of seeing abstraction, proposed by British art historian Briony Fer, based on Georges Bataille, saw in the negativity of abstraction a manifestation of psychoanalytic notions such as castration, loss, and trauma (Picasso, Miró). This conception addressed subjectivity.[51]

Following John Rajchman, Van Alphen then proposed a fourth, Deleuzian view that was dynamic and, in a sense, full of form. Here, abstraction was the exploration of what is possible yet remains unseen as soon as a particular form overwrites it. Instead of a symptom of loss or a negation of form, abstraction poses the question of radical innovation. In Rajchman's words, Deleuze and Guattari asked: "Under what conditions can new, singular forms, beyond those that already exist, be produced?" This raises the final issue of showing: can the suffering be seen, as depicted, or can it be produced?[52]

This conception, I submit, can inform our perspective on "Beautiful Suffering." For it would underlie precisely those curatorial gestures that posed the images in precarious positions relating to each other, to the galleries, to the viewers, and to the sequence of figurations, so that new possibilities emerged without exactly being (yet) produced. I contend that this exhibition is an attempt to withhold facile sentiment by making itself "abstract." It does so to the extent that viewers might wonder what is happening here and what ideas about the culture of suffering are being submitted. The exhibition stimulates reflecting along the lines sketched in this essay as well as other, still-unexplored ones. Abstraction, in this sense, is another

51. Van Alphen, "Opgenomen in abstractie," in Marian Breedveld, *Windstil* 5:25 (Staporst: Elferink, 2004). The psychoanalytic notion of abstraction is worked out in Briony Fer, "Poussiere/Peinture: Bataille on Painting," *On Abstract Art* (New Haven and London: Yale University Press, 1997).

52. John Rajchman, "Another View of Abstraction, Journal of Philosophy and the Visual Arts (5: 1995): 16–24 based on Gilles Deleuze and Félix Guattari, *A Thousand Plateaus: Capitalism and Schizophrenia*, trans. Briam Massumia (London: Athione Press, 1980 and 1994).

interpretation of what I earlier called visual philosophy—by definition, raising questions not answering them, promoting the creation of forms not creating them for us.

The "abstraction"—in the Deleuzian sense of emerging possibilities—is hinted at through some of the strategies of denaturalizing representation in this pseudo-realistic medium of photography. Seeing the show through this notion of abstraction, then, allows me to pull together the different strands of my argument as well as some of the examples alleged earlier. Some of these images are contrived, staged, cut-and-pasted. These trap viewers in the midst of their sentimental education, outlined as a militant resistance to identification. Others, we think at first sight, cannot be true. Some, like Nachtwey's **Sudan** (**PLATE 21**), are too horrible to be true. Or they seem too poorly made, like an amateur performance of the Crucifixion, for example, although we know them to be records of real torture and humiliation (see **PLATE 57**). Those have no photographer's name attached. With the recurrence of images of suffering in the everyday, visual culture of the West, it seems that less is more: the more difficult it is to actually see the suffering, the more we step into the relationality that Bennett advocates. The emergence of new, possible forms is an additional tool for this passage to relationality. This explains Bennett's preference for art that cannot be construed as realistic.

In this respect, the key work remains the rightly highlighted piece, **The Eyes of Gutete Emerita** by Chilean artist Alfredo Jaar (**PLATE 51**). Along with the display of the Afghan girl, this work is a mise-en-abyme of the exhibition. While a new genocide is going on in the Middle East, this key work recalls that other, never fully acknowledged and all-but-condoned one, in Rwanda. Three manifestations of Deleuzian abstraction are combined in this work. First, as in the works of Fazal Sheikh and others, the necessary but, by definition, insufficient supplementarity between the image and the accompanying writing produces a domain of possible forms. The alternation of full, half-empty, and near-empty frames of text insist on the wavering, unfulfilled potential of this supplementary relationship. No theorization of word/image relations has been adequate to explain this wavering. With Deleuze's help, I contend this is for the better; only *before* the realization of form can abstraction deploy its potential for the relational viewer to take up and elaborate in that unpredictable encounter between individual subject and public exhibition.

Second, Jaar's work literally, "abstracts" the figure, reducing her to only her eyes. "I am looking at the eyes that looked at the emperor," Roland Barthes said at the opening of *Camera Lucida*.[53] When Jaar commented that "I remember her eyes," he did so in the accompanying text that both spatially and temporally all but takes over the work. Through this text and its pacing, Jaar proposes the relationality of witnessing, the autobiographical act of relating, and the memorial aspect of its belatedness as a way of performing relationality. He performs the powerlessness when—always radically belatedly—we gather to witness the violence that has already killed. The reduction of figure to eyes is, of course, not incidental. Those eyes carry the imprint of witnessing the murder of Emerita's family and then her seeing of the earth where the bodies lie rotting. Traces of Emerita, these eyes are also traces of what they saw. And that includes Jaar himself, who saw her and attempted to enter those eyes and see with her. "Seeing for," as Bennett had it, to achieve "empathic unsettlement"—is this

53. Barthes, *Camera Lucida*, p. 3.

abstraction? No, in one sense it is emphatic figuration, the highlighting of a detail of the person but one that stands, synecdochically, for the person and her entire being: her body, her life, her history. On the other hand, the reduction or subtraction opens up new possible forms: we don't have the woman's physical appearance in front of us to distract us, as Adorno said, from "seeing for" her. The forms we make encompass a world of suffering that these eyes carry with them, but that we cannot appropriate. Instead, we can produce it.

The most important form of Deleuzian abstraction that this work embodies lies, however, in the shift from visual to *temporal*. Not only is the body reduced to the eyes, but those eyes flash by only very briefly. The text carries most of the weight of the piece. This brief flash, in combination with the total darkness of the built-in room, confronts the viewer with the difficulty of holding fast to the past. Like memory, this memorial to a woman who saw her family being murdered touches the viewer now and then but not at will. Much like the return of an unmasterable trauma, it offers the possibility to see the eyes and "see for" Emerita. The preposition "for," obviously, cannot mean "instead of" but "with" and thus "in support of"—support through an act, to quote Van Alphen once more, of "testimony's performative quality as a humanizing transactive process."[54]

54. Van Alphen, *Caught by History*, p. 153.

The brief flashing of Emerita's eyes is not only a confrontation with traumatic memory—hers, not ours—but also a sense-based confrontation with the difficulty of keeping in touch with the past. The speed is painful. One wants to see the eyes again. Hence, one lingers in the dark room longer and longer. Looking cannot keep up with the pace of the images that flash by us, in everyday life as much as in this exhibition, according to Jaar's piece. But the only tool we possess to counter the inuring, numbing effect of that speed is to stop and look and keep looking. Not so much "taking the time," as the phrase has it, but giving it. The utter paradox, then, of this work is that it deploys speed to bodily enforce a slowing down in looking.

The temporal abstraction that Jaar's work stages for us is, ultimately, also a statement on how little political art can really do. Just a flash. But, for want of anything better, in the face of the indifference that actively produces the disasters of war and famine that underly so much of the suffering which the show and its photographs reflect, a flash is all we have. Moreover, it is still slower than the pace of that indifference. Is it a coincidence that the economic term "interest"—a tool to make money with the instrumental help of time—is also at the root of "interesting," that utter, clichéd term of aesthetic engagement? The confusion is compounded when we consider the most widely known, and still endorsed, Kantian standard of "disinterestedness." But what is the "interest," Jaar-cum-Emerita's flashing eyes seem to say, from which Kant wanted the contemplator of beauty to take distance? Is it interest as in money; interest as in superficial, self-gratifying looking; or interest as commitment, concern that lead beyond its moment? This question brings us back to the beginning, to the first encounters this show stages for its visitors. Perhaps I should be true to my definition of a philosophical exhibition and say no more.

Beautiful Suffering

Beautiful Suffering

PHOTOGRAPHY
AND THE
TRAFFIC IN
PAIN

EXHIBITION IN RETROSPECT

WILLIAMS COLLEGE MUSEUM OF ART
JANUARY 28–APRIL 30, 2006

EXHIBITION IN RETROSPECT

An exhibition might be described, glibly, as some objects accompanied by identifying labels and, perhaps, elucidating wall texts, but it is actually a more complex and shifty convergence of artifacts and people in time and space. Even as a single photograph changes with context and caption, so an exhibition will function differently as each viewer wanders through the gallery. One visitor might contemplate images carefully but disregard words entirely; another might skim this wall text but skip that one; yet another might read the texts assiduously, like a book, while seldom glancing at the artifacts. Thus, a show's "meaning" will morph constantly.

When those artifacts are then folded into an exhibition catalogue, the reader's experience cannot be equated with that of the museum visitor. So much is lost. A wall- sized image and a snapshot enjoy parity on the page that they lack in the gallery, and both, in turn, are imprisoned between cardboard covers. Squashed, homogenized, and unceremoniously owned, the images are diminished; myriad meanings may be erased in the service of a linear narrative. This is a particularly charged transposition for an exhibition like "Beautiful Suffering," which seeks to explore, among other things, the function, proliferation, and commodification of images.

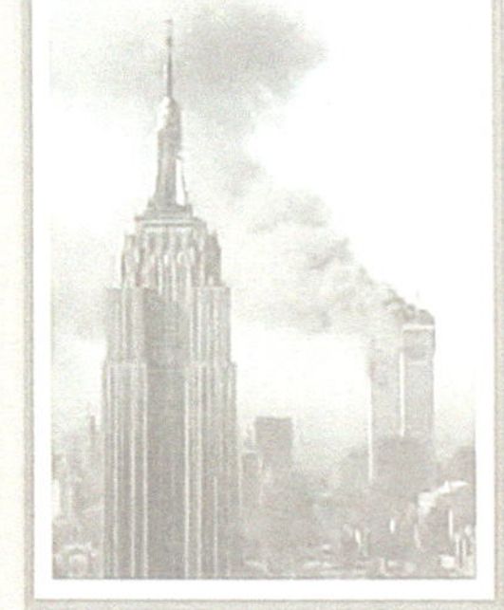

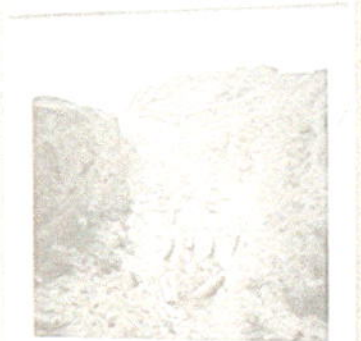

Where looking itself is problematized, the act of exhibiting is even more fraught. Framing the issues and complementing individual photographs with open-ended questions (rather than taking a polemical or omniscient stance) was therefore a taxing curatorial process. It was only with carefully composed exhibition texts that we, the curators, felt comfortable displaying such images, knowing that to do so was to run the risk of perpetuating voyeurism and capitalizing on pain. By reproducing that combination of words and pictures here, we hope to sustain our intended critique of museum display now that the show is over.

Despite all that it transforms, a book *is* well suited to documenting the interpretive moment that an exhibition represents. What follows, then, as a kind of book-within-a-book, is a compendium of plates and wall texts that approximate the sequence experienced by a visitor to the show. By documenting the event in this manner, we admit to anchoring these images in a particular set of meanings and attitudes. Such is our curatorial agenda. The images themselves, of course, have considerably more to say.

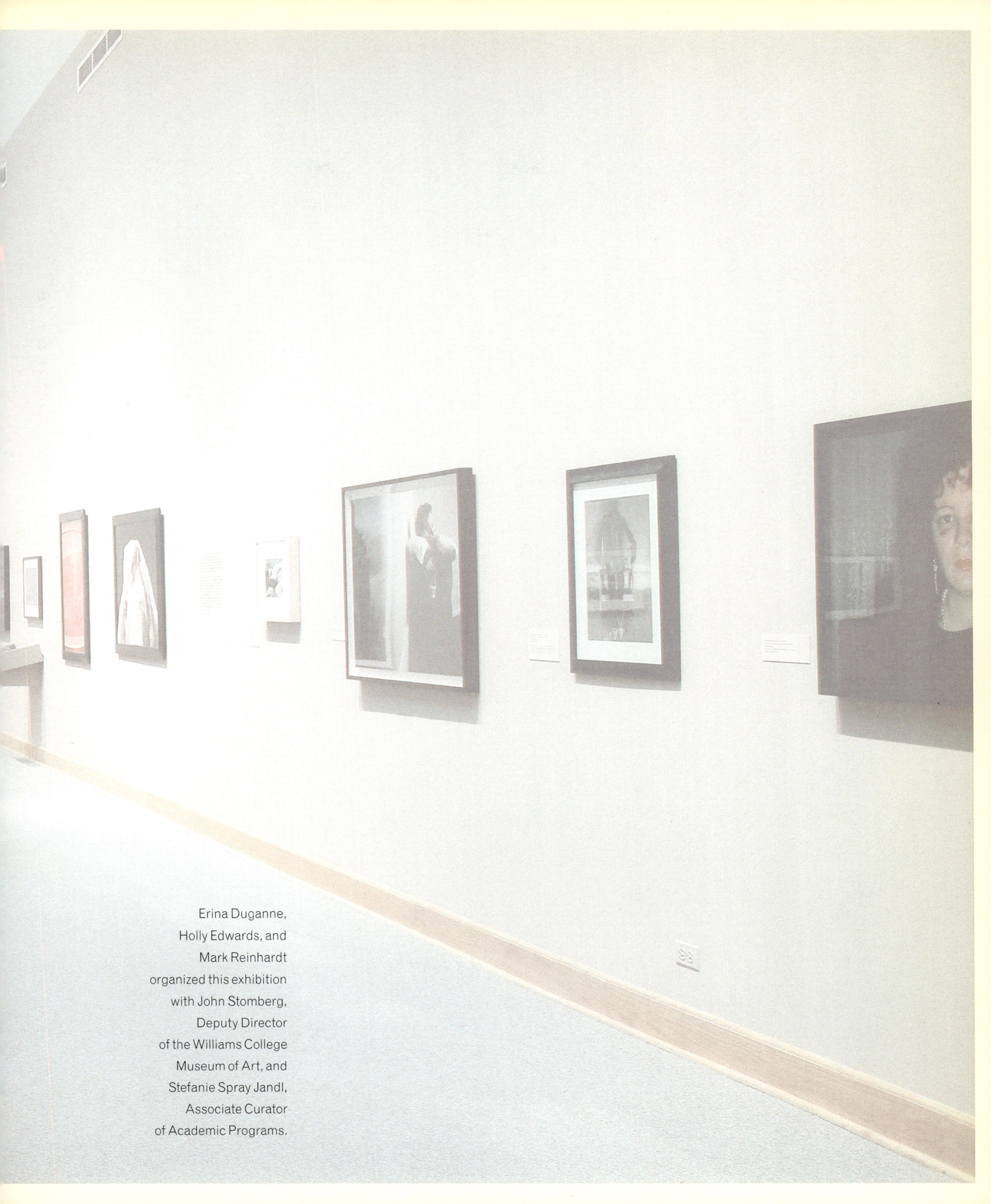

Erina Duganne,
Holly Edwards, and
Mark Reinhardt
organized this exhibition
with John Stomberg,
Deputy Director
of the Williams College
Museum of Art, and
Stefanie Spray Jandl,
Associate Curator
of Academic Programs.

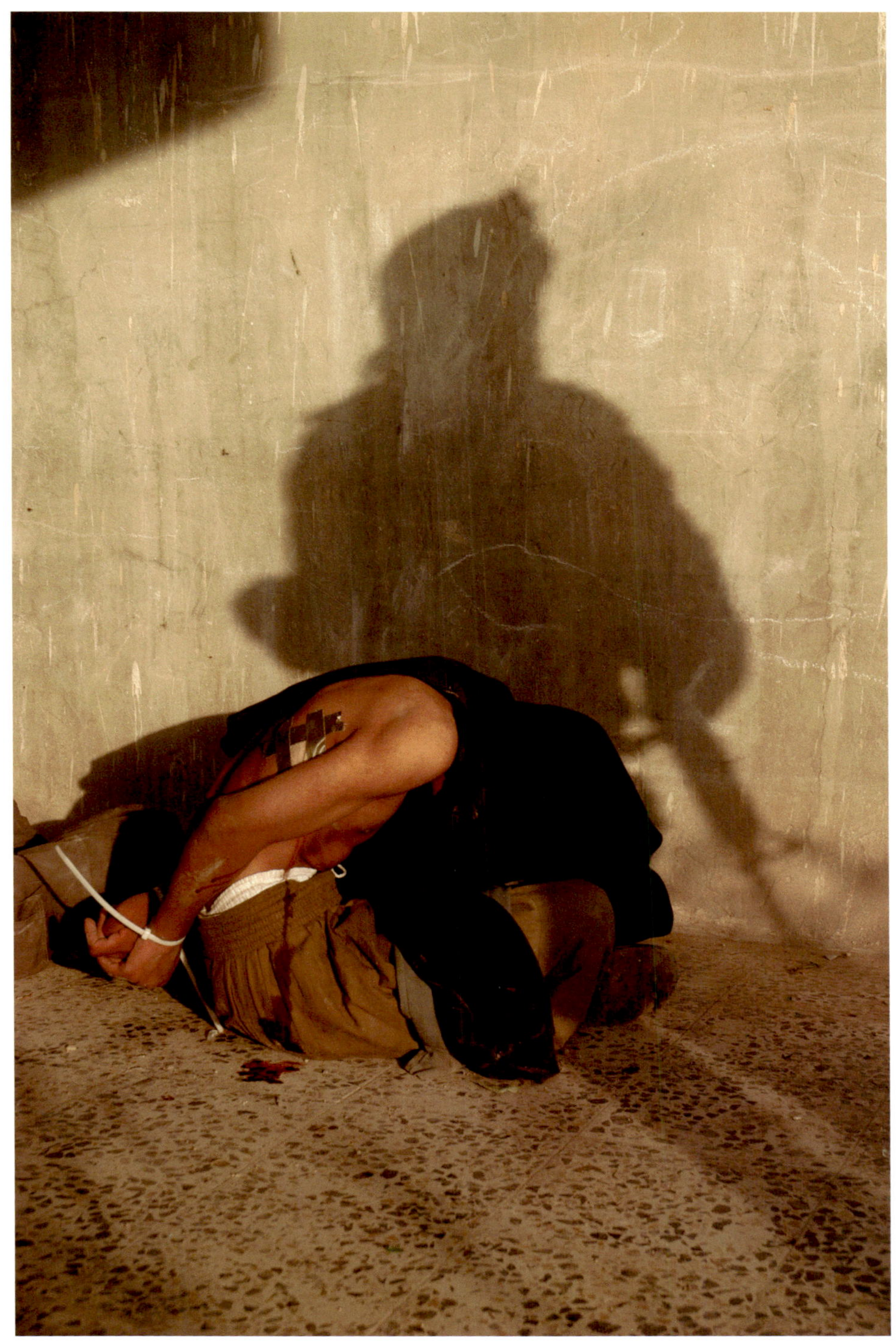

See page 112 Object label on page i

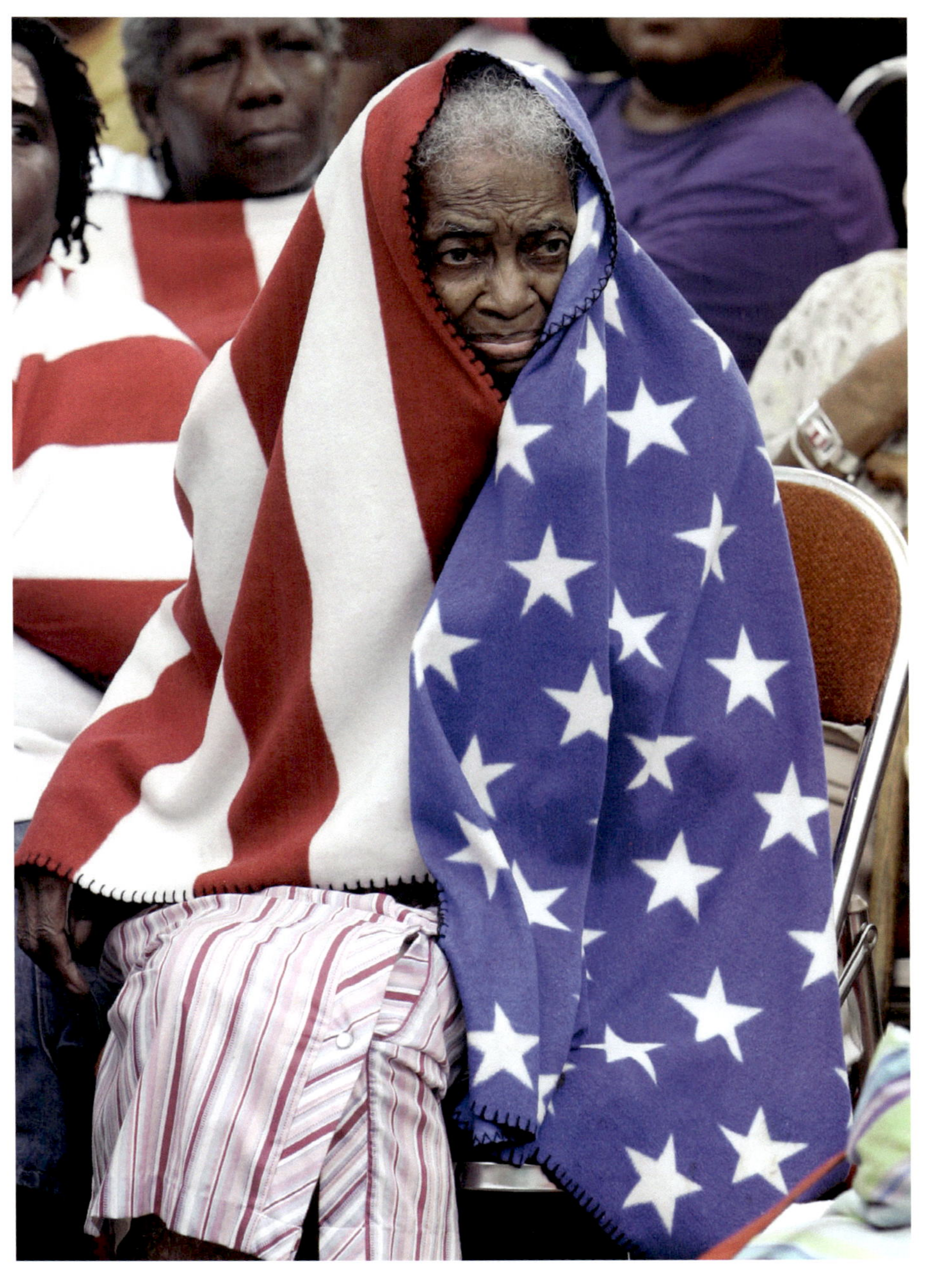

Object label on page i **plate 2**

BEAUTIFUL SUFFERING? In our fast-paced, conflict-ridden culture, it is commonplace. Every day, we encounter exquisite images of others' pain. If we miss them in the news, they are available on the web, in books, or in galleries. Sometimes, the suffering is not actually shown but just implied—the Hurricane Katrina survivor on this wall is striking but not obviously miserable. Other pictures are so explicit and ghastly that one cannot bear to look for long. Such images assault us, reveal us, and ultimately, shape us.

They also pose very tough questions. Why do we take pictures of people in pain instead of just helping them? Perhaps, you might say, photographing suffering is not perverse but rather constructive. A camera, after all, may offer the best means of bearing witness. If horrible things are documented and acknowledged, maybe they will not be so readily repeated. Making that suffering beautiful, you might even argue, ennobles the victims and honors their pain with respect. More pertinently still, the visual proof of catastrophe might generate activism or humanitarian aid.

But when a person suffers, what kind of attention is really helpful? Being the object of public scrutiny may exact its own costs. A "poster child" may never outgrow the experience of personifying a disease or representing a disaster. Photographs of the poor or socially marginal may insidiously perpetuate their powerlessness. Enshrined as victims, they may also be deprived of agency and personal dignity. The makers and viewers of such images, in turn, may be confirmed in their power and privilege even as they seek to provide meaningful aid.   Such imbalances can easily go unrecognized, disguised and reinforced by the diverse transactions of consumer society. The multiple appearances of Steve McCurry's **Afghan Girl** arrayed on the adjoining wall, for example, suggest that every time an image is reproduced in a new context, its meaning is altered and its social function changed. With each new incarnation, moreover, someone else benefits. Does additional suffering result as well? This exhibition offers you, the viewer, an opportunity to consider how we are all implicated in this traffic in pain that is endemic in our culture and manifest in our images.

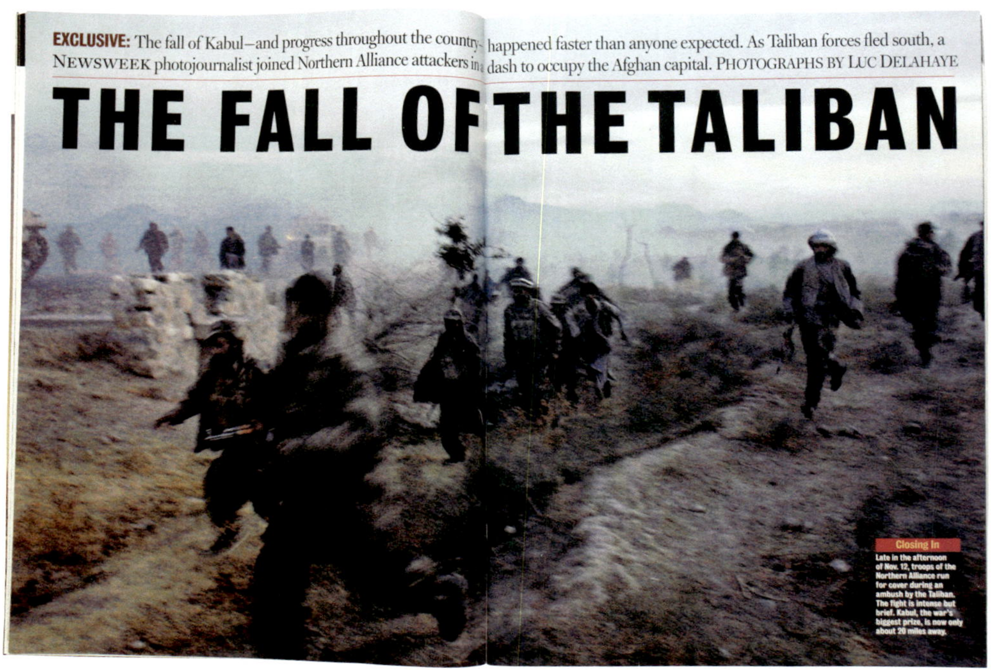

EXCLUSIVE: The fall of Kabul—and progress throughout the country—happened faster than anyone expected. As Taliban forces fled south, a NEWSWEEK photojournalist joined Northern Alliance attackers in a dash to occupy the Afghan capital. PHOTOGRAPHS BY LUC DELAHAYE

THE FALL OF THE TALIBAN

Closing In

Late in the afternoon of Nov. 12, troops of the Northern Alliance run for cover during an ambush by the Taliban. The fight is intense but brief. Kabul, the war's biggest prize, is now only about 20 miles away.

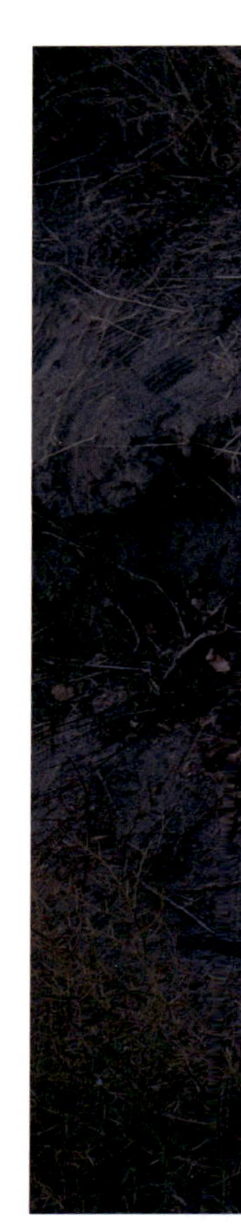

plate 3 See pages 58, 61 Object label on page i

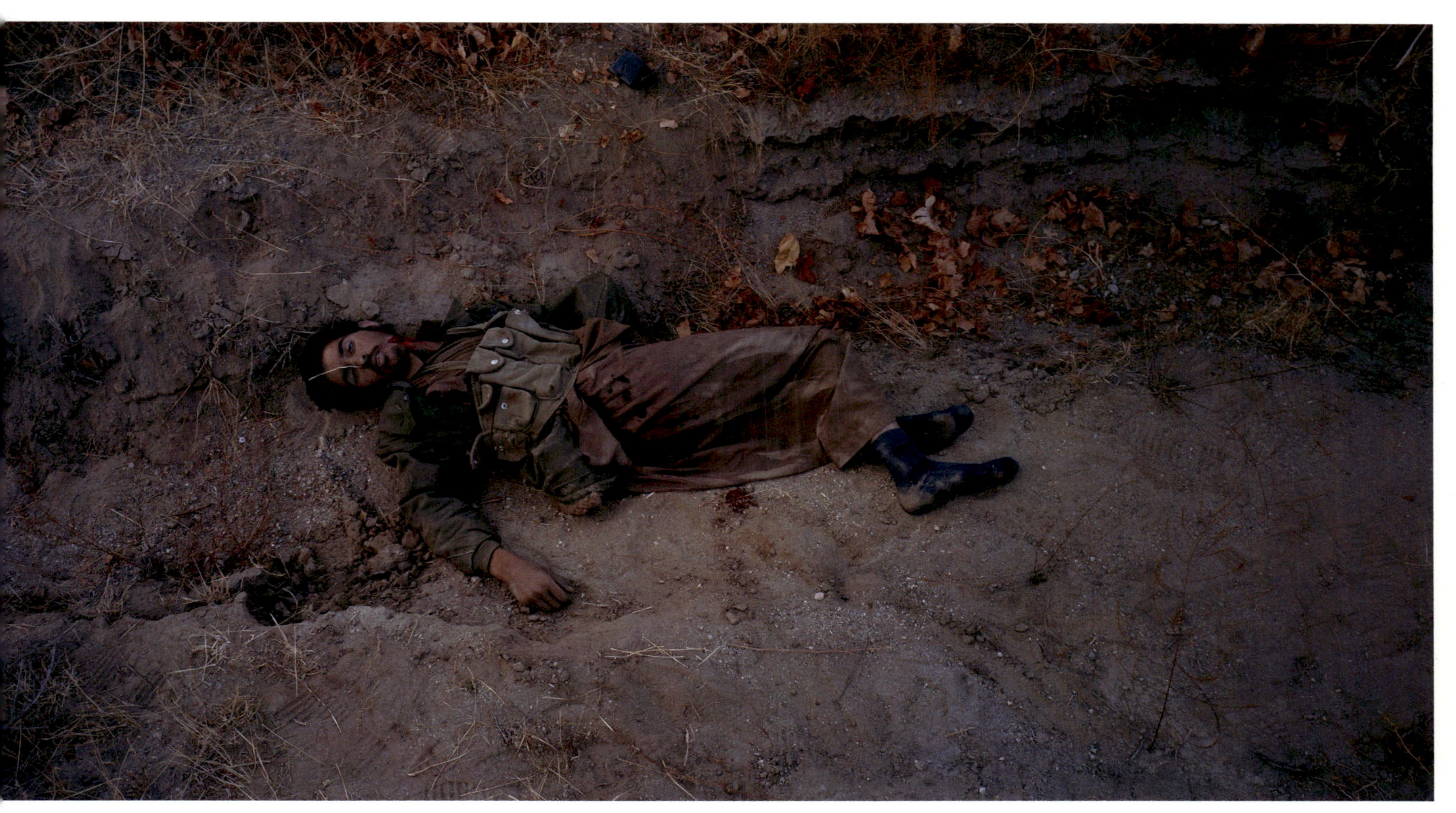

 See pages 18, 58, 61, 64, 65 Object label on page i

AFGHAN GIRL, by Steve McCurry, has morphed from documentary to "art" to advertisement to fundraiser, touching countless lives over the course of years. First published in 1985 on the cover of *National Geographic* magazine, the portrait accompanied a story about Afghans fleeing across the Pakistani border from the Russian invasion. The photograph was taken by a photojournalist intent on documenting the plight of refugees, but it effortlessly conformed to familiar conventions of fashion photography. Appearing at once beautiful and needy, the girl became the ideal "poster child" for the Afghan cause.

In the face of massive suffering in Afghanistan, using such an image for humanitarian purposes seems inevitable and even laudable, but there is irony and ethical tension in the situation as well. Living in a society that practices gender segregation, this young woman might not have chosen to show her face openly as she grew up; in the West, however, this same young woman became a "bankable" icon, even though she did not know it was happening.

Eventually, after

the Taliban came to power in Afghanistan and American forces invaded the country in the wake of 9/11, *National Geographic* launched a campaign to find the now famous but still anonymous **Afghan Girl** and recount her newly topical story. Once "found" and definitively identified by means of the FBI's forensic technology, Sharbat Gula was photographed again (veiled and unveiled), and her present life was "revealed" to magazine readers and video audiences. As if in compensation, her words are now translated and transmitted around the world in support of a fundraising campaign to benefit Afghan girls. Ironically, in a society that fetishizes youth and beauty, Sharbat Gula's older face has perhaps augmented the fundraising charisma of the earlier portrait as nothing else could. What better evidence of suffering, the cynic might say, than age and faded beauty? On the other hand, what kind of pain does bankable anonymity entail? Is that pain tolerable if, by its means, a larger humanitarian goal is reached? Has anyone asked Sharbat Gula her opinion?

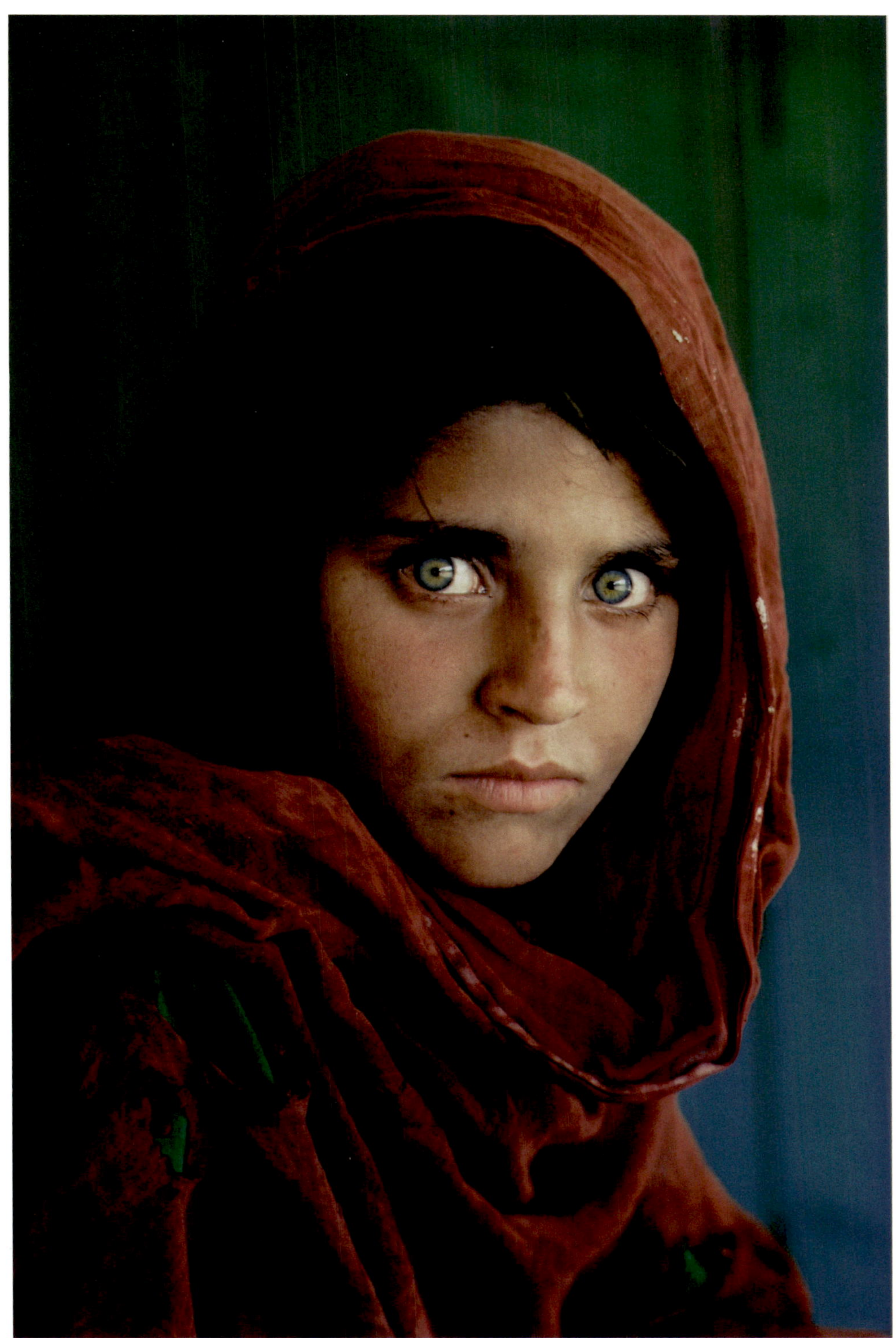

See pages 10, 75–92, 98, 99 Object label on page i

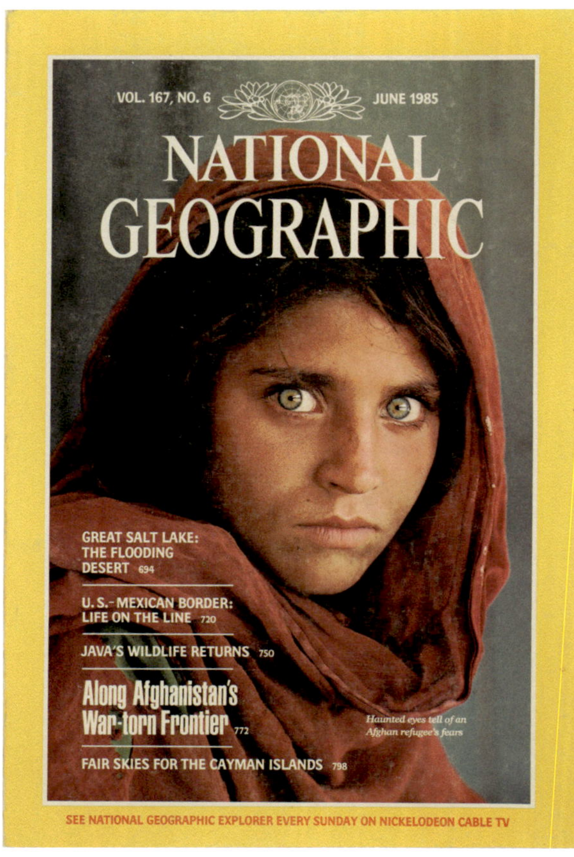
VOL. 167, NO. 6
JUNE 1985
NATIONAL GEOGRAPHIC
GREAT SALT LAKE: THE FLOODING DESERT 694
U.S.-MEXICAN BORDER: LIFE ON THE LINE 720
JAVA'S WILDLIFE RETURNS 750
Along Afghanistan's War-torn Frontier 772
Haunted eyes tell of an Afghan refugee's fears
FAIR SKIES FOR THE CAYMAN ISLANDS 798
SEE NATIONAL GEOGRAPHIC EXPLORER EVERY SUNDAY ON NICKELODEON CABLE TV

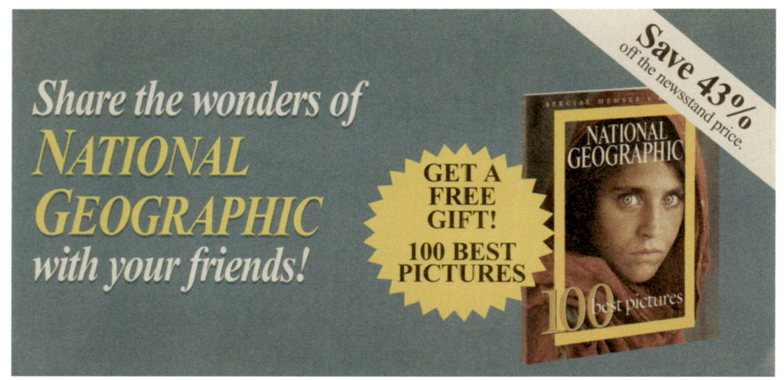
Share the wonders of
NATIONAL GEOGRAPHIC
with your friends!
GET A FREE GIFT!
100 BEST PICTURES
Save 43%
off the newsstand price.
NATIONAL GEOGRAPHIC
100 best pictures

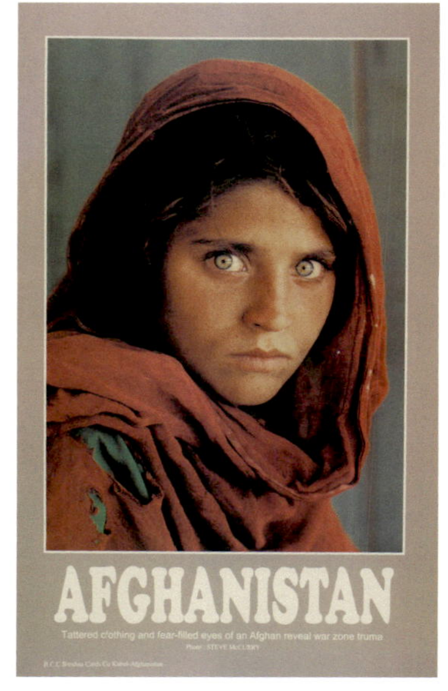
AFGHANISTAN
Tattered clothing and fear-filled eyes of an Afghan reveal war zone truma

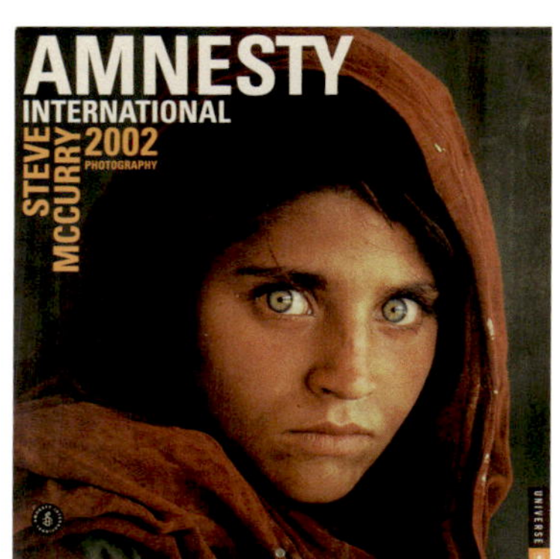
AMNESTY
INTERNATIONAL
STEVE MCCURRY
2002
PHOTOGRAPHY

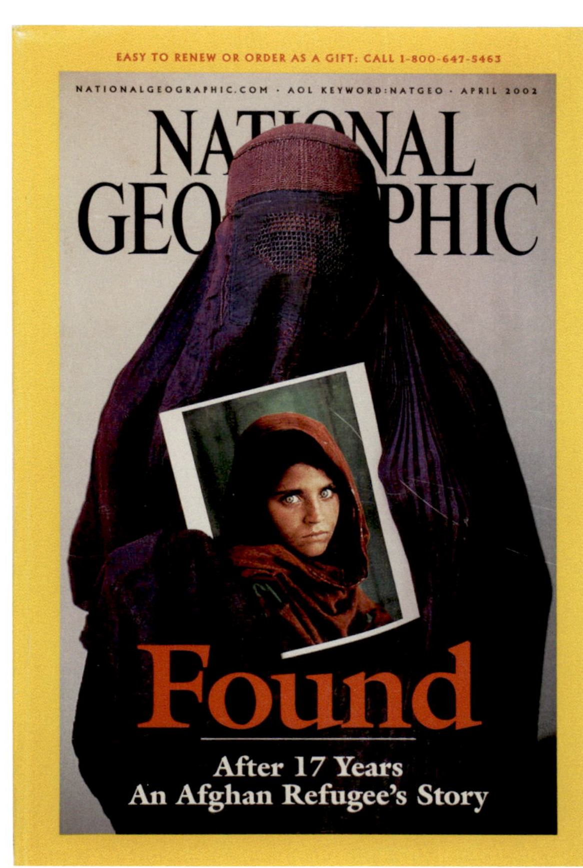

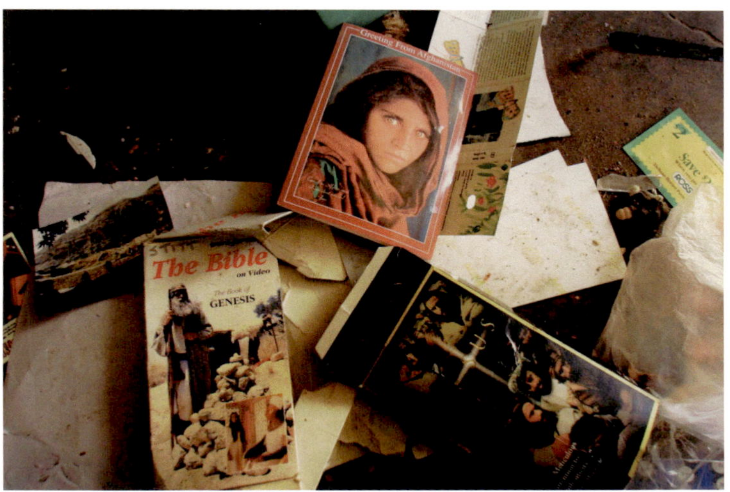

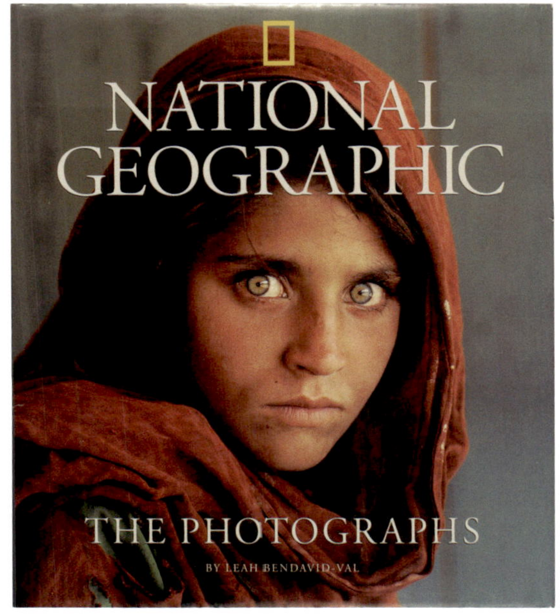

See pages 75–92 Object labels on pages i–ii **plates 10–12**

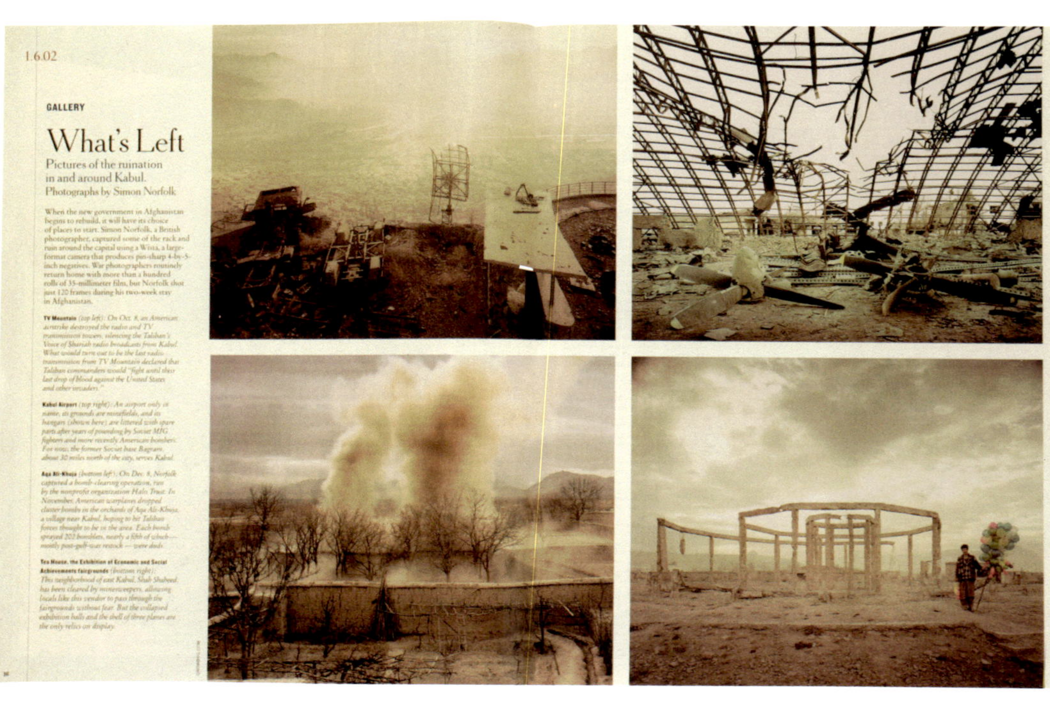

1.6.02

GALLERY

What's Left

Pictures of the ruination in and around Kabul. Photographs by Simon Norfolk

When the new government in Afghanistan begins to rebuild, it will have its choice of places to start. Simon Norfolk, a British photographer, captured some of the rack and ruin around the capital using a Wista, a large-format camera that produces pin-sharp 4-by-5-inch negatives. War photographers routinely return home with more than a hundred rolls of 35-millimeter film, but Norfolk shot just 120 frames during his two-week stay in Afghanistan.

TV Mountain *(top left): On Oct. 8, an American airstrike destroyed the radio and TV transmission towers, silencing the Taliban's Voice of Shariah radio broadcasts from Kabul. What would turn out to be the last radio transmission from TV Mountain declared that Taliban commanders would "fight until their last drop of blood against the United States and other invaders."*

Kabul Airport *(top right): An airport only in name, its grounds are minefields, and its hangars (shown here) are littered with spare parts after years of pounding by Soviet MIG fighters and more recently American bombers. For now, the former Soviet base Bagram, about 30 miles north of the city, serves Kabul.*

Aqa Ali-Khoja *(bottom left): On Dec. 8, Norfolk captured a bomb-clearing operation, run by the nonprofit organization Halo Trust. In November, American warplanes dropped cluster bombs in the orchards of Aqa Ali-Khoja, a village near Kabul, hoping to hit Taliban forces thought to be in the area. Each bomb sprayed 202 bomblets, nearly a fifth of which — mostly post-gulf-war restock — were duds.*

Tea House, the Exhibition of Economic and Social Achievements fairgrounds *(bottom right): This neighborhood of east Kabul, Shah Shaheed, has been cleared by minesweepers, allowing locals like this vendor to pass through the fairgrounds without fear. But the collapsed exhibition halls and the shell of three planes are the only relics on display.*

plate 13 Object label on page **ii**

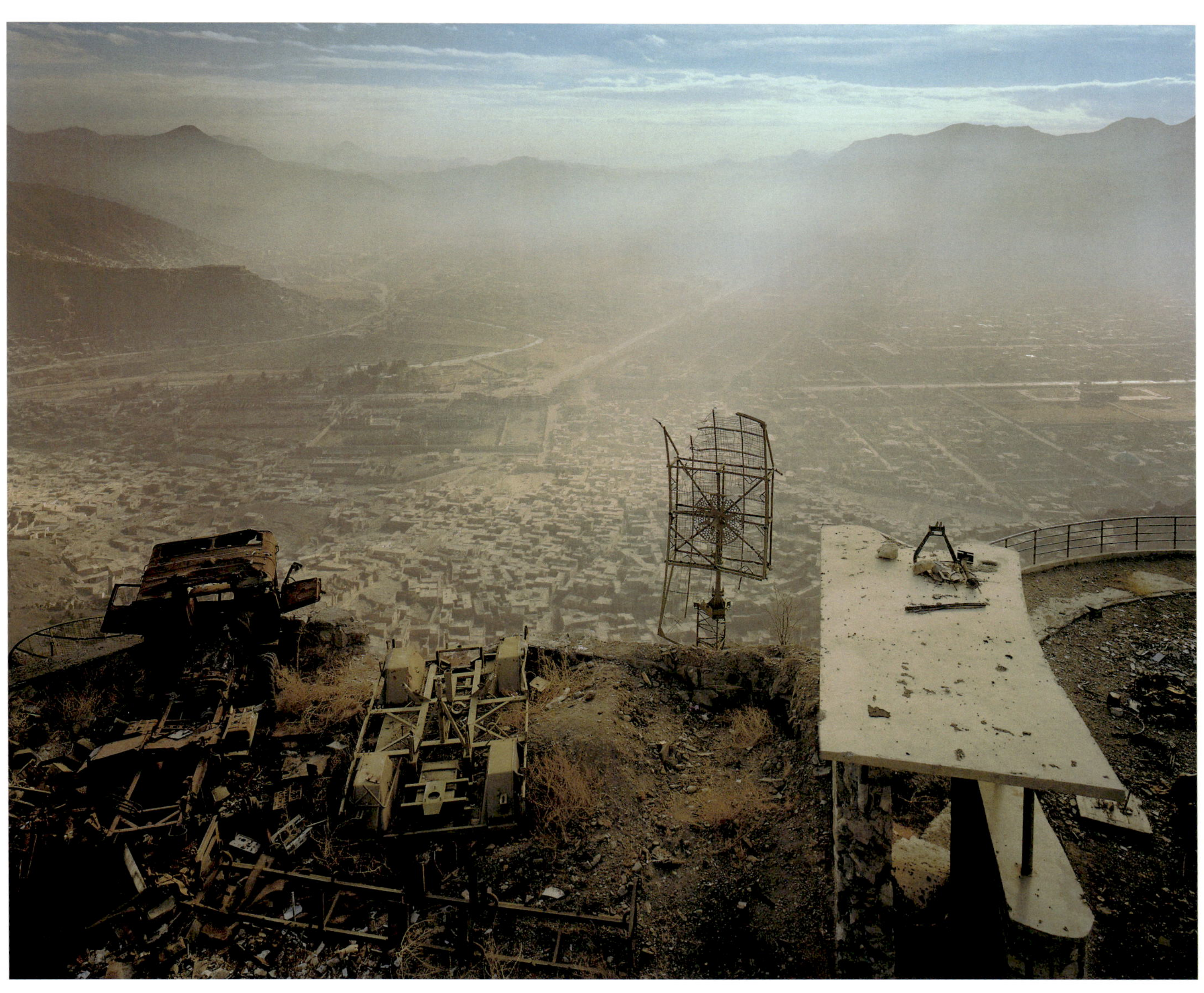

Object label on page ii **plate 14**

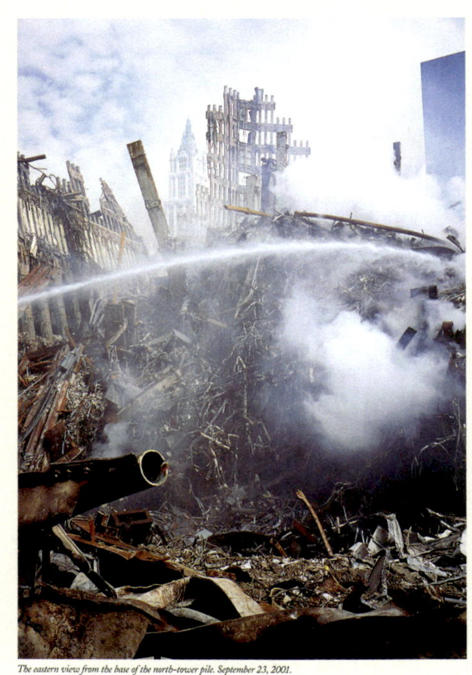

The eastern view from the base of the north-tower pile. September 23, 2001.

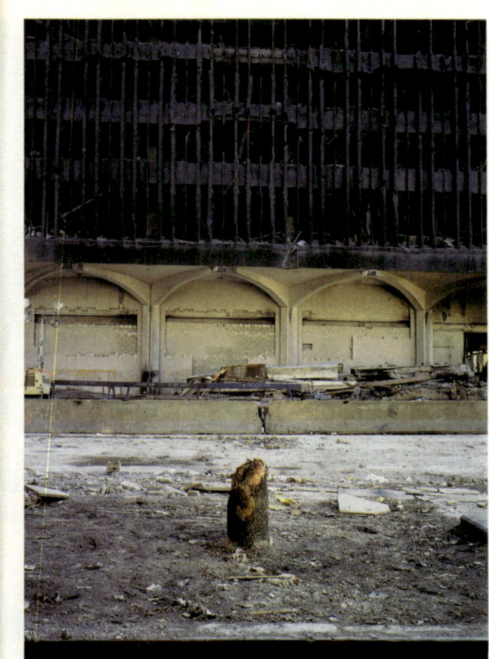

The stump of a tree destroyed on the day of the attacks, on the walk leading to the World Trade Center plaza. October 11, 2001.

plate 15 Object label on page **ii**

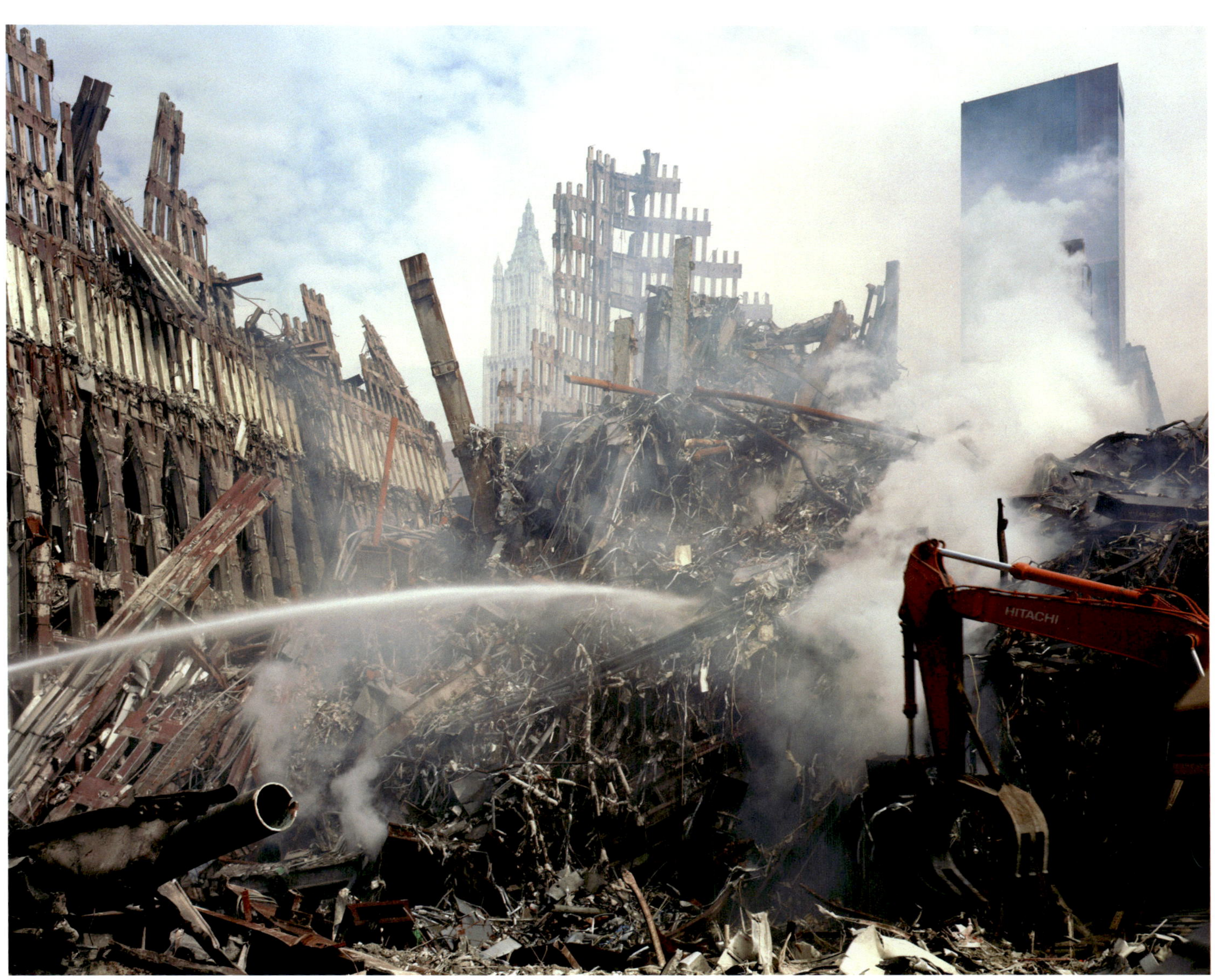
HITACHI

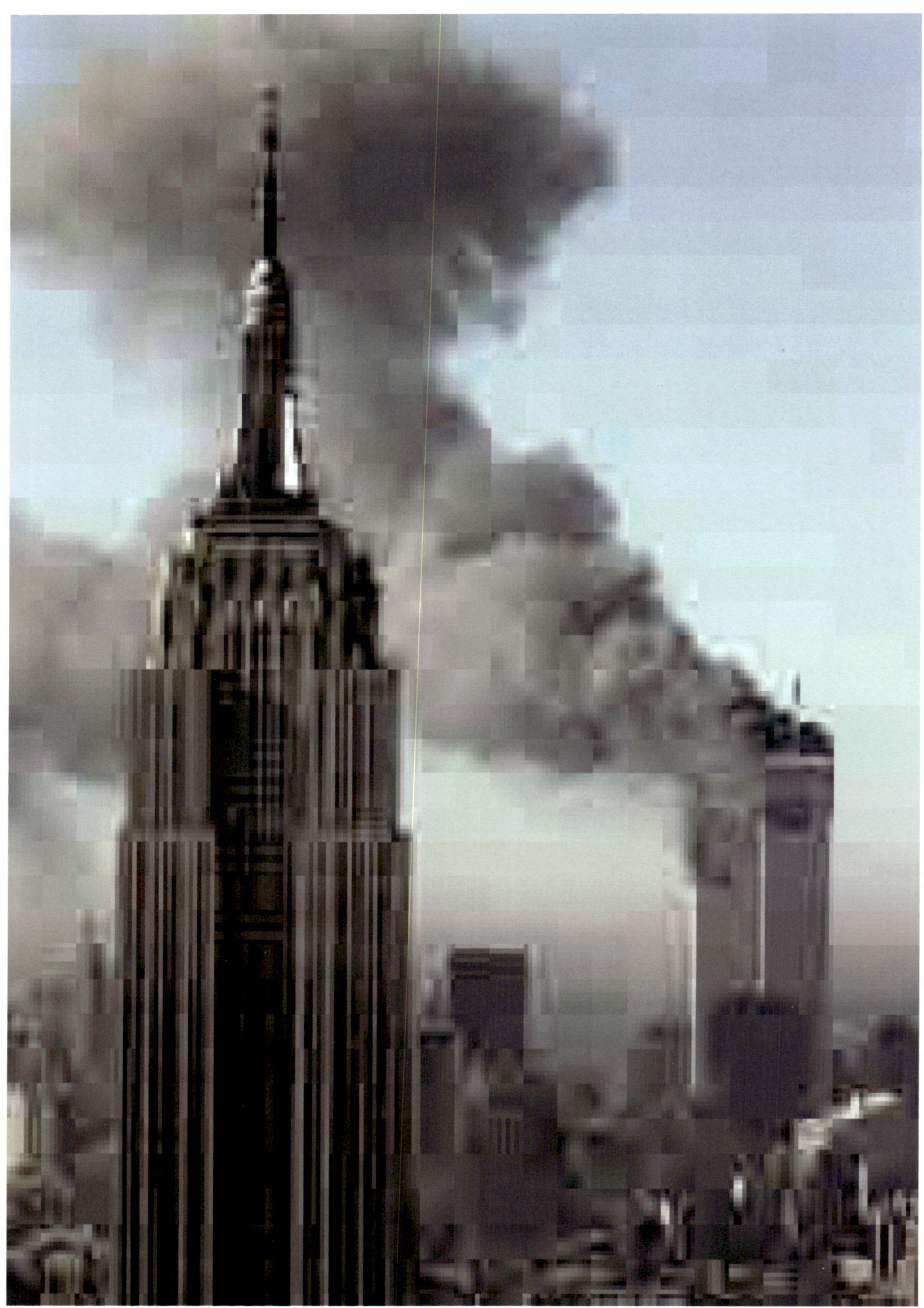

plate 17 See pages **26**, **27**, **30**, **31** Object label on page **iii**

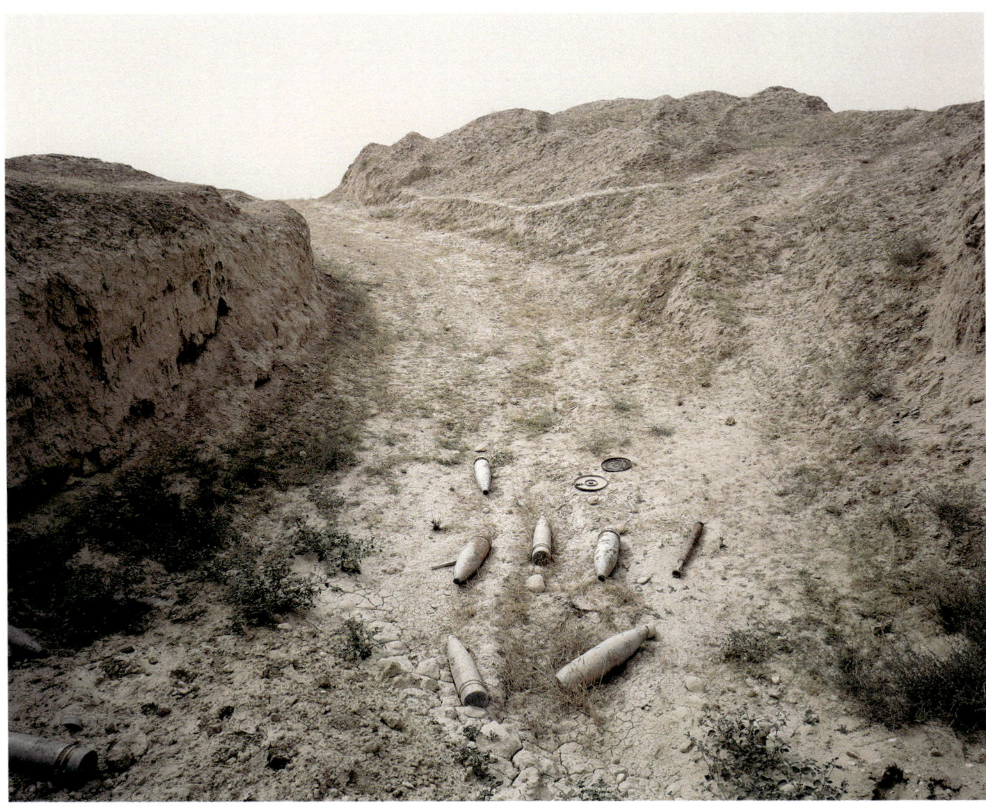

See pages 97, 112 Object label on page iii

BEAUTY IS CONTROVERSIAL. Some link it with virtue and truth, while others argue that it is tied to corruption, superficiality, and deceit. It has been deemed both essential and irrelevant to "art." History suggests, however, that beauty does wield power, often of a transformative sort. Centuries of Christian art enshrine the suffering of Jesus in beautiful images. Shrouding our dead in beauty can provide solace and respite from pain. Aestheticization of this sort is seldom a matter of airbrushing blemishes away. It is purposeful and fundamental to the meaning of the image. It may entail refined style, carefully calculated composition, or canonical iconography. Guided by such formal elegance across barriers of difference, pain, or distaste, the viewer may be able to address the causes of suffering more constructively. Alternatively, such beauty may summon too much attention, leading us to look away from pain and lulling us into passivity or lazy sentimentality. It may even lure us to erotic pleasure as we view the degradation of others. Ultimately, we must ask whether beauty deepens our critical engagement or distracts us, anesthetizing us to pain.

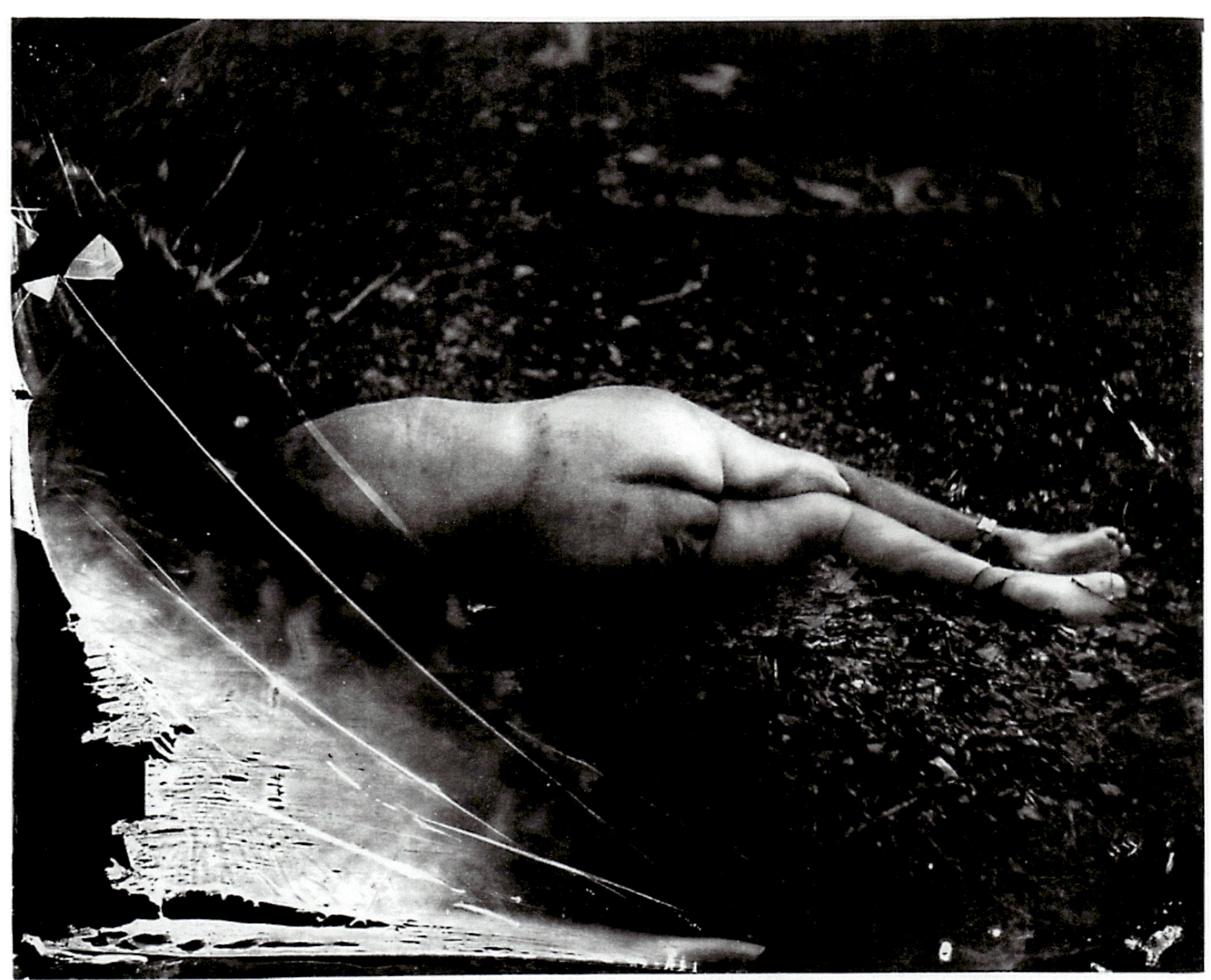

See pages 62, 63 Object label on page iii

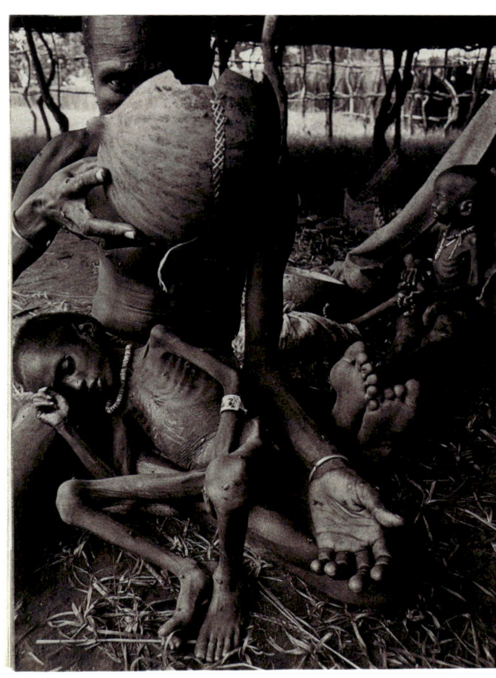

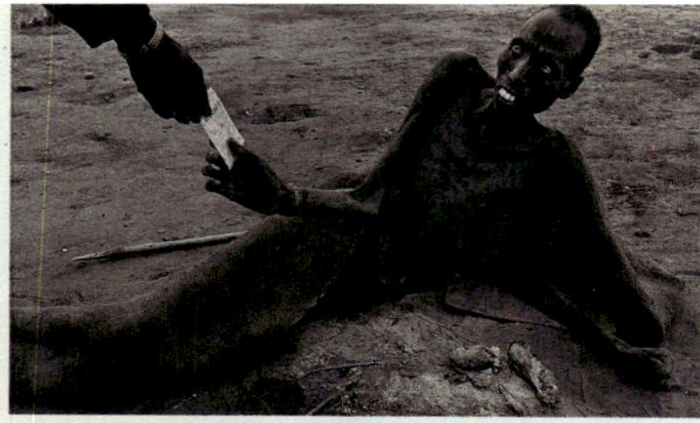

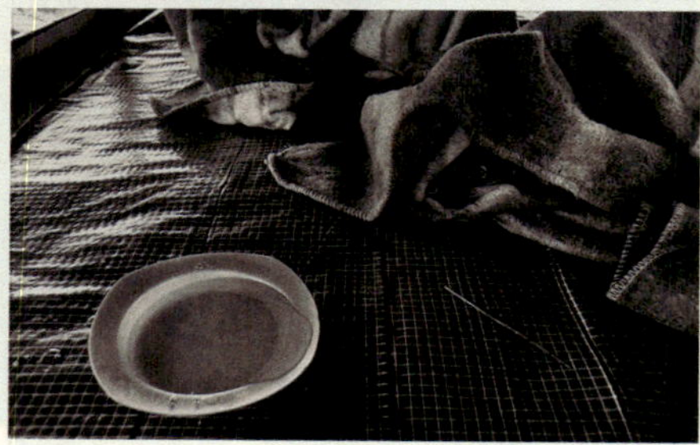

The rains have been plentiful, and the sorghum is growing. Still, in southern Sudan the old, the young and the weak are dying of starvation: a frail child is barely able to share a meager meal with his father at a feeding center; a desperately weak man stares at a bowl of water; another is huddled by the remains of a fire with a packet of rehydration salts. As earlier in Ethiopia and Somalia, this famine is in part the result of civil war. Initially the fighting pitted the Muslim government in Khartoum against Christian rebels in the south; now the rebels are also killing one another. No one knows how many are starving, but in a cycle of hatred and revenge, peace is not in sight, nor is an end to hunger.

plate 20 Object label on page **iv**

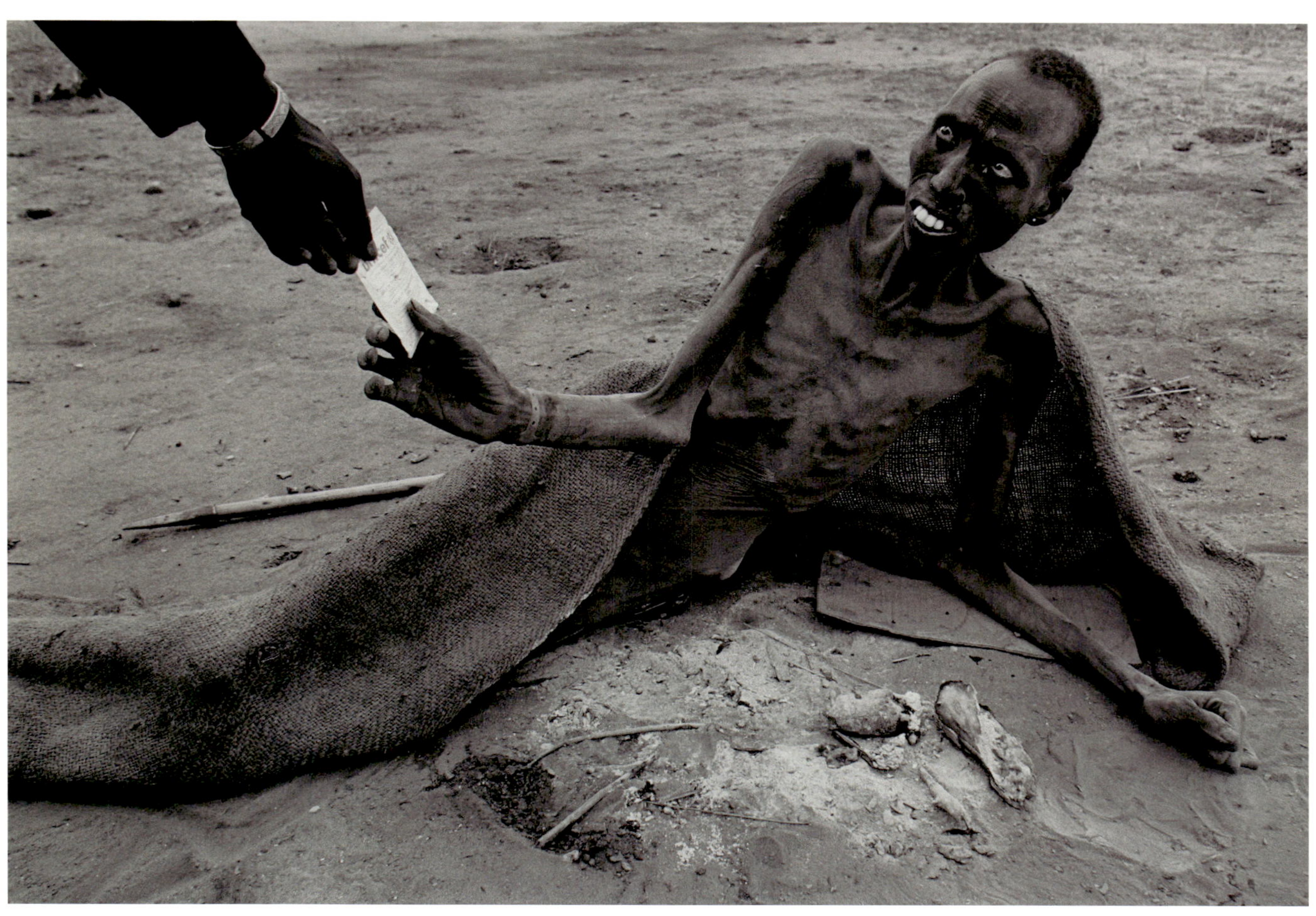

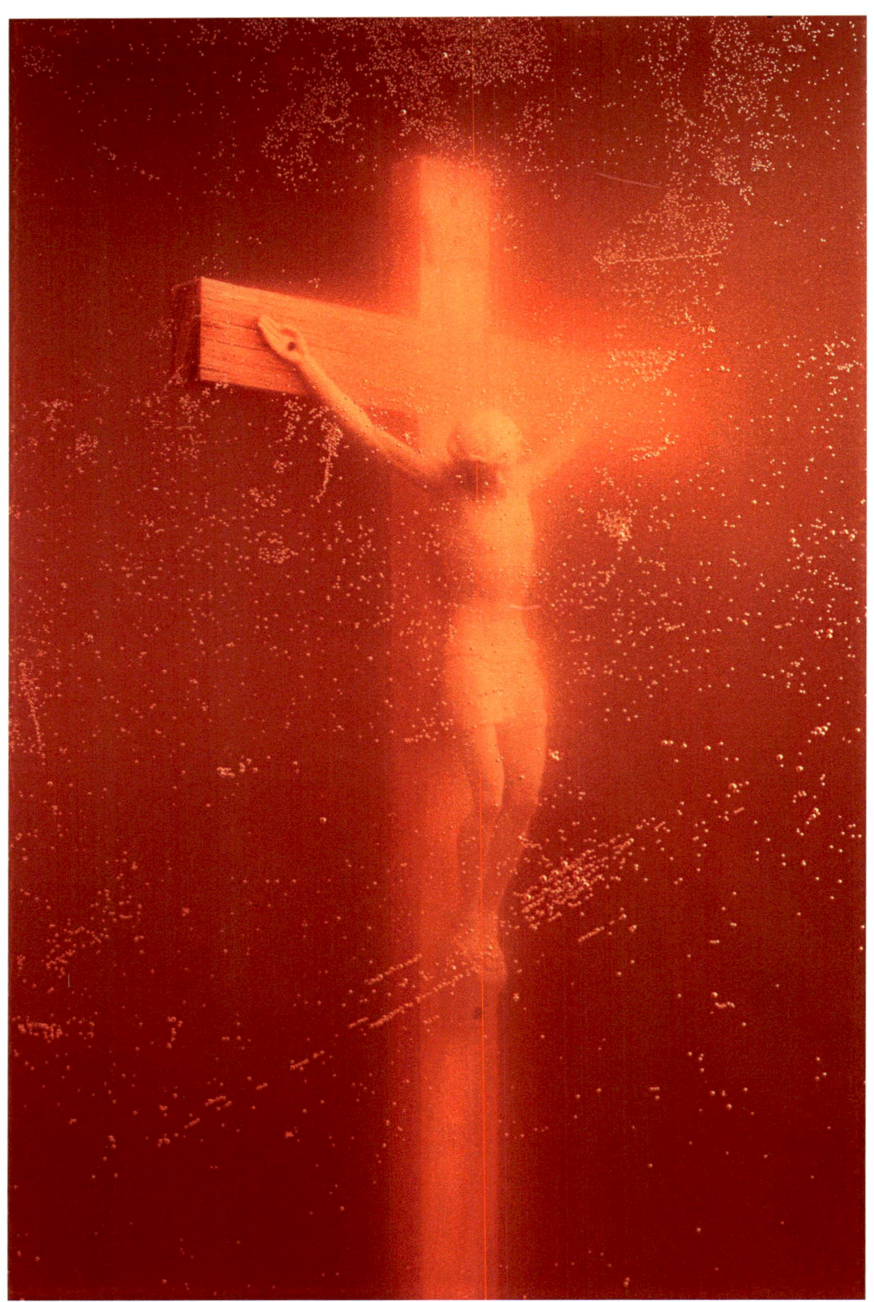

plate 22 See pages **72**, **82**, **102** Object label on page **iv**

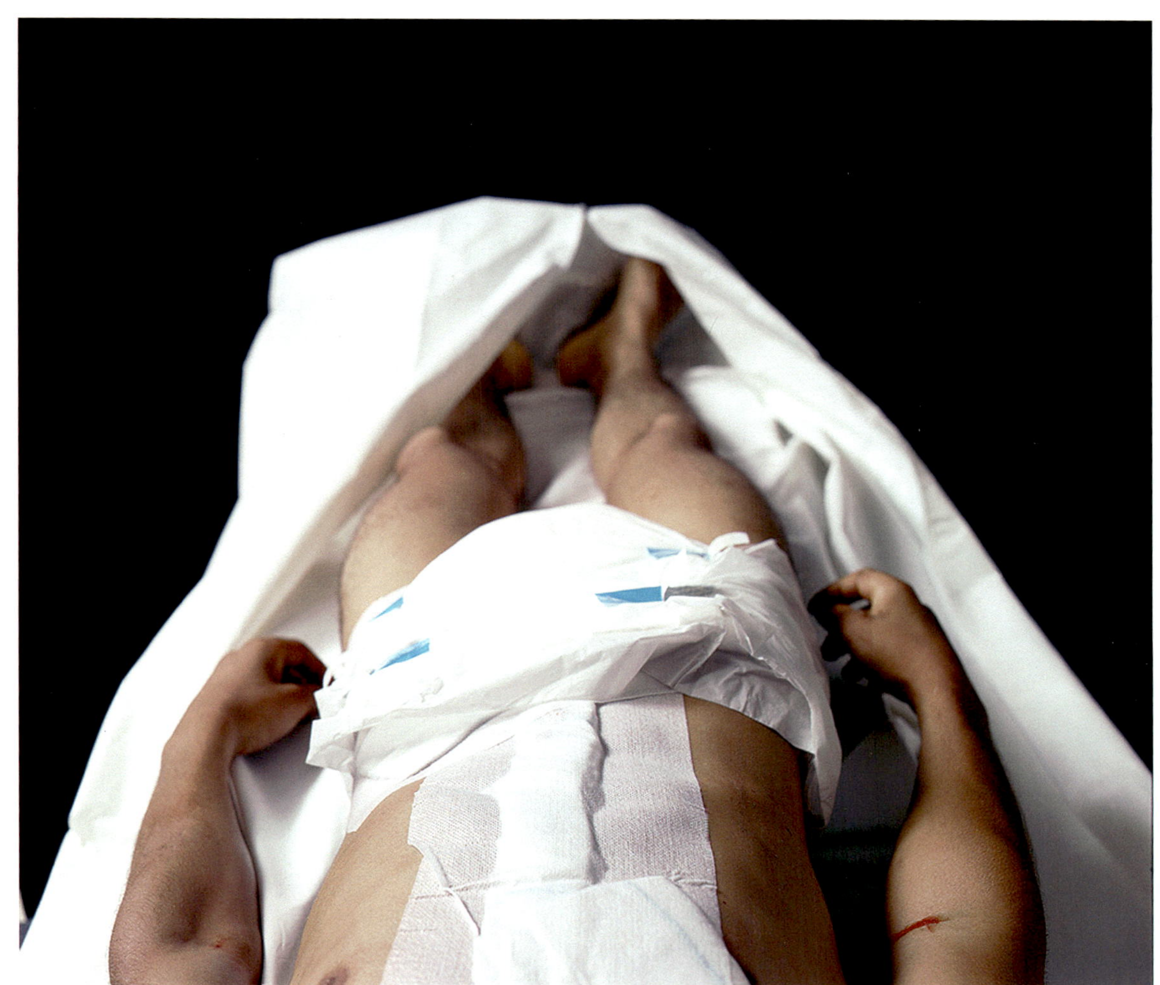

See pages 72, 112 Object label on page iv

LOADING, AIMING, SHOOTING. When applied to photography, these terms seem to imply that the act of taking someone's picture is aggressive and even violent. They suggest that photographers exercise power over their subjects and may exploit them for artistic, journalistic, or entrepreneurial gain. But what happens to the alleged hostility of the photographic act when the photographer turns the camera on her or himself, thereby documenting personal pain for public viewing? Is the power lessened or intensified if the photographer pays the subject to pose and then cites that exchange in the picture's title? Can the inclusion of texts or audio components give a voice to subjects in a way that images alone cannot? How do the culture and interests of viewers as well as photographers affect how we read the power relationships in images? Such complexities suggest that it is impossible to assess the making and viewing of photographs without considering the intricate and, at times, contradictory relations among photographers, subjects, and viewers.

letter ② The main problems of Borona Tribes 25/8/92

The Transitional Government of Ethiopia EPDRF with Their followers accomplices. Geri, Gabera, Guji and Tegree Tribes had been fighting against borona tribes in ethiopia by Burning their houses, looting their properties, killing and arresting The borona people who were living in ethiopia.

These borona tribes were detested and killed by tegree Government of ethiopia because of they are oromo people in tribe and oromo Liberation front (O.L.F) are contrary to the interests of EPDRF. there by they looked borona people like the previous regimes and supporters of O.L.F. hence the borona tribes became enemy of EPDRF in ethiopia.

For Example: the under named borona people head leaders Those who were arrested by tegree/EPDRF

1. BULEE KULLU GUYO 2. Golisa ROBA 3. DAWID DABASU These three persons are still imprisoned in ethiopia and they are going to be killed by tegree/EPDRF

most of the borona people. because of all these above mentioned problems they fled to Kenya to save their lives and Camped here in Walda the problems that they had been frightened when they were In ethiopia came with and following after them to Kenya, Walda Refugees camp and nirobi

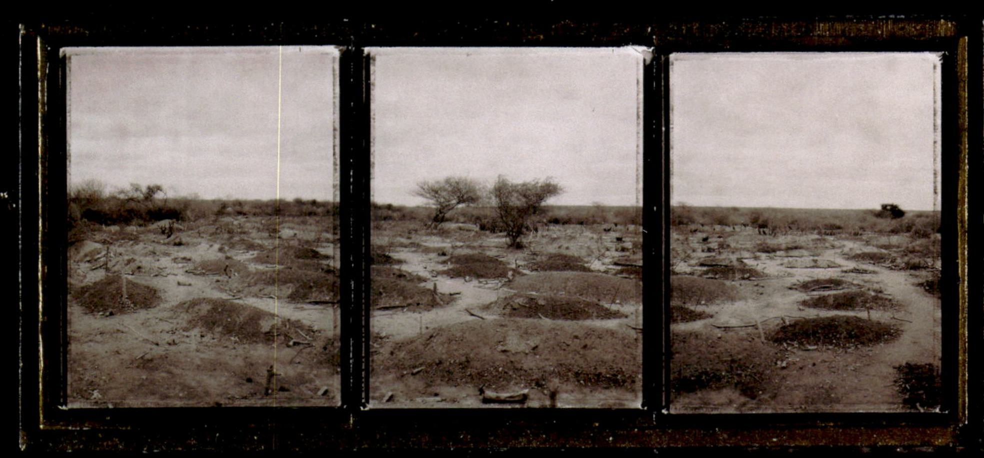

For Example! The man whose name is called Jaatani Ali Dandu who was the famous and head leader of borona people was killed by EPDRF and Geri Spies on 2/6/92 in nirobi

Here in walda from borona tribes refugees about eight (8) persons were Killed. 12 persons were disappeared, ten (10) persons were wounded by Geri tribe refugees on 29/7/92

All the deadsmen bodies were maimed to pieces and thrown away. when this accedent happened to borona tribes ten (10) other Tribes who are in Walda as a refugee from different country; UNHCR of Walda, and Walda police station were eyewitness for the above mentioned conditions. Thereby if we think to goback to ethiopia we will not able to get peace for our problems are still going on in ethiopia

From now on here in walda camp we can't stay for long time for we have been suffering and in fatal conditions.

Hence we would like to report you as soon as possible as you try to give us solution which will satisfy us and protect us from all our above mentioned problems.

We do hope as you will give us a posetive answer. We beg and ask you all above mentioned problems to get solution with in few days With Thanks

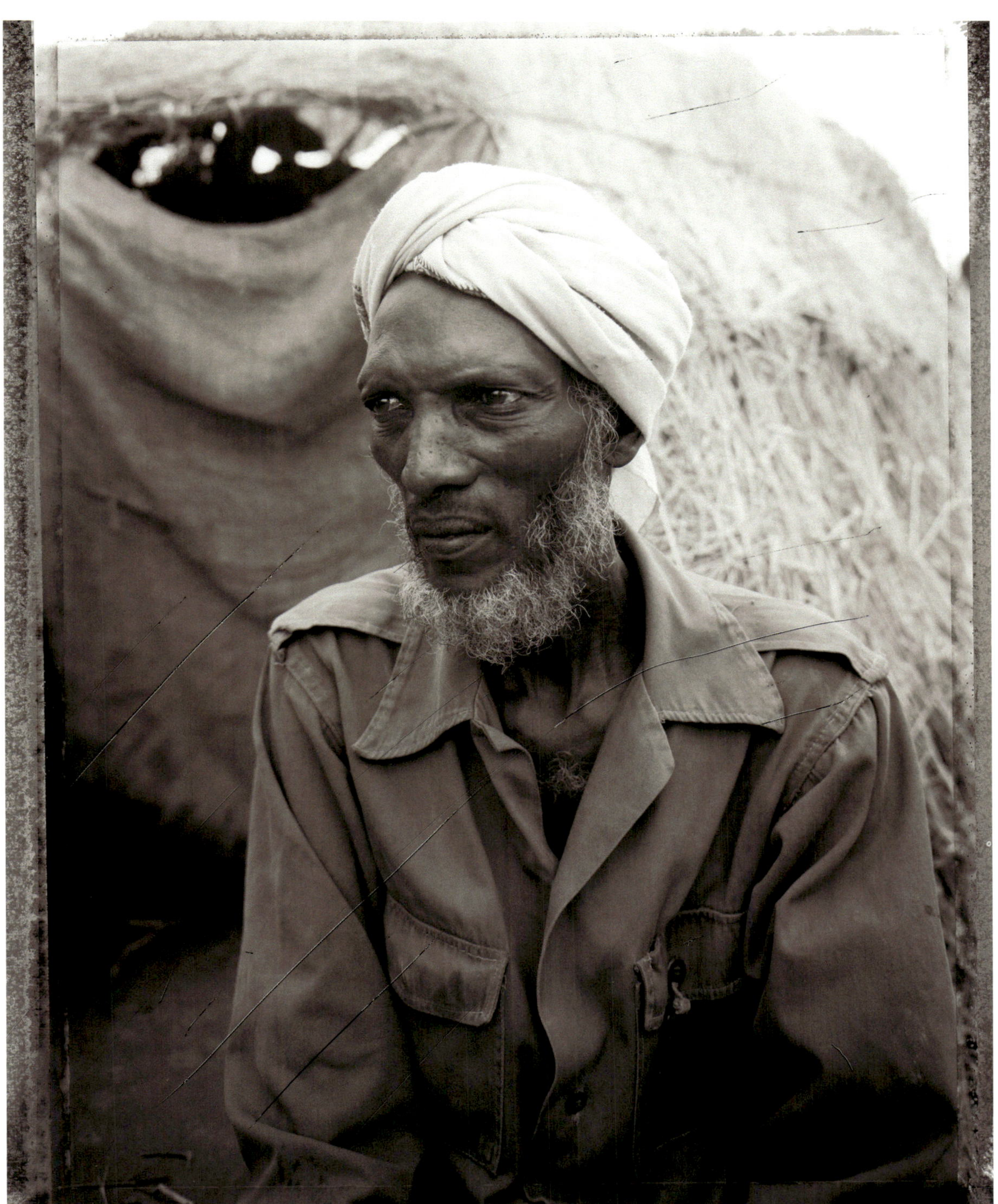

See pages 34, 97, 99, 112 Object label on page iv

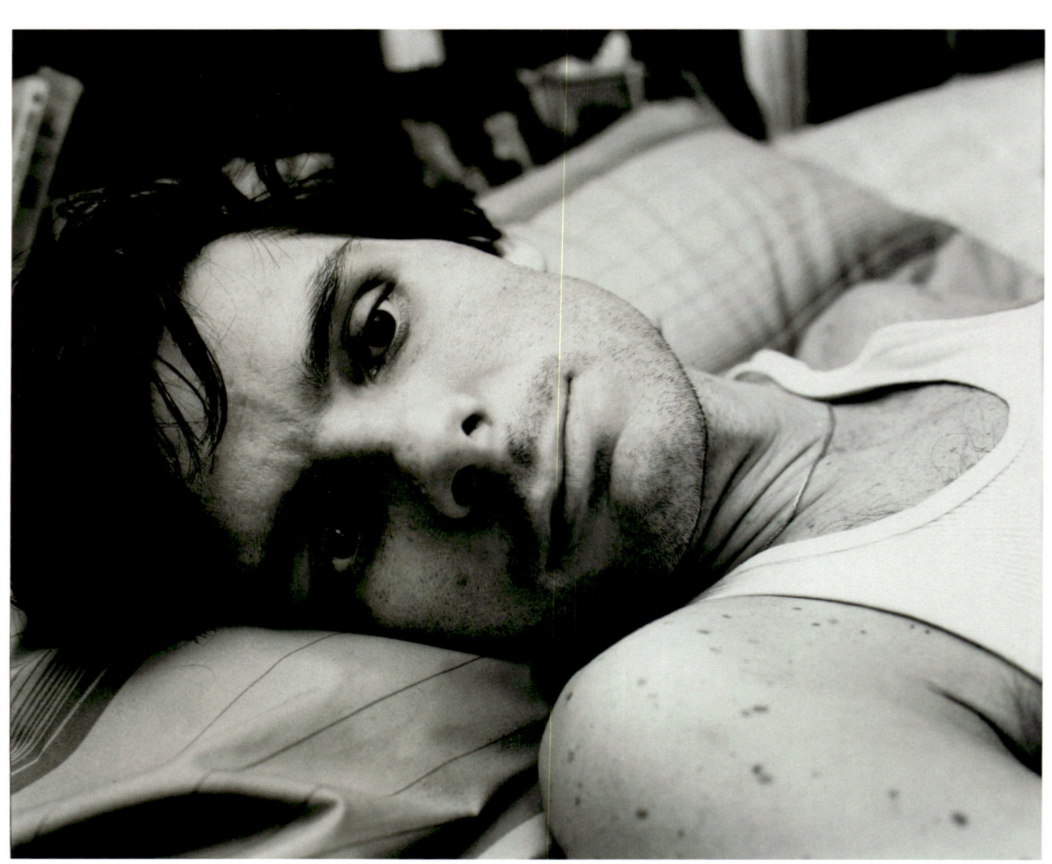

plate 25 See page **94** Object label on page **iv**

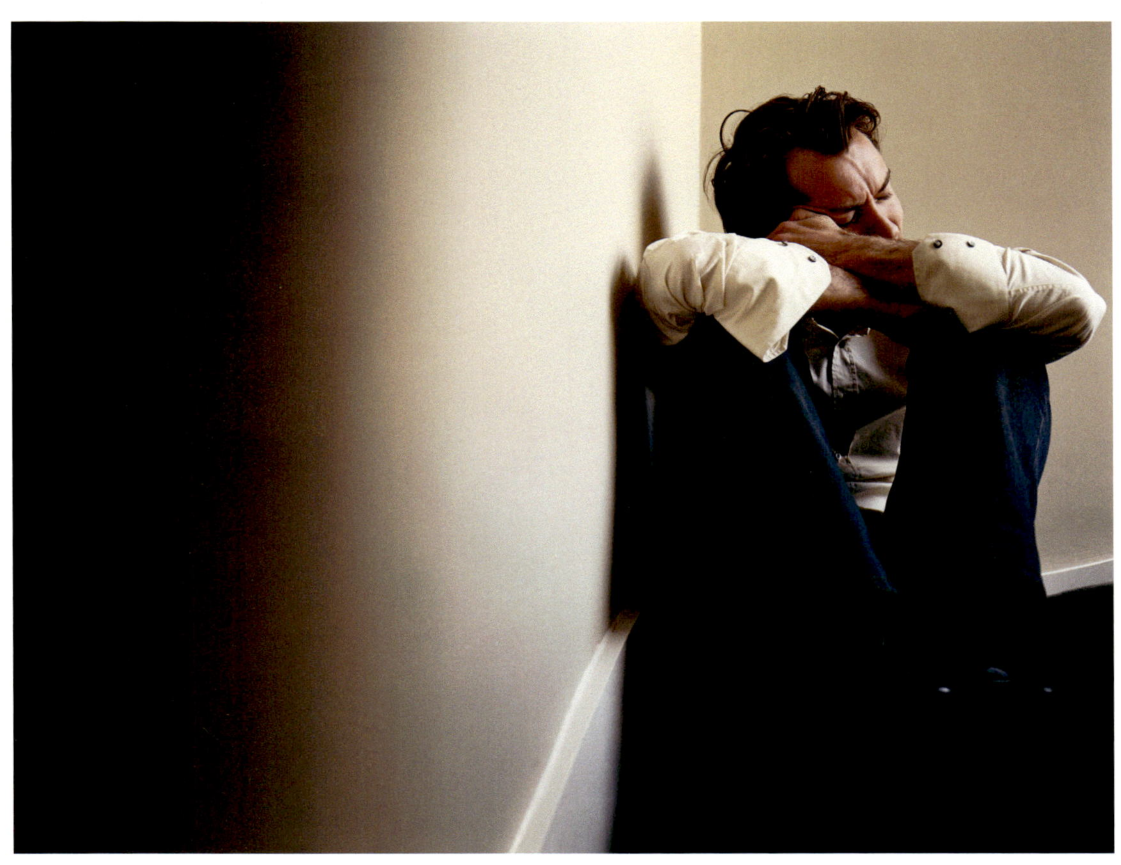

Object label on page **iv**

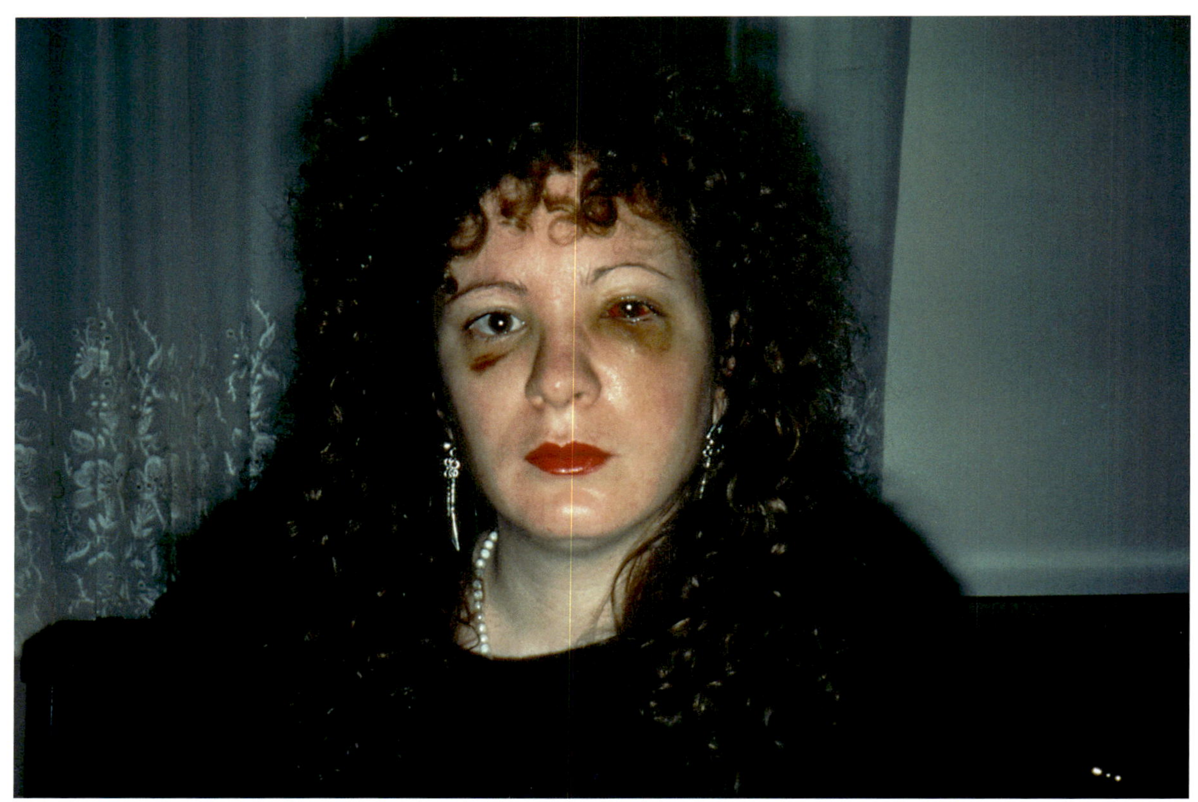

plate 27 See pages **102**, **104** Object label on page **v**

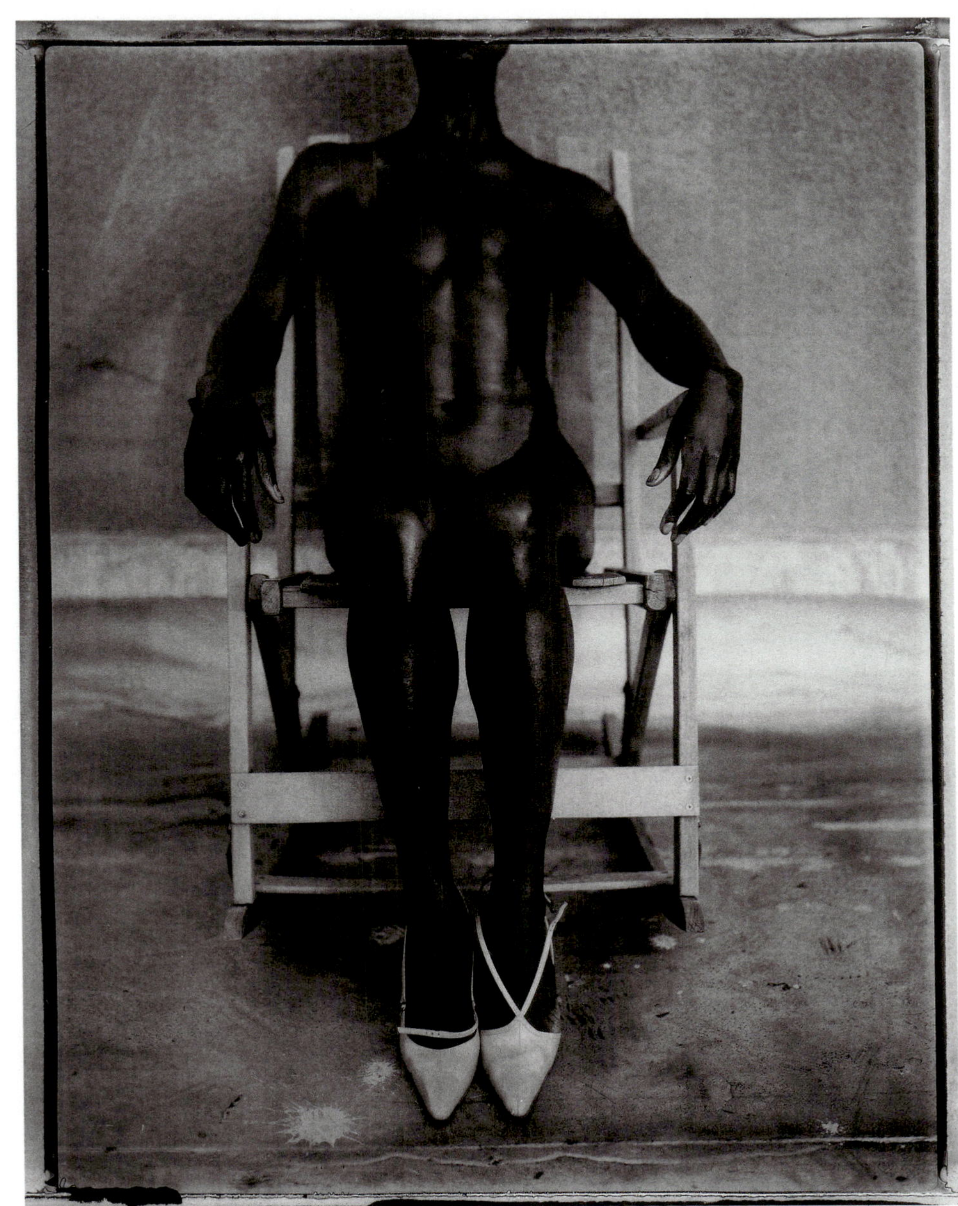

See pages 103, 112 Object label on page v

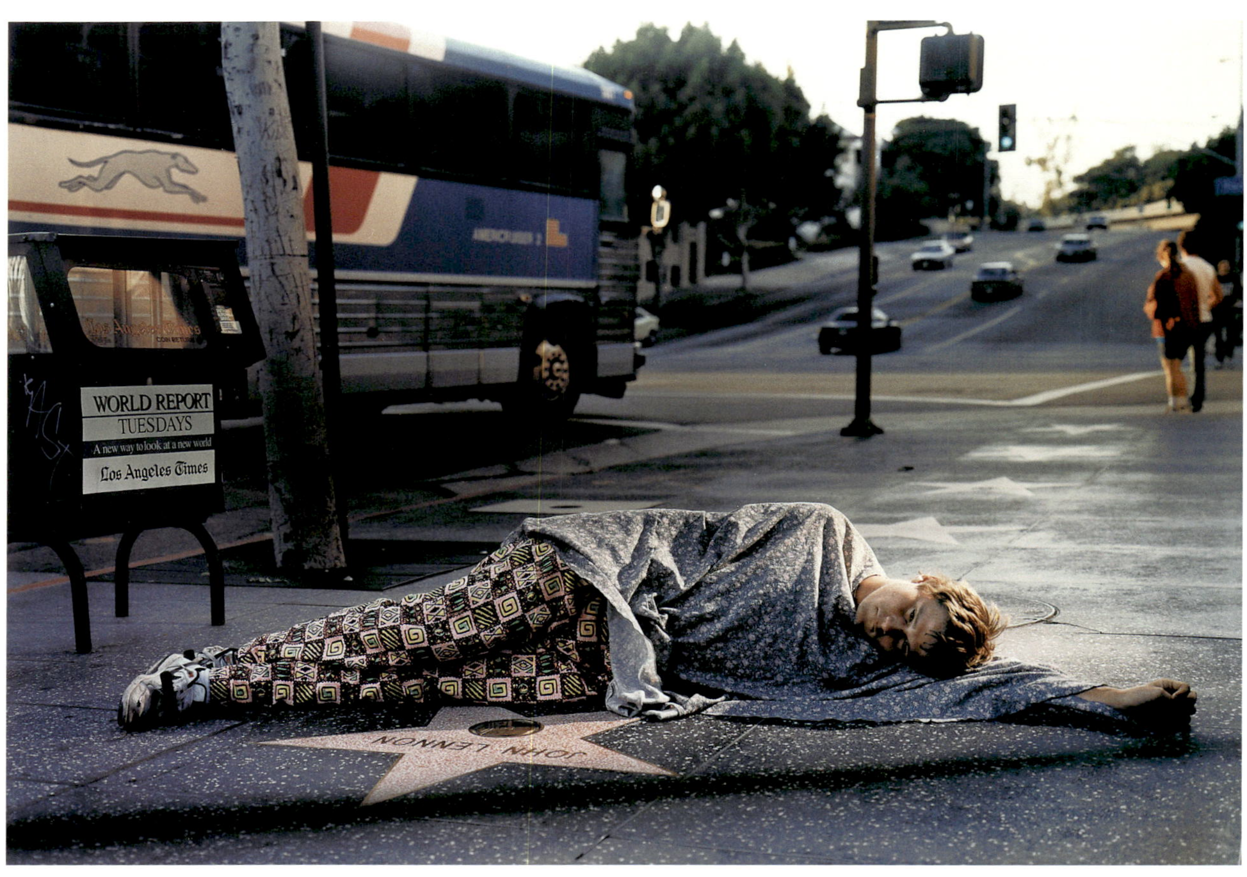

plate 29 See pages 91, 101 Object label on page v

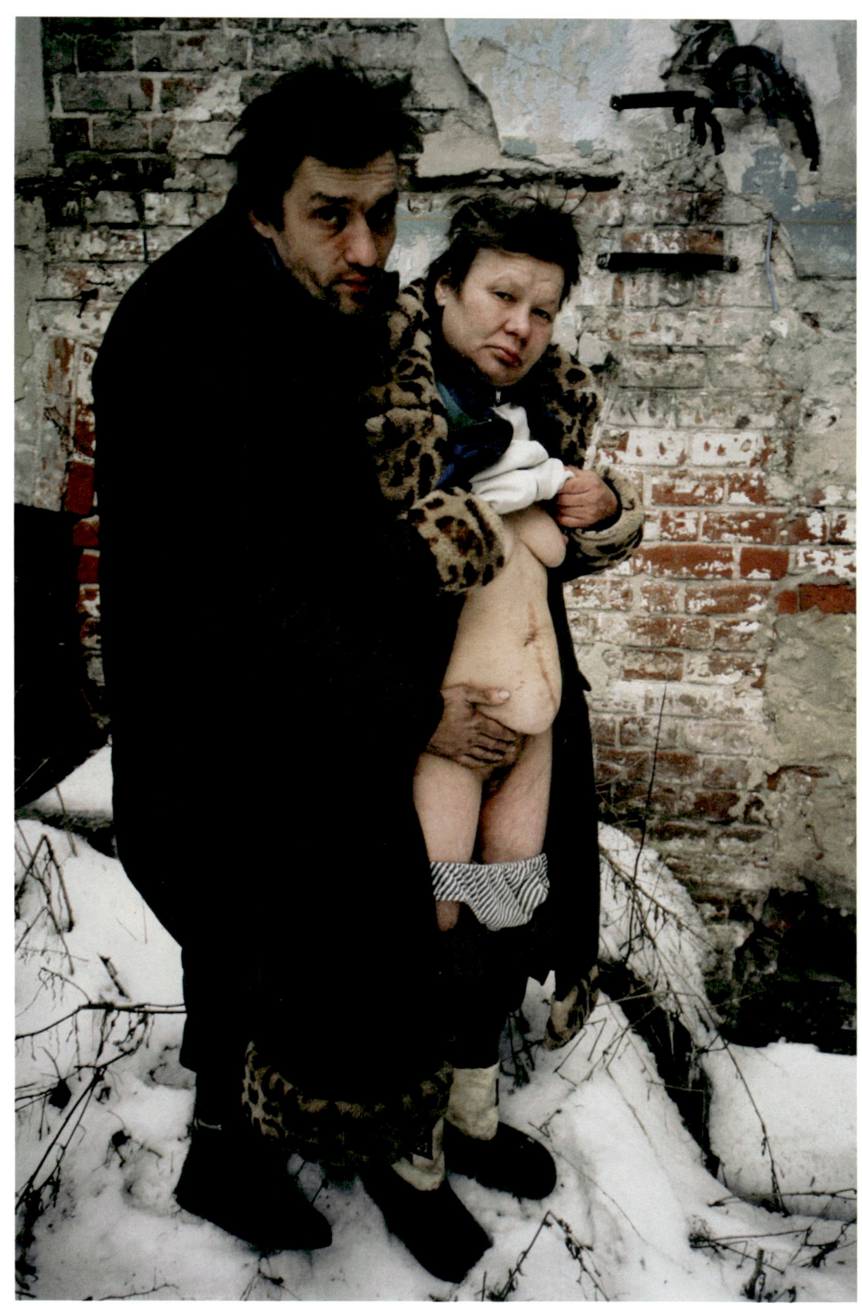

See page 102 Object label on page v

I'm on my way to a party, so I've got to talk fast. I'm going to be there all day long. I mean, actually, all night, until like 3, maybe 3:30, or 4. We're going to hang out, listen to music, eat candy—all that stuff. There'll be girls there, yeah, of course. My name is Edgardo Figueroa, and I'm fourteen.

I want to mention something about pictures, photographs. They're important, they're like memories. They bring you back if you look at them fifty years from now. I've lost a lot of pictures in my life. When we moved out of our old house, in the storage, we lost a lot of things. I've looked for them, but Mom didn't tell me nothing. I don't know where things went. I was thinking, all those moments—gone. When I realized a lot of things were lost, it's weird.

Anyway, to change the subject, my best subjects in school are social studies, English, and shop. Basically, I've already decided I want to be a cop. My older sister's in the academy now.

If I had three wishes I'd have lots of money, I'd wish I was an adult already, and I'd wish for peace in the world. I'm sick and tired of being treated like a little kid.

Look—I'm dressing up as a woman for Halloween. The idea just flicked into my brain. Of course this was only a one-day thing; it's not like I'm going to go gay. I don't want people mistaking me for a transvestite.

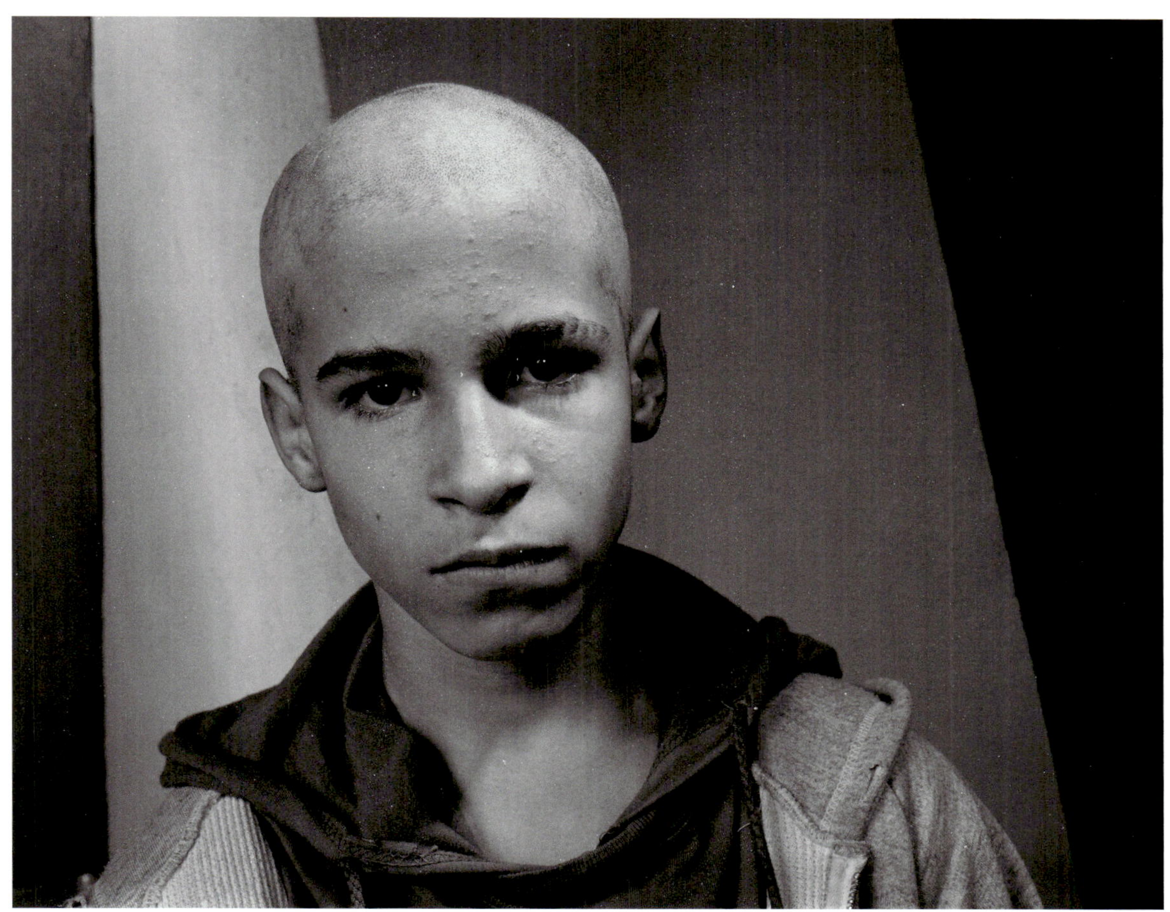

 See page 101 Object label on page v

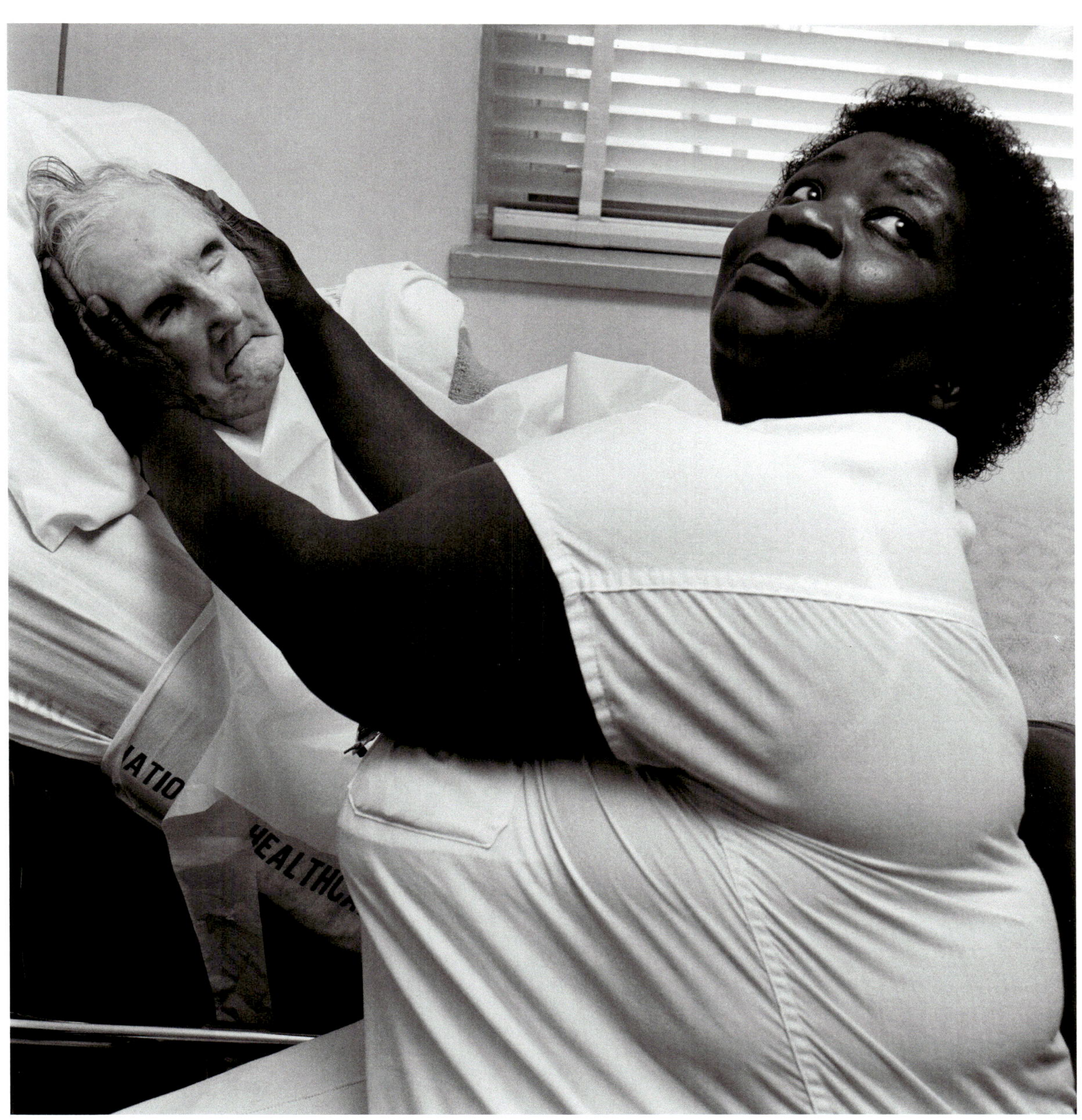

Object label on page **v**

My name is Doris. I'm 43. I've got a Bachelor's degree in Sociology, and I've been diagnosed with what used to be called Multiple Personality Disorder, what is now referred to as Disassociative Identity Disorder, or D.I.D. If... and this is kind-of a dream, if I ever get lucky, and win the Lotto—and I try, I'd buy a house of my own. It's my home, and no one can take it away from me. Because I'd feel safe; that was mine. And do nice, normal things. Maybe have a dog or a cat or two running around, or be able to cook a good meal and be able to have individuals actually appreciate... And have that freedom to be myself. As a child growing up, I didn't know if I was going to be alive the next year or not. I can remember... there was physical violence... Father who molested me; Mother was physically violent. I've got scars on my hand from my mother sticking my finger in a fan. Being pushed down flights of stairs and there was something so horrible that happened, I became deathly afraid of going into somebody else's house; to a point where I would just sit, frozen, afraid to move, and I guess, started fragmenting, and fragmenting, and fragmenting because there were so many incidents. It's like a fear of drowning. And nobody stepped in. My multiple personalities came from a need to protect myself against the shock of the traumatic occurrences I had growing up. And especially if it's a dangerous situation, it's a total blackout and all I'd got was a scary feeling left over. They start doing that to protect my mind because at a young age, I probably would've died from the shock. I'm alive because I've got my personalities. But it's dysfunctional in adult years. I've lived on the street as a homeless individual for a couple of years, trying to go from shelter to shelter and waiting and hoping that you'd finally get off the streets. There was this one time I was in Dallas, just wandering around the streets, and it was like early in the evening and the next thing I know, I'm half-way between Dallas and Texarkana and there's a car driving away.. and I don't know how the hell I got there. I'm scared to death, I can't explain why.. and it's a lot later at night.. and I did not know how the hell I got there. The public looks at individuals with mental illness like we're not even human. When I look at people who talk about that, they use terms like "Lunatic." They talk about you in the third person, like you're not even in the room. They think we're all dangerous, and they don't want to be seen in our company. They're afraid to come near us. Little kids and animals see something in me that is good. Little kids'll come up to me. And you can't really lie to a small child about that, 'cause they haven't learned to see that lie yet. I've had more dogs and cats come up to me trying to persuade me to lettin' them in my home and birds, too. And gettin' a couple of geese at the zoo to look at me and stare while I take their picture—Not everybody can do that. One thing that helped me survive all these years, and to keep goin' was the conversation I had with the Orthodox rabbi here in San Antonio. He said, "Well, if you get well, I'd convert you." He gave me the courage and the hope and just something to grasp for. And when I became Jewish, my heart and everything about me was already there. I wasn't going to let anybody take that away from me because that meant no matter where I go, they have to accept me... as a part of the community. INTERVIEWED AND EDITED BY MICHAEL NYE

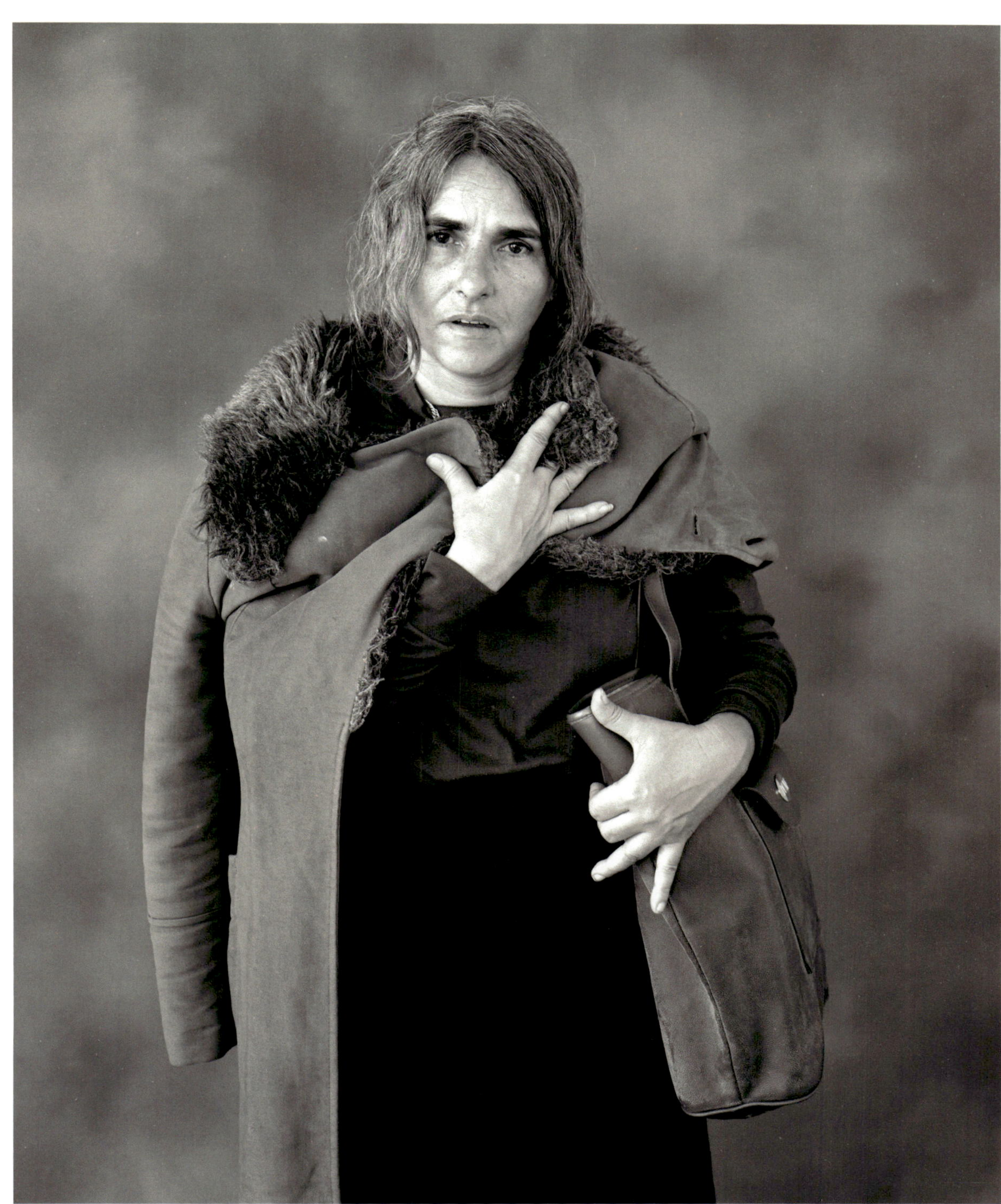

See page 34 Object label on page v

ALL PHOTOGRAPHS ARE IN SOME SENSE FABRICATIONS, but not all ask to be recognized as such. The captions and visual rhetoric employed in mainstream traditions of reportage have vested photographs with special evidentiary authority, treating images as traces of the real. So, when a famous picture of a conflict turns out to have been staged for the camera, the discovery often provokes the anger of a broken promise. The pictures on this wall, however, allow no such scandal: rather than suppressing their fabricated character, they revel in it, making it internal to the meaning of the work. Some present wholly fictitious traumas. Others return to historically important sites of violence, altering a scene the photographer never could have witnessed or transforming an iconic picture taken long ago by someone else. By refashioning histories, these works critically engage the ways images of suffering shape individual and public memory. They also raise questions about how the ethical stakes in representing suffering change when photographers abandon traditional forms of witnessing. Do questions of exploitation, sentimentality, and sensationalism vanish when the injuries in question are not "real"? Are there events or experiences for which the irony that marks many of these works is morally misplaced? Do the photographs here accomplish more, less, or just something altogether different from those we see everyday in the news?

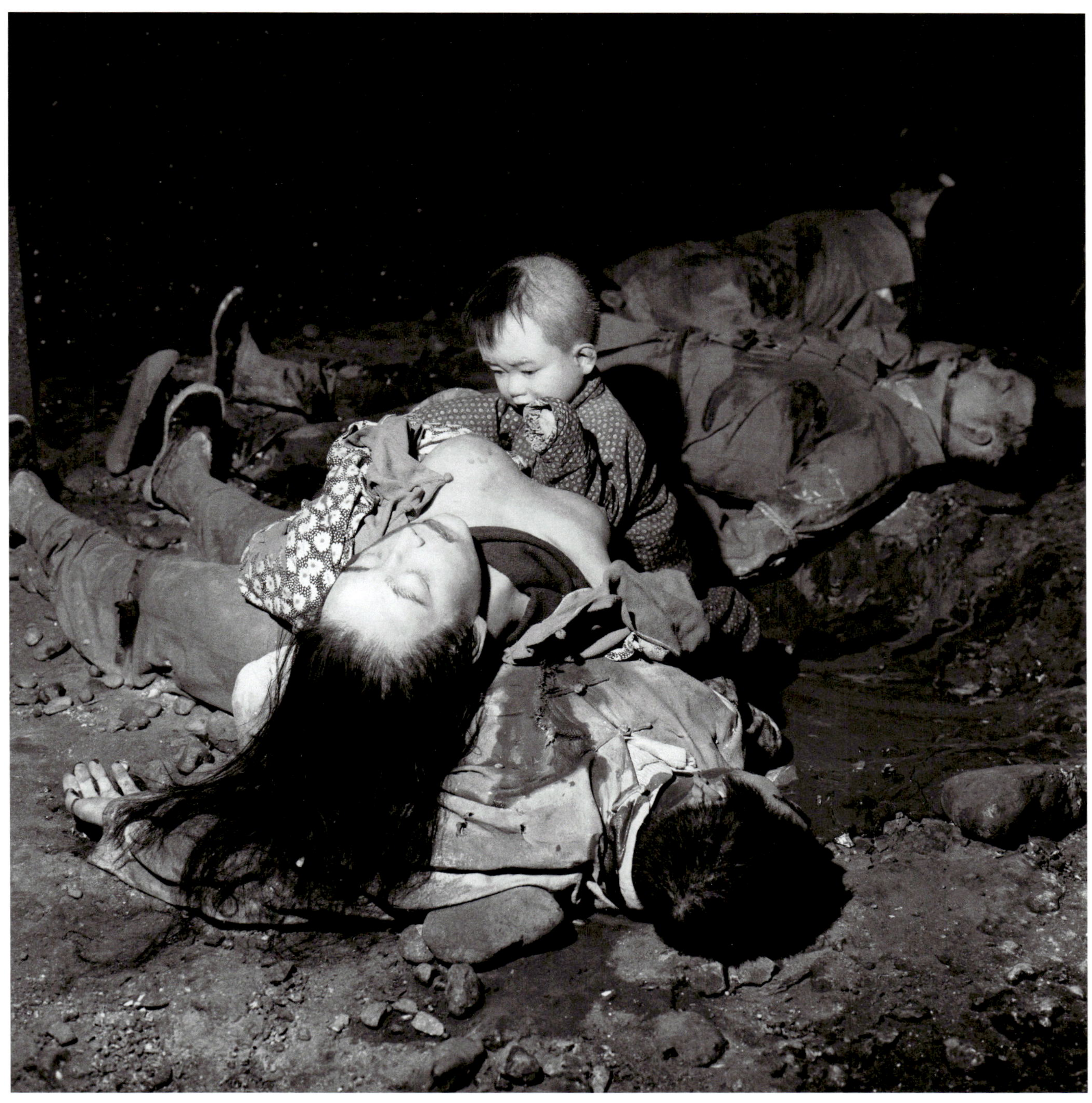

Object label on page **vi**

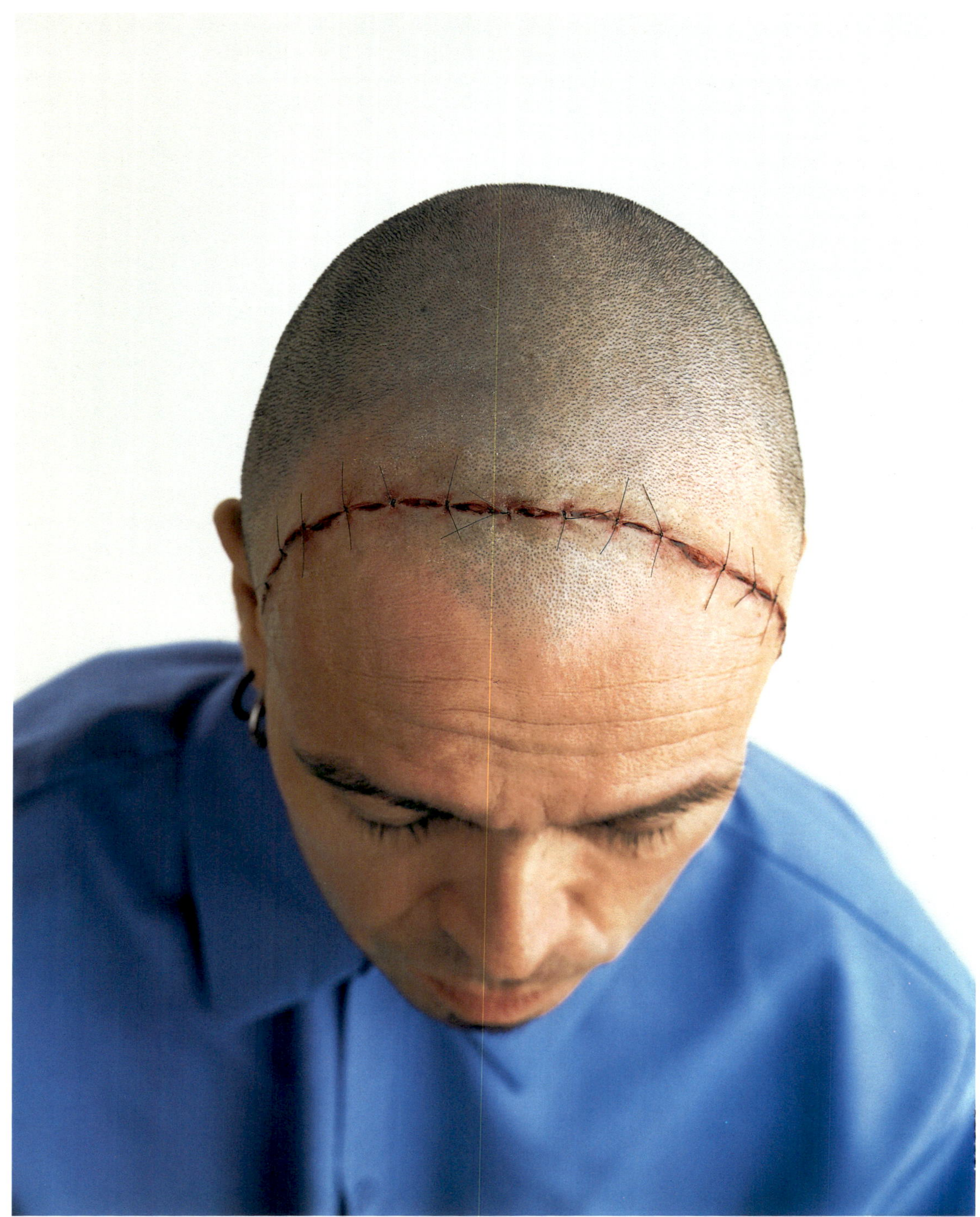

plate 35 Object label on page **vi**

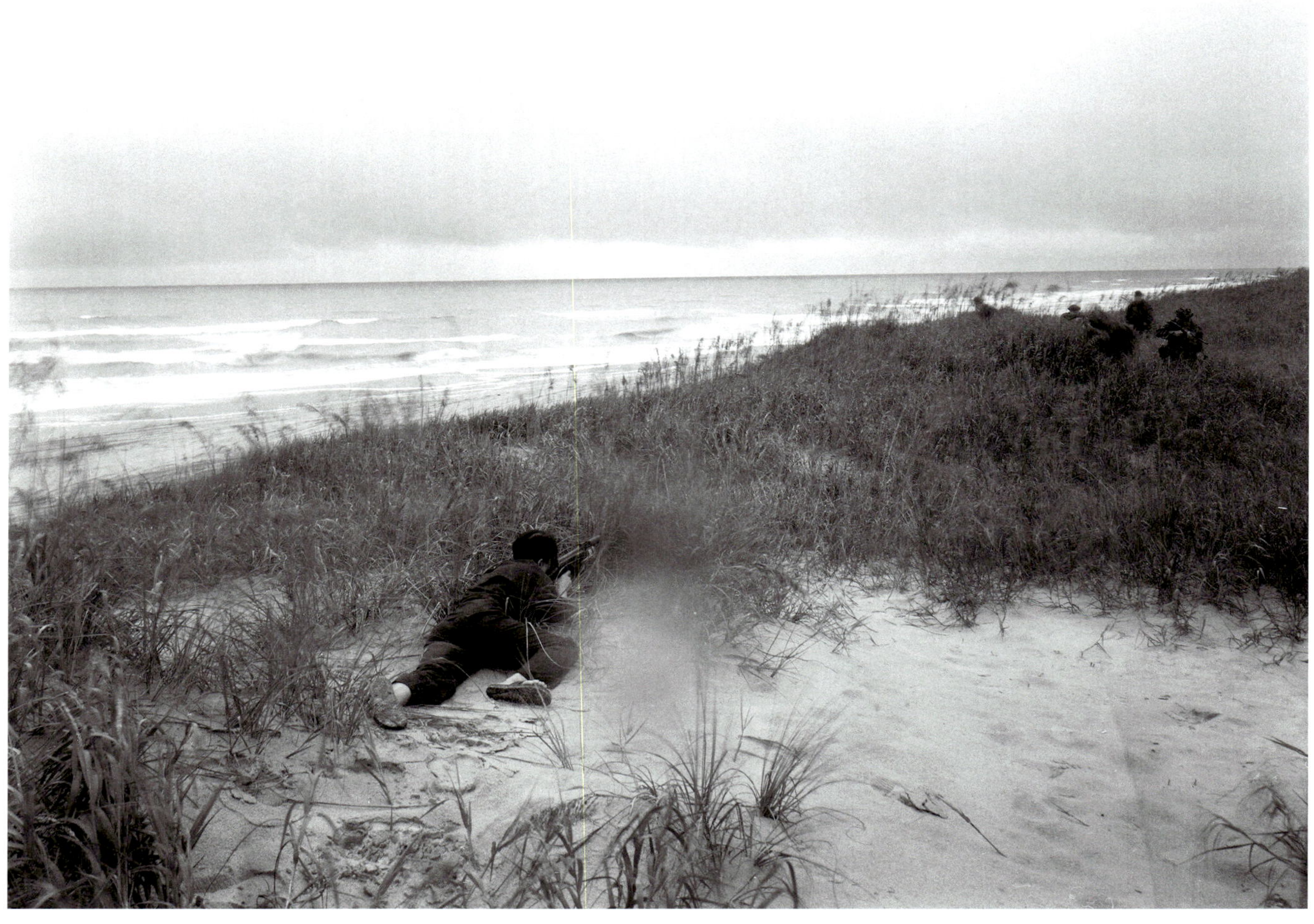

plate 36 See page 97 Object label on page vi

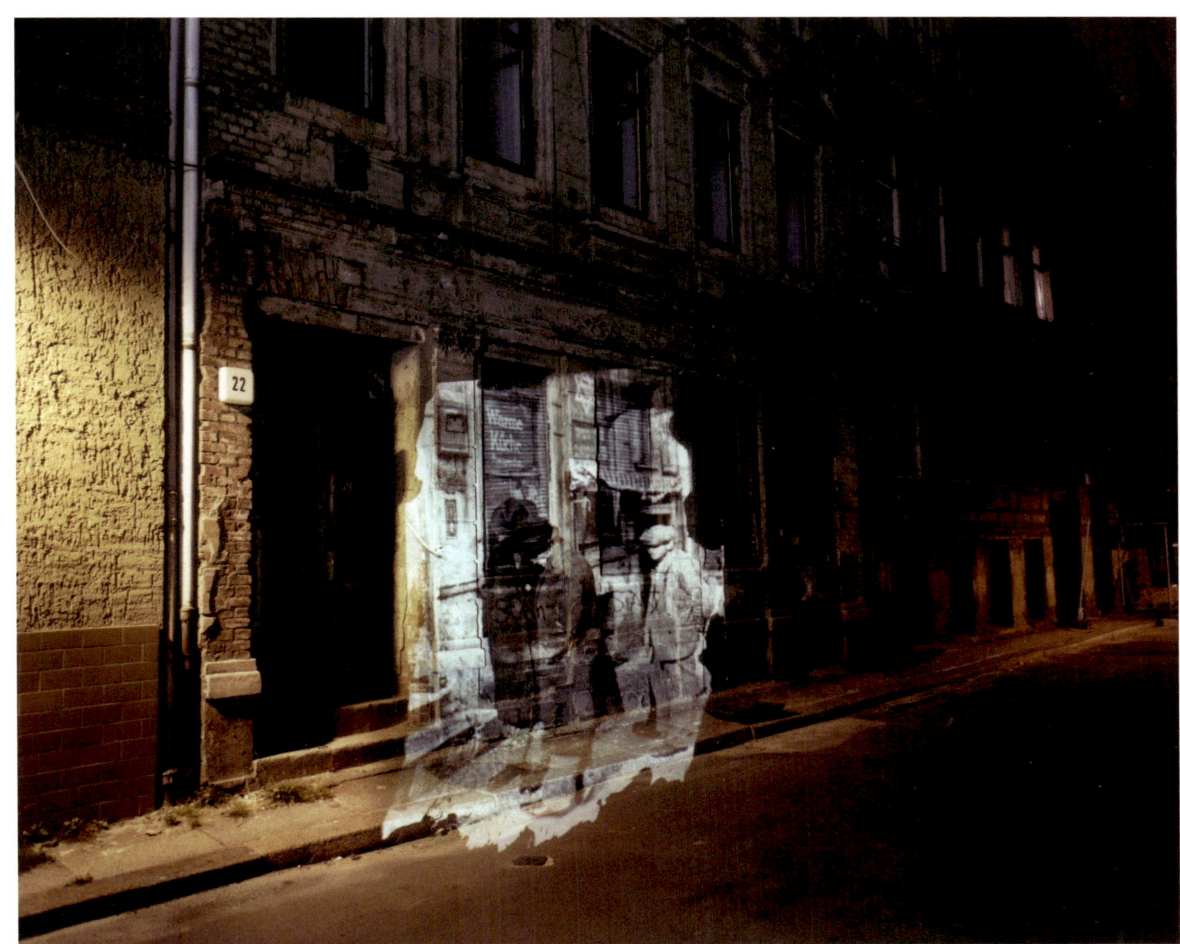

See pages 29, 30, 35, 112 Object label on page vi

Mylai, March 16, 1968

Victims of the slaughter at Mylai sprawl on a road outside the village. It was more than a year after the event that the news finally got out and Army photographer Haeberle's pictures were published.

RONALD HAEBERLE

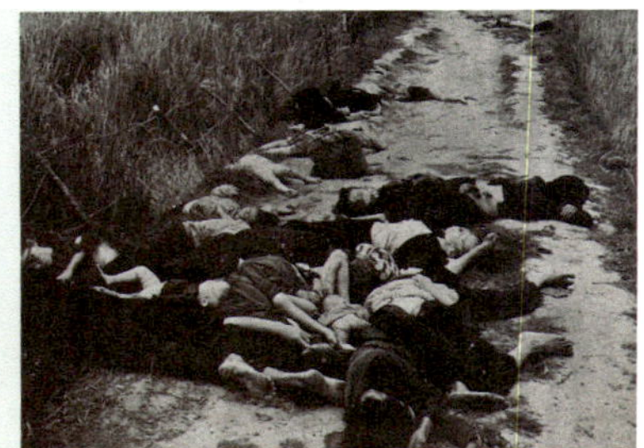

Saigon, February 1968

At the height of the Tet offensive, Saigon Police Chief Nguyen Ngoc Loan summarily executes a Viet Cong suspect. A few months later LIFE ran a picture of Loan himself wounded in a street battle.

EDDIE ADAMS

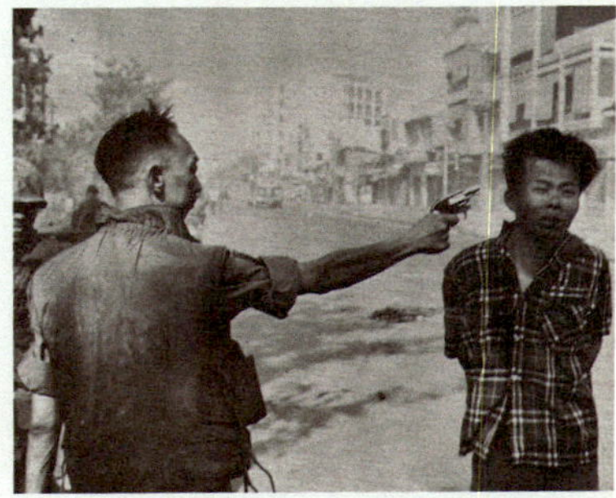

Trang Bang, June 1972

Napalmed in error by a South Vietnamese plane, Phan Thi Kim Phuc flees from the scene after tearing off her flaming clothes.

NICK UT

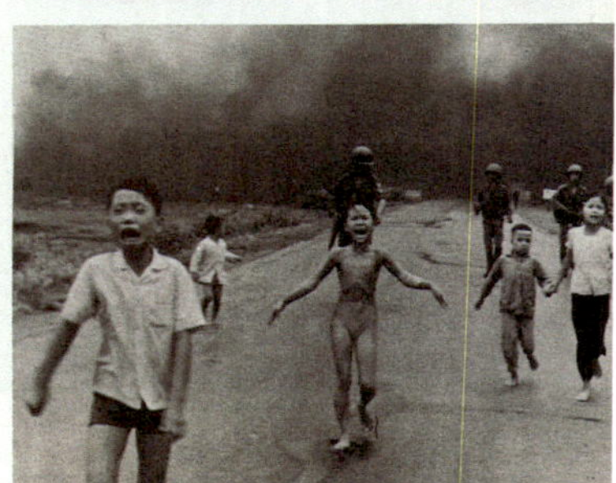

 See page 105 Object label on page vii

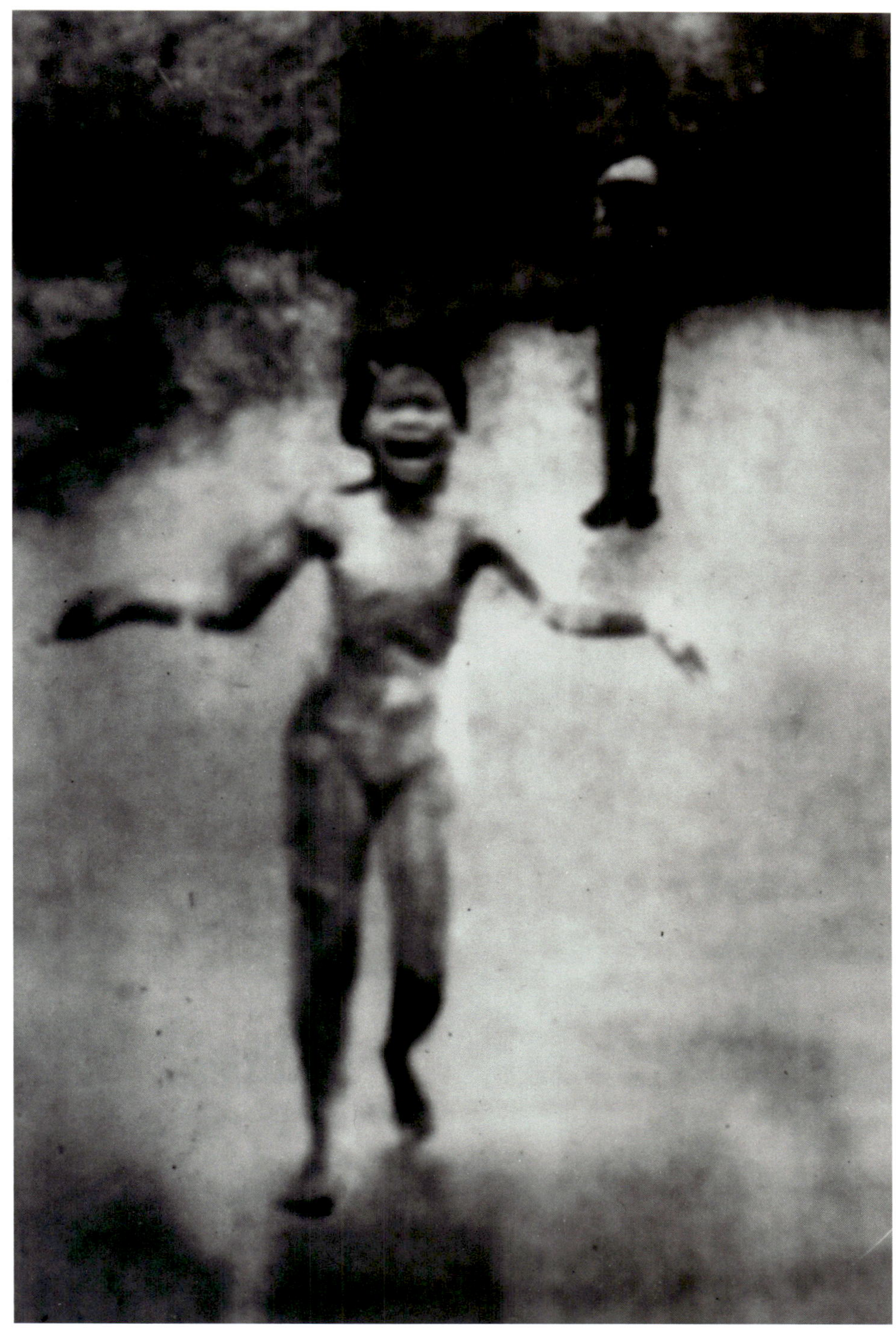

 See pages 105–107 Object label on page vii

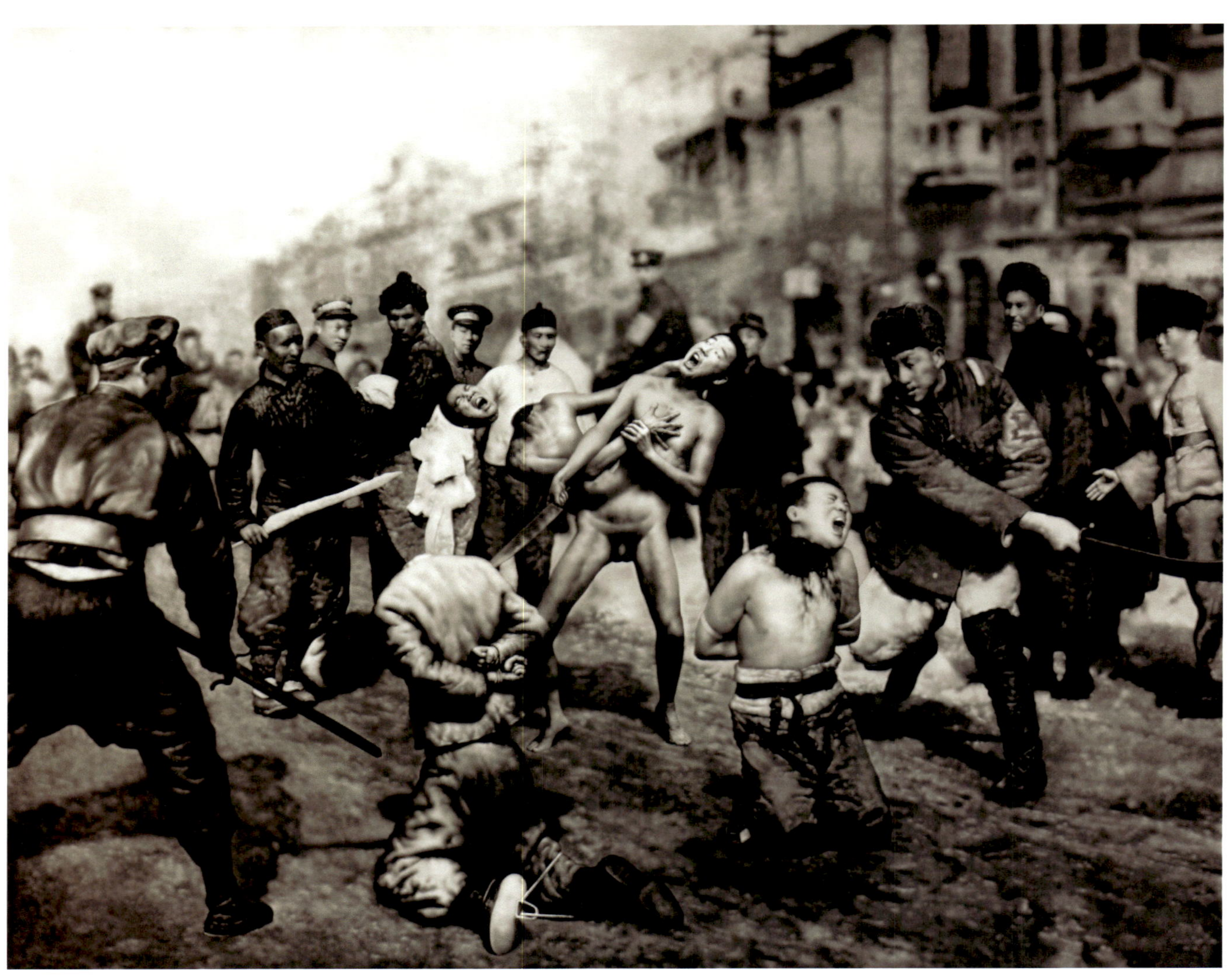

plate 40 Object label on page **vii**

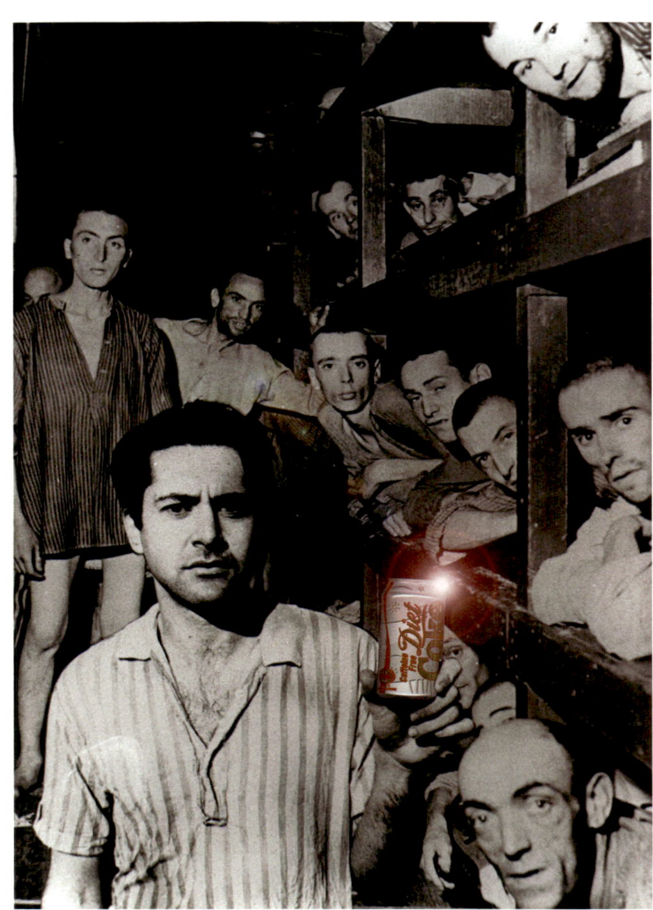

 See pages **35**, **36** Object label on page **viii**

WHAT DOES IT MEAN TO BEAR WITNESS? How can one do it effectively when crises seem to happen daily and images pass by in a blur? How can one prevent viewers from becoming numb and passive? For many photographers, bearing witness means gaining intimate knowledge of subjects and the circumstances in which they live and then disseminating what they have seen and experienced in magazines and newspapers. Working with the print media, however, limits a photographer's control over assignments and schedules. It also affects the ways that images are presented and interpreted. How can photographers, curators, and editors slow down habits of consumption and encourage viewers to think more carefully about what they see and, by extension, what they cannot see? This exhibition is one effort to do that. It is intended to suggest that distribution, consumption, and the marketplace shape the act of bearing witness as much as the intent of photographers.

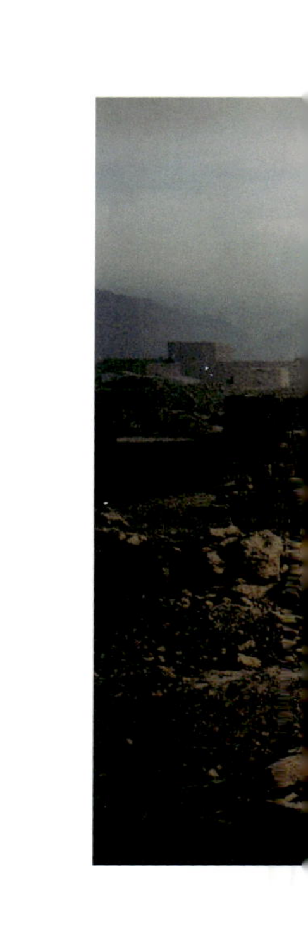

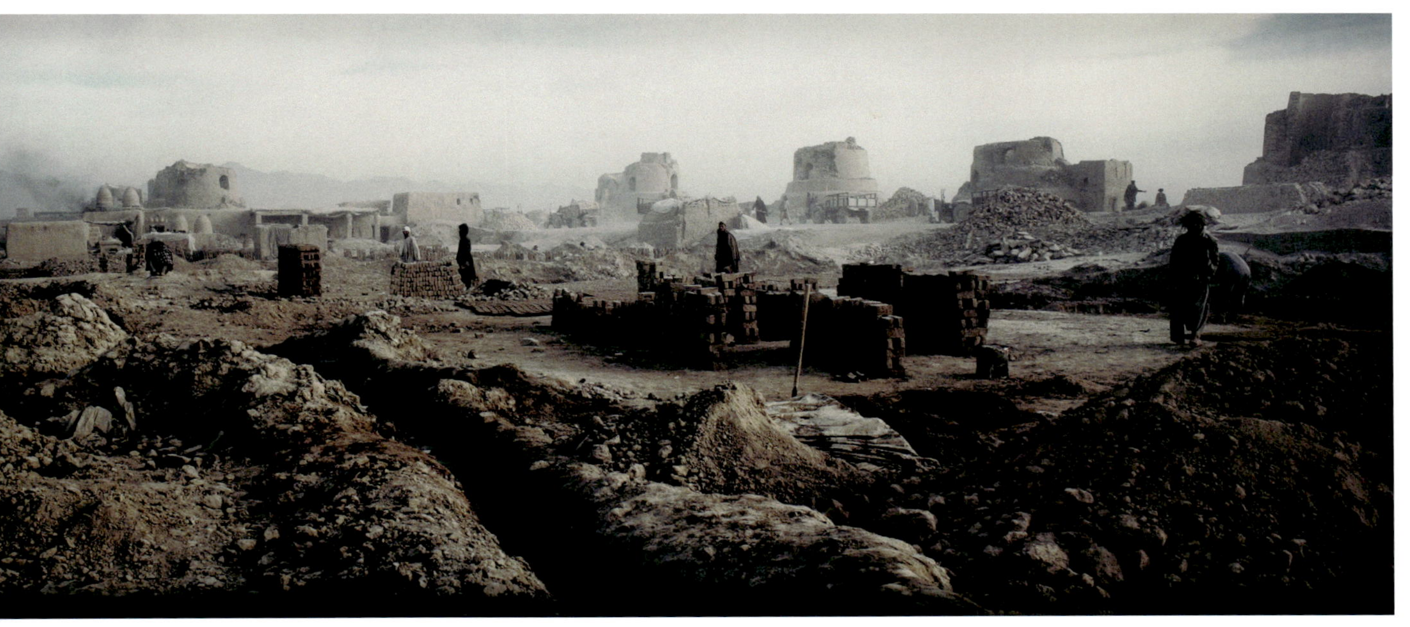

Object label on page **viii**

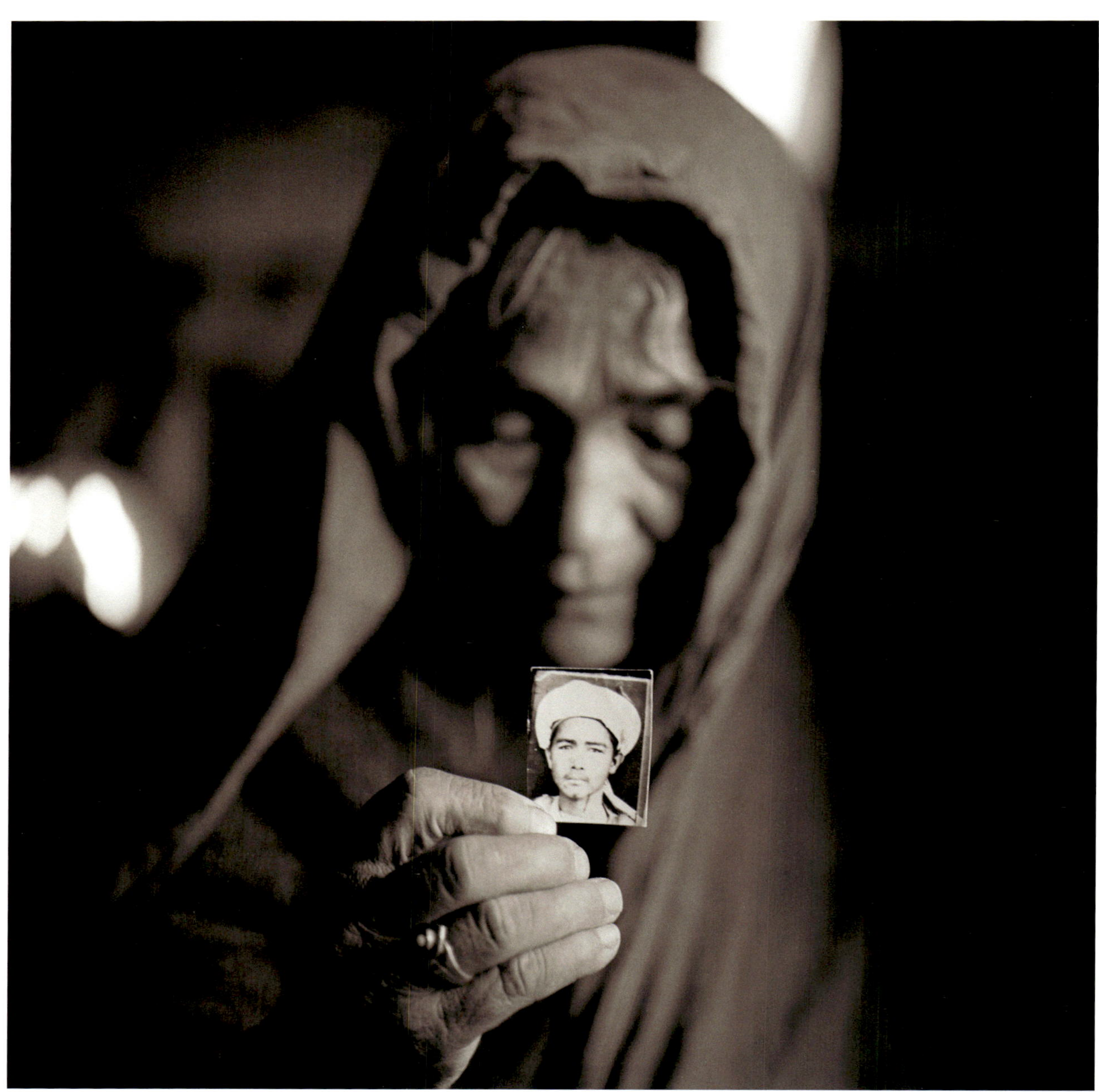

plate 43 See pages **97**, **100**, **102**, **112** Object label on page **viii**

Mula Awaz was my youngest son. In 1986, when he was eighteen years old, his group of Mujahedin attacked a communist post. In the exchange of fire, he was killed. Before the news of his death reached us, I dreamed that my son's body was being prepared for burial. When he had been washed and wrapped in white cloth, he was carried to the graveyard. They laid his body on the ground and turned his head towards Mecca. Then his body was covered with earth.

After that I did not dream of him again for several years. Then I became very ill and was taken to the hospital where I lay near death. Then I had the second dream of Mula Awaz. I was lying in my bed and I could hear the door to my hospital room opening. Mula Awaz appeared in the doorway and walked towards my bed. He had a scarf draped about his shoulders. As he approached, he took the cloth from his neck and offered it to me. He told me to wrap it about myself. Then without another word he turned away and disappeared into the corridor. I covered myself with the scarf and a sensation of warmth moved throughout my body. In the coming days, the illness left me and I was able to return home. I never dreamed of him again.

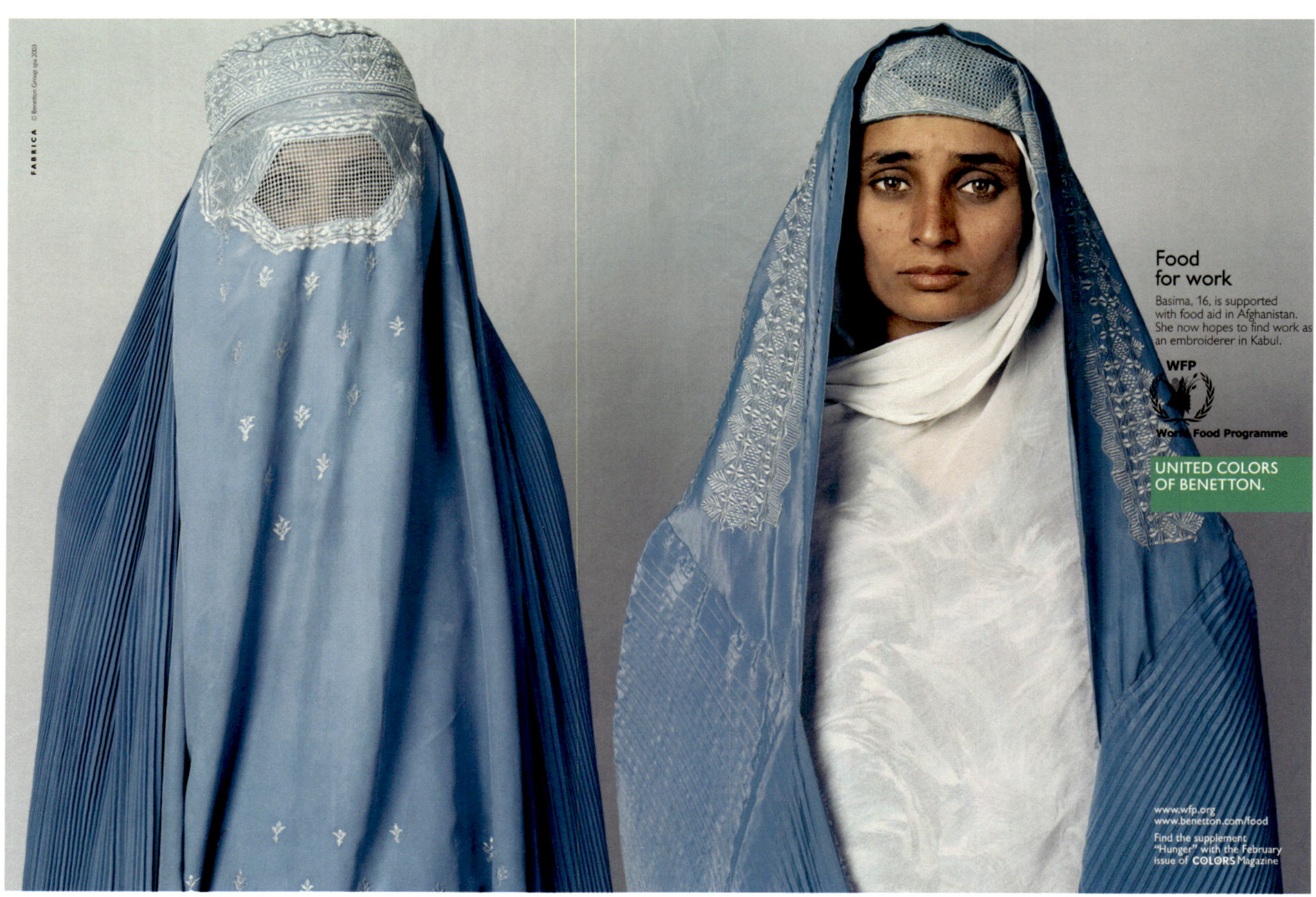

plate 44 See pages **84**, **97**, **98** Object label on page **viii**

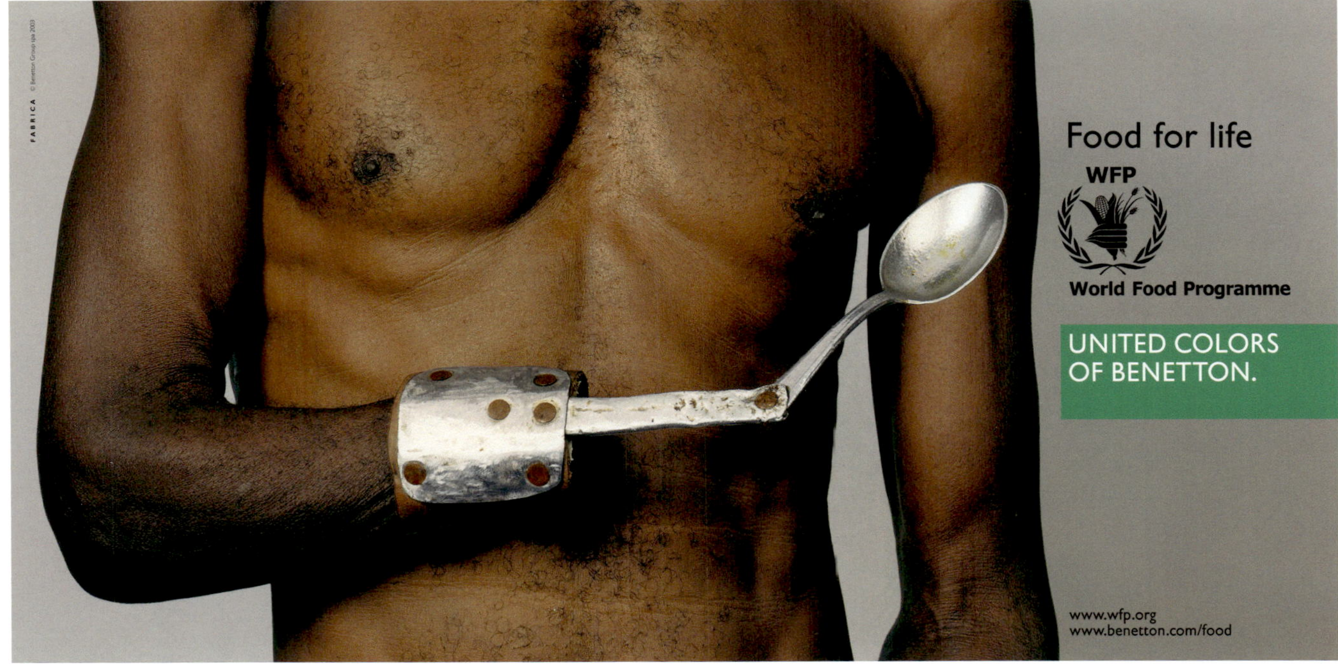

Object label on page **viii** **plate 45**

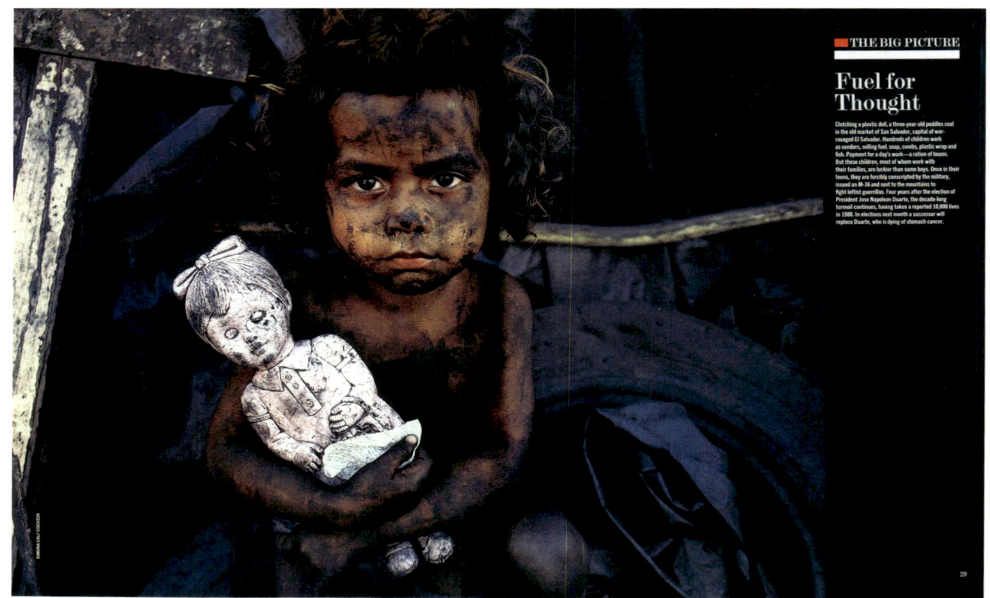

THE BIG PICTURE

Fuel for Thought

Clutching a plastic doll, a three-year-old peddles coal in the old market of San Salvador, capital of war-ravaged El Salvador. Hundreds of children work as vendors, selling fuel, soap, combs, plastic wrap and fish. Payment for a day's work—a ration of beans. But these children, most of whom work with their families, are luckier than some boys. Once in their teens, they are forcibly conscripted by the military, issued an M-16 and sent to the mountains to fight leftist guerrillas. Four years after the election of President Jose Napoleon Duarte, the decade-long turmoil continues, having taken a reported 10,000 lives in 1988. In elections next month a successor will replace Duarte, who is dying of stomach cancer.

29

plate 46 Object label on page **ix**

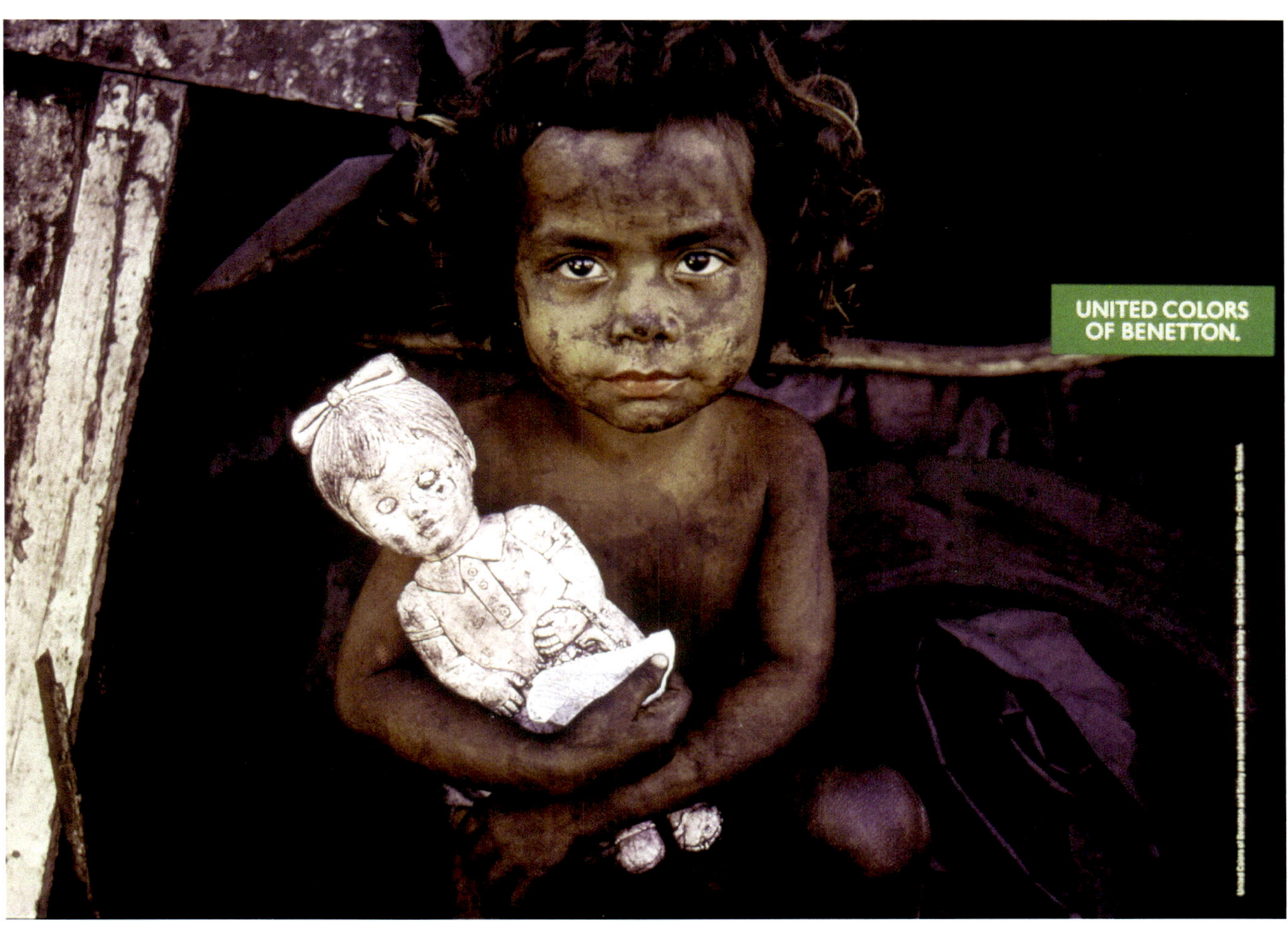

Object label on page ix

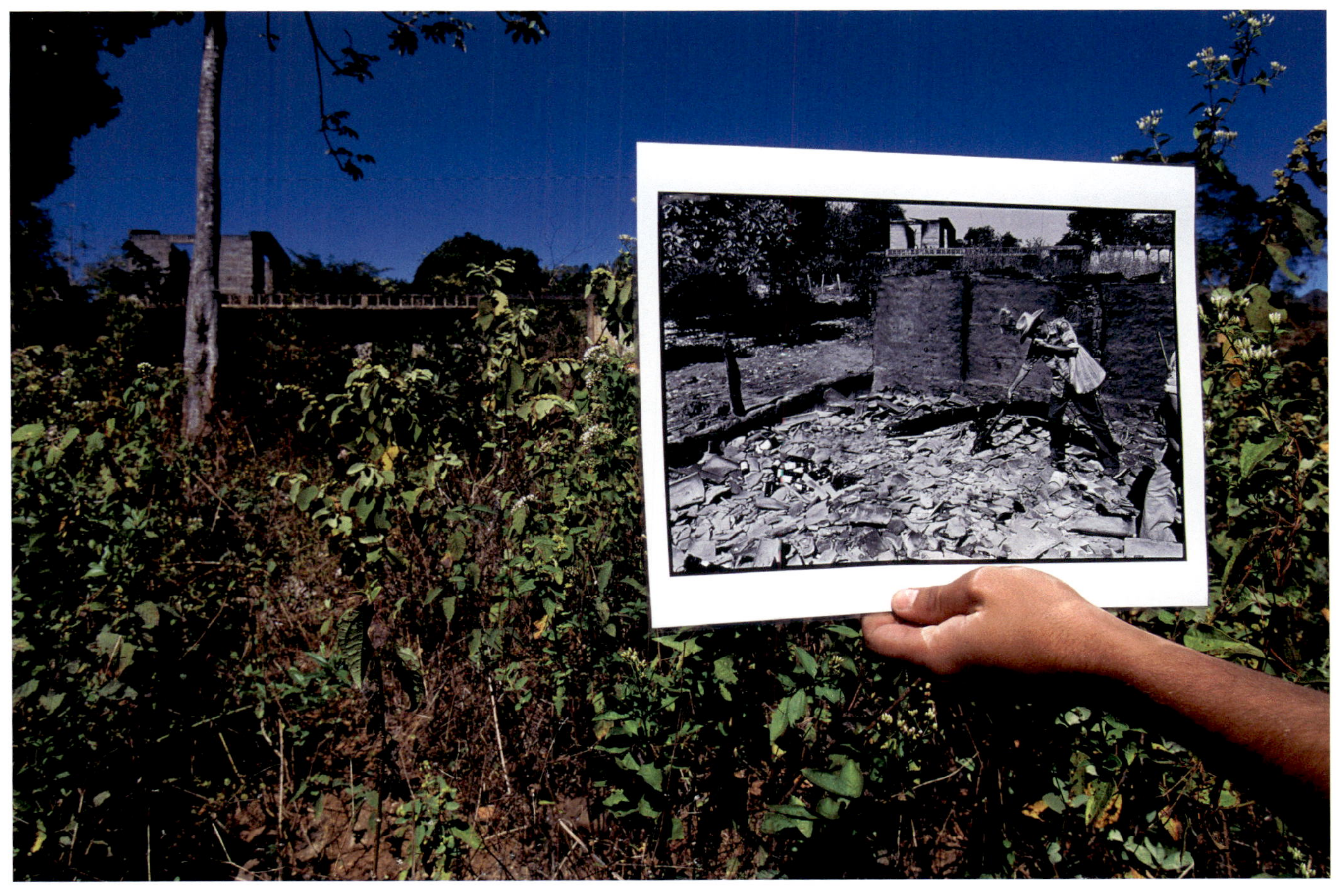

Object label on page **ix**

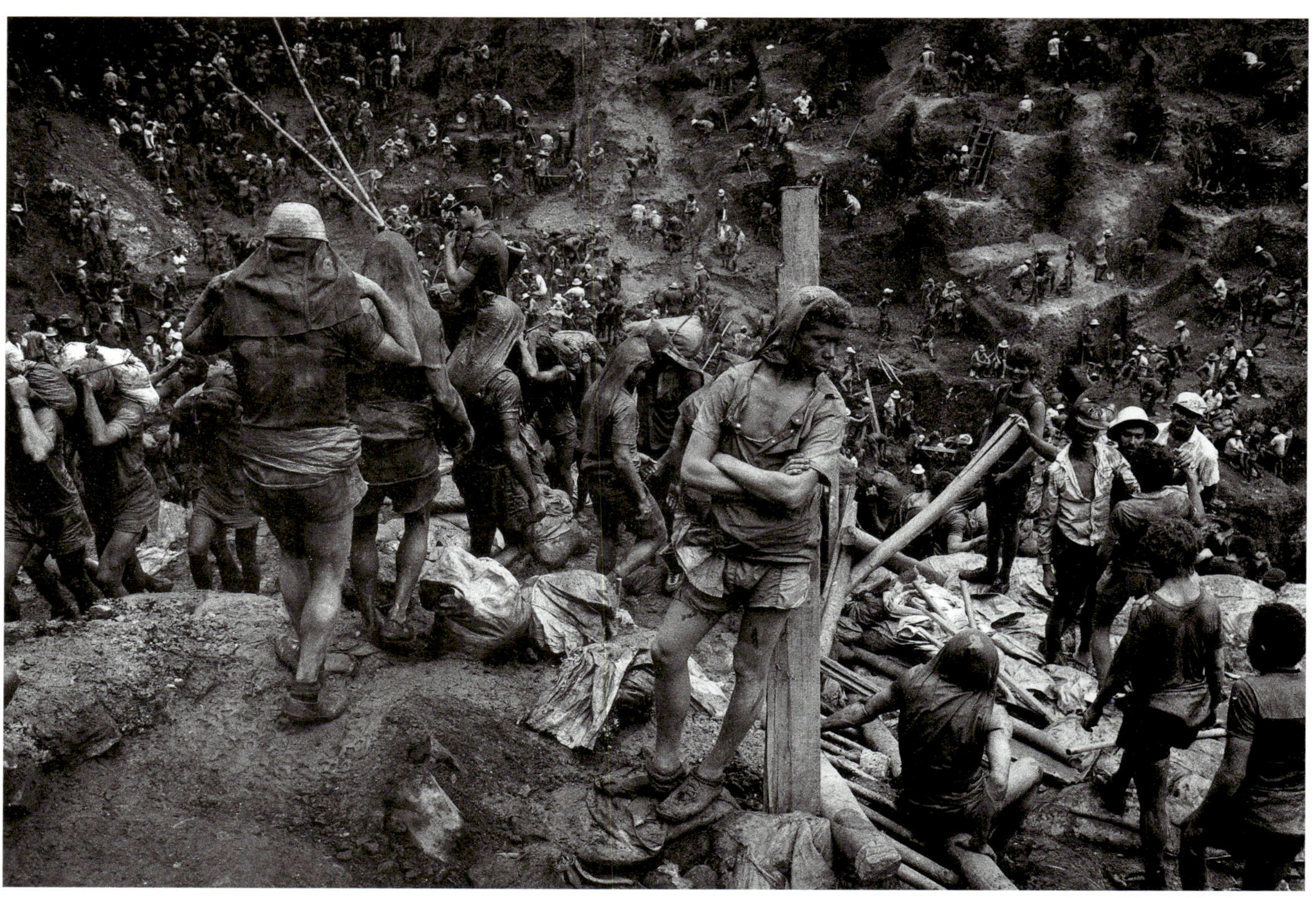

plate 49 See pages **10**, **22**, **69** Object label on page **ix**

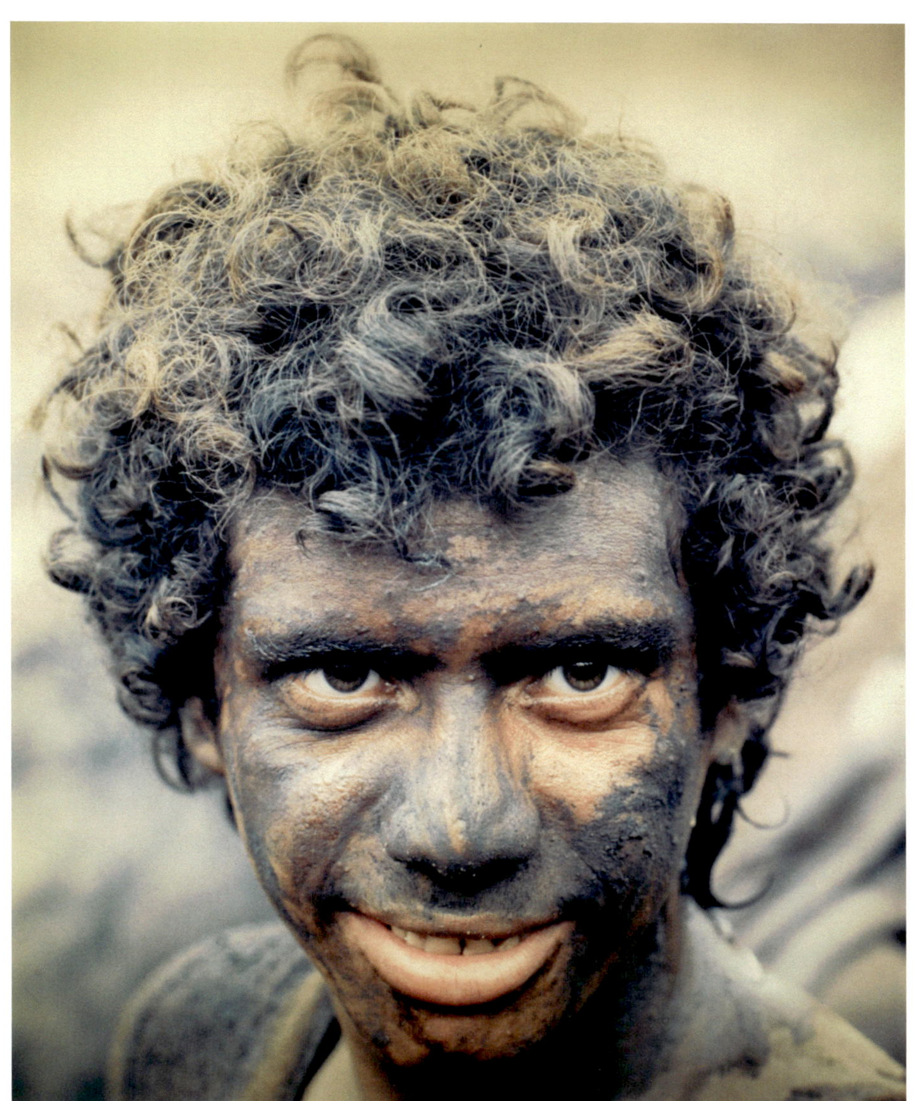

 See pages 65–69 Object label on page x

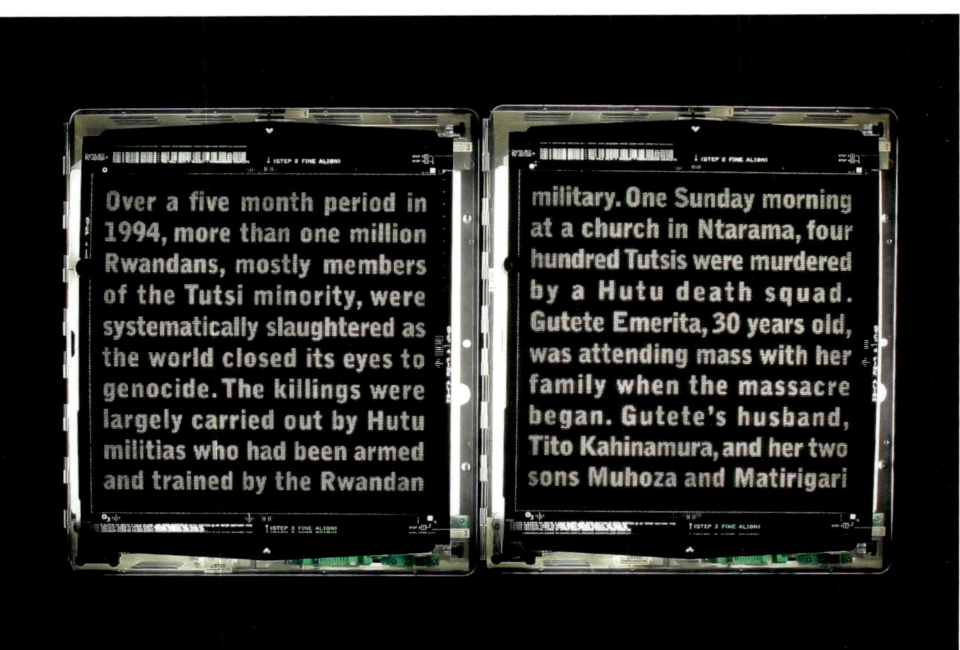
Over a five month period in
1994, more than one million
Rwandans, mostly members
of the Tutsi minority, were
systematically slaughtered as
the world closed its eyes to
genocide. The killings were
largely carried out by Hutu
militias who had been armed
and trained by the Rwandan
military. One Sunday morning
at a church in Ntarama, four
hundred Tutsis were murdered
by a Hutu death squad.
Gutete Emerita, 30 years old,
was attending mass with her
family when the massacre
began. Gutete's husband,
Tito Kahinamura, and her two
sons Muhoza and Matirigari

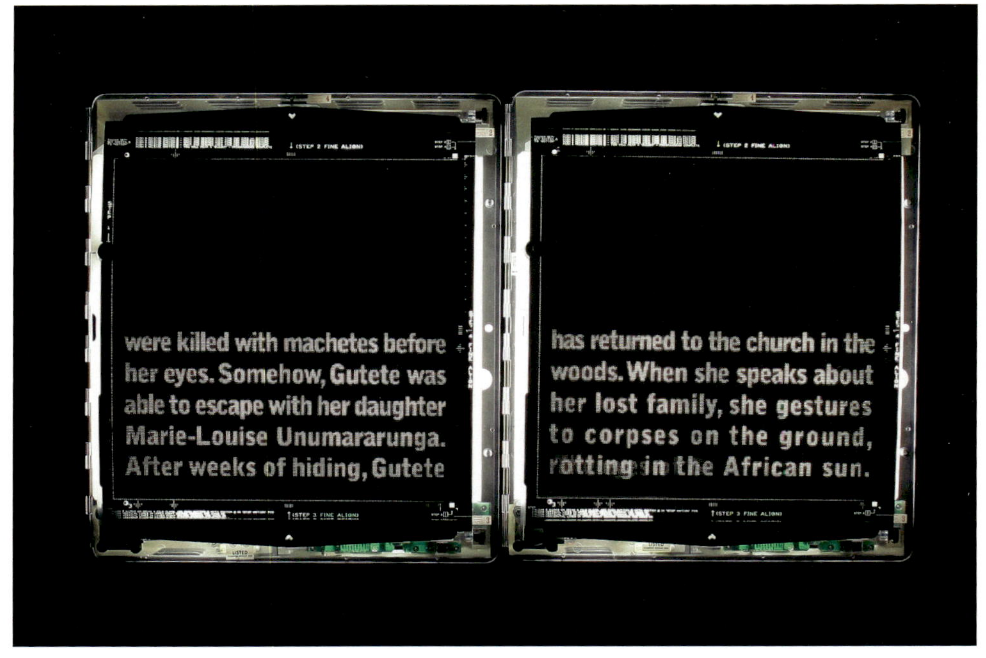
were killed with machetes before
her eyes. Somehow, Gutete was
able to escape with her daughter
Marie-Louise Unumararunga.
After weeks of hiding, Gutete
has returned to the church in the
woods. When she speaks about
her lost family, she gestures
to corpses on the ground,
rotting in the African sun.

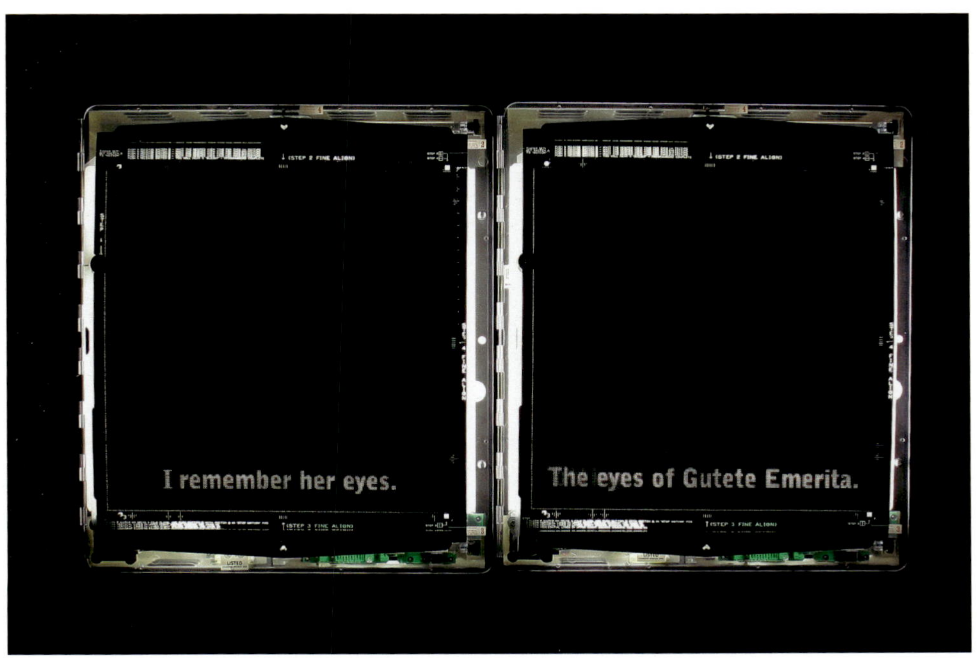

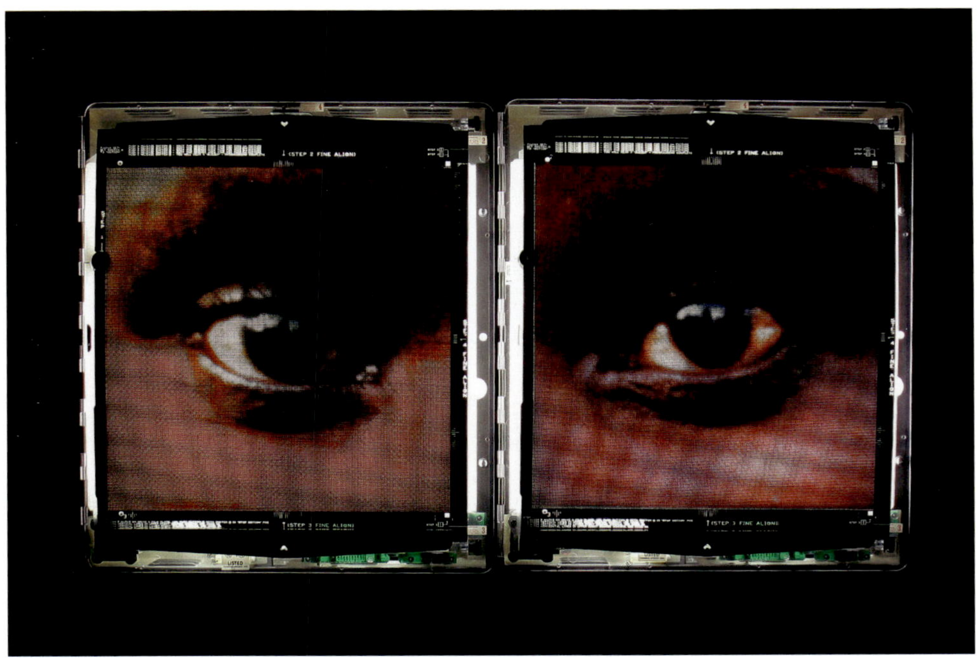

 See pages 10, 32–35, 65, 69, 70, 114, 115 Object label on page x

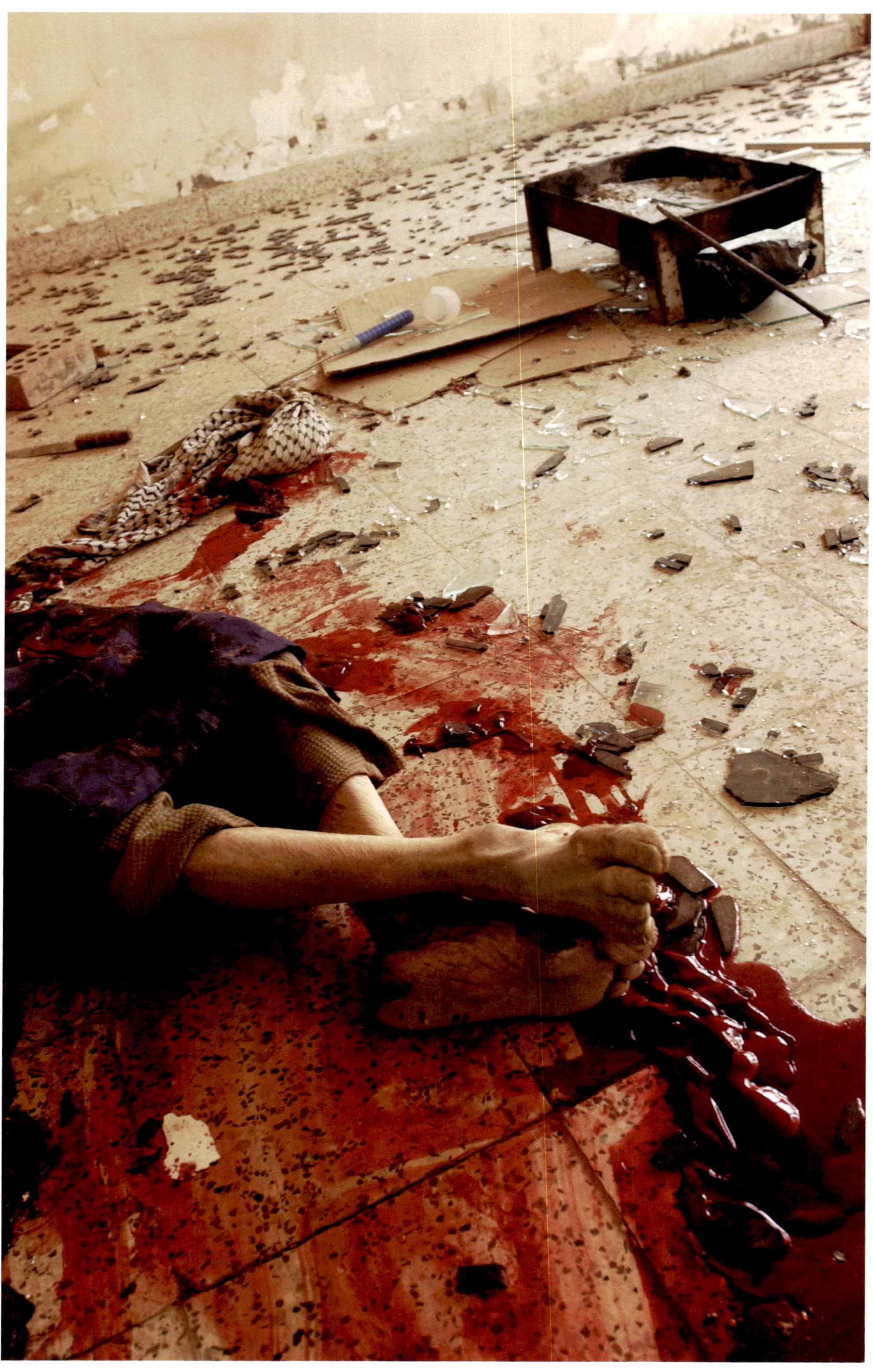

plate 52 Object label on page **x** See page **97**

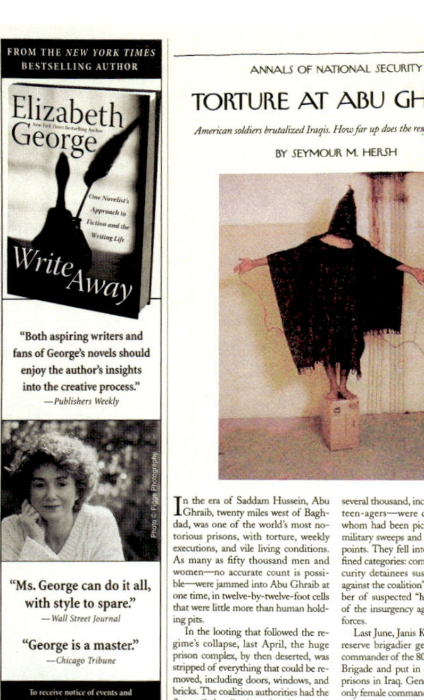

ANNALS OF NATIONAL SECURITY

TORTURE AT ABU GHRAIB

American soldiers brutalized Iraqis. How far up does the responsibility go?

BY SEYMOUR M. HERSH

In the era of Saddam Hussein, Abu Ghraib, twenty miles west of Baghdad, was one of the world's most notorious prisons, with torture, weekly executions, and vile living conditions. As many as fifty thousand men and women—no accurate count is possible—were jammed into Abu Ghraib at one time, in twelve-by-twelve-foot cells that were little more than human holding pits.

In the looting that followed the regime's collapse, last April, the huge prison complex, by then deserted, was stripped of everything that could be removed, including doors, windows, and bricks. The coalition authorities had the floors tiled, cells cleaned and repaired, and toilets, showers, and a new medical center added. Abu Ghraib was now a U.S. military prison. Most of the prisoners, however—by the fall there were several thousand, including women and teen-agers—were civilians, many of whom had been picked up in random military sweeps and at highway checkpoints. They fell into three loosely defined categories: common criminals; security detainees suspected of "crimes against the coalition"; and a small number of suspected "high-value" leaders of the insurgency against the coalition forces.

Last June, Janis Karpinski, an Army reserve brigadier general, was named commander of the 800th Military Police Brigade and put in charge of military prisons in Iraq. General Karpinski, the only female commander in the war zone, was an experienced operations and intelligence officer who had served with the Special Forces and in the 1991 Gulf War, but she had never run a prison system. Now she was in charge of three

42 THE NEW YORKER, MAY 10, 2004

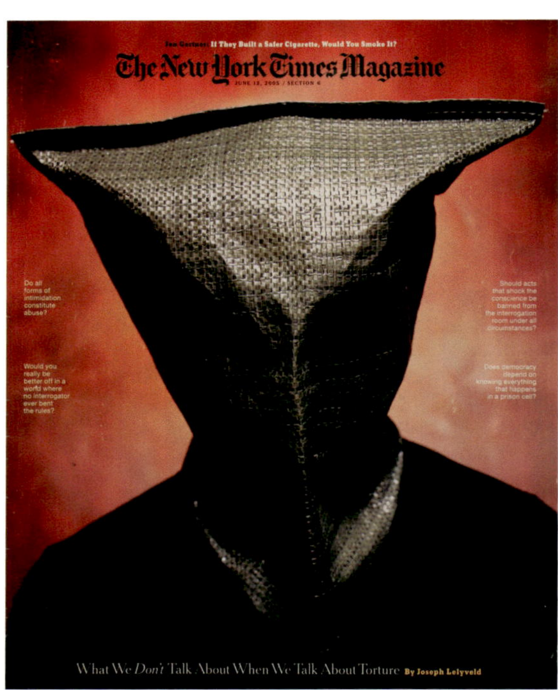

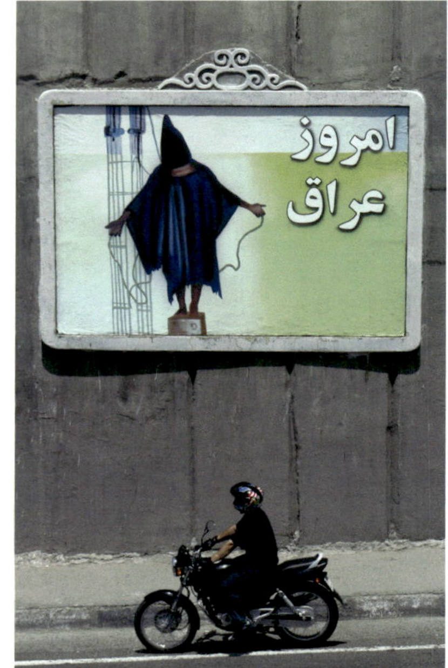

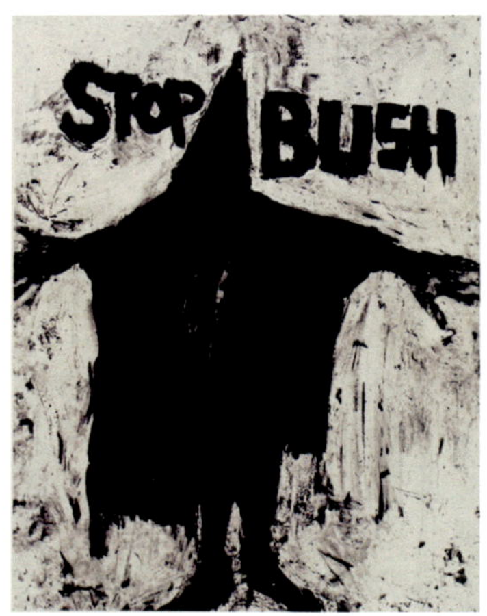

 See pages **16**, **71**, **74** Object labels on pages **x–xi**

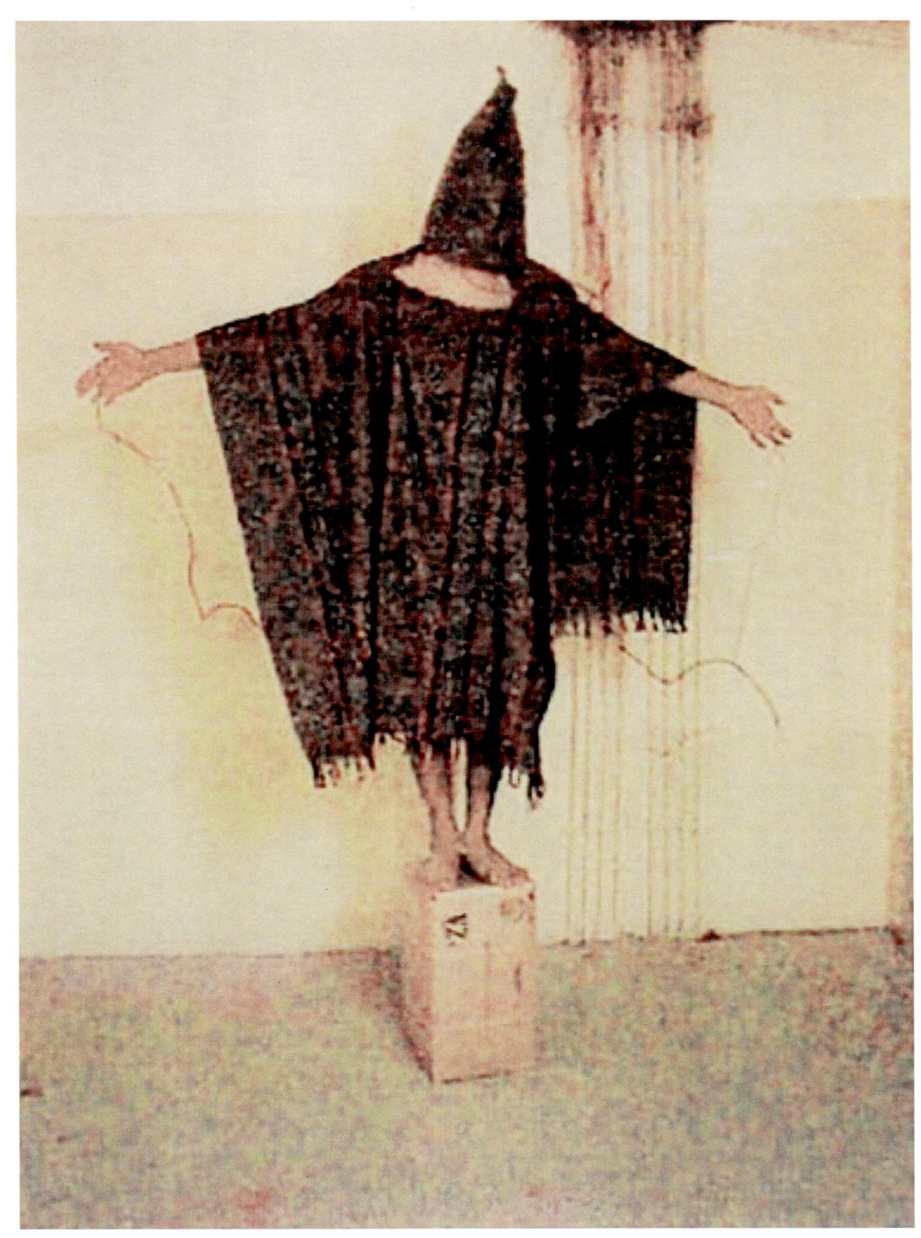

 See pages 16–20, 71, 114. Object label on page xi

THE CONFLICT IN IRAQ: A City Under Siege

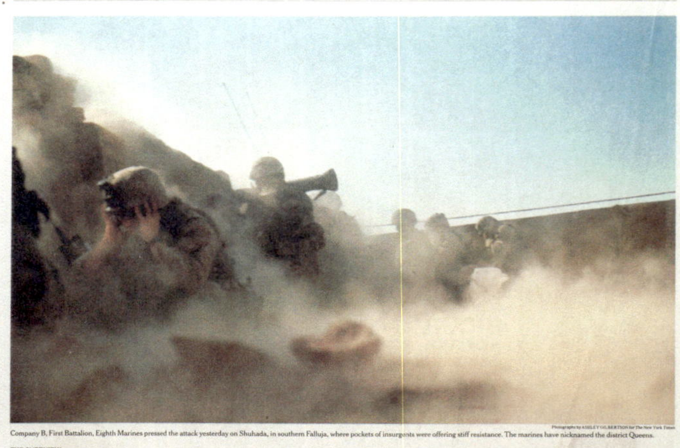

Photographs by ASHLEY GILBERTSON for The New York Times

Company B, First Battalion, Eighth Marines pressed the attack yesterday on Shuhada, in southern Falluja, where pockets of insurgents were offering stiff resistance. The marines have nicknamed the district Queens.

THE OVERVIEW

U.S. Armored Forces Make Final Push to Take Last Rebel Stronghold in Falluja

Continued From Page 1

Moktada al-Sadr, the Shiite cleric who has already led two uprisings against the Americans, said Saturday that Mr. Sadr would not take part in elections scheduled for January as long as "Iraqi cities are under attack."

Drawing Mr. Sadr into the political process has been one of the most pressing goals of the Americans and the interim Iraqi government. Mr. Sadr is mercurial, and the practical impact of his statement remains unclear. Until now, he has appeared to be committed to the political process, and the statement could be a way for him to build his support in the period leading up to the elections, given that his immense popularity is based on an uncompromising anti-American stand.

The Iraqi government announced [illegible]

[illegible] said Lt.

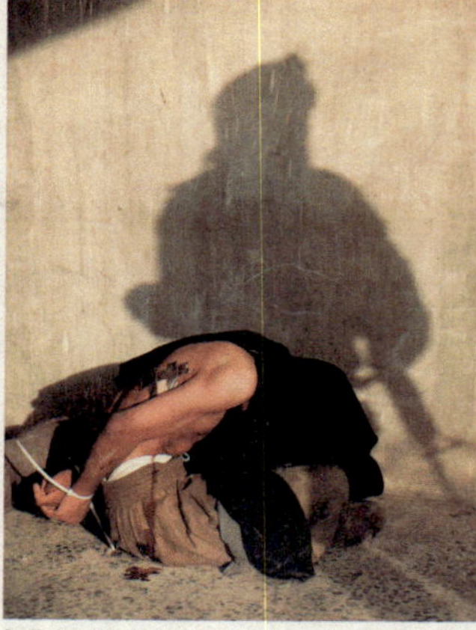

One of four Iraqis who surrendered to the marines and said they were students trying to avoid the battle.

Col. Paul Hastings, a spokesman for Task Force Olympia, charged with controlling the northern region. Hundreds of policemen fled from the guerrillas that day, and the interim Iraqi government fired the city's police chief on Friday.

Mosul has sizable numbers of Sunni Arabs, Kurds and Christians, and racial tensions have run high since the Americans invaded Iraq. It is clear that the Sunni Arabs are leading the insurgency here, while the Kurds and Christians are more sympathetic to the American forces.

A car bomb exploded next to a Kurdish patrol in the afternoon, killing at least six militiamen, witnesses said. The city's health bureau said that at least 25 people were killed and 62 wounded in violence on Thursday and Friday, though it was unknown how many of them were civilians and how many were guerrillas.

It is clear that the American-led forces were taken by surprise by the magnitude of the uprising. The Stryker Brigade, a light-armored mechanized unit based in Mosul, had to recall a battalion from the fighting in Falluja. The Iraqi government ordered four battalions of national guardsmen, all Kurds, to the city.

Up to 500 insurgents, far more than American and Iraqi intelligence had predicted, carried out the first big wave of attacks on police stations on Thursday by working in groups of 15 to 50, Brig. Gen. Carter Ham, commander of the Stryker Brigade, said in a telephone interview late Friday.

The general said he believed that the insurgency was being organized by former members of Saddam Hussein's security forces.

The Iraqi Interior Ministry appointed a new police chief in Mosul on Saturday, and police officers were returning to the stations, some of which had been set afire, Colonel Hastings said. But the police were being confined to security duties at six sites, he added, because American soldiers might not be able to tell the real police from insurgents who could be roaming the city in stolen police uniforms or body armor.

"The situation is improving," Colonel Hastings said. "That's not to paint a rosy picture, because there are still neighborhoods that are dangerous."

An American counteroffensive began on Thursday afternoon, when an airstrike hit a mortar team. By Saturday, American-led forces were making forays into some of the most dangerous neighborhoods, the colonel said, including the area around the Yarmouk traffic circle in the southwest and an area called Palestine in the east.

In Al Wehda neighborhood, insurgents slit the throats of two Iraqi National Guardsmen in the street, witnesses said.

"When I was driving back to my house through the Wehda area, I saw a huge gathering of people, so I stopped the car and went to see what was the matter," said Muhammad Hazim, a resident. "I saw a number of insurgents holding two Iraqi National Guard soldiers and reading a statement calling them traitors and collaborators with the enemy, and then they slaughtered them by slitting their throats and yelling, 'God is great!' "

General Ham, the commander in Mosul, said the performance of the Iraqi policemen on Thursday had been "very disappointing." While raiding six or seven of the city's 33 police stations, the insurgents made off with up to 40 police vehicles, hundreds of weapons, hand-held radios, computers, telephones, police uniforms and body armor. "It's several hundreds of thousands of dollars of equipment," the general said.

The dismal performance by the police forces undermined recent assertions by President Bush that Iraqi security forces will soon be able to take over policing duties from the more than 140,000 American troops here.

Two Marines were killed and one was wounded on Saturday morning when a roadside bomb exploded near them as they stood outside a vehicle in Zaidon, a rural area to the south of Falluja. Attacks on American positions to the north and south of Falluja have increased in recent days, and commanders say they believe the insurgents are trying to distract attention from the battle in the city and cut a wedge in the military cordon ringing Falluja.

To the south, tanks and armored vehicles assigned to the Marines' Second Reconnaissance Battalion could be seen waiting, part of the American military cordon that is intended to prevent any insurgents from escaping. Other American vehicles patrolled busily along the highway running north and south along the city's eastern edge.

Gazing at the battle through his binoculars, Colonel Formica said, "We're seeing the completion of the liberation of Falluja."

Reporting for this article was contributed by James Glanz and Edward Wong from Baghdad; Eric Schmitt from Washington; and Iraqi employees of The New York Times from Baghdad and Mosul.

Names of the Dead

The Department of Defense has identified 1,196 American service members who have died since the start of the Iraq war. It confirmed the deaths of the following Americans yesterday:

[illegible]

plate 58 Object label on page **xi**

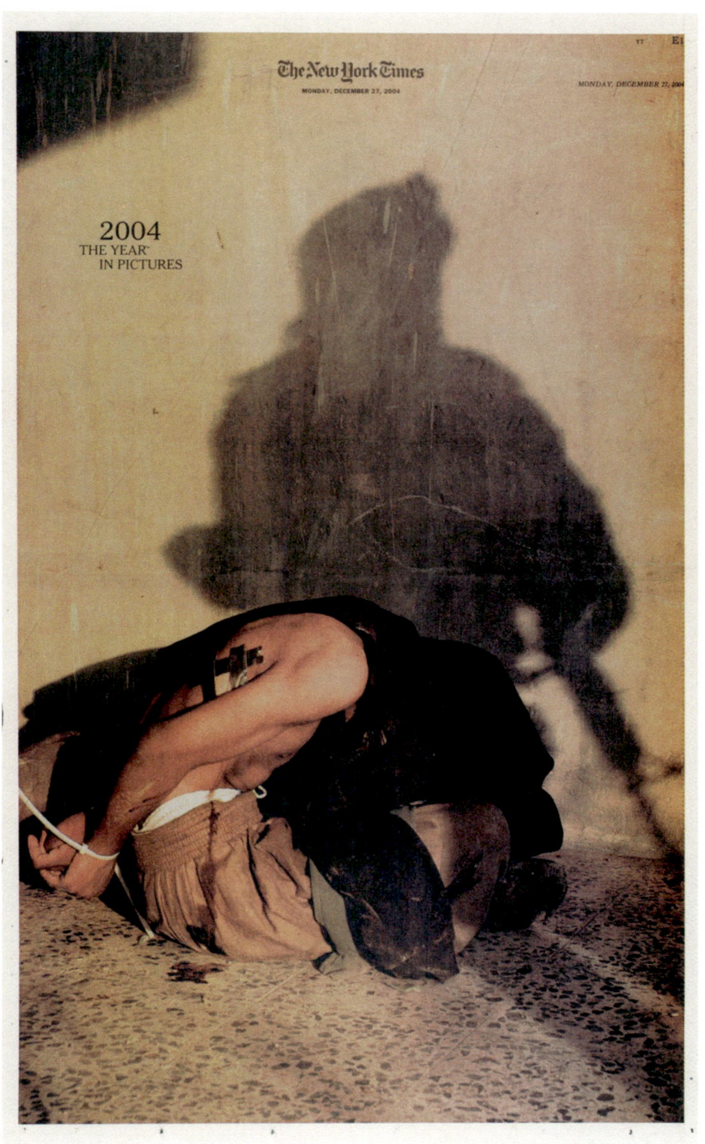

Object label on page **xi**

THIS EXHIBITION ADDRESSES THE ETHICAL COMPLEXITIES OF PICTURING THE PAIN AND SUFFERING OF OTHERS. In designing the installation and composing the accompanying texts, we, the curators, have posed the questions that trouble us most, and we have sought out photographs that engage the fundamental challenges in very different, perhaps even contending, ways. We thought this would give you, the viewer, the opportunity to consider these problems independently and come to your own conclusions. You may not have enjoyed the experience. In fact, you may have found individual images shocking and even repugnant. We would like to acknowledge that the most objectionable aspect of this exhibition may be its very existence. If it is, as some argue, perverse or irresponsible to take a photograph of someone in need or in pain, how much worse is it to put a frame around that image and hang it in a museum? If viewing suffering from a position of comfort is voyeuristic, what does it mean to indulge in that act collectively, in a public space? Are we, by enshrining these photographs here, asking you to accept all such imagery unquestioningly, as "art"? And what do we, the curators, gain from mounting an exhibition like this? Are we just as implicated in the traffic in pain that we seek to contest? While there are no easy answers to these questions, we would like to think that it is fruitful to ask them, and that ultimately, a museum is an ideal site in which to consider such social, political, and philosophical issues. We also recognize that some of the most thoughtful and provocative responses come from contemporary photographers themselves. We hope that you will express your own opinions and responses to this exhibition, whatever they are, in this room. Through this exchange, we may jointly confront the profound responsibilities as well as the rampant indulgences of our visual culture.

OBJECT LABELS

plate 1
ASHLEY GILBERTSON (Australian, b. 1978)
"One of four Iraqis who surrendered to the marines and said they were students trying to avoid the battle," 2004
digital print, 20" x 13"
© Ashley Gilbertson/Aurora

plate 2
ERIC GAY (American, b. 1961)
"Milvertha Hendricks, 84, center, waits in the rain with other flood victims outside the convention center in New Orleans, Thursday, Sept. 1, 2005," 2005
digital print, 11" x 14"
© AP Photo/Eric Gay

plate 3
Newsweek, 26 November 2001
Magazine, 10 5/8" x 16 1/8"

plate 4
LUC DELAHAYE (French, b. 1962)
Taliban, from "History," 2001
Chromogenic process color print, 43" x 93"
Chrysler Museum of Art, Norfolk, VA;
Gift of the Chrysler Contemporaries
Courtesy of the artist

plate 5
STEVE McCURRY (American, b. 1950)
Afghan Girl, 1985
color print, 20" x 16"
Museum purchase, Joseph O. Eaton Fund
M.2005.8
Courtesy of the artist and Magnum Photos

plate 6
National Geographic, vol. 167, no. 6, June 1985
Magazine, 10" x 7"
Courtesy *National Geographic* magazine

plate 7
Share the wonders of National Geographic with your friends
Magazine subscription card, 3 1/2" x 7"

plate 8
"Afghanistan: Tattered Clothing and Fear-filled Eyes of an Afghan Reveal War Zone Trauma," no date
Breshna Cards Co. Kabul, Afghanistan
Poster, 17" x 11"

plate 9
Amnesty International 2002 calendar
Publisher: Universe Calendar
Calendar, 12" x 12"

plate 10
National Geographic, vol. 201, no. 4, April 2002
Magazine, 10" x 7"
Courtesy *National Geographic* magazine

plate 11

RON HAVIV (American, born in 1967)
"Remains of confiscated material found in an office of the Taliban Ministry for the Prevention of Vice and Promotion of Virtue," 2001
Digital print, 11 7/8" x 16"
Ron Haviv/VII

plate 12

LEAH BENDAVID-VAL
National Geographic: The Photographs
(Washington, D. C.: National Geographic Society, 1994)
Book, 12 3/8" x 23 1/4"
Courtesy *National Geographic* magazine

plate 13

New York Times Magazine, 6 January 2002
Magazine, 10 5/8" x 16 1/8"
Courtesy of the artist

plate 14

SIMON NORFOLK (British, b. 1963)
Destroyed Military and Civilian Radio Installations on Kohe Asmai, in Central Kabul, from *Afghanistan: Chronotopia*, 2001
digital C-print, 20" x 24"
Courtesy of the artist and Gallery Luisotti

plate 15

The New Yorker, May 20, 2002
Magazine, 10 5/8" x 16 1/8"
© Joel Meyerowitz
Courtesy of Condé Nast Publications

plate 16

JOEL MEYEROWITZ (American, b. 1938)
North Tower and Woolworth Building, from *World Trade Center, Archive Project*, 2001
color print, 20" x 24"
© Joel Meyerowitz

After Mayor Rudy Giuliani decreed "no photography" at Ground Zero, Joel Meyerowitz sought out special permission to photograph the clean-up operation with his large-format 1942 Deardorff camera. As the only photographer granted unimpeded access to the site, Meyerowitz took over 8,000 photographs over a period of eight months. A selection of these images was subsequently sent to more than 60 countries, many of them in the Middle East and North Africa, as part of an exhibition initiated by the U.S. State Department to provide, as former U.S. Secretary of State Colin Powell explained, "a remembrance of those who perished and a reminder of our commitment to pursuing terrorists wherever they may try to hide."

plate 17

THOMAS RUFF (German, b. 1958)
Jpeg ny01, 2004
C-Print with Diasec, 100" x 74"
Courtesy of the artist and David Zwirner, New York

When Thomas Ruff began his formal education in photography, Joel Meyerowitz was one of his heroes. Yet Ruff ultimately developed a radically different approach to making pictures, as one can see by comparing the two photographers' responses to 9/11. While Meyerowitz gained exclusive access to the World Trade Center site, Ruff required only access to the Internet, where he found Patrick Sison's Associated Press photograph of the Empire State Building and the burning towers. His massive enlargement of a JPEG of Sison's picture produced an image that, by calling attention to the manipulations that made it possible, marks its distance from the event it putatively records. The work is part of a recent series of similarly enlarged and pixelated JPEGs. Ruff first thought of the larger project as a "visual encyclopedia" of contemporary history, but as the work developed he renounced the aspiration "to explain the whole world in images" as unachievable.

plate 18

PAUL SEAWRIGHT (Irish, b. 1965)
Valley, from *Hidden*, 2002
C-print on Fuji Crystal paper mounted on aluminum, 48" x 58"
Courtesy of the artist and The Kerlin Gallery, Dublin

Commissioned by the Imperial War Museum in London, Paul Seawright spent three weeks in Afghanistan taking photographs for his series "Hidden." Seawright, however, is not a photojournalist. In fact, he consciously distinguishes his approach from witnessing. Instead, like Luc Delahaye and Simon Norfolk, he prefers to photograph "after the facts." In this case, the "after" is an image of Afganistan that looks like Roger Fenton's famous photograph from the Crimean War of cannonballs scattered along a dirt road that curves to a distant void.

plate 19

SALLY MANN (American, b. 1951)
Untitled from *What Remains*, 2001
gelatin silver print with varnish, 30" x 40"
Courtesy Sally Mann

Sometimes photojournalists can go places artists can not. For her project *What Remains*, which began in response to the death of her beloved greyhound Eva, Mann wanted to photograph corpses at the University of Tennessee Forensic Anthropology Facility, or Body Farm. With the access provided by the *New York Times Magazine*, Mann was able to enter the facility and photograph decaying human corpses for a story about scientists who study these bodies to better learn how to assess times of death from decomposition. In taking the photographs for this story, however, Mann did not act like a typical photojournalist. Instead, she used a large-format camera along with the time-consuming 19th-century process known as wet-plate collodion printing.

plate 20
Time Magazine, 22 August 1993
Magazine, 10 1/2" x 8"

plate 21
JAMES NACHTWAY (American, b. 1948)
Sudan, 1993
gelatin silver photograph, 16" x 20"
Museum Purchase, Wachenheim Family Fund
M.2005.14

In this photograph, James Nachtwey depicts a famine victim receiving rehydration salts from a volunteer aid worker.

plate 22
ANDRES SERRANO (American, b. 1950)
Piss Christ, 1989
Cibachrome, silicone, Plexiglas, wood frame, 32 3/4" x 45"
Courtesy the artist and Paula Cooper Gallery, New York

plate 23
ANDRES SERRANO (American, b. 1950)
The Morgue (Homicide Stabbing), 1992
Cibachrome, silicone. Plexiglas, wood frame, 37 5/8" x 45 1/4"
Courtesy the artist and Paula Cooper Gallery, New York

plate 24
FAZAL SHEIKH (American, b. 1965)
Gulma Duba Salo, Borana elder from Arero, 1993–1996
hand-made accordion style book comprised of five gelatin silver prints, archival board, acrylic paint, varnish, and binding, 14" x 11 1/4" x 2 1/2"
Courtesy Pace/MacGill Gallery, New York

Much of Fazal Sheikh's work focuses on refugee communities, a subject matter common to photojournalism. Sheikh, however, has neither worked as a photojournalist nor allowed his images to be disseminated in newspapers or magazines. Instead, he circulates them, often accompanied by texts, in museum and gallery exhibitions, in multimedia publications, online, and in books.

plate 25
NICHOLAS NIXON (American, b. 1947)
Tony Mastrorilli, Mansfield, Massachusetts, October 1987, from *People with AIDS*, 1987
gelatin silver print, 8" x 10"
Courtesy Bernard Toale Gallery, Boston, Mass.

In 1986, Nicholas Nixon and his wife Bebe began a project to tell the personal stories of people with AIDS. They circulated a letter in the AIDS Action Committee's newsletter in Boston, requesting volunteers to be photographed and interviewed during the duration of their illness. Tony Mastrorilli was one of 15 volunteers who participated in this project.

plate 26
SAM TAYLOR-WOOD (British, b. 1967)
Jude Law, from *Crying Men*, 2002–2004
C-print, 20 1/2" x 20 1/2"
Courtesy of Amanda P. Brotman

plate 27

NAN GOLDIN (American, b. 1953)
Nan one month after being battered, 1984
Cibachrome, 30" x 40"
Courtesy the artist and Matthew Marks Gallery, New York, New York

plate 28

MFON ESSIEN (Nigerian, 1967–2001)
The Amazon's New Clothes No. 1, 1999
gelatin silver print, 20" x 16"
Courtesy of Danny Simmons

After being diagnosed with breast cancer at the age of 31 and undergoing a mastectomy, Mfon Essien used herself as the subject of her series, *The Amazon's New Clothes*. In 2001, at the age 34, Essien lost her life to cancer.

plate 29

PHILIP-LORCA DICORCIA (American, b. 1951)
Major Tom, Kansas City, $20, 1990–1992
Ektacolor print, 16" x 23 1/4"
© Philip Lorca di-Corcia
Courtesy Pace/MacGill Gallery, New York

In 1989, Philip-Lorca diCorcia received a National Endowment for the Arts fellowship. He used this funding to travel to Los Angeles, where he solicited and photographed young men that he encountered around Santa Monica Boulevard. The title of each work gives the subject's name, hometown, and the amount they were paid to pose.

plate 30

BORIS MIKHAILOV (Ukrainian, b. 1938)
Untitled from *Case History*, 1997–98
Color print, 23 2/3" x 15 3/4"
Courtesy of Barbara Gross Galerie, Munich

This photograph belongs to a series of nearly 500 that Boris Mikhailov took in his hometown of Kharkov. The image depicts two homeless people whom Mikhailov befriended and asked to pose in exchange for money. According to Mikhailov, photographing his subjects in various stages of undress ensures that they will not go unnoticed or remain invisible.

plate 31

MARY ELLEN MARK (American, b. 1941)
Edgardo Figueroa, Bronx, New York, USA, 1993
gelatin silver print, 20" x 24"
Courtesy Mary Ellen Mark

plate 32

MARY ELLEN MARK (American, b. 1941)
Leprosy Patient With Her Nurse, National Hansen's Research Center, Carville, LA, 1990
gelatin silver print, 16" x 20"
Courtesy Mary Ellen Mark

plate 33

MICHAEL NYE (American, b. 1949)
Doris, from *Fine Line: Mental Health/Mental Illness*, 2003
gelatin silver print; audio box with headphones, 24" x 30"
Collection of the artist
Courtesy of the artist

plate 34

LIU ZHENG (Chinese, b. 1969)
Waxwork in the Nanjing Massacre Memorial Museum, Nanjing, Jiangsu Province, 2000
gelatin silver print, 18" x 18"
Courtesy Yossi Milo Gallery, New York

plate 35

DANIEL J. MARTINEZ (American, b. 1957)
Self-Portrait #4 (Second attempt to clone mental disorder or How one philosophizes with a hammer), 1999
color light jet print, 60" x 40"
Courtesy of the artist and Projectile, New York

The injury pictured here is simulated, an effect of makeup and lighting. Perhaps Martinez seeks "cheerfulness in the midst of a gloomy task," believing that "nothing succeeds if prankishness has no part in it." The words are Nietzsche's, from his *Twilight of the Idols, or How One Philosophizes with a Hammer.* Whatever else Martinez does or does not owe to that witty polemic, he appropriated its subtitle. What does this literary borrowing suggest? Nothing so violent as one might suspect: Nietzsche claims to use his hammer like a tuning fork, lightly tapping prevailing ideals of beauty, morality, truth, and humanity until we hear how hollow they are.

plate 36

AN-MY LÊ (American, 1960)
Small Wars (Sniper #2), 1999–2002
gelatin silver print, 26" x 37 1/2"
Courtesy of the artist and Murray Guy, New York

For her series *Small Wars*, An-My Lê, who emigrated to the United States from Vietnam as a political refugee in 1975, worked with Vietnam War re-enactors in South Carolina, whom she photographed staging what Lê describes as "a Vietnam of the mind."

plate 37

SHIMON ATTIE (American, b. 1957)
Steinstrasse 22 (Berlin), 1993
C-print, 33" x 39"
Courtesy of the artist and Jack Shainman Gallery, New York

In 1991, Shimon Attie, recently arrived in Berlin from the U.S., combed the city's archives for photographs of life in the Scheunenviertel, the city's prewar Jewish quarter. He then made slides of the photographs and projected them at the addresses at which they had originally been taken in the 1920s and 1930s. Attie pursued this project for about a year, displaying an image for a night or two and then moving on to the next site. On each occasion, he photographed the projection. Using exposure times of several minutes, he created colors and effects that could not have been perceived by anyone present at the scene. Like the other pictures in this series, Steinstrasse 22 is thus both a record of a public installation and itself a complex and challenging work.

plate 38

David E. Scherman, ed., *The Best of Life.*
New York, Time-Life Books, 1973
Book, 13 1/4" x 10 3/4"

One of the first books that Vik Muniz bought after he came to the United States was *The Best of Life*. In 1989, seven years after he purchased the book at a garage sale outside of Chicago, he misplaced it. Feeling that he had "lost his link to humanity," Muniz began to draw photographs in the book from memory, including this famous Pulitzer Prize winning image by Nick Ut. It depicts nine-year old Vietnamese Kim Phuc running naked toward the camera after having been scorched by Napalm accidentally dropped by South Vietnamese pilots. After completing the drawings, Muniz photographed them and then printed them according to the duotone screen in which he had first seen them.

plate 39

VIK MUNIZ (Brazilian, b. 1961)
The Best of Life Memory Rendering of Tram Bang Child, 1989
gelatin silver print, 11" x 14"
Courtesy of Kitty Bowe Hearty

plate 40

CHEN CHIEH-JEN (Taiwanese, b. 1960)
Revolt in the Soul and Body: Self-Destruction, 1996
digital print, 41 ¼" x 51 ¾"
Museum Purchase, Wachenheim Family Fund
M.2005.20

In 1996, Chen Chieh-jen made this work by digitally combining and altering two historical photographs of massacres of Chinese Communists by Chang Kai-shek's Nationalist soldiers. The figure on the far left and the kneeling victim with his back to the viewer are from a picture taken by an unknown photographer in the streets of Shanghai in 1928. Much of the rest is from a photograph taken in 1927 by the American Consul to Canton, Jay Calvin Huston, who sent his many pictures of the carnage in Canton to the State Department in Washington. Neither historical image, of course, contained the naked figure with two dueling torsos. Here, the artist has put himself—much transformed—into the center of the violence. The face of a soldier peering from the background is his, too.

plate 41

ALAN SCHECHNER (British, b. 1962)
It's the Real Thing—Self Portrait at Buchenwald, 1993
digitally manipulated photograph, dimensions variable
Courtesy of the artist

Alan Schechner, some of whose relatives were killed in the Nazi concentration camps, has repeatedly explored the ideological uses of Holocaust imagery. In *It's the Real Thing*, he digitally inserts himself, gleaming can of Diet Coke in hand, into a photograph taken by Margaret Bourke-White during the liberation of Buchenwald. Viewers often find Schechner's gesture shocking, even inexcusable, but he considers it integral to his engagement with the politics of memory and the construction of Jewish identity. Strangely, few have noted how the controversy over Schechner echoes a dispute about his source material. Originally published in *Life*, Bourke-White's photographs of Buchenwald were among the first to reveal the horrors of mass extermination to a wide public. Some of the pictures not included in *Life*'s initial coverage, including the one appropriated here, are now among this famous photojournalist's most renowned works. Yet her elegantly composed pictures also provoke charges of aestheticization and exploitation, helping to shape the continuing debate about the ethics of representation.

plate 42

ZALMAÏ AHAD (Swiss, b. 1964)
Kandahar, from *Return, Afghanistan*, 2003
color print, 21 9/16" x 60"
Museum Purchase, Wachenheim Family Fund
M.2005.19

plate 43

FAZAL SHEIKH (American, b. 1965)
Qurban Gul holding a photograph of her son Mula Awaz, Afghan refugee village, Khairabad, north Pakistan, 1998
gelatin silver print, 16" x 16"
Courtesy Pace/MacGill Gallery, New York

plate 44

United Colors of Benetton
From *Food for Work* Campaign, 2003
Digital print, 11" x 17"
Courtesy of United Colors of Benetton

plate 45

United Colors of Benetton
Colors 54, February–March 2003
From *Food for Life* Campaign, 2003
Magazine, 11 3/8" x 18 1/4"
Courtesy of United Colors of Benetton

plate 46

Life, February 1989
Magazine, 12 1/4" x 20 1/4"

The relationships between the social and commercial ambitions of the clothing company Benetton's use of extreme images of suffering has raised controversy over the years. In 1992, for instance, Benetton turned its advertising campaign away from displays of the company's products and began to appropriate images from the print media and stock agencies. Cali Cocuzza's photograph of a three-year old girl peddling coal in El Salvador, which circulated in picture magazines such as *Life*, was part of this campaign. Benetton described their new approach as "reality advertising," since they were using "real" photographs to replace the "fantasy" of traditional advertising with social commentary. In 2003, Benetton, in collaboration with the World Food Programme, initiated a different campaign intended to demonstrate "how food can become a catalyst for reconciliation and development, a tool capable of revolutionising the lives of hungry individuals." These images were taken by James Mollison, a photographer working for Fabrica, Benetton's "communication research center."

plate 47

United Colors of Benetton
From *Shock of Reality* Campaign, 1992
Digital print, 8" x 10"
Courtesy of United Colors of Benetton

plate 48

SUSAN MEISELAS (American, b. 1948)
El Mozote, Morazon, El Salvador, 2001
color print, 16" x 20"
Courtesy of the artist

A month after the 1981 El Mozote massacre in El Salvador, Susan Meiselas traveled with journalists from the *New York Times* and the *Washington Post* to document what remained. Twenty years later, a photograph that Meiselas took there is being used by a member of a team evaluating possible burial locations of the over 800 people that went missing.

plate 49

SEBASTIÃO SALGADO (Brazilian, b. 1944)
Serra Pelada Mine, Brazil, 1986
gelatin silver print, 16" x 20"
Courtesy The Yancey Richardson Gallery

plate 50

ALFREDO JAAR (Chilean, b. 1956)
Gold in the Morning, 1985
Duratrans transparency and light box,
20 3/8" x 32 1/4"
Williams College Museum of Art;
Museum purchase, Kathryn Hurd Fund
93.3.4.A–B

In 1985, Alfredo Jaar used funding that he received from the John Simon Guggenheim Memorial Foundation to finance a trip to the Serra Pelada gold mine in Brazil, where he spent time getting to know and photographing the workers mining there. A year later, Sebastião Salgado photographed the same miners while working concurrently on assignment for two German magazines in South America. While Salgado's Serra Pelada photographs were distributed in over 25 picture magazines, including *The New York Times Magazine*, Jaar selected only five of the over 1,000 images that he took in Serra Pelada, displaying them as color transparencies in light boxes.

plate 51

ALFREDO JAAR (Chilean, b. 1956)
The Eyes of Gutete Emerita,
from *The Rwanda Project*, 1996
two quadvision lightboxes with six black-and-white text transparencies, and two color transparencies, 26" x 23 1/4" x 6 1/8"
Courtesy of the artist and Galerie Lelong, New York

plate 52

BENJAMIN LOWY (American, b. 1979)
Untitled from *Preemptive War*, 2003
color print, 19 1/4" x 13 1/8"
© Benjamin Lowy

plate 53

New York Times Magazine, 12 June 2005
cover photograph by Andres Serrano
Magazine, 11 5/8" x 19 1/4"
Courtesy of the artist and *New York Times*

One of the ways that the general public first learned about the torture of Iraqi prisoners at Abu Ghraib was through the widespread circulation of photographs of the abuses in newspapers and magazines such as the *New Yorker*. As people around the world sought to condemn and resist the horrific actions depicted in these photographs, many of the images were rapidly appropriated in contemporary art, murals, and other public displays. The hooded figure on the cover of this *New York Times Magazine* clearly refers to these responses. At the same time, as a photograph staged by Andres Serrano in collaboration with the editors at the *Times Magazine*, it neither provides evidence of the gruesome events that occurred at Abu Ghraib nor passes judgment on those responsible for them.

plate 54
New Yorker, 10 May 2004
Magazine, 10 5/8" x 16 1/8"
Photograph reprinted by permission
of International Creative Management, Inc.
©2006 by Seymour Hersh

plate 55
RICHARD SERRA (American, b. 1939)
Stop Bush, 2004
digital image downloaded from
PleaseVote.com, 8" x 10"

plate 56
BEHROUZ MEHRI
"An Iranian Motorist with the U.S. Flag on his helmet rides past a mural depicting a scene from the torture of Iraq prisoners by US soldiers at the Abu Ghraib prison, 1 June 2004
digital print, 8" x 10"
Courtesy Behrouz Mehri/AFP/Getty Images

plate 57
Abu Ghraib Prison, 2004
digital image downloaded from the Internet,
dimensions variable

plate 58
ASHLEY GILBERTSON (Australian, b. 1978)
"One of four Iraqis who surrendered to the marines and said they were students trying to avoid battle"
From the *New York Times*, Sunday,
14 November 2004
Newspaper: image 8 1/8" x 3 3/8";
sheet 22 1/2" x 13 1/2"
Courtesy of the artist and *New York Times*

plate 59
ASHLEY GILBERTSON (Australian, b. 1978)
"An Iraqi man captured by American forces during fighting in the Sunni enclave of Falluja sits bound and hooded near a heavily armed marine. The soldiers returned to Falluja in November, seven months after pulling out"
From the *New York Times "2004: The Year in Pictures,"* Monday, 27 December 2004
Newspaper: image 21" x 12 7/8";
sheet 22 1/2" x 13 1/2"
Courtesy of the artist and *New York Times*

ACKNOWLEDGMENTS

This book and the exhibition from which it grew have been, from the beginning, collaborations between the Williams College Museum of Art and the Oakley Center for the Humanities and Social Sciences. The Center's mission is to promote interdisciplinary scholarship; as a teaching museum, the Williams College Museum of Art seeks to facilitate study and provoke serious academic conversation about art and visual culture. We like to think that this project advances both aims. "Beautiful Suffering: Photography and the Traffic in Pain," which ran at the Williams College Museum of Art from January 30 through April 28, 2006, was produced by a team of scholars and museum professionals whose specialties include political science, Islamic art, and the history of photography. We all sought to make the exhibition a form of philosophical inquiry, a way of questioning and exploring the traffic in pain that is so central to contemporary visual culture. The book seeks both to preserve this form of inquiry, documenting the exhibit as a kind of case study, and to push the analysis further.

Tackling such contentious topics and haunting images has its hazards, but we found the nearly two years of collaboration to be not only stimulating and rewarding, but marked by generosity and goodwill. For this we especially thank our partners, Erina Duganne, Holly Edwards, and Stefanie Jandl. For her many contributions to the project, not least her ambitious essay in this volume, we also extend special thanks to our other main collaborator, Mieke Bal.

At the outset, some knowledgeable interlocutors questioned whether a project pursing our critical questions about the taking and circulation of photographs could gain the cooperation of galleries and photographers. We were gratified to find that so many artists, institutions, and collectors were willing to lend us work and, indeed, to do all they could to help make the show and book possible. We extend our sincere gratitude to the following artists: Zalmaï Ahad, Shimon Attie, Chen Chieh-jen, Luc Delahaye, Philip-Lorca diCorcia, Mfon Essien, Eric Gay, Ashley Gilbertson, Nan Goldin, Alfredo Jaar, An-My Lê, Benjamin Lowy, Sally Mann, Mary Ellen Mark, Daniel J. Martinez, Steve McCurry, Behrouz Mehri, Susan Meiselas, Joel Meyerowitz, Boris Mikhailov, Vik Muniz, James Nachtwey, Nicholas Nixon, Simon Norfolk, Michael Nye, Thomas Ruff, Sebastião Salgado, Alan Schechner, Paul Seawright, Richard Serra, Andres Serrano, Fazal Sheikh, Sam Taylor-Wood, Liu Zheng. We also extend our gratitude to the following lenders: Shimon Attie and Jack Shainman Gallery, New York, Kitty Bowe Hearty, Amanda P. Brotman, Chrysler Museum of Art, Norfolk, VA, Philip-Lorca diCorcia and Pace/MacGill Gallery, New York, Holly Edwards, Nan Goldin and Matthew Marks Gallery, New York, Alfredo Jaar and Galerie Lelong, New York, An-My Lê and Murray Guy, New York, Benjamin Lowy, Sally Mann and Gagosian Gallery, New York, Mary Ellen Mark, Daniel J. Martinez and Projectile, New York, Susan Meiselas, Joel Meyerowitz, Boris Mikhailov and Barbara Gross Galerie, Munich, Nicholas Nixon and Bernard Toale Gallery, Boston, Simon Norfolk and Gallery Luisotti, Santa Monica, Michael Nye, Thomas Ruff and David Zwirner, New York, Sebastião Salgado and The Yancey Richardson Gallery, New York, Alan Schechner, Paul Seawright and The Kerlin Gallery, Dublin, Andres Serrano and Paula Cooper Gallery, New York, Fazal Sheikh and Pace/MacGill Gallery, New York, Danny Simmons, Liu Zheng and Yossi Milo Gallery, New York.

The project is indebted to the support of the Oakley Center for Humanities and Social Sciences, the Williams College Museum of Art, and the Andrew W. Mellon Foundation.

For assistance of various kinds on the individual essays, thanks to: Laurie Balfour, Lauren Berlant, Susan Buck-Morss, Jodi Dean, Peggy Diggs, Bregje van Eekelen, Bryan Frank, Jason Frank, Allison Harding, John Hunt, Martin Jaffee, Tom Kohut, Rosemary Lane, Molly Magavern, Paul Passavant, Noa Roei, Amelie Rorty, Diane Rubenstein, George Shulman, Christian Thorne.

The vision and support of two successive WCMA Directors, Marion Goethals and Lisa Corrin, were crucial, and the staff of WCMA made this project come to life in many ways. Thanks to Michele Alice, John Anderson, William Blaauw, Michael Chapman, Robert Kove, Dorothy Lewis, Tina Maher, Nancy Mathews, Allison Mondel, Christine Paglia, Vivian Patterson, Judy Pellerin, Kathryn Price, Deborah Rothschild, Edith Schwartz, Suzanne Silitch, Greg Smith, Rachel Tassone, Amy Tatro, and Theodore Wrona. Martine Neider provided extensive research and curatorial assistance throughout the project and along with Rebecca Burditt provided programming assistance. As well, Graduate Assistants Jessica Fripp and Rebecca Uchill provided research assistance, while Aimee Hirz worked full-time as a production assistant on this book. Special thanks to Diane Hart, Registrar of WCMA for her work on the many loans for the exhibition and Hideyo Okamura, WCMA Exhibition Designer and Chief Preparator for his creativity and flexibility in designing and constructing the exhibition.

Barbara Glauber and Emily Lessard, of Heavy Meta, designed this book. We thank Barbara not only for her characteristic flair but also for understanding how to find a visual form so in tune with the substantive concerns and arguments explored in these pages. We gratefully acknowledge as well our intrepid copy editor, Gilian Shallcross. Finally, at the University of Chicago Press, we thank Anthony Burton—and, especially, Susan Bielstein, for enthusiastically embracing the risks and provocations of this book.

Mark Reinhardt
DIRECTOR
THE OAKLEY CENTER FOR THE HUMANITIES AND
SOCIAL SCIENCES, WILLIAMS COLLEGE

John Stomberg
DEPUTY DIRECTOR AND SENIOR CURATOR FOR EXHIBITIONS
WILLIAMS COLLEGE MUSEUM OF ART

CONTRIBUTORS

MIEKE BAL, a well-known cultural critic and theorist, is Professor of the Theory of Literature in the Faculty of Humanities at the University of Amsterdam. Her many books include *Quoting Caravaggio: Contemporary Art, Preposterous History* (University of Chicago Press 1999) and *Concepts in the Humanities: A Rough Guide* (University of Toronto Press, 2002). *A Mieke Bal Reader* was published earlier this year by the University of Chicago Press. She is also a video artist. Her video installation, Nothing is Missing, is currently touring internationally.

ERINA DUGANNE is Assistant Professor of the History of Art at Texas State University. She is currently working on a book project entitled *Looking In, Looking Out: Photography and the Black Subject*. Articles relating to this research have been published in the anthology *New Thoughts on the Black Arts Movement* (Rutgers University Press, 2006) and in *Visual Research Methods: Image, Society, and Representation* (Sage, forthcoming).

HOLLY EDWARDS is Senior Lecturer in Islamic art at Williams College. Author of *Noble Dreams, Wicked Pleasures: Orientalism in America, 1870–1930* (Princeton University Press, 2000) and a forthcoming study of commemorative architecture in the Indus Valley (Oxford University Press), she has curated exhibitions on topics ranging from 19th century photography in Iran to contemporary transnational art. Prior publications include studies of Arabic epigraphy, Qajar lacquerware, and Ghurid architecture. She has recently embarked on a new project concerning the visual culture of Afghanistan.

MARK REINHARDT is Professor of Political Science and Director of the Oakley Center for the Humanities and Social Sciences at Williams College. Author of *The Art of Being Free: Taking Liberties with Tocqueville, Marx, and Arendt* (Cornell University Press, 1997) and the forthcoming *The Strange Case of Margaret Garner* (University of Minnesota Press), he has also curated several exhibitions and is co-editor of *Kara Walker: Narratives of a Negress* (MIT Press, 2003). His work has appeared in such publications as *Critical Inquiry, The Nation, Political Theory*, and *Theory & Event*.

JOHN STOMBERG is Deputy Director and Senior Curator for Exhibitions at the Williams College Museum of Art and Lecturer in Art at the College. He has published in a variety of journals including *Winterthur Portfolio, Bostonia, American Art Review*, and *Art New England*, as well as in the *Encyclopedia of Twentieth-Century Photography* and several exhibition catalogues. The author of *Power and Paper: Margaret Bourke-White, Modernity, and the Documentary Mode* and *Looking East: Brice Marden, Michael Mazur, Pat Steir*, he is currently working on a study of photographers who attempt to characterize nations through series of individual portraits.

Designed by Barbara Glauber & Emily Lessard/
Heavy Meta, New York
Printed in Canada by Transcontinental Litho Acme

front cover:
ASHLEY GILBERTSON (Australian, b. 1978)
"One of four Iraqis who surrendered to the marines and said they were students trying to avoid battle"
From *The New York Times*, Sunday, 14 November 2004
Newspaper: image 8 1/8" x 3 3/8"; sheet 22 1/2" x 13 1/2"
Courtesy of the artist and *The New York Times*
Newspaper photographed by Rick Schwab

back cover:
ALFREDO JAAR (Chilean, b. 1956)
The Eyes of Gutete Emerita, from *The Rwanda Project*, 1996
two quadvision lightboxes with six black-and-white text transparencies, and two color transparencies, 26" x 23 1/4" x 6 1/8"
Courtesy of the artist and Galerie Lelong, New York